The Lafayette Flying Corps
Volume 2

Pilots of the Escadrille Lafayette attacking a German patrol over the Champagne Sector, (March 26, 1918)

The Lafayette Flying Corps Volume 2
During the First World War

Edited by
James Norman Hall
&
Charles Bernard Nordhoff

The Lafayette Flying Corps Volume 2
During the First World War
Edited by James Norman Hall & Charles Bernard Nordhoff

First published under the titles
The Lafayette Flying Corps Volumes 1 & 2

Leonaur is an imprint of Oakpast Ltd

Copyright in this form © 2014 Oakpast Ltd

ISBN: 978-1-78282-331-5 (hardcover)
ISBN: 978-1-78282-332-2 (softcover)

http://www.leonaur.com

Publisher's Notes

The views expressed in this book are not necessarily those of the publisher.

Contents

Biographical Sketches: Friends of the Corps   7
Biographical Sketches: The Corps   34
Appendix   370

THE LAFAYETTE FLYING CORPS

Biographical Sketches: Friends of the Corps

Jarousse de Sillac

Shortly after Norman Prince arrived in France, self-charged with the difficult task of organising an *escadrille américaine* for the French service, he was introduced, through the courtesy of Mr. Robert Bliss, to M. Jarousse de Sillac. Viewed in the light of subsequent results, it would seem that no happier connection could have been made; for it was almost entirely due to the efforts of M. de Sillac that the consent of the French Government to the plan for an American squadron was gained. A man of keen intelligence and broad vision, he saw at once the importance of organising in the French Army a unit of American combatants, which would become a centre of pride and of interest to all Frenchmen and to all Americans. He gave to the project his immediate and effective support. His profound belief in it, coupled with his reputation for patriotism and prudence, won the confidence of the War Office, and encouraged the French Military authorities to agree to the formation of the squadron at a time when American neutrality and the widespread fear in France of spies and secret agents made the undertaking a difficult one.

Assuming as he did, almost alone, the responsibility for the patriotism and the good faith of the American volunteers, M. de Sillac made it clear to them that he was staking not only his honour, but in a large measure the welfare of his country upon their loyalty to France. One disloyal member, in the position of an aviator at the Front, with easy access from the air to the German lines, could work immeasurable harm. Realising this, and knowing the infinite ramifications of the German Secret Service, the early reluctance of the French Government is not to be wondered at. But, as the result proved, M. de Sillac's confidence was not misplaced. The greatest caution was exercised by the Executive Committee, in its examination of candidates. From February 24, 1915, the date of General Hirschauer's acceptance of American aviators, until the close of the war, there is not a single instance of disloyalty to the Allied Cause on the part of any member of the Lafayette Corps.

It was on February 20, 1915, that the now historic letter of M. de Sillac to Colonel Bouttieaux, of the French War Office, was written. The early acceptance of an American squadron was urged, and the names of six Americans—Norman Prince, Frazier Curtis, William Thaw, Elliot Cowdin, James J. Bach, and Bert Hall—already enlisted or about to enlist in the French Aviation Service, were attached in a separate memorandum. These were the men then available as possible members of the squadron. Four days later, Colonel Bouttieaux's favourable reply was received; but it was many months, more than a year in fact, before the *Escadrille Américaine* was actually formed. Throughout this long and wearisome interval M. de Sillac gave generously of his time and his energy in bringing about the wished-for result. Norman Prince was opposed to the plan for an enlarged corps. That it was enlarged, its pilots fighting in many French squadrons along the entire Western Front, in Italy and in Macedonia, was due chiefly to the efforts of four men: M. de Sillac, Dr. Gros, William K .Vanderbilt, and Frazier Curtis.

M. de Sillac came in personal contact with all of the American volunteers. In company with Dr. Gros he made many visits to the aviation schools where they were preparing for service. No one of them will ever forget these occasions, enduring memories now. In their eyes M. de Sillac stood for France. He represented to them the type of great and noble-minded Frenchmen for whom and with whom they were to fight. His love for America was an inspiration to them and made the stronger their own love for France. Neither can they forget his unwavering belief that ultimately the United States would be fighting side by side with Frenchmen in the great struggle for Right.

M. de Sillac has given long and valuable service to his own country and to the cause of peace throughout the world. At the age of twenty-five he already held an important post in the diplomatic world, as *attaché* of Embassy. He was soon afterward appointed Secretary of the First Peace Conference at The Hague, and from that time he has taken part in all of the great peace movements until the Conference of the Society of Nations at Versailles, where he acted as technical expert and

THE GUESTS AT A BANQUET GIVEN TO MR. W. K. VANDERBILT, AT THE INTERALLIED CLUB, PARIS, OCTOBER 9, 1918

Seated, left to right: M. René Viviani, former President of Council; Mr. William Sharp, American Ambassador; Mr. W. K. Vanderbilt; Mr. Jacques Dumesnil, Minister of Aeronautics. Standing, left to right: Major Edmund Gros, Vice-President and Director of Lafayette Flying Corps; Mr. Lawrence Slade, Treasurer, L.F.C.; Colonel Halsey Dunwoody, C.O., U.S. Air Service, Paris; Count de Fels; Rene Besnard, Former Sub-Secretary of Aeronautics; Lieutenant Arthur Evans, Assistant Treasurer, L.F.C.; M. Flandin, Deputy; Senator Menier; Captain Ray C. Bridgman, U.S.A.S.; Captain Charles Turnure, U.S.A.S.; Lieutenant George Kyle, U.S.A.S.; Mr. Paul Rockwell; Captain Thénault, C.O. Escadrille Lafayette; Lieutenant Granville Pollock, U.S.A.S.; Commandant Brocard; Sergent Everett T. Buckley; General Patrick, C.A.S. A.E.F.; Sergeant Sidney Veil, L.F.C.; Captain Boulanger, Bureau Interallie, Sec. Aeronautics; Colonel Girod, Chief of French Aviation Schools; Mr. Elmer Roberts, Associated Press; Lieutenant Commander Frederick Allen, Director for America, L.F.C.; Sergent James A. Connally, L.F.C.

adviser. But to all Americans, both in present and in future days, his name will be held in most grateful remembrance because of his steadfast and loyal friendship for the American volunteers of the Lafayette Flying Corps.

William K. Vanderbilt

In the early days of the war, when the American Ambulance opened its doors to hundreds of French soldiers brought into Paris from the battlefields of the Marne, Mr. William K. Vanderbilt gave his generous support, and Mrs. Vanderbilt all her sympathy and tenderness, to the work of caring for the wounded. Throughout the year 1915 the thoughts and energies of both Mr. and Mrs. Vanderbilt were centred in this work. The receiving station at Le Chapelle railway terminus was improved, hospital trains were equipped, surgical dressings collected and distributed to advanced *postes de secours*—their generosity found vent in scores of practical ways having a common object, the relief of suffering.

Like other Americans abroad who were in close touch with the war, Mr. Vanderbilt was strongly opposed to the neutrality of the United States. He was one of the warmest admirers of the American volunteers who were fighting in the Foreign Legion. He took a keen interest in their welfare, regretting that there was nothing which he could do to show them his appreciation of the stand which they had taken. One evening, in December, 1915, Dr. Edmund Gros called at his home in Paris and told him of the plan, then on the point of realisation, for organising a corps of one hundred volunteer American airmen for the French Service. Dr. Gros spoke earnestly and with conviction, feeling that the support of Mr. and Mrs. Vanderbilt would mean the success of the undertaking; and he was not disappointed. Both were greatly interested. There was no need for pleading, and Dr. Gros left them with a contribution which placed the corps upon a firm basis.

From that time until long after the signing of the Armistice, Mr. Vanderbilt assumed, almost alone, the financial responsibilities of the Lafayette Flying Corps. His generosity made it possible to distribute monthly allowances to the volunteers, many of whom were without private means, to give them uniforms, to contribute to their mess funds, and in many other ways to make their life, both in the aviation schools and at the Front, pleasant and comfortable. Mr. Vanderbilt gave with no thought of reward or acknowledgment. Many of those interested in the Lafayette Corps will here learn for the first time of the important part which he played in its success. But although he kept always in the background, he took a friendly personal interest in every pilot. He not only foresaw the importance of the influence which the corps would have upon public opinion in America, but he realised its value to the United States in the event of war. He believed firmly in the plan for an enlarged organisation, and made it clear to the Executive Committee that his contributions would be limited only by the needs of the corps. Having this assurance, the committee, under the leadership of Dr. Gros, was able to continue the work of recruiting and enlisting. The obligations which Mr. Vanderbilt had to meet became increasingly heavy during the last two years of the war. He met them all gladly. It is not too much to say that through him at least one hundred pilots were added to the personnel of the corps.

On October 9, 1918, the French Government conferred upon Mr. Vanderbilt the Cross of the Legion of Honour. In presenting the decoration, Monsieur Dumesnil, Minister of Aeronautics, said:

> The Government of the Republic is happy to express its appreciation and gratitude to one of the citizens of America who, from the very first hour, has been a warm and valued friend to France.

This sentiment for Mr. Vanderbilt is shared by every member of the Lafayette Corps. They will remember him not only with appreciation and gratitude, but with feelings of sincere respect and friendship.

Edmund Gros

Upon his arrival in Paris, the candidate for enlistment in the Lafayette Flying Corps reported at 23 Avenue du Bois de Boulogne, where he was ushered into a small and busy waiting-room. While he waited his turn, his eyes and thoughts were kept busy, for around him, smoking and talking shop, there was always to be found an interesting group of flyers: *élèves-pilotes* from Avord, proudly telling of their first solo flights; newly breveted men who had just completed their training at Pau; and most fascinating of all, veterans from the Front, not unconscious of the awesome halo surrounding them. When at last the door opened, and the neophyte's name was called, he found himself in the presence of a man whose kindly manner and cordial hand-clasp put him at his ease at once. It was Dr. Edmund Gros.

There were hours each day when his office resembled a recruiting bureau at the Invalides rather than a doctor's waiting-room. Volunteers, newly arrived from America, from the Ambulance, or the Legion, went there to sign their enlistment papers for the Air Service. Men already in the service dropped in to consult with him whenever they were in Paris. Some needed medical advice or attention, which he gave freely. Others called for letters or parcels sent in his care. Yet others, about to be returned to civilian life because of some unintentional breach of camp or field discipline, called to ask his intervention. No matter what the difficulty, it was always to Dr. Gros they came for counsel and he was always accessible, ready to help in some practical way.

Early in 1915, when Dr. Gros was one of the heads of the American Ambulance, Norman Prince was working, despite many discouragements, to carry out his plan of forming an American squadron. Elliot Cowdin and Frazier Curtis were giving him loyal and effective aid, and it was Curtis who introduced Dr. Gros to M. de Sillac, the warm friend of the American volunteers. Dr. Gros had for some time, quite independently of the others, been considering the same idea, having seen the splendid material among the scores of American lads flocking overseas to drive ambulances—men splendidly fitted to play the part of combatants in the war, who loved adventure and were with France heart and soul. Upon meeting M. de Sillac, and a little later, Norman Prince, Dr. Gros joined forces with them, and from that time on took an increasingly active and important part in the organisation and development of what was to become the Lafayette Flying Corps. He had lived in Paris for many years. French was to him a second mother tongue, and he understood the French people, their customs, and their politics as few Americans are fortunate enough to do.

It was Dr. Gros who on July 8, 1915, planned the now historic luncheon at the house of Senator Menier, where General Hirschauer agreed to form the *Escadrille Américaine*. It was Dr. Gros who interested Mr. Vanderbilt in the corps and obtained from him the funds which have made its existence possible. He likewise did most of the work of the Executive Committee handling the funds, attending to the correspondence, publishing pamphlets, and arranging all the details for making the existence of the corps known to Americans at home. He examined every candidate upon his arrival in Paris, sent him off, as a full-fledged *soldat de deuxième classe*, to Buc or Avord, and kept a fatherly eye upon him throughout his entire period of service in France.

Dr. Gros has done more for the Lafayette Flying Corps than any

DR. EDMUND GROS

other one man who has been connected with it. Norman Prince conceived the idea of forming an American squadron to serve with the French. William K. Vanderbilt, with unfailing generosity, furnished the funds without which the corps could not have continued to exist. Dr. Gros, from the time of his meeting with M. de Sillac, has carried on the burden of the work, giving unselfishly his time, his enthusiasm, and his rare ability as an organiser. Few Lafayette men realise, perhaps, how whole-heartedly he has worked in their interests. He stood in the relationship of a parent, saw to it that they had enough money to enable them to live in comfort, got them out of scrapes, rejoiced with them in their triumphs. His pleasure and pride in the honours bestowed upon Lafayette men was every whit as keen as that of the recipients.

When the United States declared war upon Germany, Dr. Gros was commissioned Major, and afterward promoted to Lieutenant-Colonel in the United States Air Service. In the midst of his new duties and responsibilities, he did not forget the American volunteers with whom he had been associated for so long a time. He saw that in the Lafayette Corps there existed a nucleus of trained and seasoned pilots about which to build the Pursuit Branch of our own Aviation Service. Two things only were necessary: to persuade the French to release the men and to convince the American authorities of the advisability of taking them. The business seemed simple, but military affairs of all nations move with notorious slowness. Although Colonel Gros set to work to effect the transfer almost immediately after our declaration of war, the first telegram recommending Lafayette men for commissions was not sent from Washington until November, 1917. In the end, Colonel Gros was instrumental in transferring ninety-three pilots to the United States Air Service and twenty-three to the United States Naval Air Service, all of these men trained and ready for immediate service, many of them having already had long and valuable experience at the Front. Had he done nothing else in the war, Colonel Gros could feel that he had done his full share. He was also chief of the Liaison Section, United States Air Service, at the American Headquarters in Paris, where much of the business between the French and American Aviation passed through his hands.

In recognition of his services to the Allied cause Dr. Gros has been awarded the American Certificate of Merit, the French Legion of Honour and Reconnaissance Française, and the Italian Order of the Knights of SS. Maurizio e Lazzaro.

Twenty-eight Lafayette men remained in the French service. Colonel Gros kept in touch with them as long as they were in France, helping them with all available funds, looking after their interests, corresponding with their families in case of imprisonment or death. All through the history of the Lafayette Corps, whenever a casualty was reported, Colonel Gros wrote at once to the Squadron Commander asking for details. In the case of a wounded man, he saw that every care was given him, and immediately reassured his family. If a Lafayette man was shot down back of the enemy lines, he sent details, including the number of the machine, motor, etc., to the American Red Cross in Berne, Switzerland, where a committee existed which made immediate inquiries in Germany. In the files of the Lafayette Corps are to be found copies of letters written to the parents of the men who have been killed, every one of them showing, in its fine sympathy of thought, the patient care which has been given to it, letters written by a busy man who was never too busy to send a word of comfort to a sorrowing mother or father.

Now that the war has ended in victory and the members of the Lafayette Corps have returned to civilian life, the great debt of gratitude which they owe to Colonel Gros will not be forgotten. At future reunions, when old memories are revived and healths are drunk, the first toast will be: "To our wise counsellor and loyal friend; to the father of the Lafayette Corps, Dr. Edmund Gros."

Mrs. Georgia Ovington

The measure of Mrs. Ovington's services to France and to her own country cannot be set down in black and white. She found her place, and gave without stint or thought of self, her time, her energy, her tact and charm—and, in the end, her only son.

A small part of her accomplishment is expressed in the warm and respectful admiration with which she is regarded by the members of the corps. Nothing she could do for her "boys" was too much—she forwarded mail, held and delivered packages from home, replied to a thousand letters from anxious relatives, and wrote words of comfort—breathing true feeling and sympathy—to the families of those who lost their lives. Sometimes, at the Front, when the war seemed eternal, and one wondered dully what it was all about and whether all friendly and human things had disappeared forever, the *courrier* brought a letter from Mrs. Ovington. How she found time to write, in the midst of

Mrs. Ovington

her endless and exacting duties, has never been explained, but somehow—in the odd moments which most of us devote to rest—she sent off scores of these kindly and interesting little messages. They gave news of old comrades, now serving with far-off *escadrilles*, enabled us to share with our friends the pleasure of victories and decorations, and told of those who were in hospital or visiting Paris on leave. They were letters which might have been written by a mother or elder sister; with a delicate personal touch that has brought new courage to many a tired and homesick American, brought a fresh realisation of the cause for which one fought.

There is no woman with a better understanding of the realities of war flying than Mrs. Ovington; but when the time came and her son asked permission to join the Corps, she did not hesitate. Landram and his mother were united by the strongest ties of love and comradeship. She was able to realise, as not every mother can, what her own feelings would have been in his position. Her permission was granted with a smile; and when her son gave his life in combat, she bore the loss with a proud fortitude more touching than any demonstration of grief, continuing her duties with scarcely a sign of the suffering which must have tortured her. Men's tongues are tied where their feelings are concerned, but one wishes that Mrs. Ovington could see the face of any Lafayette man light up at the mention of her name.

Commandant Philippe Féquant

Commandant Philippe Féquant, known to all the American volunteers as the commanding officer of *Groupe de Combat* 13, began his military career in 1903 when he entered the Saint-Cyr Military School. He made a choice of the Colonial Infantry, and was sent as a second lieutenant to Tonkin where he took part in the operations against the Tonkinese pirates. He became interested in aviation some time before the experiments of the Wright brothers in France and transferred to the Air Service in 1913. He was sent on an aviation mission to Africa and after making the campaign in Morocco, he returned to France in 1915 to participate in the war against Germany. He was at once attached to an *escadrille de bombardement*. He took part in many of the most famous raids of the early part of the war, upon Ludwigshafen, Karlsruhe, Sarrebruck, Trèves, and during one of the expeditions was wounded in the arm by a shell fragment.

For several months he was attached to the bureau of Monsieur Rene Besnard, Sub-Secretary of State, and at this post was in a posi-

Commandant Féquant

Commandant Féquant at the Front

tion to give valuable assistance to the cause of the American volunteers at the time when the Escadrille Lafayette was created under the name of the *Escadrille Américaine*. He returned to the Front in April, 1916, and early in May, during the Battle of Verdun, took command of the Escadrille N. 65, the first squadron to receive the *fourragère* with the colours of the *Médaille Militaire*. It was at Verdun that Commandant Féquant first met the pilots of the *Escadrille Américaine*.

During the heavy aerial battles of this period the Americans fought side by side with the pilots of N. 65, and when in October, 1916, they again met at Cachy on the Somme and *Groupe de Combat* 13 was created, both the N.65 and the N. 124 were included in it, under the command of Commandant Féquant. *Groupe* 13 took part in all of the important engagements of 1916-17: on the Somme, the Aisne, at Verdun and in Flanders. Commandant Féquant was a splendid leader, admired and respected by all of his pilots. As commanding officer of a *groupe de combat*, he had heavy responsibilities. It was an unusual thing for a Group Commander to take part in actual patrol work; but Commandant Féquant often did. When the fighting was heaviest, his Spad with its anchor insignia would be seen far beyond the enemy lines, making its way calmly through the *éclatementes* of enemy anti-aircraft shells. It was a heartening, an inspiring sight. One of the reasons for Commandant Féquant's success as a leader was that he shared with his pilots their dangers as well as their successes; and he did this, when, as a Group Commander, his duties on the ground almost forbade his taking any part in activities over the lines.

Early in 1918, before the German offensive was imminent, a large aviation group comprising several combat and bombardment groups, was formed to operate in the region between Soissons and Rheims. Commandant Féquant was placed in command and the formation designated as "*le Groupe Féquant.*" This group played a glorious role during the early days of the German offensive which began on March 21, gained undoubted supremacy of the air, and then concentrated all its forces against the enemy land troops. It was owing in large measure to its relentless attacks against the enemy infantry and artillery, that the German advance was retarded and that the attempt to separate the French and British armies failed.

The *Féquant Groupe* was then sent wherever the need was greatest: to Beauvais, in rear of the Chemin des Dames in May; to Montdidier in June; to Château-Thierry in July, 1918. Meanwhile other pursuit and bombardment units had been added, and the *Groupement* became the 2nd Aviation Brigade, composed of the First Pursuit and the First Bombardment *Escadres*. The brigade took part in the Mangin offensive of July 18, 1918, when the American troops gave so splendid an account of themselves and which marked the final turning-point of the war. After this battle the Germans were continually beaten farther and farther back.

Commandant Féquant was then appointed Chief of General Staff of the Aerial Division, to General Duval, and at the Battle of Saint-Mihiel, some of his old pilots of the Escadrille Lafayette again had the privilege of meeting him. In 1916, in almost the same region, there had begun that fraternity between French and American aviators which existed on so much larger scale at the battle of Saint-Mihiel. In 1916, squadrons were fighting side by side, America represented only by the Escadrille Lafayette. At Saint-Mihiel, in 1918, the association was of Wings and *Escadres*.

At the time of the signing of the Armistice, Commandant Féquant was sent as a delegate to the International Commission at Spa, and was later appointed as a member of the Military Mission of the President of the French Republic. Throughout his career in French Aviation he never ceased to be in close touch with the pilots of the Lafayette Flying Corps, and in particular with those Americans who. were for so long under his direct command in the Escadrille Lafayette. They will always remember him as a wise and fearless leader under whose orders it was not only their duty, but their privilege and pleasure to serve.

Captain Georges Thénault

It was during the spring of 1915, while both were members of the Escadrille C.42, that William Thaw and Georges Thénault laid the foundation for the friendship which was to have such important results for the Lafayette Squadron. Lieutenant Thénault, as he then was, although a young man in years, was already a pilot of wide experience and proven ability at leadership. He was raised to the rank of Captain in May, 1915, and placed in command of the C.42 on July 31 of the same year.

He held this position until April 9, 1916, when, upon Thaw's recommendation, he was chosen to take command of the Escadrille Lafayette, then ready for service. With the exception of one month of detached duty, in 1917, he led the American unit until January, 1918, when its pilots were being transferred to the United States Air Service.

SERVICE RECORD

GEORGES THÉNAULT, Paris, France

SERVICE IN FRENCH AVIATION:
From the beginning of the war.
École d'Avord, January 12 to March 23, 1915.
At the Front: Escadrille C.11, August to December 1, 1914.
Escadrille, C.34, March 25, 1915.
Escadrille C.42 (as Commanding Officer), July 31, 1915.
Escadrille Lafayette, (as Commanding Officer), April 9, 1916, to January 18, 1918.
Chief Pilot, School of Aerobacy at Pau January 18, 1918 to Armistice.
Final Rank: Captain.

DECORATIONS:
Légion d'Honneur.
Croix de Guerre, with four Palms.

CITATIONS

Au G.Q.G., le 27 août, 1914
Citation à l'Ordre de l'Armée:

GEORGES THÉNAULT, Lieutenant à l'Escadrille C.11:

A exécuté plusieurs reconnaissances au cours desquelles son appareil a été atteint par des projectiles.

Au G.Q.G., le 19 octobre, 1914

A fait presque journellement des reconnaissances à longue portée et des réglages de tir d'artillerie bravant le feu de l'ennemi et se prodiguant sans compter pour remplir les missions qui lui étaient confiées.

Légion d'Honneur:

Ancien et habile pilote qui depuis le début de la campagne compte plus de 300 heures de vol au dessus de l'ennemi, entraîne par son exemple quotidien les pilotes et ses observateurs de son escadrille dont il obtient le rendement maximum. Le 21 février, 1916, revenant d'un mission de bombardement avec 4 avions de son escadrille a attaqué et abattu dans nos lignes un avion ennemi.

His leadership during the whole of this period was never an irksome one. His association with his pilots, who regarded him as a friend and good comrade as well as their captain, was intimate and cordial. He performed his duties with kindliness and tact, delegating much of his authority to his French seconds-in-command, Lieutenants de Laage de Meux, de Maison-Rouge, and Verdier-Fauvety, and to Thaw and Lufbery. After his pilots had served their apprenticeship at the Front, it was only occasionally that he took part in the patrols and combats of the squadron; but this was due chiefly to the fact that there was always a nucleus of older men, equipped both by natural endowment and long training as flight leaders of the first order. He knew and trusted in their ability, and in time came to exercise only a nominal leadership in matters of the air.

CAPTAIN THÉNAULT AND FRAM

A sketch, however brief, of Captain Thénault would be incomplete without mention of Fram, his *"bon chien"* and inseparable companion. The fine comradeship, the love of the one for the other, was known to pilots throughout the entire French Service, and all of them envied Captain Thénault the loyalty and unwavering faithfulness of his dog. No lover of a brave and splendid animal could see Fram without desiring him. But he was firm in his allegiance, and although friendly to others, one always felt that it was merely out of courtesy to the wishes of his master.

The month of January, 1918, marked for the Lafayette Squadron, the transition period from the French to the American Service. It was at this time that Captain Thénault said goodbye to the pilots of his old command and was sent to new duties as Chief Pilot at the School of Acrobacy and Combat at Pau. An association of nearly two years' standing was thus brought to an end. For the members of the N. 124 it is an association never to be forgotten. Their memories of Captain Thénault, of his good-fellowship, of his thoughtful consideration for them upon innumerable occasions, through days of danger and great strain, must always remain among the happiest which they have of the Great War.

SERVICE RECORD

Alfred de Laage de Meux, Lieutenant (French); Clessé (Deux Sèvres), France.

Previous Service: 14th Dragoons, August, 1914, to March 25, 1915.

Service in French Aviation:
  Date of enlistment: March 25, 1915.
  Service with Escadrille Lafayette: April 20, 1916, to May 23, 1917.
  Killed in line of duty: May 23, 1917, at Ham (Somme).

Decorations:
  Croix de Guerre, with two Palms and two Stars.

CITATIONS

Le 1 septembre, 1914
Citation à l'Ordre de l'Armée:

De Laage de Meux, Alfred, Sous-Lieutenant de Réserve au 14ème Régiment de Dragons, a exécuté 31 août une reconnaissance fructueuse dans des conditions difficiles; a repris trois fois et pendant plusieurs heures le contact d'une importante colonne ennemie (deux régiments de cavalerie accompagnés de mitrailleuses); atteint d'une balle à la cuisse et ayant eu ses vêtements traversés par d'autres balles n'en a pas moins continué sa reconnaissance rapportant lui, même le dernier renseignement, a ensuite continué son service à son escadron, malgré sa blessure.

IIe Armée, État-Major.   *Au G.Q.G., le 14, août, 1916*

Le Général Commandant la IIe Armée cite à l'Ordre de l'Armée:

  Le Lieutenant de Laage de Meux, Alfred, Pilote à l'Escadrille N. 124

Pilote d'élite qui est un véritable modèle de bravoure. Faisant partie d'un groupe de chasse depuis le début de la bataille de Verdun a livré de nombreux combats allant chercher ses adversaires loin dans leurs lignes, et les attaquant quelqu'en soit le nombre. Le 27 juillet a abattu un avion allemand à proximité du front.

Groupe d'Armées de l'Est
  État-Major.   *Au G.Q.G., le 28 octobre, 1916*

  Le Lieutenant de Laage de Meux, de l'Escadrille N. 124

Officier pilote très courageux. A pris part, le 12 octobre, à l'opération de bombardement d'Oberndorf. A dégagé plusieurs fois les appareils qu'il était chargé de protéger, en attaquant, de très près, les appareils ennemies qui s'approchaient.

Le 21 avril, 1917

De Laage de Meux, Alfred, Lieutenant, Pilote (active) à l'Escadrille N. 124, a été nommé dans l'Ordre de la Légion d'Honneur au grade de Chevalier.

Pilote de chasse de premier ordre. Après s'être très brillamment conduit à Verdun et sur la Somme, s'est à nouveau distingué de la manière la plus remarquable au cours des récentes opérations, exécutant de nombreux vols à faible altitude pour obliger l'ennemi à se découvrir et rapportant au commandement de précieux renseignements. Le 8 avril, 1917, a livré successivement trois durs combats et abattu deux appareils ennemis, dégageant ainsi un avion et un ballon français violemment attaqués. Déjà quatre fois cité à l'ordre de l'armée.

Citation à l'Ordre de l'Armée: Le 6 *juin*, 1917

DE LAAGE DE MEUX, ALFRED, Lieutenant, Pilote de l'Escadrille N. 124

Pilote de chasse d'une bravoure et d'une adresse remarquable, se dépensant sans compter, avex un joyeux courage. N'a cessé d'être pour ses camarades un magnifique exemple d'entrain et d'esprit de sacrifice. Mortellement blessé dans une chute d'avion le 23 mai, 1917.

Alfred de Laage de Meux

Alfred de Laage de Meux, who was long the beloved second-in-command of the Escadrille Lafayette, was descended from an old Orleanist family. He was born at Clessé (Deux Sèvres) and in peacetime had been interested in scientific farming. When called for his military service he responded gladly, and at the outbreak of the war, was a second lieutenant in the 14th Regiment of Dragoons. He took part in all of the war of movement until August 31, 1914. While on a reconnoitring expedition on that day he had his horse killed under him, and was himself wounded in the leg. His orderly Jean Dressy, who later followed him in Aviation, and served him until his death, carried him back on his own horse and de Laage reported in person to his chief.

After his convalescence in the spring of 1915, the war of trenches having immobilized the cavalry, he entered the Aviation Corps, and was sent as an observer to the Escadrille C. 30. His service here was exceptionally fine in quality and won him his second citation *à l'ordre de l'armée*. The duties of an observer did not satisfy him, however. He wished to become a pilot, and accomplished the unusual feat of learning to fly while at the Front, and while carrying on his work as an observer and machine-gunner. He was one of very few French pilots who had never a day of training in an aviation school. For the next few months he piloted a Farman and gained his first victory while flying this machine. His contempt for danger was such that his fellow pilots of that squadron predicted an early death for him. But he seemed invulnerable. On two occasions his machine-gunner was killed. Often his *avion* was so badly damaged by bullets as to be past repair. He then transferred to an *escadrille de chasse*, and during the first Battle of Verdun distinguished himself by a series of combats which are memorable even in the long list of brilliant actions which make up the history of French Aviation.

It was at this time that Captain Thénault, who had just taken command of the newly formed *Escadrille Américaine*, first met him, and asked that he be transferred to this unit. The change was effected. Lieutenant de Laage took up at once his duties as second-in-command, joining the squadron at Luxeuil, on April 20, 1916, the day of its original muster. He represented all that is best in French character and had a power of personal magnetism which made him a natural leader. He gave to his pilots a new conception of the meaning of patriotism, and it is not the least exaggeration to say that the love which the Americans had for him bordered upon adoration. He led them out to their first battles, flew with them individually and in groups of two or three, instructing them in the tactics of combat, which, in those early days, had to be learned at the Front. It was at about this time that Kiffin Rockwell wrote to his brother Paul of a combat he had had while flying with Lieutenant de Laage:

> Very early one morning, Lieutenant de Laage and I went on patrol together. Over Étain, I saw a Boche underneath me. I immediately dove on him, and when I was just about ready to open fire, two other Germans, whom I had not seen, attacked me, filling my machine full of holes. I thought that my last hour had surely come. Lieutenant de Laage had already had a combat and his machine gun was jammed. But although it was impossible for him to fire even one shot, he dove on the two Boches who were trying to bring me down and drove them off. I am certain that at that moment he saved my life as he has done many times before.

Upon another occasion, one of the Americans wrote of him: "De Laage had three combats on the 8th of April and destroyed two planes which were officially confirmed. The whole Squadron shares in his joy, for he is the most devoted and self-sacrificing airman one could hope to see. He has had any number of successful combats which have not been officially accredited him, because far on the other side of the lines; but one can say, with absolute confidence, that the enemy machines were destroyed."

One could quote indefinitely from letters of the early volunteers, in which reference is made to Lieutenant de Laage. They would give even an outsider, who knew neither the pilots nor their leader, a lasting impression of an unusual comradeship, precious beyond any other gift which life has to offer. Nearly all of the men who knew him best are dead. Those who took their places at the Front had all too short a time to enjoy the heritage of friendship.

He had earned the right to die in the midst of combat. He was killed in one of those stupid accidents which take the bravest and most skilful of airmen together with the timid and unskilful. Toward the end of the afternoon of May 23, 1917, he left the aerodrome at Ham (Somme) for a trial flight in a new Spad. Gathering terrific speed, as he left the ground, he pulled up in a steep climbing turn, as he loved sometimes to do. At that instant his motor failed him, and before he could straighten out in *ligne de vol,* he lost flying speed. Had he been fifty metres higher he could have saved himself. As it was, his Spad crashed to the ground in a half *vrille,* the fall killing him instantly.

THE FUNERAL OF LIEUTENANT DE LAAGE DE MEUX

Many of his ancestors had been killed in battle, and he once said that he believed he too would be killed in this way. We did not know of this conviction of his, until after his death. Even though we had known of it, we should not have believed that it could be confirmed. He had come unscathed through so many combats. Our confidence in his invulnerability was more than confidence. It was almost a faith in a kindly Providence which would not and could not let him die.

He was buried in the soldiers' cemetrey at Ham. Captain Thénault spoke fittingly and briefly of his life and of his service to France; and at the end he said:

> *Adieu, mon cher de Laage. Dors en paix. Ta vie aura été un exemple et nous n'on aurons pas de plus beau á suivre. Ton souvenir restera impérissable parmi nous et ton nom demeurera glorieux.*
> *Et maintenant, Vive la France!*

SERVICE RECORD

ARNOUX DE MAISON-ROUGE, Lieutenant (French).

PREVIOUS SERVICE: Cavalry, 1914-15.

SERVICE IN FRENCH AVIATION:
  Date of enlistment: 1915.
  Breveted: November 5, 1915 (Maurice Farman).
  At the Front: Escadrille N. 67, September 22, 1916, to May 27, 1917.
    Escadrille Lafayette, May 28 to October 6, 1917.
    Escadrille Spa. 78, January 14 to May 31, 1918.
  Killed in combat: May 31, 1918.

CITATION

Par Ordre N° 186, du 27 juin, 1917, le Chef d'Escadron, Chef du Service Aéronautique au G.Q.G., cite à l'Ordre du Groupe de Combat N° 13:

ARNOUX DE MAISON-ROUGE, Lieutenant à l'Escadrille N. 67

Très bon pilote de chasse. A fait preuve pendant la bataille de la Somme et la retraite allemande des belles qualités d'ardeur et de bravoure. A eu de nombreux combats au cours desquels il a forcé plusieurs appareils ennemis à atterrir désemparés dans leurs lignes. A eu plusieurs fois son appareils atteint dans les parties essentielles.

Arnoux de Maison-Rouge

In common with Lieutenant de Laage de Meux, whom he succeeded as the French second-in-command of the Escadrille Lafayette, Lieutenant de Maison-Rouge was a former cavalry officer. Before the war and during the open fighting of the summer and autumn of 1914, the cavalry had been the *corps d'élite* of the French Service. When the need for mounted troops had passed, many cavalrymen became aviators. They were of the finest blood of France, fearless and splendid fighters, and brought to their new service high qualities of leadership which placed them, almost immediately, in positions of responsibility. Lieutenant de Maison-Rouge was sent to the Lafayette Squadron from the N. 67, joining the Americans at Ham on May 28, several days after the death of Lieutenant de Laage de Meux. He had a difficult position to fill, for the pilots of N. 124 were heart-broken at the loss of Lieutenant de Laage, and could not be reconciled to the thought of having any one attempt to take his place.

But Lieutenant de Maison-Rouge was a man of great tact and undertook his new duties so quietly and in so friendly a spirit that resentment soon changed to liking. He was an excellent pilot and patrol leader, and distinguished himself, particularly at Verdun, by acts of courage which gained him the whole-hearted respect of all the pilots in the squadron. Although he had the greatest consideration for the men under his command, and was, if anything, too careful not to tax them beyond their powers, he was unsparing of himself. He was not a strong man physically, but he had an unconquerable spirit which kept him at his duty long after his strength was exhausted. In the autumn of 1917 he became seriously ill and was compelled, against his will, to rest. On October 6, he left the Escadrille Lafayette, greatly to the regret of all the pilots, and when he was again ready for active duty, was assigned to a French squadron, Spad 78. During the heavy fighting of May, 1918, he was shot down in a splendid battle against heavy odds, and fell to his death far behind the enemy lines.

THE ESCADRILLE LAFAYETTE AT CHAUDUN, JULY, 1917
LIEUTENANT DE MAISON-ROUGE STANDING ON RIGHT

Louis Verdier-Fauvety

Lieutenant Verdier-Fauvety, who followed Lieutenants de Laage de Meux and Maison-Rouge as second-in-command of the Escadrille Lafayette, had long been a member of the same *Groupe de Combat—*13. His war service dates from October 10, 1914, when he was *adjudant* in a cavalry regiment, the 8th Hussars. He was severely wounded in the left shoulder during the first autumn of the war, while making a reconnaissance of the enemy trenches, and after spending several months in hospital, was transferred to the Aviation Service and sent to Spad 65, later to become one of the most famous of French combat squadrons, and the first to receive the *fourragère* of the *Médaille Militaire*. It was at this time that the American pilots first came to know Lieutenant Verdier; and to know him was to admire him as an airman and to love him as a friend and comrade.

SERVICE RECORD

Louis Verdier-Fauvety, Lieutenant (French); Meaux, Seine-et-Marne, France.

Previous Service: 8th Hussards, October 10, 1914, to February 20, 1916.

Service in French Aviation:
Date of enlistment: February 26, 1916.
Aviation Schools: February 26 to November 16, 1916, Pau, Juvisy, G.D.E.
At the Front: Escadrille N. 65, November 18, 1916, to October 1, 1917.
Escadrille Lafayette, October 6, 1917, to February 18, 1918.
Commanding Officer, Escadrilles Spad 124, 163, 65, from February 18 to August 21, 1918.
Wounded: October 12, 1914.
Killed in line of duty: August 21, 1918.

Decorations:
Légion d'Honneur.
Croix de Guerre, with four Palms.

CITATIONS

Ve Corps d'Armée, Brigade de Cavalerie.   14 novembre, 1914

Verdier-Fauvety, Louis, Sous-Lieutenant au 8e Régiment de Hussards

Le 12 octobre, a été grièvement blessé d'un coup de feu à l'épaule dans une reconnaissance qu'il dirigeait, en se portant très courageusement en avant, pour reconnaître les tranchées ennemies.

29 mai, 1917

Verdier-Fauvety, Louis, Lieutenant (Cavalerie), Pilote à l'Escadrille N. 65

Le 24 avril, 1917, protégeant une mission photographique bien qu'ayant sa mitrailleuse enrayée, a réussi à tenir à distance un monoplace adverse.
Le 2 mai, a attaqué trois avions de réglage ennemi et contraint l'un d'eux à atterrir.
Le 4 mai a attaqué un biplace allemand et l'a obligé à rentrer désemparé dans ses lignes.

(*Signé*)   *Général* Maistre

29 août, 1917

Verdier-Fauvety, Louis, Lieutenant de Réserve de Cavalerie, Pilote à l'Escadrille N. 65 a été nommé dans l'Ordre de la Légion d'Honneur au grade de Chevalier:

Pilote de chasse remarquable par sa haute conception du devoir, son courage et sa hardiesse. Le 28 juillet, 1917, à la tête d'une patrouille de combat, a abattu un avion ennemi dans nos lignes. Déjà blessé et deux fois cité à l'Ordre de l'Armée.

(*Signé*)   *Général* Debeney

G.A.R. du 25 mai, 1918

Le Général Commandant le G.A.R. cite à l'Ordre du Corps d'Armée:

Verdier-Fauvety, Louis, Lieutenant détaché du 8e Hussards à l'Escadrille Spa. 65

Pilote de chasse d'une grande bravoure.

Le 6 mai, 1918, étant chef de patrouille, a attaqué un avion ennemi et coopérée efficacement à sa chute.

21 *août*, 1918

Verdier-Fauvety, Louis, Lieutenant, Pilote à l'Escadrille N. 65

Officier d'une grande élévation morale et d'une admirable bravoure, animé par un amour profond de sa patrie et par le plus sublime esprit de sacrifice.

> Admiré et aimé de tous ceux qui ont lutté à ses côtés, a combattu sans trêve pendant quatre ans et laissé un magnifique exemple des plus hautes qualités d'un soldat: conscience, modestie, mépris de la mort.
> Tombé glorieusement pour la France le 21 août, 1918, en se portant au secours de son escadrille soumise à un violent bombardement.

In August, 1917, Lieutenant Verdier had a most remarkable escape from death, when, in the midst of a combat, his plane collided with that of one of his comrades of Spad 65, at a height of 12,000 feet. The stabilizer and the right half of his elevating planes were torn away so that he fell out of control the entire distance of more than two miles. His *avion* crashed in a wood and he escaped with only a few injuries. On October 6, 1917, to the great joy of all the pilots in the Escadrille Lafayette, he was attached to that unit as second-in-command. It was a pleasure to follow him in combat. He attacked with superb skill, and never for a moment lost his head, even under the most trying conditions. Although he was under no obligation to do so, he always undertook the most dangerous of missions, particularly the work of machine-gunning trenches and roads from low altitudes. His presence inspired confidence, made men courageous in spite of themselves. He had this quality—and there is no greater in a leader—in common with Lieutenant de Laage de Meux, whose place he so splendidly filled. The respect and love which the men of the Escadrille Lafayette had for him, may best be shown in the following extract from a letter written shortly after Lieutenant Verdier arrived at the squadron:

> We have a new second-in-command, Lieutenant Verdier-Fauvety, who has been a pilot with Spad 65, another squadron in our group. Some of the older men have known him for a long time. They were overjoyed at our luck in getting him. He is one of the finest Frenchmen I have ever met, and is so cheery and self-possessed at all times, that one is ashamed to mope in his presence. We do a little too much of this sometimes. Nerves have a way of getting jangled, and then, too, we have lost three men quite recently, which has made us all feel rather gloomy and sad.
> The change since Lieutenant Verdier's arrival has been really remarkable. It isn't due to anything he says, but simply because he has such a healthy, wholesome outlook on life. And he is never at all flustered in the air. He has been with us only a few weeks, but already the older men speak of him as a second de Laage de Meux. I notice that all of the men are keen to have his good

LIEUTENANT LOUIS VERDIER-FAUVETY

THE RESULT OF ONE OF HIS COMBATS

opinion. He keeps us up to the mark, and he does it without a word either of praise or blame.

Another Lafayette pilot wrote as follows of a ground-strafing patrol, led by Lieutenant Verdier:

The French made an attack on our sector (the Aisne) this week, which has given our group plenty of exciting work. Four of us were out this afternoon doing very low patrol near the Aisne-Marne canal and back of the Chevregny reservoir. I have never cared much about this low work. It means landing in Germany in case of motor trouble; and then, too, we are always under machine-gun fire from the ground as well as in constant danger of attack from enemy planes above. But today, strangely enough, I didn't mind it at all. On the contrary, I actually enjoyed it, which is saying a good deal for ground-strafing. The patrol was led by Lieutenant Verdier, who is now our French second-in-command. We have all learned, through much flying with him, that he is never taken by surprise, and so follow him with the greatest confidence. Today, for example, we crossed the lines at 800 metres, and flew for over an hour between 200 and 400 metres, and nearly all of the time back of the new enemy positions.

Lieutenant Verdier would dive down on some wreck of a village filled with German reserves, all of us following him in turn, blazing away like mad. Then he would circle around until we were in formation again, and take on another village or bivouac. We were chased twice by large patrols of enemy single-seaters. But Lieutenant Verdier saw them each time, long before they could reach us, so that we never gave them a chance for a decent shot. We dislike this dodging, but today our work was on the ground, hunting for enemy infantry. At first we were a little worried because of the numbers of enemy planes above us. But as a flight leader, Lieutenant Verdier is one in a thousand. He sees everything and led us to some corking targets in villages and forests almost under the patrols of enemy machines. We came home without a round of ammunition left, and, thanks to him, were not once in any real danger from above.

On February 18, 1918, the Escadrille Lafayette became the 103rd Pursuit Squadron of the United States Air Service. Lieutenant Verdier was then made Commanding Officer of the new Spad 124; afterward, of Spad 163, and finally, on April 4, 1918, he was placed in command of his old squadron, Spad 65.

After nearly four years of service at the Front, he was killed, on August 21, 1918, during a night bombardment of his aerodrome. At his death the French Air Service lost one of the finest of its pilots. There was scarcely a French squadron on the entire Front where he was not known and loved; and nowhere, surely, was he more deeply and sincerely mourned than by his old pilots and friends of the Escadrille Lafayette.

SINGLE COMBAT OVER RHEIMS

Biographical Sketches: The Corps

SERVICE RECORD

WAINWRIGHT ABBOTT, Pittsburgh, Pennsylvania.

SERVICE IN FRENCH AVIATION:
  Date of enlistment: April 2, 1917.
  Aviation Schools: April 3 to September 15, 1917.
    Avord, Pau, G.D.E.
  Breveted: August 7, 1917 (Nieuport).
  At the Front: Spad 154, September 18, 1917, to
    September 3, 1918.
  Final Rank: Sergent.

SERVICE IN U.S. AVIATION:
  Commissioned First Lieutenant, U.S. Air Service, August 15, 1918. On duty as tester at Headquarters, Paris, and at Colomby-les-Belles, September 3, 1918, to Armistice.

DECORATIONS:
  Croix de Guerre, with Palm and Star.

CITATIONS

Le 9 juin, 1918
Citation à l'Ordre du Groupe de Combat N° 11:
  Le Chef d'Escadrons Duseigneur, Commandant le Groupe de Combat N° 11, cite à l'Ordre du Régiment:

  Caporal ABBOTT, WAINWRIGHT, Pilote à L'Escadrille Spad 154

A montré au cours des dernières opérations les plus belles qualités de courage et de dévouement. Le 2 juin, 1918, a assuré une protection efficace à deux pilotes de l'escadrille chargés d'attaquer un drachen allemand qui a été incendié.

(*Signé*)   DUSEIGNEUR

Citation à l'Ordre de l'Armée: 27 juillet, 1918
  Sergent ABBOTT, WAINWRIGHT

  Pilote américain, s'est engagé au début de 1917 comme volontaire dans l'Armée Française; est venu en escadrille, où il montre tous les jours l'esprit de sacrifice et de dévouement. Avec deux autres pilotes a incendié deux drachens.

Wainwright Abbott

Wainy Abbott is one of the few Americans who were breveted on Nieuport. As he was with the famous Erlich in a squadron which specialized on *saucisses*, his life at the Front has not been devoid of excitement. On the Marne in the summer of 1918, with Erlich, Coiffard, and Lahoulle, Abbott made many perilous expeditions after the German gasbags at a time when the pyromaniacs often had to fight their way home through swarms of Fokkers. Wainy was so long with the French that he loved to *expliquer les coups*—an amiable weakness which consists in telling just how one did it, with appropriate sweeping gestures of the hands, signifying dives, zooms, and side-slips. One can easily picture him, forty years from now—grandchildren gathered around his knee—explaining with vivid gestures how grandfather used to shoot down *ballons* in the Great War.

SERVICE RECORD

JOHN RUSSELL ADAMS, Jersey City, New Jersey.

PREVIOUS SERVICE: Norton-Harjes Ambulance, 1916.

SERVICE IN FRENCH AVIATION:
Date of enlistment: February 20, 1917.
Aviation Schools: February 27 to August 10, 1917, Avord, Pau, G.D.E.
Breveted: June 14, 1917 (Nieuport).
At the Front: Spad 95: August 12 to October 12, 1917.
Spad 81: December 31, 1917 to March 13, 1918.
Final Rank: Caporal.

SERVICE IN U.S. AVIATION:
Commissioned Second Lieutenant, March 29, 1918.
Ferry-pilot, American Acceptance Park, Orly, April 4, 1918, to Armistice.

John Russell Adams

No one who was at Plessis in August, 1917, will ever forget Adams's plaintive request to the *Chef de Piste*, as he climbed in and out of his first Spad, for a machine with fewer disconcerting instruments and levers. Going to Escadrille N. 95 a short time later, he passed two quiet months at the Front and then went on leave to America. Coming back in November, he did not return to his old squadron, but was attached in December to Spad 81. Commissioned and ordered to active service in the United States Army in April, 1918, he gained fame at Orly as the only pilot in the Air Service who opened a bank account from his mileage returns as a ferry-pilot.

At the signing of the Armistice, Adams was in charge of the school for ferry-pilots at this same aviation centre.

SERVICE RECORD

ALAN N. ASH, Urbana, Illinois.

SERVICE IN FRENCH AVIATION:
Date of enlistment: June 15, 1917.
Aviation Schools: June 19, 1917, to February 20, 1918, Avord, Crotoy, G.D.E.
Breveted: November 3, 1917 (Caudron).
At the Front: Br. 134: February 23 to May 31, 1918.
Killed in combat: May 31, 1918, north of Oulchy-le-Château (Aisne).

Alan N. Ash

Writing to Major Gros a few days after Ash's death, the commanding officer of his squadron said:

"It is a heavy loss to the squadron—even in the short time he was with us he had made himself loved and admired to an extraordinary degree." Ash liked people, and there were few who failed to respond to his genuine good-nature and kindliness. The small children in the villages around Avord used to come running to greet their friend "Alash"—pronounced breathlessly, all in one word. At the *café* in the Gypsy Camp, frequented by Americans after the morning's work on the Blériot field, Ash might have been the proprietor; the family was devoted to him; he smoothed over difficulties with tired and irritable clients, and acted as intermediary between dining-room and kitchen when one's *deux ceufs sur le plât* were slow in making their appearance.

He learned to fly on the Blériot, was breveted on Caudron, and was beginning the Nieuport perfection work when he decided to apply for bombing, instead of *chasse*. There was no mistaking Ash's serious interest—the commandant willingly granted his request—and he was soon taking the Sopwith training, which he completed, with exceptionally good notes, at Le Crotoy. On February 23, 1918, he reached the Front, assigned to the Escadrille Br. 134.

ALAN ASH AT AVORD

The German advance of the following month kept the day-bombers constantly in the air, flying regardless of weather on missions of the most desperate character. In May the enemy struck south from the Chemin des Dames, and on the 31st, the fifth day of the attack, Ash fell in combat, shot down north of Oulchy-le-Château.

SERVICE RECORD

JAMES J. BACH, Paris, France.

PREVIOUS SERVICE: Foreign Legion, Infantry, August 24 to December 10, 1914.

SERVICE IN FRENCH AVIATION:
Date of enlistment: December 10, 1914.
Aviation Schools: March 10 to August 29, 1915, Pau, R.G.A.
Brevet: July 4, 1915 (Caudron).
At the Front: Escadrille M.S. (later N.) 38, August 29 to September 23, 1915.
Final Rank: Caporal.
Prisoner in Germany: September 23, 1915, to Armistice.

James J. Bach

Jimmie Bach has the distinction—a doubtful one in his opinion—of being the first member of the Lafayette Flying Corps, and also the first American, taken prisoner in the Great War. He enlisted in the Foreign Legion, Infantry Section, with Thaw, Soubiran, Bouligny, Kiffin Rockwell, Dowd, Trinkard, and other Americans who answered the call in August, 1914; was transferred to Aviation and first went to the Front as a pilot in a French squadron of Morane Saulniers, *biplace* monoplanes, which were used in those days, for both *chasse* and reconnaissance. On September 23, 1915, he was sent on special mission with Sergent-Pilote Mangeot, their duty being to land two French soldiers, dressed in civilian clothes, behind the enemy lines in the vicinity of Mézières. The two soldiers carried with them a large quantity of explosives with which they were to destroy a section of the railway line between Mézières and Hirson. After gathering information as to the disposition of enemy troops, they were to try to make their way back across the lines.

Plans were laid carefully, and the start was made. Landing-ground had already been chosen by the two soldiers, who knew the country well, but being soldiers of earth, they had selected a field not at all suitable from the airmen's point of view. It was rough and covered with bushes and small trees. However, a landing was made without accident, and a moment later, the soldiers with their load of explosives were on their way toward the railroad.

FRAZIER CURTIS, JAMES BACH, BERT HALL, AND NORMAN PRINCE AT PAU MARCH, 1915

Bach put on full gas and was off immediately, making toward the French lines. Looking back, he saw that Sergent Mangeot's machine had turned over on the ground. He landed again, picked up the French pilot, who was unhurt, but in taking off the second time, one wing of his Morane struck the limb of a tree. The machine crashed, of course, and although neither was hurt, they were face to face with a very serious situation. If the four men should be captured, and it could be proved that the two soldiers had been landed by the airmen, death was certain for all of them. Bach and his companion remained hidden in the woods until they were sure that the soldiers were far from the neighbourhood. Then they started homeward.

They were captured a few hours later and taken to Laon. Suspicion against them was strong, and they were twice court-martialled, on October 20 and October 30, 1915. The first time there was no verdict, and the second, owing largely to the able defence of a German lawyer, they were found not guilty.

Bach spent more than three years as a prisoner in various German camps. By right of seniority he becomes the *Herr Direkto*r of the *Amerikanischer-Kriegsgefangenen* Club. His eligibility for this office is no fault of his own, however. He made several attempts to escape, but was recaptured each time. He came back, after the Armistice was signed, the same quiet, genial fellow his old comrades had known, in the Foreign Legion, and in Aviation, long before the Escadrille Lafayette was organised.

SERVICE RECORD

PAUL FRANK BAER, Fort Wayne, Indiana.

SERVICE IN FRENCH AVIATION:
Date of enlistment: February 20, 1917.
Aviation Schools: February 27 to August 12, 1917, Avord, G.D.E.
Breveted: June 15, 1917 (Caudron).
At the Front: Spad 80, August 14, 1917, to January 10, 1918.
Escadrille Lafayette: January 10 to February 18, 1918.
Final Rank: Caporal.

SERVICE IN U.S. AVIATION:
Commissioned First Lieutenant, November 5, 1917.
At the Front: 103d Pursuit Squadron: February 18 to May 22, 1918.
Shot down and wounded in combat:
May 22, 1918, near Armentières.
Prisoner in Germany: Until the Armistice.

DECORATIONS:
Distinguished Service Cross, with Bronze Oak Leaf.
Légion d'Honneur.
Croix de Guerre, with seven Palms.

CITATIONS

G.H.Q., A.E.F. *April 10, 1918*

The Distinguished Service Cross is awarded to

    PAUL FRANK BAER, First Lieutenant, A.S.U.S.A., pilot, 103d Aero Squadron

On March 11, 1918, alone attacked a group of seven enemy pursuit machines, destroying one which crashed to the ground near the French lines northeast of Rheims. On March 15, 1918, he attacked two enemy two-seaters, one of which fell in flames, striking the ground in approximately the same region.

By command of General PERSHING

IVe ARMÉE, ÉTAT-MAJOR. *Le 8 avril*, 1918

Le Général Commandant la 4e Armée cite à l'Ordre de l'Armée les militaires dont les noms suivent: . . .

    Lieutenant BAER, PAUL F., de l'Escadrille Américaine, "Lafayette 103"

Pilote américain, engagé dans l'Armée Française, se révèle de suite comme un pilote de premier ordre, livrant de nombreux combats au cours desquels il met toujours l'ennemi en fuite. A abattu un avion ennemi.

Le Général Commandant la 4e Armée
GOURAUD

IVe ARMÉE, ÉTAT-MAJOR. *Le 11 avril*, 1918

Le Général Commandant la 4e Armée cite à l'Ordre de l'Armée les militaires dont les noms suivent: . . .

    Lieutenant BAER, PAUL, de l'Escadrille Lafayette (Groupe de Combat 21)

Pilote d'une merveilleuse ardeur, livrant combat sur combat à chaque sortie. Le 6 avril a livré trois combats à un ennemi supérieur en nombre, au cours desquels un ennemi est abattu en flammes et deux autres tombent desemparés dans leurs lignes.

Le Général Commandant la IVe Armée
GOURAUD

IVe ARMÉE, ÉTAT-MAJOR. *Le 11 avril*, 1918

Le Général Commandant la IVe Armée cite à l'Ordre de l'Armée les militaires dont les noms suivent: . . .

    Lieutenant BAER, PAUL, de l'Escadrille Lafayette (Groupe de Combat 21)

Pilote d'une merveilleuse audace, n'hésite jamais à engager le combat avec un ennemi supérieur en nombre. A abattu un avion ennemi (seconde victoire en quatre jours).

Le Général Commandant la IVe Armée
GOURAUD

VIe ARMÉE, ÉTAT-MAJOR. *Le 29 avril*, 1918

Le Général Commandant la VIe Armée cite à l'Ordre de l'Armée:

    BAER, PAUL FRANK, Lieutenant Pilote à l'Escadrille Américaine 103 (Lafayette)

Pilote de tout premier ordre, se signalant sans cesse par son audace. Le 12 et le 23 avril a réussi à abattre deux avions ennemis.

(Signé) *Le Général Commandant la Sixième Armée*

Q.G., *le 11 mai*, 1918

Le Général DE MITRY, Commandant le Détachement d'Armée du Nord, cite à l'Ordre de l'Armée:

    Le Lieutenant BAER, PAUL FRANK, Pilote à l'Escadrille Lafayette

Pilote remarquable d'audace, a exécuté dans la même journée six vols de chasse, au course desquels il a abattu deux avions ennemies.

(Signé) DE MITRY

DÉTACHEMENT D'ARMÉE DU NORD, ÉTAT-MAJOR. Q.G., *le 4 juin*, 1918

Le Général DE MITRY, Commandant le Détachement d'Armée du Nord, cite à l'Ordre de l'Armée:

Le Lieutenant BAER, PAUL FRANK, de l'Escadrille Lafayette
A abattu son huitième avion ennemi; le lendemain n'a pas hésité à attaquer dans les lignes ennemies une patrouille supérieure en nombre à laquelle il a livré un combat acharné, au cours duquel il a disparu.

(Signé)   DE MITRY

GRAND QUARTIER GÉNÉRAL DES ARMÉES
FRANÇAISES DE L'EST, ÉTAT-MAJOR.
BUREAU DU PERSONNEL.   Ordre No. 17,522 "D"
Après approbation du Général Commandant en Chef les Forces Expéditionnaires Améri-

caines en France, le Maréchal Commandant en Chef les Armées Françaises de l'Est, cite à l'Ordre de l'Armée:
Lieutenant BAER, PAUL
Pilote courageux et adroit. A été un très bel exemple pour ses camarades dans l'Escadrille Lafayette. A abattu 9 avions ennemis.

AU GRAND QUARTIER GÉNÉRAL.   Le 17 mai, 1919
Le Maréchal Commandant en Chef les Armées de l'Est.
Par decret du Président de la République en date du 9 avril, 1919, le Lieutenant BAER a été promu Chevalier de la Légion d'Honneur.
Cet promotion a été fait avec le motif de ce citation.

(Signé)   PÉTAIN

Paul F. Baer

When Baer was taken prisoner in the spring of 1918, our Aviation lost a man who would surely have run up a long string of victories. He has all the qualities that make an Ace: the coolness, the skill, the endurance, and the courage that never counts cost. Always on the offensive, Baer cruised far within the enemy lines in search of the enemy, and never hesitated to attack against heavy odds or under unfavourable circumstances. During the few months he was at the Front, he was officially credited with eight victories, winning for himself the reputation of a fighting-pilot of the very first order. His keenness and endurance are shown by the fact that in one day he has been known to make six patrols over the lines—a truly remarkable feat, as every aviator knows. Baer's resistance to fatigue is undoubtedly due to his simple habits. He took excellent care of his health and kept himself in all-round training like an athlete. He is, however, a thoroughly companionable fellow, always ready for a good time, frank and unaffected in manner, and much loved by his comrades.

In May, 1918, while a member of the 103rd Pursuit Squadron (formerly the Escadrille Lafayette), Baer met with a mishap which put him out of the war. At about nine o'clock on the 22nd, Lieutenants Giroux, Turnure, Wilcox, and Dugan, led by Baer, set out on patrol. Baer took them across the lines about sixteen kilometres southwest of Armentieres. They were flying at 5000 metres, when below them and some distance in the German lines, they saw five German singleseaters. As the Americans dove to attack, they saw three other German machines above them. Baer, with Giroux, close behind him, plunged headlong on one of the lower machines; next moment, the other four enemies dove on the two attackers. The three Germans of the big patrol *piqued* at once into the *mêlée*, and a fast and bitter combat ensued, during which Giroux was brought down and killed, and Baer had his controls cut by a bullet, after bringing down a German in flames. The other three Americans, heavily outnumbered and caught in a tight place, disengaged themselves with difficulty and reported on landing at the squadron that, when last seen, Baer was descending normally and was probably a prisoner.

The fact is that with his controls cut and two Albatross on his tail, shooting at him all the way down, Baer fell from 4000 metres and had a frightful crash, from which he escaped only by a miracle.

PAUL F BAER

Though he seldom speaks of it, Baer's experience as a prisoner in Germany was of exceptional interest. He was fairly well treated at the headquarters of the squadron which brought him down, but while being taken to the rear to receive treatment for his knee (which had been broken in the crash), he was noticed by a German infantry officer of very forbidding aspect. Frowning heavily, he approached the wounded American and, pointing to the ribbon of his *Croix de Guerre*, asked the meaning of the palms attached to it. Baer shook his head, not understanding at first, but another German standing nearby said,

"Each one of those Palms represents a *Deutscher flieger* shot down."

At this announcement the German, forgetting all tenets of military courtesy, reached over and pulled the decoration from Baer's breast with such violence that the pin ripped a hole in his tunic.

On another occasion, still badly crippled by his wounded knee, Baer showed his pluck by attempting to escape, far up in northern Germany. After several days of exposure and fatigue, he was captured by a body of the lowest type of German soldiers, and taken, in company with two escaped British officers, into a cellar where the soldiers were carousing with a number of women. In this place Baer, crippled and half dead with fatigue, was singled out for the heavy gibes and insults of his captors, and at last, unable to resist, was so severely beaten and mauled that he considers himself lucky to have escaped with his life.

Now that the war is over and he is safely in America once more, Baer should feel well satisfied with the part he has played in the struggle, for few members of the Lafayette Flying Corps have had more thrills or have made a finer record at the Front.

SERVICE RECORD

BENJAMIN H. BAIRD, New York City.

SERVICE IN FRENCH AVIATION:
Date of enlistment: June 25, 1917.
Aviation Schools: June 29, 1917, to March 1, 1918, Avord, G.D.E.
Breveted: September 26, 1917 (Caudron).
Final Rank: Caporal.

SERVICE IN U.S. NAVAL AVIATION:
Commissioned Ensign.
On duty in Italy, April to June, 1918.
On duty at Brest (Finisterre), August, 1918.

Benjamin H. Baird

Baird was breveted on Caudron at Avord, but instead of taking the Nieuport training, he decided to specialize in bombing work. After a course on Sopwith, he was sent—like Kyle, Corey, and Bluthenthal—to the Schmidt division. All the men who trained at Avord will remember the Schmidts: the huge and beautifully finished machines which were to be seen daily skimming low over the trees of the Blériot field—rapidly and with the sound of a six-cylinder automobile. They were considered one of the most difficult of all planes to land. Baird used to say that on a windy day it was next to impossible to bring down his Schmidt without touching one or the other of the long lower wings. He found the Bréguet easy after piloting these delicate birds, and was at the G.D.E., awaiting assignment to the Front, when he received notice that his application for transfer to the Navy had gone through, and that he had been commissioned Ensign. As a naval aviator, Baird saw service both in France and in Italy; it is unfortunate that no detailed information with regard to his later career is available.

SERVICE RECORD

H. CLYDE BALSLEY, San Antonio, Texas.

PREVIOUS SERVICE: American Ambulance, 1915.

SERVICE IN FRENCH AVIATION:
Date of enlistment: September 16, 1915.
Aviation Schools: October 1, 1915, to February 1, 1916, Pau, Ambérieu.
Breveted: January 2, 1916 (Blériot).
Attached to Air Guard of Paris as pilot with Escadrille V. 97, February 15 to April 1, 1916.
At Reserve Général Aéronautique, April 1 to May 26, 1916.
At the Front: Escadrille Lafayette: May 29 to June 18, 1916.
Seriously wounded in combat, June 18, 1916, incapacitated for further service at the Front.
Reformé from French Aviation.
Final Rank: Sergent.

SERVICE IN U.S. AVIATION
Commissioned Captain.
Attached to Pursuit Division, U.S.A.S., at Washington, D.C.

DECORATIONS:
Médaille Militaire.
Croix de Guerre, with Palm.

CITATION

LE MINISTRE DE LA GUERRE.   PARIS, *le 23 juillet,* 1916

Vu le Décret du 13 août, 1914. Sont inscrits aux tableaux spéciaux de la Médaille Militaire les militaires dont les noms suivent: . . . Pour prendre rang du 19 juin, 1916.

BALSLEY (H.C.) Caporal Pilote à l'Escadrille N 124, engagé pour la durée de la guerre: Jeune pilote plein d'allant et de courage. Le 18 juin, 1916, a attaqué plusieurs avions de chasse ennemis dans leurs lignes. Blessé très grièvement au cours du combat, a réussi à ramener son appareil dans nos lignes.

La nomination ci-dessus comporte l'attribution de la Croix de Guerre avec Palme.

(*Signé*)   ROQUES

H. Clyde Balsley

There are not many pilots in the Lafayette Corps who know Clyde Balsley personally, but there are very few of them who have not heard of him, and of the combat which came so near to costing him his life. He is one of the old-timers, one of the Pilgrim Fathers of the Escadrille Lafayette. Previous to his enlistment in the Aviation Section of the Foreign Legion in September, 1915, he had been a member of the American Ambulance Service. After receiving his *brevet militaire* in French Aviation, he and Chouteau Johnson spent six weeks at Le Bourget as members of the Air Guard of Paris. On May 29, 1916, they were both sent to N. 124, and one month later, June 18, to be exact, Balsley was shot down in one of the squadron's earliest battles. As a matter of fact it was his own first combat, for up to that time he had been flying back of the French lines, learning the country and getting "air sight." Four Lafayette pilots, Captain Thénault, Norman Prince, Kiffin Rockwell, and Balsley, were sent out on a *vol de protection* with several artillery *réglage* machines. They were well over on the German side of the lines, at 3500 metres, when they met a large enemy patrol, and the battle became general at once. Balsley dived on a two-seater *Aviatik* whose pilot didn't see him. He got within fifty metres of it before opening fire, and then his Lewis gun popped just once! A jammed Lewis gun, mounted (as they were in those days) on the top plane of a 15-metre Nieuport, was a difficult thing to arm in the air. In order to do it it was first necessary for the pilot to get out of the scrap.

Clyde was following this part of the procedure, with the *Aviatik* chasing him, firing briskly, when he was attacked from above by a second enemy plane. He was struck in the hip by an explosive bullet which made a terrific wound. Luckily for him, he was two thousand metres from the ground, for he could not use his right leg. (He learned afterwards that the sciatic nerve had been injured.) He tried to work the rudder bar by grasping his leg in his hands, but this was useless. Finally he managed to come out in *ligne de vol*, and not a minute too soon, for he was very close to the ground. He landed in a field of wild wheat, back of the French second lines, his Nieuport turning over and throwing him out. Dragging himself along for a few yards, he lay there, not knowing whether he was in French or German territory. Artillery began searching for his machine, which did nothing to relieve the strain of a terrible situation; for he was severely wounded, as badly hurt, almost, as a man can be and live. Then he was found by soldiers—in French uniform!

After a long period in a French evacuation hospital at Vadelaincourt, near Verdun, his life was despaired of, and he was sent to the American Ambulance Hospital at Neuilly. Here he was operated upon five or six times, during the course of the year, for his body was filled with tiny fragments of explosive bullet. He grew weaker and weaker, and would probably have died had it not been for the tireless, patient, splendid care of Miss Wolf, his American nurse. She pulled him through, and finally, in the autumn of 1917, nearly a year and a half after his combat, he was well enough to return to America.

Balsley will always be remembered by Americans, who were in

France in the early days of the war, as the airman *blessé*; for he was the only one who had been severely wounded at that time. Strange though it may seem, by the mere fact of being wounded, he rendered a great service to his country, one far-reaching in its ultimate effect. For he helped to make clear and unmistakable to the French people, America's friendship and her desire to help.

After recovering from his wound, although permanently crippled, he offered his services to the United States, was commissioned Captain, and did excellent work in the Pursuit Division, United States Air Service, at Washington.

SERVICE RECORD

LEIF NORMAN BARCLAY, New York City.

PREVIOUS SERVICE: American Ambulance, 1915-16.

SERVICE IN FRENCH AVIATION:
 Date of enlistment: May 22, 1916.
 Aviation Schools: June 20, 1916, to April 9, 1917, Buc, Avord, Cazeaux, Pau, G.D.E.
 Breveted: October 6, 1916 (Blériot).
 At the Front: Escadrille N. 82: April 12 to June 1, 1917.
 Final Rank: Sergent.
 Killed in line of duty: June 1, 1917, at Chaux, near Belfort.

DECORATIONS:
 Croix de Guerre, with Palm.

CITATION

VIIe ARMÉE. *Le* 24 *juin*, 1917

Le Général Boissoudy, Commandant la VIIe Armée, cite à l'Ordre de l'Armée, le Sergent BARCLAY, LEIF, du 1er Étranger, M^{le} 38920, Pilote à l'Escadrille N. 82:

Sujet américain qui a servi en France depuis le début de la guerre; d'abord à l'Ambulance Américaine et ensuite engagé volontaire à la Légion Étrangère, comme pilote aviateur. Pilote depuis le 12 avril, 1917, a fait l'admiration de tous par son habileté, son entrain, son mépris absolu du danger. A livré de nombreux combats aériens. Tué le 1er juin, 1917, à la suite d'un accident au départ pour une patrouille.

(*Signé*) DE BOISSOUDY

Leif Norman Barclay

The *élèves-pilotes* who were at Buc when the school there was discontinued, and who were sent to Pau, will always remember and be grateful for Barclay's assistance upon their arrival at the latter camp. He had been there for several weeks, and was the only one of all the earlier Americans who took an interest in the new arrivals. He secured bedding, quarters, and food for them, and helped them through the tedious routine which is inevitable in the French Army when a soldier changes his post. This is a trifling incident, and is mentioned only because it is typical of Barclay's kindly, unselfish nature. He was always ready to help, no matter what the inconvenience to himself.

BARCLAY AT BELFORT, MAY, 1917

He was killed in an accident six weeks after his arrival at the Front. While doing acrobacy over the field at Chaux, the muzzle cup of his machine gun came loose, striking the propeller and shattering it. Fragments were thrown against the wing bracings, tearing them loose and allowing the wings to collapse. The following address was delivered at his grave by his French squadron commander. It is a brief and eloquent resume of Barclay's service for France, and of the qualities which endeared him to his comrades:

> Le Sergent Barclay à qui nous avons l'immense peine de rendre aujourd'hui les derniers honneurs, était l'un de ces héroiques Américains venus en si grand nombre se battre pour nous des les premiers jours de la guerre.
> Accouru en France avec les premiers d'entre eux, il a pendant près de deux ans prodigué ses soins à nos blessés. Remarqué plusieurs fois par ses chefs pour sa superbe attitude sous de violents bombardements, il a trouvé cependant que ce n'était pas assez servir notre pays.
> Engagé volontaire à la Légion Etrangère et versé dans l'Aviation, il devint rapidementun excellent pilote.

Dès son arrivée en Escadrille, il a fait notre admiration à tous par son entrain, son adresse, son mépris absolu du danger, par la haute noblesse de ses sentiments.

Toujours volontaire pour les missions les plus périlleuses, impatient de se signaler par quelque action d'éclat, navré lorsqu'un jour se passait sans qu'il ait pu combattre, il fallait constamment modérer son ardeur. Il est tombé glorieusement avant d'avoir pu donner tout ce que promettait son courage, victime d'une manoeuvre trop hardie demandant à son appareil un trop violent effort.

Sergent Barclay, infiniment reconnaissants envers votre Patrie d'avoir fait pour notre cause le sacrifice d'hommes tels que vous, plus sûrs encore si possible du prochain triomphe puisque tous vos frères combattent maintenant à nos côtés, nous nous inclinons tous avec émotion et respect devant votre tombe ouverte et nous garderons pieusement votre souvenir.

(Discours prononcé par M. le Capitaine Échard, Commandant l'Escadrille N. 82, aux obsèques du Sergent-Pilote Barclay, Leif, mort glorieusement pour la France, le 1er juin, 1917.)

SERVICE RECORD

CHARLES CHESTER BASSETT, JR., New York City.

SERVICE IN FRENCH AVIATION:
 Date of enlistment: June 17, 1917.
 Aviation Schools: June 30, 1917, to February 10, 1918, Avord, Pau, Cazeaux, G.D.E.
 Final Rank: Caporal.

SERVICE IN U.S. NAVAL AVIATION:
 Commissioned Ensign.
 Promoted Lieutenant (Junior Grade).
 At the Front: U.S. Naval Air Station, Dunkirk, February 14 to September 3, 1918.
 Attached to 218th Squadron, British Royal Air Force.

Charles Chester Bassett, Jr.

The name of Bassett recalls the dining-room of the Hôtel Bordérieux at Avord—eight o'clock of a cool September evening; a table in the pleasant warmth of the fireplace, tended by the deft and ornamental Marcelle; Bassett, Neal Wainwright, Don Eldredge, and Jim

McMillen, lingering over an excellent dinner while the day's flying was discussed. Sometimes one of the Blériot *moniteurs*—Vireau, de la Tourasse, or de Curnieu—sat down for a *liqueur*; sometimes little Mademoiselle Bougeassie, whose brother lay in the hospital, injured in a severe Nieuport crash, came in to entertain the Americans with her pretty attempts to speak English. They were pleasant evenings—not soon to be forgotten.

While at the G.D.E., awaiting his turn to go to the Front, Bassett was released from the French Army, and commissioned an Ensign in the U.S. N.A.S. The land Aviation lost an exceptional single-seater pilot when he transferred, for at Pau and Cazeaux he had shown a real mastery of the Nieuport. With the navy he had the good fortune to see plenty of active service: flying hydros at the United States Naval Air Station at Dunkirk, and doing day-bombing work, attached to the 218th Squadron of the Royal Air Force. His promotion to the rank of Lieutenant (Junior Grade) is evidence of the quality of his service.

SERVICE RECORD
Henry A. Batchelor, jr, Saginaw, Michigan.
Service in French Aviation:
  Date of enlistment: August 1, 1917.
  Aviation Schools: August 1, to December 14, 1917. Avord, Tours, Pau, G.D.E.
  Breveted: October 14, 1917 (Caudron).
  At the Front: Escadrille Spad 103, December 16, 1917, to March 1, 1918.
  Final Rank: Caporal.
Service in U.S. Naval Aviation:
  Commissioned Ensign.
  Promoted to Lieutenant (Junior Grade).
  Assistant Chief Pilot and later Chief Pilot, U.S. Naval Air Station, Moutchic-Lacanau (Gironde), March 10, 1918, to Armistice.

Henry A. Batchelor

Batchelor was sent to a French squadron, when the last of the frequently altered plans had been made for the transfer of Lafayette men to the United States Air Service. It was an unfortunate time, and, to make matters worse, he had an accident at his aerodrome, which robbed him of six weeks of service at the Front with the French.

He was eager to be getting experience as a combat pilot, but after a month in hospital, and while waiting to be returned to his squadron, he received his commission in the United States Naval Air Service with orders to report to the Aviation Instruction Centre at Moutchic-Lacanau. As chief pilot at this school, he did excellent work; but he was bitterly disappointed, and fretted constantly under the compulsion of remaining in the rear.

Batchelor would have made a fine record at the Front, but like many another American pilot he was deprived of his opportunity because of the great need of our Air Force for capable instructors.

SERVICE RECORD

James Henry Baugham, Washington, North Carolina.

Service in French Aviation:
Date of enlistment: July 10, 1917.
Aviation Schools: July 19 to December 24, 1917, Avord, Juvisy, Pau, G.D.E.
Breveted: October 17, 1917 (Caudron).
At the Front: Escadrille N. 157, December 26, 1917, to June 27, 1918.
Escadrille Spad 98, June 27 to July 2, 1918.
Final Rank: Sergent.
Wounded in combat: July 1, 1918, over the forest of Villers-Cotterets.
Died in hospital: July 2, 1918.

Decorations:
Médaille Militaire.
Croix de Guerre, with Palm.

CITATIONS

IVme Armée, État-Major.   5 juin, 1918
Citation à l'Ordre de l'Armée:
Sergent Baugham, James Henry, du 1er Régiment Étranger, détaché à l'Escadrille Spa. 157 (sujet américain):
Pilote adroit et audacieux. Le . . . a attaqué un drachen ennemi oblige l'observateur à sauter en parachute. A recommence la même mission le. . . . Le même jour, a attaqué un avion ennemi, l'a obligé à atterrir dans les lignes après avoir mis le mitrailleur hors de combat.

19 juin, 1918

La Médaille Militaire a été conférée:
Au Sergent Baugham, James Henry (Active), du 3e Groupe d'Aviation, Pilote à l'Escadrille 157
Jeune pilote d'un rare courage. Depuis son arrivée à l'escadrille a abattu deux avions ennemis. Au cours d'un violent combat contre un appareil allemand, a été contraint d'atterrir entre les lignes par suite d'avaries à son moteur; a réussi à regagner les lignes françaises sous une grêle de balles en ramenant une partie de l'équipement de son appareil. Une citation.

James Henry Baugham

Baugham had taken a civilian pilot's license at Newport News before his departure for France, and had piloted both flying boats and land machines with great success. His intention at that time was to enter the American Army as a flying officer, but so impatient was he for action that he decided to start at once overseas to join the Lafayette Flying Corps.

He was a fine type of Southerner, keen, alert, and full of courage. He came of old American stock, the kind that loves danger for its own sake and fights to the last ditch. Breveted on Caudron at Juvisy, his performances on the staid G. 3 were the marvel of both students and instructors, and on more than one occasion were almost the means of obtaining several *jours d'arrêt*. He did vertical spirals, *renversements*, and loops in a machine which was never designed for acrobacy, and when he left the school was considered among the most skilful and daring pilots who had trained there.

From the G.D.E. he was sent to the Escadrille Spad 157. During the few months he was on the Front he fulfilled all the prophecies that had been made by his instructors.

Before his death he undoubtedly shot down four Germans, although two of them were too far within the enemy lines to be confirmed, and was decorated with the *Croix de Guerre* and *Médaille Militaire*, this last for a remarkable adventure, during which he landed between the lines and escaped to friendly territory under a storm of bullets.

Finally, on July 1, 1918, exactly one year after his arrival in France, he made his last flight. It was at 4.30 in the afternoon. Flying over the Forest of Villers-Cotterets, he attacked, single-handed, three Germans, and during a very fierce point-blank combat received two grievous wounds. Faint from loss of blood and pain, he managed to reach the French lines, but he was beyond human aid, and died on July 2.

SERVICE RECORD

Frank L. Baylies, New Bedford, Massachusetts.

Previous Service: American Ambulance, France and at Salonica, February 1916, to May, 1917.

Service in French Aviation:
Date of enlistment: May 21, 1917.
Aviation Schools: May 26 to November 15, 1917, Avord, Pau, G.D.E.
Breveted: September 20, 1917 (Caudron).
At the Front: Escadrille Spad 73, November 17 to December 18, 1917.
Escadrille Spad 3, December 18, 1917, to June 17, 1918.
Final Rank: Sergent.
Killed in combat: June 17, 1918, near Rollot (Somme).

Decorations:
Médaille Militaire.
Croix de Guerre, with Six Palms and One Star.

L'Armée Française d'Orient
57⁰ Division, Service de Santé.
Le Général Jacquemot, Commandant la 57⁰ Division d'Infanterie, cite à l'Ordre de la Division, les Militaires dont les noms suivent: ...

CITATIONS

Baylies, Frank, volontaire américain, Section Sanitaire Automobile Américaine No. 3
    Deux fois volontaire sur le front de France, puis pour l'Armée d'Orient, ont mis au service des blessés un dévouement et une intrépidité parfaite, journellement éprouvées du 19 décembre, 1916, au 26 mars, 1917, dans les évacuations du Secteur de Monastir, faits au mépris des bombardements de la ville, de la route, et du Cantonnement même de la Section.

II⁰ Armée, État-Major.   Le 9 mars, 1918
Le Général Commandant la II⁰ Armée cite à l'Ordre de l'Armée:
Le Caporal Baylies, Frank, M^le 12186, du 1er Régiment Étranger, Pilote à l'Escadrille Spad 3
    Citoyen américain engagé dans l'Armée Française avant la déclaration de guerre des États-Unis. Passé sur sa demande dans l'aviation de chasse; fait preuve du plus bel entrain. Le 18 février, 1918, a abattu, seul, un avion ennemi qui s'est écrasé dans ses lignes.
                                          (Signé)   Hirschauer

                                                             Le 6 mai, 1918
Le Général Commandant la 1er Armée cite à l'Ordre de l'Armée:
                Baylies, Frank, M^le 12186, Sergent 1er Régiment Étranger
    Excellent pilote de chasse, n'a pas voulu entrer dans l'aviation américaine comme officier pour ne pas quitter son Escadrille Française. Y livre journellement des combats. Vient d'abattre seul son 2me avion.

Citation à l'Ordre de l'Armée: 16 mai, 1918
Baylies (Frank), M^le 12186, Sergent du 1er Régiment Étranger, Pilote a l'Escadrille, Spa. 3
    Pilote de chasse de grande classe. Ne cesse de rechercher l'ennemi et entraine merveilleusement la patrouille dont il est chef. Le 2 mai, 1918, a abattu seul son cinquième avion ennemi. Dès le lendemain, a remporté sa sixième victoire.
                              Le Général Commandant la 1ère Armée
                                     (Signé)   Debeney

Citation à l'Ordre de l'Armée: 25 mai, 1918
Baylies, Frank, M^le 12186, Sergent au 1er Régiment Étranger, Pilote à l'Escadrille Spa. 3
    Excellent pilote de chasse. Le 28 mars, son avion touché dans ses parties essentielles, a atterri entre les lignes; dégagé par une patrouille d'infanterie, est revenu avec debris de son avion, malgré le feu ennemi, et a rapporté ses instruments de bord. Le 11 avril a abattu en feu son troisième avion ennemi.
                              Le Général Commandant la 1ère Armée
                                     (Signé)   Debeney

Citation à l'Ordre de l'Armée: 29 mai, 1918
Baylies, Frank, Sergent au 1er Régiment Étranger, Pilote à l'Escadrille Spa. 3
Brillant pilote de chasse. Les 9 et 10 mai, 1918, a abattu son septième et huitième ennemi.
                              Le Général Commandant la 1ère Armée
                                   (Signé)   Debeney

Frank L. Baylies

Baylies, Putnam, Lufbery, these are great names in the Lafayette Flying Corps, a trio of superb pilots and keen fighting men. Lufbery, the best known of all, combined a cool caution with his skill in shooting and combat tactics, rarely attacking at a disadvantage. Putnam was a bitter and reckless fighter, dashing to the attack regardless of risk. The genius of Baylies is more difficult to define; the French pilots of the *Cigognes*, who watched and tutored him, declared that he possessed the qualities of the greatest Aces, the straight shooting, the skill in manoeuvre, the instinct for taking the enemy at a disadvantage. Even in the school, we recognised in him a true individual touch in flying and an absolute disregard of danger. His contemporaries will remember our horror and the monitor's despair when Baylies did a *vrille* in an ancient Blériot, unparalleled feat!

From the G.D.E., he went to the Front in the famous Spad 3, the Squadron of Dorme, Heurteaux, Deuillin, and Guynemer, where the newly fledged American corporal soon made a name for himself as a pilot of extraordinary worth. His French comrades, critics of the keenest, predicted for him a brilliant career, and he was not slow in confirming their expectations. His *escadrille* was patrolling the most active sectors of the Western Front, pitted against the best of Germany's fighting pilots. At Noyon, Montdidier, and on the Somme, the *Cigognes* found their dreamed-of happy hunting grounds, and in desperate combats against the formidable "Rednoses," "Checkerboards," and "Tangos," Baylies soon made himself one of the wonders of an *escadrille d'élite*. His tactics were faultless; he was a dead shot, and rarely broke off a combat until his opponent was plunging earthward, dead in his cockpit or enveloped in flames.

Once, in his anxiety to make sure of a victory, he descended almost to the ground, far behind the German lines. His victim crashed, but while returning, Baylies had his machine riddled by bullets from the ground and his motor ruined. Volplaning down with propeller stopped, he landed between the French and German lines, only a few yards from the latter. Undoing his belt before the wheels touched ground, he leaped from the still moving machine, dodged two Germans who tried to catch him, and sprinted to a French advance post, escaping, by some miracle, through a storm of lead from the enemy lines.

Toward the end, Baylies was considered almost invincible. In attacking, he held his fire until at point-blank range, when his first burst was usually fatal. In three months he scored twelve official victories and many others, undoubtedly shot down, but too far in the enemy lines for official confirmation under the strict French system.

Personally, Baylies was the most attractive of men, frank, kind, and jolly, the kind of a chap who is always good company. In a crowd he did not often speak seriously, but his close friends knew that beneath his bluff manner ran a vein of thoughtfulness and genuine idealism; it was not for pure love of adventure that he worked so honourably as an ambulance driver, joined the Aviation, and made at last the greatest sacrifice. His modesty was always charming; no amount of success could turn his head or alter his simple statement that his victories were due to luck.

He was killed during the bitter fighting along the west side of the Marne Salient. We shall never know the exact circumstances. It was five o'clock on the afternoon of June 17, in the region between Crevecoeur and Lassigny. Adjudant Parsons, of the *Cigognes*, reported that Baylies fell in flames after being attacked by four German *monoplaces*. Sinclaire, of the Spad 68, was flying with a comrade over the same region. He saw a patrol of Germans well within their lines, and as he turned to attack them he saw three Spads, bearing on their sides the famous insignia of the *Cigognes*, heading eastward after a second patrol of Fokker triplanes, still farther in.

When his combat broke off, Sinclaire caught a glimpse of a distant machine, which he feared was a Spad, going down in flames. This was undoubtedly Baylies, cut off in the prime of his skill and fame; sincerely mourned by his comrades and by the entire Aviation of France.

SERVICE RECORD

JAMES ALEXANDER BAYNE, Grand Rapids, Michigan.

SERVICE IN FRENCH AVIATION:
Date of enlistment: July 10, 1917.
Aviation Schools:
  July 19, 1917, to February 26, 1918, Avord, Tours, Pau, Cazeaux, G.D.E.
Breveted: October 19, 1917 (Caudron).
At the Front:
  Escadrille Spad 85, March 1 to March 3, 1918.
  Escadrille Spad 81, March 3 to March 29, 1918.
Final Rank: Caporal.

SERVICE IN U.S. AVIATION:
Commissioned First Lieutenant: March 29, 1918.
At the Front: Attached to the French Squadron Spad 81, March 29 to May 8, 1918.
Killed in line of duty: May 8, 1918.

James Alexander Bayne

Bayne was a fine example of the serious, successful young American who felt it his duty to take an active part in fighting the German aggressors. A sportsman in civil life, he had sailed racing craft and driven high-speed motor boats for several years; he took naturally to aviation and made it a serious study. His interest in motors and the technical side of flying made him stand out among his more irresponsible comrades, and unlike many of the technically inclined, he developed into a skilful and daring pilot.

Bayne went to the Front, in the Escadrille Spad 85, on March 1,

1918, and was commissioned a First Lieutenant in the United States Army while on service with Spad 81. During the short time he was with the squadron, he showed great promise, but on May 8, 1918, while testing a 220 H.P. Spad, he met his death. The exact cause of the accident cannot be determined.

At 2000 metres above the field, he was seen to go into a steep dive, which continued for about 1000 metres when suddenly the four wings came off the machine and the fuselage plunged into the ground, killing Bayne instantly. It is possible, as happens sometimes to the strongest, that he fainted and went into a dive with full motor; it is possible also that there was some defect in the construction of his machine.

We shall never know the truth. The accident cost us a fine comrade, loved and respected by a wide circle of friends, and a pilot who would have rendered good service to his country.

SERVICE RECORD

PHILIP P. BENNEY, Pittsburgh, Pennsylvania.

SERVICE IN FRENCH AVIATION:
Date of enlistment: May 31, 1917.
Aviation Schools: June 18 to December 10, 1917, Avord, Tours, Pau, G.D.E.
Breveted: October 16, 1917 (Caudron).
At the Front: Escadrille Spad 67: December 12, 1917, to January 26, 1918.
Final Rank: Caporal.
Seriously wounded in combat:
Near Montfaucon, January 25, 1918.
Died in hospital: January 26, 1918.

DECORATIONS:
Croix de Guerre, with Palm.

CITATION

Citation à l'Ordre de la IIe Armée, N° 1080:

Le Brigadier Pilote BENNEY, PHILIP, Pilote à l'Escadrille Spa. 67

Jeune pilote américain, engagé volontaire dans l'Armée française, a toujours fait preuve du plus bel entrain. A été blessé très grièvement le 25 janvier, 1918, dans un dur combat contre un groupe d'avions ennemis. Mort glorieusement pour la France le 26 janvier, 1918, des suites de cette blessure.

Le Capitaine Commandant l'Escadrille Spa. 67
(Signé)   J. D'INDY

Philip P. Benney

The circumstances of Phil Benney's death form a stirring commentary on his own splendid pluck, and the self-sacrifice of the French who tended him. On the 25th of January, at three o'clock in the afternoon, Benney was on patrol with four comrades far beyond the enemy lines before Verdun.

All at once a German patrol, which had stolen up unperceived, attacked them from beneath, and in the first exchange of shots Benney was grievously wounded—an explosive bullet in the calf and another in the thigh. Bleeding profusely and feeling his consciousness slipping from him, he managed, by a superb effort of coolness and will power, to regain the lines and land in friendly territory. Kind-hearted *poilus* ran to aid him, lifted him from the machine, stanched his wounds as best they could, and rushed him to the hospital at Glorieux.

BENNEY (LEFT) AND SPENCER

There he was able to talk to his comrades who came to the bedside as fast as the touring car could bring them; he seemed cheerful, and even told Tailer to keep the news from his family. But he had lost great quantities of blood, and Dr. Henriot, the kind and skilful French surgeon in command, saw that an immediate transfusion would be necessary.

With fine self-sacrifice, Sergent Cazé at once offered his blood, and that not being sufficient, the Aide Major Reinhold stepped forward to make up the deficit. It was in vain. Benney was beyond human aid and died quietly in the night, mourned by all his comrades and by the French who had worked so nobly to save him.

SERVICE RECORD

Leo E. Benoit, Attleboro, Massachusetts.

Service in French Aviation:
 Date of enlistment: June 10, 1917.
 Aviation Schools: June 22 to November 15, 1917, Avord, Juvisy, G.D.E.
 Breveted: September 22, 1917 (Caudron).
 At the Front: Escadrille Spad 84, November 18 to December 2, 1917.
  Escadrille Spad 228, February 1 to April 1, 1918.
 Wounded: December 13, 1917.
 Final Rank: Sergent.

Service in U.S. Aviation:
 Commissioned Second Lieutenant: April 23, 1918.
 At the Front: Attached to French Escadrille Spad 228, May 1 to August 25, 1918.
  213th Pursuit Squadron, August 25, 1918, to Armistice.

Decorations:
 Croix de Guerre.

CITATION

Ière Armée
Service Aéronautique.   Le 8 avril, 1919

Le Sergent Pilote Benoit, Leo, No. 5880 cité à l'Ordre du Jour la Ière Armée

Engagé volontaire au service de la France, pilote très adroit et d'un sang-froid extraordinaire, a rempli sans arrêt d'une façon parfaite les nombreuses missions de guerre que lui furent confiées.

Le 6 avril, 1918, au cours d'une mission lointaine dans les lignes ennemies, il fut attaqué par une patrouille de quatre avions ennemis, le Sergent Benoit fut blessé par une balle phosphoreuse; malgré sa blessure douloureuse, continua sa mission, et rapporta des photos de la plus importance.

Le Sergent Benoit a un avion ennemi à son actif.
Cette citation lui porte la Croix de Guerre.

Leo E. Benoit

Benoit is one of the Lafayette men who took the Caudron training at Juvisy. Breveted September 22, he did well at Pau, and went to the Front on November 18, in Escadrille Spad 84. On one of his first patrols he got lost and had a "smash" near Meaux; slightly injured in the accident, he was sent back to the G.D.E., where he trained on the Spad *biplace*, and returned to the Front on February 1, 1918, in Escadrille Spad 228.

In April, 1918, Benoit was transferred to the United States Air Service with the rank of Second Lieutenant, and, at the request of his Squadron Commander, was allowed to remain as an American officer attached to his old French squadron. He was afterward sent to the 213th Pursuit Squadron, and from August 25 until the Armistice was employed as a pilot with his squadron and as a tester at the First Air Dépôt at Colombey-les-Belles.

SERVICE RECORD

CHARLES J. BIDDLE, Andalusia, Pennsylvania.

SERVICE IN FRENCH AVIATION:
Date of enlistment: April 8, 1917.
Aviation Schools: April 13 to July 26, 1917, Avord, Pau, G.D.E.
Breveted: June 2, 1917 (Caudron).
At the Front: Escadrille Spad 73, July 28, 1917, to January 10, 1918.
Escadrille Lafayette, January 10 to February 18, 1918.
Final Rank: Sergent.

SERVICE IN U.S. AVIATION:
Commissioned Captain, November 7, 1917.
Promoted Major, November 1, 1918.
At the Front: 103d Pursuit Squadron, February 18 to June 22, 1918.
Commanding Officer, 13th Pursuit Squadron, June 22, to October 24, 1918.
Commanding Officer, 4th Pursuit Group, October 25, 1918, to Armistice.
Wounded in combat: May 15, 1918.

DECORATIONS:
Légion d'Honneur.
Croix de Guerre, with three Palms.
Ordre de Léopold (Belgium).

CITATIONS

Ière ARMÉE, ÉTAT-MAJOR. *Au Q.G.A., le 27 janvier*, 1918

Le Général Commandant la Ière Armée cite à l'Ordre de l'Armée:

BIDDLE, CHARLES, M^{le} 12137, Caporal au Ier Régiment Étranger, Pilote à l'Escadrille S. 73 Américain engagé volontaire avant l'entrée en guerre des États-Unis. Excellent pilote de chasse; fait preuve journellement d'audace, d'énergie, et de mépris du danger. Le 5 décembre, 1917, a abattu un avion ennemi dans nos lignes.

(Signé) DEBENEY

VIe ARMÉE, ÉTAT-MAJOR. *Q.G., le 29 avril*, 1918

Le Général Commandant la VIe Armée cite à l'Ordre de l'Armée:

BIDDLE, CHARLES JOHN, Capitaine Pilote à l'Escadrille Américaine N° 103 (Lafayette) Officier pilote remarquable. Le 12 avril, a réussi à abattre un avion ennemi.

DÉTACHEMENT D'ARMÉE DU NORD, ÉTAT MAJOR. *Q.G., le 4 juin*, 1918

Le Général de MITRY, Commandant le Détachement d'Armée du Nord, cite à l'Ordre de l'Armée:

Le Capitaine BIDDLE, CHARLES JOHN, de l'Escadrille Lafayette

Pilote d'un allant merveilleux. A attaqué successivement dans leurs lignes deux biplaces ennemis, a probablement abattu le premier. Blessé et désemparé au cours du 2ème combat a réussi à force d'énergie à atterrir entre les lignes et a pu après avoir passé la journée dans un trou d'obus regagner de nuit les tranchées alliées.

(Signé) DE MITRY

GRAND QUARTIER GÉNÉRAL DES ARMÉES
FRANÇAISES DE L'EST, ÉTAT-MAJOR. *Le 17 mai*, 1919

Après approbation du Général Commandant en Chef les Forces Expéditionnaires Américaines en France, le maréchal Commandant en Chef les Armées Françaises de l'Est cite à l'Ordre de l'Armée:

Capitaine BIDDLE, CHARLES J.

Citoyen américain engagé dans la Légion Étrangère. Excellent pilote qui n'a pas cessé de faire preuve des meilleures qualités de courage et de dévouement. A rendu les plus grands services comme pilote à l'Escadrille Lafayette.

Le Maréchal en Chef des Armées de l' Est
PÉTAIN

Par Decret du Président de la République en date du 9 avril, 1919, le Capitaine BIDDLE a été promu Chevalier de la Légion d'Honneur.
Cette promotion a été fait avec le motif de cette citation.

Charles J. Biddle

Charles J. Biddle's brilliant record in French aviation schools was even more brilliantly fulfilled at the Front. The *moniteurs* at Avord, Pau, and at G.D.E. regarded him as an unusually fine pilot. He completed all of his training—Penguins, Blériot, Caudron, Nieuport—and the final advanced work in acrobacy and combat in less than three months, and had almost a month to spare at Le Plessis-Belleville awaiting his orders for assignment to a squadron. At Plessis one's time was for the most part free, and it was the custom of many pilots to spend a large share of it on French leave in Paris, which was only an hour distant by train. Biddle might have followed the crowd, for he enjoyed good, wholesome amusement as much as anyone. But to him flying was the most fascinating of all amusements, and he never lost his zest for it. Furthermore, he knew, as all of us knew, that most of the deaths in aviation, whether by accident or in combat, were due to inexperience, and that a very large percentage of them occurred during the pilot's early weeks at the Front. He had no desire to die for France. He much

BIDDLE AT THE FRONT

preferred to live and to accomplish results for her.

Therefore, at the G.D.E., as elsewhere, he kept steadily before him his purpose, which was so to perfect himself in the management of combat planes that he could be reasonably certain of getting results when he should be sent on active duty. Had all the members of the Lafayette Corps been as keen for their work, and as serious in their desire for success in it, the total of accomplishment would have been more than doubled. But this is, perhaps, too broad a statement, and does not make sufficient allowance for differences of temperament and individuality. Charles Biddle is both a theorist and a man of action, and the qualities of such opposite types are rarely combined, as he combined them, successfully.

His first service at the Front was with the French squadron, Spad 73. Oliver Chadwick was sent with him to this unit. The two men had much in common, and all of us who knew them and their excellent records in the aviation schools predicted great things for them. Both were fearless and accomplished combat pilots and were among the very few of whom it could be said that they had got all that could be got from their training. But in war there are no certainties, and Chadwick was killed in an unequal combat while saving another Allied plane from destruction. Biddle splendidly avenged his death on December 5, 1917, when he shot down an Albatross two-seater near Langemarck in Belgium. This was his only official victory during his five months' service with the French, but he actually destroyed other enemy machines which were as surely victories and which added as certainly to the losses of the German Air Force.

During these early months of active service, Biddle made a careful study of combat tactics. Actual experience gained in his own battles had taught him much, and he corrected or confirmed his findings by consulting the most famous of the French pilots with whom he came in contact. The result of this study was a monograph on aerial combat which was later adopted for use in the instruction of pilots in the U.S. Air Service. It had the merit of being a thoroughly readable and interesting as well as a practical study, and was but one of Biddle's many ways of being useful to his country in time of war.

He was commissioned as Captain in the U.S. Air Service on November 7, 1917, and in common with most of the Lafayette men was compelled to waste valuable time in inactivity while awaiting active duty orders. He remained with Spad 73 until early in January, and a month later was sent to the Escadrille Lafayette which was then on the point of becoming the 103rd American Pursuit Squadron. That was a happy time in the history of the *escadrille*. All of the pilots were in American uniform, although still under French orders. William Thaw, the best of C.O.'s, was in charge, with Lieutenant Verdier-Fauvety second-in-command. We had good Spads and plenty of them. Beside the regular daily patrols there were many voluntary ones, for every pilot was eager to secure the first official victory for the U.S. Air Service. The honour fell to Paul Baer, who shot down an Albatross near Rheims on March 11, 1918. Biddle, who was always the first to suggest a voluntary patrol, brought down the 103rd's seventh plane on April 12, a two-seater Halberstadt, which fell at Corbeny on the Chemin-des-Dames. Under ordinary conditions a battle with a two-seater is far more of a sporting proposition than a single-seater and requires twice the skill at manoeuvring. Biddle made good theory meet with sound practice—the result being that three of his seven official victories were the result of battles with two-passenger machines.

While he was with the Escadrille Lafayette on the Champagne sector, the German airmen on the opposite side of the lines destroyed a good many French observation balloons. They made their attacks with exasperating frequency and success. Their incendiary bullets seemed flawless and rarely if ever failed in igniting a gas bag. Finally, when no attempt at retaliation was made by the French Q.G., Biddle decided to call the matter to the attention of Commandant Féquant, and to ask that he and one of his comrades of the 103rd be permitted to concentrate their energies on German balloons. The two men were told, what they had already learned by experiment, that the incendiary bullets, then in use by the French, would not ignite the gas in German balloons, and that while a more satisfactory kind of bullet would soon be ready, none were at hand at that time. This was a great disappointment to Biddle. It was unfortunate that his plan could not be carried out, for he left nothing to chance and would undoubtedly have destroyed many German balloons.

On May 15, 1918, he had one of the most unpleasant as well as the most thrilling experiences which can happen to an airman. He was shot down, wounded, in No Man's Land. The enemy machine was flying at 600 metres over the desolate battlefields between Langemarck and Ypres where the opposing lines are no more than a series of shell-holes joined together. Biddle described it as:

The slowest bus I ever saw, with a rounded body, a square tail, and the lower wing much shorter than the upper, like many English two-seater observation planes. Whether or not this fellow was what I think he was (an armoured plane of the new Junker type), he certainly got the best of me, and I don't feel at all vindictive about it, as it was a perfectly fair fight, but just the same it would give me more satisfaction to bring that boy down than any five others. It would also be interesting to see whether his hide is thick enough to stand a good dose of armour-piercing bullets at close range. An incendiary bullet in his gas tank might also make his old boiler factory a warm place to fly in. . . . The observer did the quickest and most accurate bit of shooting I have yet run up against, and his very first shot came crashing through the front of my machine above the motor and caught me just on top of the left knee. It felt more like a crack on the leg from a fast pitched ball than anything else I know of, except that there is also a sort of penetrating feeling one gets from a bullet.

RUMPLER TWO-SEATER
BROUGHT DOWN BY MAJOR CHARLES BIDDLE. AUGUST 16, 1918

With his motor rendered useless by bullets, he was compelled to land at once, his machine crashing in a maze of barbed wire and overlapping shell-holes, less than seventy yards from the enemy trenches and several hundred from the British. Under heavy shell and machine-gun fire, he crawled and ran and waded to a British observation post, covering the last fifty yards, despite his wound, in about .02 flat, to give his own estimate.

In less than a month he was again at the Front as C.O. of the 13th Pursuit Squadron, and on August 1, brought down his third and fourth enemy machines at Preny, north of Pont-à-Mousson, both Albatross single-seaters. On August 16, in a single combat with a Rumpler two-seater, he killed the enemy observer and forced the pilot to land in the French lines near Bouxières-aux-Dames, near Nancy. The plane was intact. His sixth official victory was over a Fokker single-seater, shot down at Flabas, near Verdun, on September 26; and his seventh the result of a Battle over Banthéville, in the Argonne sector, where another Fokker was destroyed.

On October 25, Biddle was placed in command of the Fourth Pursuit Group and a few days later he was promoted to the rank of Major. There was no man in the Lafayette Corps more richly deserving of recognition or more competent to fill a position of great responsibility. From the date of his enlistment until his demobilisation in 1919, he served both France and America with distinction and honour. He could not have done otherwise.

SERVICE RECORD

JULIAN CORNELL BIDDLE, Ambler, Pennsylvania.

SERVICE IN FRENCH AVIATION:
Date of enlistment: May 25, 1917.
Aviation Schools: June 2 to August 8, 1917, Avord, Pau, G.D.E.
Breveted: June 20, 1917 (Blériot).
At the Front: Escadrille Spad 73, August 11 to August 18, 1917.
Final Rank: Caporal.
Killed in line of duty:
August 18, 1917, near Dunkirk.

Julian Cornell Biddle

None of his contemporaries at Avord will forget Julian Biddle. His quiet and pleasant manner concealed a burning determination to get to the Front—a zeal to fight for the Allied cause which made him an inspiration to his comrades.

At home Biddle was well known as a cross-country rider and athlete. He took up aviation as a sport in the early days of the war, receiving his pilot's license in 1916. Impatient to fly and to fight, he crossed to France early in the following year, joined the Lafayette Flying Corps, and arrived at Avord on June 2. Even though he was already a pilot, his performance in the Blériot School was remarkable, for he was breveted on June 20. On July 13 he arrived at Pau, finished the course in fourteen days, went to the Front on August 11, and made his last *sortie* on August 18. No pilot ever left a briefer or finer record in the schools, and none gave promise of a more brilliant future at the Front.

The exact circumstances of Biddle's death will never be known. At 10.45 in the morning he left the aerodrome for a short practice flight and fell into the sea a few kilometres west of Dunkirk; fragments of his Spad were found floating in the water, and it is probable that he fell in an encounter with a German bombing flight which raided the south coast of England that day. At his death the Lafayette Flying Corps lost a man who would surely have added to its laurels, and he will always be mourned by the many friends who admired his modesty, his determination, and fine courage.

SERVICE RECORD

STEPHEN BIGELOW, Boston, Massachusetts.

SERVICE IN FRENCH AVIATION:
Date of enlistment: April 13, 1916.
Aviation Schools: June 9, 1916, to January 20, 1917, Buc, Avord, Cazeaux, Pau, G.D.E.
Breveted: September 8, 1916 (Blériot).
At the Front: Escadrille Spad 102, January 24 to February 8, 1917.
Escadrille Lafayette, February 8 to September 11, 1917.
Final Rank: Sergent.
Wounded in combat: August 20, 1917.

DECORATIONS:
Croix de Guerre, with Star.

CITATIONS

G.C. 13, ESCADRILLE N. 124.
Citation à l'Ordre de l'Aéronautique:
Par décision du Chef d'État-Major de la 2ᵉ Armée, en date du 31 août, 1917, le militaire dont le nom suit a été cité à l'Ordre de l'Aéronautique:
BIGELOW, STEPHEN, matricule 11737, Sergent Pilote à l'Escadrille N. 124 (G.C. 13)

Citoyen américain engagé au service de la France, au cours d'une protection de bombardement a soutenu le combat contre 6 appareils ennemies qui venaient attaquer un de nos avions. A dégagé et a été légèrement blessé au cours du combat.

Stephen Bigelow

Enlisting on April 13, 1916, Bigelow was trained on Blériot at Buc and at Avord, and got to the Front on January 24, 1917, assigned to the *Escadrille* N. 102. A few days later he was transferred to the N. 124, with which he served until autumn, when his health gave way and he was invalided out of the army. His most memorable experience at the Front was probably as a member of the patrol sent to protect a large group of Sopwiths on a bombing raid into enemy territory—the day that Lovell got a Boche in flames and Willis was made prisoner. In the free-for-all combat over Dun-sur-Meuse, Bigelow earned a wound stripe and a citation—in his successful defence of a Sopwith against the attacks of six Albatross.

SERVICE RECORD

Charles Raymond Blake, Westerly, Rhode Island.

Previous Service: American Ambulance, 1917.

Service in French Aviation:
Date of enlistment: June 4, 1917.
Aviation Schools: July 19, 1917, to March 8, 1918, Avord, Tours, G.D.E.
Brevetté: October 27, 1917 (Caudron).
At the Front: Escadrille Br. 29, March 11 to April 18, 1918.
Final Rank: Caporal.

Service in U.S. Aviation:
Commissioned First Lieutenant: March 17, 1918.
At the Front: Attached to his former French unit, Br. 29, April 18 to September 3, 1918.
7th A.I.C., Clermont-Ferrand, September 7, 1918, to Armistice.

Decorations:
Distinguished Service Cross.
Croix de Guerre, with Palm and Star.

CITATIONS

Le 10 août, 1918
Escadre 12, Escadrille Br. 29, G.B. 9.
Le Chef d'Escadron Vuillemin, Commandant l'Escadre de Bombardement N° 12, cite à l'Ordre de l'Escadre:

Le Premier Lieutenant Pilote Américain Blake, Raymond, de l'Escadrille N. 29.

Officier pilote américain, plein de bravoure et d'entrain, a effectué plus de 15 bombardements depuis son arrivée à l'Escadrille.
Marchant jusqu'à trois fois dans une journée, notamment les 30 et 31 mai, 1918, dans des circonstances les plus périlleuses en dépit des attaques violentes des avions ennemis.
(Signé) Vuillemin

G.H.Q., A.E.F.

First Lieutenant Charles Raymond Blake, Pilot, Air Service

Near Lassigny, France, on August 9, 1918, Lieutenant Blake, with Second Lieutenant Earl W. Porter, observer, while on a reconnaissance expedition at a low altitude far beyond the enemy lines, was attacked by five German battle planes. His observer was wounded at the beginning of the combat, but he maneuvered his plane so skillfully that the observer was able to shoot down one of their adversaries. By more skillful maneuvering he enabled his observer to fight off the remaining planes and returned safely to friendly territory.
By order of General Pershing

G.Q.G., 10 *décembre*, 1918
1ᵉʳ Lieutenant Pilote Charles Raymond Blake, à l'Escadrille Br. 29

Officier plein d'allant, ayant à son actif plus de 30 bombardements. Le 9 août, 1918, au cours d'une expédition à faible altitude, s'est trouvé seul aux prises avec cinq avions. Bien qu'ayant son observateur blessé, a réussi, après avoir abattu un de ses adversaires, à se dégager et à rentrer dans nos lignes.

Charles Raymond Blake

Blake served six months with the American Field Service before enlisting in the Lafayette Flying Corps on July 1, 1917. Breveted at Tours, he took a course at the French bombing school at Sacy-le-Grand, and was sent to the Escadrille Bréguet 29 in March, 1918. After being commissioned in the United States Army, he was reassigned to his *escadrille*, where he made 37 official bombing raids, covering the whole Front between Arras and Château-Thierry.

Bréguet day bombers in formation

On August 9, 1918, Blake had a very close call. He became separated from his formation and went on alone to the objective, where he dropped his bombs from an altitude of 1500 metres. As he started to return home, he was attacked by five Fokkers. His observer, Lieutenant Earl W. Porter, was shot through the jaw and the neck in one of the first bursts of fire, but very pluckily continued to defend the Bréguet, which enabled Blake to bring his machine back to our lines, almost shot to pieces by German bullets. For this feat, both observer and pilot received the D.S.C. as well as a citation to the order of the French Army.

SERVICE RECORD

ARTHUR BLUTHENTHAL, Wilmington, Delaware.

PREVIOUS SERVICE: American Ambulance on service in Macedonia, 1916.

SERVICE IN FRENCH AVIATION:
Date of enlistment: June 1, 1917.
Aviation Schools: June 9, 1917, to March 15, 1918, Avord, G.D.E.
Breveted: September 22, 1917 (Caudron).
At the Front: Escadrille Bréguet 227, March 17 to June 5, 1918.
Final Rank: Sergent.
Killed in combat: June 5, 1918, near Maignelay (Oise).

DECORATIONS:
Croix de Guerre, with Star (American Ambulance).
Croix de Guerre, with Palm (Aviation).

CITATIONS

9 *juin*, 1918
BLUTHENTHAL (ARTHUR), M^{le} 12203
Caporal au 1er Régiment Étranger, à l'Escadrille Br. 227

Pilote américain de premier ordre. S'est engagé dans la Légion Étrangère, pour pouvoir servir en France dans l'aviation. S'est fait remarquer, dès ses débuts, par son esprit de discipline et son courage réfléchi. A voulu continuer à servir dans une escadrille française, au cours de la bataille actuelle, avant de passer dans l'aviation américaine. Le 5 juin, pendant un réglage lointain, a été tué en combat. Cette citation comporte l'attribution de la Croix de Guerre avec palme.

Arthur Bluthenthal

The following letter, written by an Englishman, Captain Inness-Brown, appeared in the Paris *Herald* of June 29, 1918—a tribute to the memory of a lovable comrade and a very gallant soldier.

In the death of Arthur Bluthenthal, killed in an aerial battle some few days ago, France and America lose one of their stanchest patriots. To come to death alone, high in the air, with no friend to tell the story of the struggle and to be buried in a lonely spot near the Front, unofficially, with little publicity, would have been the fate that Bluthenthal would have desired, could he have chosen. At all times he shunned being considered a hero, and when a friend said to him jokingly that his fear of publicity amounted almost to conceit, he replied: 'Conceit, it may be, but I've always taken serving France so seriously that I hardly ever want to talk about it.'

This feeling of serving France, just for herself and nothing more, is not an unfamiliar one. It has been expressed by many of her own people who have felt that to have accomplished the deed for France was enough. This spirit was shared by such men as Jim McConnell, another of America's sons to die for France. It seemed to be the mainstay of Bluthenthal, through his two long years of service, first with the American Field Service and then in the capacity of a bombing pilot. Just before he was killed, he wrote to one of his friends: 'I am not doing much in the line of fighting, not nearly so much as I would like. Being too heavy for an *avion de chasse*, they've shipped me into a bombing squadron. It's pretty good fun, and moreover, though every now and then it's boring, it has its exciting moments. Anyhow, I am glad to be alive.'

But Bluthenthal did not only serve as a bomber. His loyalty to France and to the spirit which prompted him to aid her, made him Her champion wherever her name was mentioned. No one could speak of her depravities in his presence, and really be in earnest about it. His short, stocky frame, his massive shoulders, his heavy neck, told in a moment's glance his strength. His determination to make those about him realise that gossiping about the good name of France was not to be tolerated, though it made him some enemies, won him many, many friends. His strength and bravery gave him an advantage in an argument that few people tried to overcome. Those that did try generally found themselves wishing that they had not. This was his serious side.

However much he was a Frenchman at heart, Bluthenthal was at the same time a loyal and stanch American. He used to say, when others criticized the United States for not coming into the war: 'Well, give 'em time, they'll wake up.' While he was always putting forth the side of France, not once have I known him to say anything that could be interpreted as disloyal to America. He was one of the pioneers, yet he never lost that poise, the lack of which in the beginning of things made a great many forget for a moment their own country.

SERVICE RECORD

PIERRE BOAL, Boalsburg, Pennsylvania.

PREVIOUS SERVICE: First (French) Regiment of Cuirassiers, August, 1914, to May 1, 1916.

SERVICE IN FRENCH AVIATION:
Date of enlistment: May 24, 1916.
Aviation Schools: June 5, 1916, to February 1, 1917, Buc, as *élève-pilote* and afterward as interpreter for the American volunteers training in this school.

SERVICE IN U.S. AVIATION:
Commissioned Captain: March 10, 1917.
Brevetted: U.S. Aviation School, San Antonio, Texas (Curtiss).
Adjutant to Chief of Training Division, U.S.A.S., Washington, D.C.
On duty in France as Officer in Charge of American pilots assigned to French squadrons.
Attached to Groupe Weiller, French G.H.Q. (Long distance reconnaissance.)

Pierre Boal

Pierre Boal enlisted in the very early days of the war, in the First (French) Regiment of Cuirassiers, and served at the Front with this unit until his transfer to the Lafayette Flying Corps on May 24, 1916. He was among the first of the little group of Americans to be sent to Buc for training on the Blériot monoplane. Proving inapt—as most *élèves-pilotes* did at first—at handling alone, this difficult machine, he was proposed for *radiation*, but instead of accepting his discharge from service as he might have done, he remained at the school at his own request, acting as interpreter for the other American pilots. His knowledge of French and his own experience at flying Blériots were at the service of all later comers, and it was Boal who saved more than one of them from being released because of early awkwardness in learning to fly. In January, 1917, when the Blériot School was moved from Buc to Avord (Cher), he went to America on leave, but his interest in the Lafayette Corps never waned. He served there as he had in France, giving invaluable cooperation to the Executive Committee of the corps in Paris.

Sometime later he received a captain's commission in the U.S. Air Force and gained his wings at an American flying field. After serving for several months in America, he was sent again to France where he was placed in charge of all of the American pilots who were temporarily assigned to French units at the Front; and worked with Major Gros as Aviation Liaison Officer between the French and American Air Services.

SERVICE RECORD

ELLISON CONVERSE BOGGS, New York City.

SERVICE IN FRENCH AVIATION:
Date of enlistment: August 4, 1917.
Aviation Schools: August 5, 1917, to April 18, 1918, Avord, Tours, Pau, Cazaux, G.D.E.
Brevetted: October 23, 1917 (Caudron).
At the Front: Escadrille Spad 81, April 21, 1918, to Armistice.
Final Rank: Sergent.

DECORATIONS:
Croix de Guerre, with Star.

CITATIONS

Citation à l'Ordre de l'Aéronautique du 22 juillet, 1918
Le Commandant de l'Escadre cite à l'Ordre de l'Aéronautique:
BOGGS, ELLISON, Sergent Pilote à l'Escadrille Spa. 81

Très bon pilote de chasse, adroit et brave. S'est déjà signalé dans de nombreux et durs combats. Le 15 juillet, 1918, a contribué à l'incendie d'un drachen enflammé malgré l'intervention de nombreux Fokkers.
(Signé)   *Le Commandant de l'Escadrille Spa.* 81

Ellison Boggs

Ellison Boggs, with Tommy Hitchcock, shared the distinction of being the youngest members of the Lafayette Flying Corps. He was also the last of the Americans accepted for enlistment in the French Aviation Service. Breveted at Tours, on October 23, 1917, he arrived at the G.D.E. on January 10 of the following year, but illness prevented his going to the Front until April 21, when he was sent to Escadrille Spad 81. During eight months of service with this squadron, Boggs gave an excellent account of himself and got along particularly well with his French comrades.

SERVICE RECORD

VERNON BOOTH, JR., New York City.

SERVICE IN FRENCH AVIATION:
  Date of enlistment: June 3, 1917.
  Aviation Schools: June 10, 1917, to January 8, 1918, Avord, Pau, G.D.E.
  Breveted: October 26, 1917 (Caudron).
  At the Front: Escadrille Spad 96, January 10 to June 25, 1918.
  Final Rank: Sergent.
  Wounded in combat: Near Longpont (Aisne) June 25, 1918.
  Died in hospital: At Royaumont, July 10, 1918.

DECORATIONS:
  Médaille Militaire.
  Croix de Guerre, with Palm.

CITATIONS

GRAND QUARTIER GÉNÉRAL DES ARMÉES DU NORD ET DE NORD-EST
ÉTAT-MAJOR.   *Le 27 juillet,* 1918
En vertu des pouvoirs qui lui sont conférés par la décision ministérielle N° 12285 K du 8 août, 1914, le Général Commandant en Chef a fait, à la date du 27 juillet, 1918, dans l'Ordre de la Légion d'Honneur, les nominations suivantes: . . .

En outre, le Général Commandant en Chef a conféré la Médaille Militaire, aux Militaires dont les noms suivent: . . .

À la date du 4 juillet, 1918:

BOOTH, VERNON, M¹⁵ 41494 (active), Sergent au 1ᵉʳ Régiment de la Légion Étrangère, Pilote Aviateur Esc. Spa. 96

Pilote d'un splendide courage. Au cours d'un combat contre quatre avions ennemis a été grièvement blessé, son appareil ayant pris feu en l'air, a pu grâce à sa présence d'esprit et malgré de fortes brûlures éteindre l'incendie et atterrir normalement entre les lignes à quarante mètres des tranchées ennemies. A incendié son appareil et regagné les positions françaises malgré un feu violent des canons et des mitrailleuses.

Les nominations ci-dessus comportent l'attribution de la Croix de Guerre avec palme.

Le Général Commandant en Chef
PÉTAIN

Vernon Booth

To those of us who enjoyed the privilege of Booth's close friendship, it is oftentimes impossible to realise that he is gone. He was so gay, so merry, so vitally alive—a charming companion and a friend to count on through thick and thin. On the *boulevards*, in the haunts of former happy leaves, we caught ourselves scanning half unconsciously the passing faces in hopes of seeing "Vernie's" quizzical smile of welcome and hearing his jolly voice. Late in the spring we heard of his marriage and the whole corps joined in sympathy with his happiness; when the news came to us that he was gone, the thought of his widow—a bride only a few weeks before—added an extra pang to our grief. Even in the schools we knew Booth for a man of the coolest courage and absolute disregard of danger, but knowing him as we did we were still forced to marvel at his last exploit—certainly one of the finest examples of cold daring the war has produced.

DAVIS AND BOOTH AT NICE

On June 25, above the fighting to the south of Soissons, Booth was engaged in bitter combat with a swarm of Fokkers. Hemmed in, outnumbered and manoeuvring desperately, always on the offensive, Booth's machine was suddenly set on fire by an incendiary bullet, and at the same instant an explosive ball shattered his right leg, inflicting a terrible wound. Enveloped in flames and, in an agony of pain, he still kept his head, and after a straight plunge of 6000 feet succeeded in putting out the fire. But by now the motor had stopped for good, forcing him to land near Longpont, by misfortune at a point exactly between the lines, forty yards from the Germans—thirty from the French. The Germans promptly turned rifles, machine guns, and even 37 mm. cannon on the Spad, but in spite of a storm of lead and bursting shell, severely burned and dragging a mangled leg, Booth painfully extricated himself from his plane, *deliberately set fire to what remained of it*, and crawled to the French lines. In the hospital, on July 4, this splendid act of courage was rewarded with the *Médaille Militaire,* and on July 10 Booth died from the effects of his wounds. He was the best-loved of comrades and a soldier who upheld with honour the finest traditions of his country.

EDGAR BOULIGNY (IN REAR) WITH SERGENT FOUCHER HIS MACHINE-GUNNER

Attached to American Aviation in France from June 14, 1918.

DECORATIONS:
 Croix de Guerre, with Star.

SERVICE RECORD

EDGAR J. BOULIGNY, New Orleans, Louisiana.

PREVIOUS SERVICE:
 August 6, 1914, to May 1, 1917. Foreign Legion (Infantry). Wounded four times.

SERVICE IN FRENCH AVIATION:
 Date of enlistment: May 15, 1917.
 Aviation Schools:
  June 7, 1917, to March 30, 1918. Étampes, Châteauroux.
 Breveted: July 13, 1917 (Farman).
 At the Front:
  Escadrille N. 501 (Army of the Orient), April 14 to June 14, 1918.
 Final Rank: Sergent.

SERVICE IN U.S. AVIATION:
 Commissioned Second Lieutenant: October 14, 1918.

CITATION

2ᵉ CORPS D'ARMÉE COLONIAL RÉGIMENT DE MARCHE
1ᵉ DIVISION, 1ᵉ BRIGADE. DE LA LÉGION ÉTRANGÈRE

Citation à l'Ordre de la Division :
Le Général Dégoutte, Commandant la Division, cite à l'ordre de la Division :

BOULIGNY, EDWARD, Sergent, Mˡᵉ 42612

 Motif de la citation: Excellent sous-officier, énergique et dévoué. Blessé dans la tranchée par un éclat de grenade à la jambe gauche, a continué à assurer son service pendant toute la nuit. Ne s'est fait panser que le lendemain matin et a été immédiatement évacué. Déjà blessé en Champagne en septembre, 1915.

(*Signé*) METZ

Edgar J. Bouligny

Edgar Bouligny, as his name would indicate, is of French descent. One of his grand-uncles, Dominique Bouligny, commanded a regiment of French troops in the Louisiana Territory, and when the land was sold by Napoleon to the United States, he became an American citizen and later a member of the U.S. Senate. Edgar Bouligny responded to the prompting of his French blood and joined the Legion on August 6, 1914 During his two years and eight months as an infantryman he was wounded four times, first by a fragment of shell casing, then by a *coup de couteau* during a hand-to-hand fight in No Man's Land with a patrol of Germans; the third time by a machine-gun bullet; and the fourth in the explosion of a hand grenade when he came dangerously near losing a leg as the result of his injuries. He received the *Croix de Guerre* and the *galons* of a sergeant while serving in the Legion and was the last of the American *légionnaires* to transfer to the Aviation Service.

In the spring of 1918 he returned to the Front as a pilot, being sent to the French Squadron N 501 of the Army of the Orient. His unit was a combined combat and reconnaissance squadron, flying both Farmans and Nieuports, and Bouligny was engaged in all kinds of aerial missions on both the Serbian and Albanian Fronts. There was no man in the Lafayette Corps more justly entitled to generous recognition on the part of the American Government for his long and splen-

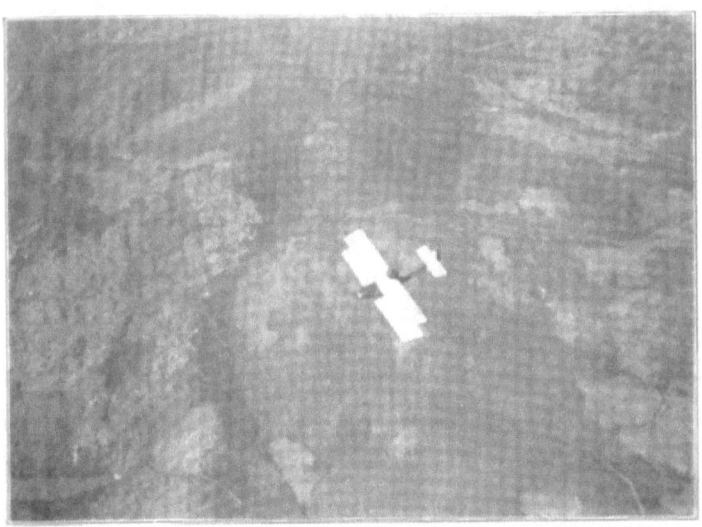

OVER THE MACEDONIAN FRONT

did service. He had been constantly on active duty in the Infantry and in Aviation for more than four years, and yet, upon his transfer to our own Air Service, he was commissioned only as a Second Lieutenant. The fault is partly his own, however. Much as he knew of war he was sadly ignorant of the delicate art of wire-pulling which is often so necessary in securing military preferment. Furthermore, he was always at the Front, and had no time to further his own interests at G.H.Q.'s and other centres of intrigue. But it is impossible to imagine Bouligny talking about or for himself. A modest and brave soldier, he carried on at his post of duty and let the plums fall where they would. His record speaks for itself more eloquently than any military award.

SERVICE RECORD

LESTER STRAYER BRADY, Lock Haven, Pennsylvania.

SERVICE IN FRENCH AVIATION:
Date of enlistment: May 28, 1917.
Aviation Schools: May 28, 1917, to February 23, 1918, Avord, Juvisy, Pau, G.D.E.
Breveted: November 6, 1917 (Caudron).
At the Front: Escadrille Spad 26, February 23 to April 13, 1918.
Final Rank: Caporal.

SERVICE IN U.S. AVIATION:
Commissioned Second Lieutenant: April 16, 1918.
On duty in Paris: April 13 to June 7, 1918.
Ferry-Pilot: American Acceptance Park, Orly, June 7 to July 16, 1918.
At the Front: First Observation Group, July 16 to August 21, 1918.
135th and 27th Pursuit Squadrons, August 30, 1918, to Armistice.

Lester Strayer Brady

In the schools Brady seemed to bear a charmed life; twice he escaped unhurt from crashes of the most disastrous and sensational character. From the G.D.E. he was sent to the Escadrille Spad 26 on February 23, 1918, and served with that unit until his transfer to the American army. He was assigned first to Orly for duty as a ferry-pilot, and from July 16 until the Armistice was on various duty both at the Front and in Paris.

SERVICE RECORD

Ray Claflin Bridgman, Lake Forest, Illinois.

Service in French Aviation:
  Date of enlistment: July 24, 1916.
  Aviation Schools: August 10, 1916, to April 10, 1917, Buc, Juvisy, Avord, Cazeaux, Pau, G.D.E.
  Breveted: December 5, 1916 (Caudron).
  At the Front: Escadrille N. 49, April 13 to April 27, 1917.
    Escadrille Lafayette, May 1, 1917, to February 18, 1918.
  Final Rank: Sergent.

Service in U.S. Aviation:
  Commissioned Captain: February 4, 1918.
  At the Front: Flight Commander of 103d Pursuit Squadron, February 18 to August 15, 1918.
    Commanding Officer 22d Pursuit Squadron, August 15, 1918, to Armistice.

Decorations:
  Croix de Guerre, with Star.

CITATION

29 octobre, 1917

Par décision du Chef d'E.M. de la VIme Armée

Le Sergent Pilote Bridgman de la Spad 124

est cité à l'Ordre de l'Aéronautique de la VIme Armée avec le motif suivant:

Citoyen américain engagé le 7 août, 1916, dans l'Aéronautique. Arrivé à l'Escadrille Lafayette le 2 mai, 1917.

Pilote de chasse adroit, modeste, et consciencieux, a toujours rempli avec beaucoup d'allant les missions qui lui ont été confiées.

A plusieurs fois mitraillé les réserves de l'Infanterie ennemie au cours de la dernière attaque.

Ray Claflin Bridgman

The French citation of Ray Bridgman appeared under the date of October 29, 1917. It is quoted below and the only reason for speaking of it here is that in the text of that brief description you have "Bridgman" absolutely true to life.

A combat pilot, skilful, modest and conscientious; has always fulfilled with the greatest keenness the missions which have been entrusted to him.

French official praise often errs on the side of generosity. Not so in "Bridgie's" case. Ask any of his old comrades of Spad 124 who have flown with him, followed him on patrol, fought with him. He was one of the keenest pilots, one of the most aggressive fighters the Squadron ever had, and this despite the fact that he hated war with his whole soul.

For a long time he was the luckiest of unlucky men. He had any number of combats, but the inevitable result would be that he would come limping homeward *de loin chez les Boches*, with no decision in his favour, at least no victory which could be officially confirmed.

There was never any doubt about the nature of his battles or the closeness of his contact with enemy planes. His Spad was always a battle-scarred old bird, and if he happened to be flying a new machine, in a week's time wings and fuselage would be plastered over with patches of fabric. One reason for this was that it appeared to be his fortune always to attack two-seaters. Many an enemy machine-gunner has sprayed bullets in Bridgman's direction with a good deal of accuracy while his pilot dove headlong into the German lines.

A pilot's record in enemy planes destroyed is never a criterion of the real quality of his service. This is particularly true of Ray C. Bridgman. When he was leading a patrol, enemy *réglage*, reconnaissance, and photographic planes had an anxious time of it. They were never able to carry out their routine work, but had to spend all their time fighting rear guard actions. The result was that enemy batteries were deprived of their eyes, and enemy chiefs of staff, of much-needed information relative to the disposition and movements of Allied troops.

From the first of April, 1917, until the end of the war, he was always on active duty at the Front. It is difficult to speak with restraint of his service to the Allied cause. It was so immeasurably fine in kind. One must have known him intimately, in the *popote*, on patrol, in combat. No American volunteer has tried harder to live up to an ideal duty. It was an almost impossible task because of the loftiness of the ideal. In his own opinion, no doubt, he failed, but it was a failure most men would call splendid success.

SERVICE RECORD

JASPER C. BROWN, New York City.

SERVICE IN FRENCH AVIATION:
Date of enlistment: June 19, 1917.
Aviation Schools: June 20, 1917, to February 1, 1918, Avord, Pau, G.D.E.
Breveted: November 6, 1917 (Caudron).
At the Front: Escadrille Spad 67, February 3 to March 29, 1918.
Final Rank: Caporal.

SERVICE IN U.S. AVIATION:
Commissioned Second Lieutenant: March 29, 1918. Promoted First Lieutenant October 22, 1918.
At the Front: Attached to the French Squadron Spad 67, March 29, 1918, to Armistice.

DECORATIONS:
Croix de Guerre, with Palm.

CITATION

GRAND QUARTIER GÉNÉRAL DES
ARMÉES FRANÇAISES DE L'EST
ÉTAT-MAJOR.   25 janvier, 1919

Le Maréchal de France, Commandant en
  Chef les Armées Françaises de l'Est,
  cite à l'Ordre de l'Armée:

Lieutenant JASPER BROWN à l'Escadrille Spa. 67

Officier pilote de grande valeur, ayant fait preuve des plus belles qualités militaires. Depuis 10 mois à l'Escadrille a affirmé son adresse et son courage au cours de nombreuses patrouilles et de nombreux combats, où il s'est toujours montré sur de lui-même. D'une conscience et d'un dévouement absolus, a conquis l'estime de tous.

(Signé)   PÉTAIN

Jasper C. Brown

Brown was one of the last Blériot men to be breveted at Avord, and after going through Pau was sent to the Spad 67. After his transfer to the American army, he was allowed to continue in his French squadron until the end of the war, and did good work all through the summer's severe fighting.

Brown is a genuine *numero*—full of dry humour, always ready for any sort of prank, always entertaining. At Avord, during the long spell of bad weather, he was to be found at the *café* known as "The Old Lady's," where his drolleries kept a roomful in good humour. He presided over the little *coterie* which dined each night in the back room—A. Ash, Phil Davis, Charlie Chapman, and Bill McKerness. All these good fellows are gone, but Brown has carried on, saddened without doubt, but still the same droll and cheerful comrade.

During the heavy fighting of March and April, 1918, in the region of Montdidier, Brown had an exceptionally broad experience of the thrills of ground-*strafing*, and during the autumn, in the battles to the north of Châlons, he shot down two Hanovranners in pieces—both too far within the enemy lines for official confirmation.

SERVICE RECORD

EVERETT T. BUCKLEY, Kilbourne, Illinois.

SERVICE IN FRENCH AVIATION:
  Date of enlistment: January 6, 1917.
  Aviation Schools: January 16 to July 30, 1917,
      Buc, Pau, Avord, G.D.E.
  Breveted: June 2, 1917 (Blériot).
  At the Front: Escadrille Spad 65, August 3 to
      September 6, 1917.
  Final Rank: Sergent.
  Shot down and wounded in combat: September 6,
      1917, over Dun-sur-Meuse.
  Prisoner in Germany: Until July 1, 1918. Escaped
      into Switzerland.

Everett T. Buckley

Everett T. Buckley had the good fortune to be sent to the crack French squadron Spad 65, the *escadrille* of Lieutenant Nungesser. *Groupe de Combat* 13 was then at Senard on the Verdun sector. Throughout the summer of 1917, this was the liveliest part of the French Front for airmen, and throughout the war always a dangerous salient for the young pilot. Enemy patrols could cross it on two sides, and with the sun behind their backs, they often swooped in from the east, attacking French patrols which were coming into the sun, crossing again into German-held territory on the northern side.

Here Buckley gained experience rapidly and without question would have made a splendid record at the Front. Unfortunately, he was shot down five weeks after his arrival there and fell far within the German lines. Two months later news came that he was a prisoner, but what had actually happened to him was not known until July, 1918, when he escaped into Switzerland. His adventures in Germany were briefly as follows:

In the combat of September 6, 1917, his plane was badly damaged by bullets and he fell out of control at Dun-sur-Meuse. He was knocked unconscious in the crash, and upon coming to, found himself surrounded by German infantrymen.

After eighteen days of bread-and-water diet in a fortress, he was sent to the notorious Karlsruhe "Hotel" for the usual sojourn, while being interrogated by German intelligence officers. He was then sent to a prison camp at Heuberg, and escaped two months later, by breaking through the fence.

Caught at the Swiss frontier, he was escorted back to Heuberg and then sent to Donaueschingen to work on a farm. Two days later he escaped while at work in the fields, and was recaptured while trying to cross the Danube. Back he went (under considerable compulsion) to Heuberg.

The hopeful enemy, after giving him time for reflection in solitary confinement, tried farming him out again, sending him this time to Waringenstadt. Here he worked very hard—the first night, with seven other prisoners. They cut the bars out of a window and were well away from the neighbourhood before daybreak. All were recaptured and returned to Heuberg. Solitary confinement for thirty-one days as before.

The fourth attempt was successful. While working in a field cutting hay, Buckley and a French prisoner made a last break for freedom. They

EVERETT BUCKLEY
IN HIS GERMAN PRISON GARB

were immediately pursued by a crowd of German farmers, but eluded them in a wood. Profiting by former experiences in approaching the frontier, they dodged the three lines of German sentries and continued walking until certain that they were well beyond the last posts. Two Swiss musicians first gave them the news of their safety, and directed them to the military police, who sent them on to Berne and Paris.

SERVICE RECORD

THOMAS B. BUFFUM, New York City.

PREVIOUS SERVICE: American Ambulance, 1917.

SERVICE IN FRENCH AVIATION:
Date of enlistment: June 15, 1917.
Aviation Schools: June 27, 1917, to March 20, 1918, Avord, Pau, Cazeaux, G.D.E.
Breveted: October 31, 1917 (Caudron).
At the Front: Escadrille Spad 77, March 24 to May 4, 1918.
Final Rank: Caporal.
Shot down in combat: May 4, 1918, east of Montdidier.
Prisoner in Germany: Until the Armistice.

Thomas B. Buffum

Long before our declaration of war, Buffum was serving with distinction in Macedonia, driving an ambulance under the most difficult and trying circumstances. On June 15, 1917, he enlisted in the Lafayette Flying Corps and made a brilliant record both at Avord and at Pau. Arriving at the G.D.E. at a time when squadron assignments were made with exceptional slowness, Buffum did not get to the Front until March 24, 1918, when he joined the Escadrille Spad 77. His first flights convinced his superiors that he was a young pilot of great promise, as all his friends had long believed, but less than three weeks later he was shot down in flames behind the enemy lines. In the Lafayette Corps Buffum's frank and manly character had made him extremely popular, and all along the lines, as the news spread, isolated groups of Americans mourned him for dead. Some time later the news came from Switzerland that he had escaped with his life and was a prisoner, unharmed. In company with several fellow prisoners he escaped from Trausnitz Castle at Landshut, Bavaria. After fourteen nights of tramping they were recaptured at the Austrian border.

SERVICE RECORD

EUGENE BULLARD, Columbus, Georgia.

PREVIOUS SERVICE: 1915-16, Foreign Legion (Infantry).

SERVICE IN FRENCH AVIATION:
Date of enlistment: November 15, 1916.
Aviation Schools: November 30, 1916, to August 20, 1917, Cazaux, Tours, Avord, G.D.E.
At the Front: Escadrille Spad 93, August 27 to September 13, 1917.
Escadrille Spad 85, September 13 to November 11, 1917.
Final Rank: Caporal.
Returned to duty with 170th (French) Infantry Regiment, January 11, 1918.

DECORATIONS:
Croix de Guerre, with Star.

Eugene Bullard

The writer will never forget one occasion when he was waiting at 23 avenue du Bois to see Dr. Gros. Suddenly the door opened to admit a vision of military splendour such as one does not see twice in a lifetime. It was Eugene Bullard. His jolly black face shone with a grin of greeting and justifiable vanity. He wore a pair of tan aviator's boots which gleamed with a mirror-like lustre, and above them his breeches smote the eye with a dash of vivid scarlet. His black tunic, excellently cut and set off by a fine figure, was decorated with a pilot's badge, a *Croix de Guer*re, the *fourragère* of the Foreign Legion, and a pair of enormous wings, which left no possible doubt, even at a distance of fifty feet, as to which arm of the Service he adorned. The *élèves-pilotes* gasped, the eyes of the neophytes stood out from their heads, and I repressed a strong instinct to stand at attention.

There was scarcely an American at Avord who did not know and like Bullard. He was a brave, loyal, and thoroughly likable fellow, and when a quarrel with one of his superiors caused his withdrawal from the Aviation, there was scarcely an American who did not regret the fact. He was sent to the 170th French Infantry Regiment in January, 1918, from which date all trace of him has been lost.

SERVICE RECORD

WILLIAM GRAHAM BULLEN, Chicago, Illinois.

SERVICE IN FRENCH AVIATION:
Date of enlistment: July 14, 1917.
Aviation Schools: July 27, 1917, to March 10, 1918, Avord, Juvisy, Pau, G.D.E.
Breveted: September 29, 1917 (Caudron).
At the Front: Escadrille N. 162, March 13 to April 17, 1918.
Final Rank: Sergent.

SERVICE IN U.S. NAVAL AVIATION:
Commissioned Ensign: November 3, 1918.

William Graham Bullen

Gay Bullen is one of the men who have helped particularly to make and maintain good feeling between Americans and French. Speaking the language fluently, he understood the customs and manners of our Allies, all of whose good points he appreciated. In his Squadron Spad 162, he was immensely popular both with officers and pilots, as he was a keen and aggressive man in the air and a particularly pleasant comrade in mess or billets. Wherever he went, Bullen carried with him an excellent library of French and English books, and on returning from a patrol, one found him in the bar, absorbing the poetry of Meredith or something equally literary. In the air he had his full share of excitement, as on one occasion, when a German anti-aircraft battery registered a hit on him and forced him to come down slightly wounded.

SERVICE RECORD

PHILIP N. BUSH, Schenectady, New York.

SERVICE IN FRENCH AVIATION:
 Date of enlistment: May 9, 1917.
 Aviation Schools: May 23, 1917, to January 13,
  1918, Avord, Pau, G.D.E.
 Breveted: October 3, 1917 (Caudron).
 At the Front: Escadrille Spad 73, January 19 to
  May 2, 1918.
 Final Rank: Sergent.

SERVICE IN U.S. AVIATION:
 Commissioned First Lieutenant: May 8, 1918.
 At the Front: Attached to his former French
  Squadron Spad 73, May 8 to
  July 21, 1918.
 On duty at Paris, Choisy-le-Roy and American
  Acceptance Park, Orly, July 22, 1918, to
  Armistice.

DECORATIONS:
 Croix de Guerre, with Palm.

Philip N. Bush

Unlike those of us who imitated the *poilu* in dress and manner, Bush strove to live up to the *midinette'* s idea of an aviator; none of his contemporaries at Avord will forget his spotless and natty uniforms, his superb boots—his general air of military smartness. We often suspected that his presence in our ranks saved us from many a menial task; it was unthinkable that one with the presence of a small field-marshal should pick up stones, build gasoline tanks, or push tired Blériots back to their roosting-places. Despite his air of casual elegance, Bush piloted a Blériot with the best—his landings were faultless; he had an easy, daring style which showed the natural flyer. At Pau, too, he went through the acrobatics as though he had done them all his life, and without outward sign of the slight preliminary trepidations usual on such occasions. On January 19, 1918, he reached the Front, assigned to the Escadrille Spad 73. In May he was commissioned a First Lieutenant in the Air Service, and had the pleasure of being returned to his French squadron, fighting with it through some of the bitterest actions of the war.

SERVICE RECORD

LOUIS LESLIE BYERS, Philadelphia, Pennsylvania.

SERVICE IN FRENCH AVIATION:
 Date of enlistment: June 13, 1917.
 Aviation Schools: June 27, 1917, to July 10, 1918,
  Avord, Pau, Cazeaux, G.D.E.
 Breveted: December 5, 1917 (Caudron).
 At the Front: Escadrille Spad 38, July 13 to
  July 18, 1918.
 Final Rank: Caporal.
 Taken prisoner near Marquises: July 18, 1918.
 Prisoner of war until the Armistice.

Louis Leslie Byers

Byers showed a fine determination in going in for flying, for he realised that he was much handicapped by defective eyesight. In spite of this he did well at Avord, at Pau, and at Cazeaux. On July 13, 1918, he was assigned to the Escadrille Spad 38, and five days later, in the region of Marquises, was taken prisoner by the Germans. A long and tiresome training, five days of life at the Front, and four months of particularly hard imprisonment in Germany: that is Byers's experience of the war.

SERVICE RECORD

ANDREW COURTNEY CAMPBELL, JR., Chicago, Illinois.

SERVICE IN FRENCH AVIATION:
Date of enlistment: July 20, 1916.
Aviation Schools: September 8, 1916, to April 10, 1917, Buc, Juvisy, Avord, Cazeaux, Pau, G.D.E.
Breveted: November 22, 1916 (Caudron).
At the Front: Escadrille Lafayette, April 15 to October 1, 1917.
Final Rank: Sergent.
Killed in combat: October 1, 1917, north of Soissons.

DECORATIONS:
Croix de Guerre, with Star.

CITATION

Le Chef d'Escadron, Chef du Service Aéronautique au G.Q.G., cite à l'Ordre de l'Aéronautique:

CAMPBELL, ANDREW COURTNEY, Sergent Pilote à l'Escadrille N. 124

Citoyen américain engagé au service de la France. Pilote plein d'audace ayant déjà livré plusieurs combats avec une fougue admirable.

Le 7 juillet, 1917, a perdu complément un des plans de son avion à 1800 m. d'altitu de. Par son sang-froid et son adresse, s'est rétabli dans la chute et a réussi à atterrir indemne.

Andrew Courtney Campbell

One of the most remarkable accidents in the history of French aviation happened to Courtney Campbell during his service with the Escadrille Lafayette. While a patrol was assembling over the aerodrome at Chaudun, on the Aisne sector, he lost completely a lower wing of his Nieuport, brought the machine to the ground, and landed it beautifully. Theoretically the thing couldn't be done, but owing to great presence of mind and a most fantastic bit of luck, Courtney did it.

Throughout his period of service at the Front, his adventures were of a piece with this experience in landing a three-winged Nieuport. They were always richly humorous, beyond those of any other pilot, because of his rare gift at making them so in the narration. He was a born jester, a jester in the Shakespearean sense. Sometimes, after a hard and disappointing day, when dinner at the *popote* was passing glumly—Tiffin and Percy tiptoeing around the tables, serving with painfully obvious attempt at silence lest they should jar some one's already jangled nerves—Courtney would shatter the gloom with one of his ridiculous comments.

Then he would look around the table with a quizzical smile; and if he didn't get a "rise," he would go serenely on until he jolted us out of a sullen mood, forced us to grin against our wills. "Darn you, Campbell! Shut up, will you?"—someone would shout, through clenched teeth. He rode his jests as he rode his old Nieuport. He would pique *à la verticale* on a metaphor, zoom up after a play on words, get "under the tail" of some stale old joke, and bring it triumphantly down, flaming with new absurdity.

CAMPBELL WITH HIS THREE-WING NIEUPORT

Many a time we swore at Courtney openly, while secretly thanking the good lord of wits who sent him to N. 124. And we admired him as a pilot, for, despite his furious fun at his own expense, he never failed a comrade in combat, and was a skilful and courageous fighter. He was shot down within the enemy lines, on October 1, 1917, and so ended a complete, useful, and happy career.

SERVICE RECORD

H. GORDON CAMPBELL, Denver, Colorado.

PREVIOUS SERVICE: Norton-Harjes Ambulance, 1916-17.

SERVICE IN FRENCH AVIATION:
* *Date of enlistment:* June 27, 1917.
  Aviation Schools: July 24, 1917, to January, 1918, Avord, Pau, Cazeaux, G.D.E.
  Breveted: December 3, 1917 (Caudron).
  At the Front: Escadrille de Saint-Pol, Dunkirk.
  Final Rank: Sergent.

SERVICE IN U.S. NAVAL AVIATION:
  Commissioned Ensign.
  At the Front: Attached to the French Escadrille de Saint-Pol.

DECORATIONS:
  Légion d'Honneur.
  Croix de Guerre, with Two Palms.

H. Gordon Campbell

Campbell is one of the many Lafayette men who transferred to aviation from Ambulance work. After an honourable term of service with Section 5 of the Norton-Harjes Ambulance Corps, he was accepted in June, 1917—and sent to Avord on July 24.

His record in the schools was excellent, for he is the type that flies naturally—young, alert, and fearless. Before going to the Front with the French, he was transferred to the U.S. Navy and was fortunate enough, as an Ensign, to be attached to the Escadrille of SaintPol, where he gave a fine account of himself, and was cited for bringing down a German plane. Unfortunately no details of his adventures are available.

SERVICE RECORD

THOMAS G. CASSADY, Spencer, Indiana.

SERVICE IN FRENCH AVIATION:
  Date of enlistment: July 10, 1917.
  Aviation Schools: August 5 to December 24, 1917, Avord, Tours, Pau, G.D.E.
  Breveted: October 6, 1917 (Caudron).
  At the Front: Escadrille Spad 157, December 26, 1917, to February 16, 1918.
  Final Rank: Sergent.

SERVICE IN U.S. AVIATION:
  Commissioned First Lieutenant: February 22, 1918.
  Promoted Captain March 13, 1919.
  At the Front: Attached to French Squadron Spad 163, May 14 to September 8, 1918.
    28th Pursuit Squadron, September 8, 1918, to Armistice.

DECORATIONS:
  Distinguished Service Cross, with Bronze Oak Leaf.
  Légion d'Honneur.
  Croix de Guerre, with three Palms and one Star.

GROUPE DE COMBAT 21   23 *juin*, 1918

Le Général Commandant la IVe Armée cite à l'ordre de l'Armée:

   Lieutenant CASSADY, THOMAS G., de l'Escadrille Spad 163

 Premier Lieutenant de l'Armée Américaine venu sur sa demande dans l'Aviation Française. Toujours volontaire pour les missions dangéreuses. A, le 28 mai en tête de sa patrouille, abattu un avion ennemi.

Le Général Commandant IVe Armée
(*Signé*)   GOURAUD

L'ARMÉE DE L'EST, ÉTAT-MAJOR.   *Au G.Q.G., Ordre N°* 12,780

Le Général Commandant l'Armées de l'Est cite à l'Ordre de l'Armée:

   Lt. CASSADY, THOMAS G., de l'Escadrille Spa. 163

 Officier d'un esprit remarquable. Toujours volontaire pour les missions périlleuses. Le 11 août, 1918, il a abattu un avion ennemi qui est tombé dans les lignes Allemands.

Par ordre de la Général Commandant
(*Signé*)   BREAT

GRAND QUARTIER GÉNÉRAL DES ARMÉES
DU NORD ET DU NORD-EST, ÉTAT-MAJOR.   30 *octobre*, 1918

Le Général Commandant en Chef les Armées Françaises du Nord et du Nord-Est, cite à l'Ordre de l'Armée:

   CASSADY, THOMAS, Lieutenant Pilote à l'Escadrille Spa. 163

 Merveilleux pilote de chasse. A fait preuve d'un courage et d'un entrain inlassables. À la tête de sa patrouille le ... a abattu un monoplace ennemi.

Le Général Commandant en Chef
(*Signé*)   PÉTAIN

7 *November*, 1918

 The Commander-in-Chief, in the name of the President, has awarded the Distinguished Service Cross to the following named officer for the act of extraordinary heroism described after his name:

   First Lieutenant THOMAS G. CASSADY, A.S., U.S.A., Flight Commander,
    28th Aero Squadron N° 1022

 For extraordinary heroism in action near Fismes, 29 May, 1918, and near Épieds, France, 5 June, 1918. On 29 May, 1918, Lieutenant Cassady, single-handed, attacked an L.V.G. German plane, which crashed near Fismes. On 5 June, 1918, as patrol leader of five Spads, while being attacked by twelve German Fokkers, he brought down one of the enemy planes near Épieds and by his dash and courage broke the enemy formation.

A BRONZE LEAF

 For the following act of extraordinary heroism:

 On 15 August, 1918, near Saint-Maire, while acting as protection for a Salmson, he was attacked by seven Fokkers, two of which he brought down and enabled the Salmson to accomplish its mission and return safely.

AÉRONAUTIQUE MILITAIRES, G.C. 21.   ESCADRILLE SPA. 163

PROPOSITION POUR LA LÉGION D'HONNEUR POUR LE LIEUTENANT CASSADY, THOMAS
1er Lieutenant de l'Armée Américaine

 Venu servir la France au moment où aucune obligation militaire ne l'y contraignait. Objet dans une Section Sanitaire d'une brillante citation et grièvement blessé.

 Passé depuis dans l'Aviation; s'y est imposé à tour par l'élévation de son caractère, ses qualités de pilote, son insouciance absolue du danger.

 Vainqueur officiel de cinq avions ennemis.

Le Lieutenant Commandant d'Escadrille
(*Signé*)   CLAUDE CHÉREAU

(NOTE. Lieutenant Cassady was awarded the Legion of Honor, his Citation having the text of the above proposition.)

Thomas G. Cassady

Cassady, with Larner and Ponder, was attached to *Groupe de Combat* 21, where the three Americans upheld splendidly the finest traditions of our army. He served with the N. 157 during January, 1918, was transferred to the American Army, and on May 14, 1918, returned with which he served until September 8, 1918. From that time until the Armistice he was with the 28th Pursuit Squadron.

Cassady has shot down and had confirmed nine enemy planes, three of which have fallen in our lines, a rare satisfaction to the victor.

His good fellowship won the liking of the French, as his skill and courage won their respect, and he has done more than his share to promote good feeling with our Allies. In addition to a *Croix de Guerre* with three palms, Cassady has been decorated with the D.S.C., and on leaving the *escadrille*, Captain Villeneuve proposed him for the Legion of Honour, the highest compliment the French can pay an American officer. The award was approved by the French military authorities, and the American General Headquarters, and the decoration conferred after the Armistice. Cassady's record from beginning to end has been a splendid one and is a matter for pride to all the members of the Lafayette Corps.

SERVICE RECORD

OLIVER M. CHADWICK, Lowell, Massachusetts.

SERVICE IN FRENCH AVIATION:
  Date of enlistment: January 17, 1917.
  Aviation Schools: January 23 to July 25, 1917,
    Buc, Avord, Cazeaux, Pau,
    G.D.E.
  Brevetd: May 4, 1917 (Blériot).
  At the Front: Escadrille Spad 73, July 28 to
    August 14, 1917.
  Final Rank: Caporal.
  Killed in combat: North of Bixschoote, August
    14, 1917.

Oliver M. Chadwick

Oliver Chadwick was one of the last of the 1916 volunteers who began Blériot training at Buc shortly before that school was removed to Avord. It was strange how quickly his influence made itself felt in Lafayette affairs, and yet not strange either, to those who knew him, or who came to know him afterward. He took up his work with an intensity of purpose which had a wholesome effect upon all of his comrades and raised to a high level the general standard of flying efficiency.

He went to the Front with Charles Biddle in July, 1917. Three weeks later while flying alone, he encountered a British Sopwith which was being badly handled by an Albatross. Although there were two other Albatross hovering high above the scene of the combat, he attacked the German at once, saved the British plane, but was in turn attacked by the higher machines as he must have foreseen that he would be. In the unequal contest which followed, and before the British pilot in his slower *avion* could come to his aid, he was shot down and fell just in front of the enemy trenches near Bixschoote. The following account of Chadwick's death is taken from a letter written at the time, by Charles Biddle. His estimate of his worth as a man and as a pilot is held by every member of the Lafayette Corps who knew Chadwick.

> The next morning, August 14 (1917), Oliver and I were not scheduled to fly until the afternoon, but as we were both anxious to get all the practice possible, we went to the field in the morning in the hope that they might need an extra man. A patrol was just going out, and being short one man they asked Oliver to fill up. I saw him off and was a little disappointed that he had gotten the job instead of myself, as he had already had an hour or two more over the lines than I. He went out with three Frenchmen and never came back. They reported that at about 9.45, shortly after they had reached the lines, they had lost track of Oliver while manoeuvring near some clouds. Shortly after lunch we received a telephone message, that the infantry had seen a machine of the type Oliver was flying shot down in the course of a combat from about 2000 metres and fall about 1200 metres north of Bixschoote at a place known as the 'Ferme Carnot.' According to the report, the French machine went to the assistance of an English one that was being attacked by a Boche, and at the same time was itself attacked from the rear by two other Boches. The French machine was *nettement descendu*, as they say, and took a sheer fall of over 6000 feet, until it crashed into the ground.
>
> I had hoped against hope that there might be some mistake; that the machine was merely forced to land, or perhaps that it was not Oliver's machine at all, or that he might be only a prisoner. I have been doing everything I could think of to get all the detailed information possible, as it will mean so much to

his family to know just what happened and whether or not he is really dead. The commander has been very kind in trying to help me to collect this information, but it has seemed almost impossible to trace what clues we have. Where so many thousands are being killed and have been for the past three years, a dead man, no longer able to help in the fight, is nothing, and men busy with the great business of war have no time to spend in trying to find one.

Oliver fell between the lines, but very close to the German. The recent French advance has, however, put the spot just within our own lines, and I wanted to go up myself and have a look, but it seems impossible. I thought perhaps I might be able to find his body or the machine or something. Even though I could not do this, my efforts seem to be bearing fruit, and there seems to be no longer any doubt that the machine was his.

Today I received a photograph of the machine taken by a priest attached to the infantry and also some details of what happened when the machine fell.

It seems that both the Boche and French soldiers rushed out of their trenches to try and get possession of it, and a fight followed in which both were forced to retire. The picture was taken after the advance a day or so later and shows a tangled mass of wreckage and beside it the dead body of a Boche. No trace could be found of Oliver's body, but this is easily explained by the fact that pilots often have papers on them of military importance, and his body would therefore have been taken and searched. This would have been easy for the Germans to do at night, as the machine was so close to their front-line trenches. I am now trying to get the number of the fallen machine and to find some one who actually saw it fall. I think then we shall have everything. What chance has a man who falls like that from such a height? I have seen the result of a fall of one tenth the distance or less, too often not to know. I have a large-scale map showing the spot where he fell. It will, of course, always be impossible to find out where he is buried.

I wish you could have known Oliver Chadwick, as I am sure he would have appealed to you as he did to me. He was the kind of a man that it takes generations to make and then you only get them once in a thousand times. A man with a great deal of brains, he was also a very hard worker and had learned much about aviation and had made himself the best pilot I have ever seen for one of his experience. He was one of the very few I have met over here who came over long before America entered the war, simply because he felt it was his duty to fight for what he knew was right. That was why he was fighting and what he was fully prepared to die for. His ideals were of the highest and he was morally the cleanest man I have ever known. Physically he had always been a splendid athlete and was a particularly fine specimen. Absolutely fearless and using his brains every minute, if he had only had a chance to really get started and to gain a little experience, he should have developed into the best of them all. The Boche that got him certainly did a good job from their point of view, for if he had lived long enough to become really proficient, they would have known it to their sorrow, and I doubt if they would ever have gotten him.

We were in the Law School together, but I never saw much of him there, as we lived far apart and had a different set of friends. Since I came over here, however, and went to the aviation schools, we had been almost constantly together. We had lived together, eaten together, flown together, and planned all our work together. Always a gentleman and thinking of the other fellow, he was the most congenial man to me that I had ever known. I had come to regard him as my best friend, and it is astonishing how well you can get to know one with whom you work in this business, whom you often rely on for your life and who you know relies on you in the same way.

There is nothing I would not have done for Oliver Chadwick and I know he would have done the same for me. He was the finest man of his age that it has ever been my good fortune to meet and was my idea of what a gentleman should be. I am very glad to have known him, and I think it did me a great deal of good. When a man of this rare stamp goes down almost unnoticed, it seems, it makes one appreciate what this war means. To me, personally, his death naturally leaves a pretty big hole, but I am glad that if he had to die, he died fighting, as he wanted to. I know he himself never expected to survive the war, but his only fear was that he might be killed in some miserable accident. He was a great favourite with all the instructors, both because of his amiability and because they could not help but admire his skill and his fearlessness. The commander here re-

CHADWICK AT AVORD

CHADWICK'S GRAVE IN FLANDERS

garded him as one of the most courageous men he had ever had, which is saying a great deal in this organisation.

One of the officers tried to tell me that Oliver should not have left his patrol and gone to help out the other machine. I think he did exactly what he should have done. He could not well stand by when he saw a comrade in trouble and leave him to shift for himself. What one admires in a man more than anything else is the doing of his duty regardless of the consequences to himself, and this was Oliver all over. As soon as I heard what had happened I felt sure that it was he. My great regret is that I could not have been on the same patrol, as we usually stuck pretty close together and might have been able to help one another out.

Chadwick died as he would have wished, in the French service. At the time, when many of us were dreaming of commissions in the American aviation, he had written to Major Gros:

> I wish to associate myself as closely as possible with the cause of France, for I feel that a few Americans scattered here and there among the French *escadrilles* can do a greater service to the United States than if all were together; but with General Pershing already here I am well aware that conditions may be different from the past. Therefore I wish to let you know of my inclinations before acting upon them, and should welcome any advice which you may choose to give. I am more interested in getting into the fight where I can be of service, than in advancement under either of the flags which it has been my privilege to serve.

He was killed less than two months after this letter was written. His body lies in French soil which was the scene of some of the heaviest fighting of the war.

SERVICE RECORD

CYRUS F. CHAMBERLAIN, Minneapolis, Minnesota.

SERVICE IN FRENCH AVIATION:
Date of enlistment: June 3, 1917.
Aviation Schools: June 6 to December 8, 1917, Avord, Pau, G.D.E.
Breveted: October 15, 1917 (Caudron).
At the Front: Escadrille Spad 85, December 12, 1917, to January 9, 1918.
Escadrille Spad 98, January 9 to June 13, 1918.
Final Rank: Sergent.
Killed in combat: Near La Ferté-Milon (Aisne), June 13, 1918.

DECORATIONS:
Croix de Guerre, with Palm.

CITATION

Le 29 juin, 1918

VIe Armée, Aéronautique
Citation à l'Ordre de l'Armée:

Chamberlain, Cyrus, Sergent Pilote à l'Escadrille Spa. 98

Sujet américain engagé dans l'Armée Française. Soldat modeste et brave. Pilote de chasse de tout premier ordre, a été tué dans un combat aérien livré contre un ennemi supérieur en nombre.

Le Général Commandant la VIe Armée
Degoutte

Cyrus F. Chamberlain

Chamberlain was older than most of his contemporaries at Avord, and had seen more of the world. His intelligence and sense of humour made him a delightful companion when he chose to talk; none of his friends will forget the pleasant evenings at the Café des Aviateurs, where he dined nightly in company with Booth, Forster, and Ferguson. His chief interest at that time, of course, was flying, but he was a man of many hobbies—shooting, fishing, music, literature. . . . Sometimes, when a dense *brouillard* shrouded the Blériot field, and we sat dismally in the lee of a hangar, waiting for the sun, he carried us far away from our surroundings with his tales of canoe trips into the wilderness north of Lake Superior. He loved every mood of Nature, and could make one feel the solemn hush of the forest, or the thrill of a rush down roaring and uncharted rapids. A very few of his friends—for he was almost furtive in doing good—knew of his frequent unostentatious acts of kindness to needy or unfortunate comrades, both at Avord and at the Front.

Possessing the curious combination of caution and recklessness which makes a pilot of the first order, Chamberlain proved that in his case age was no handicap; he flew with a sure and delicate touch, went through the schools without a crash, and on the Front gave promise of a future of exceptional brilliancy. When the Germans drove south from the Chemin des Dames, his squadron was sent to oppose the formidable enemy aviation. The morning of June 13, 1918, found a patrol of Spads weaving back and forth above the lines at La Ferté-Milon—Chamberlain with five French comrades on the lookout for Boches. It was ten o'clock: a warm summer forenoon with the sky almost cloudless. The Spads were at 12,000 feet.

CHAMBERLAIN AND AMERICANS' ROOM AT AVORD

Suddenly, a thousand metres below, appeared a small patrol of German machines. All dove to the attack, and the French leader, glancing behind him as he rushed downward, saw a dozen enemy single-seaters plunging from above. A quick turn, a faint rattle of machine guns, and one Spad continued its dive—on and down, a fading dot above the battle-field. It was Chamberlain, killed in his seat by an unlucky burst. In our memories, he will live forever in the simple words of his citation to the order of the army: "*Soldat modeste et brave*."

SERVICE RECORD

CHARLES W. CHAPMAN, JR., Waterloo, Iowa.

SERVICE IN FRENCH AVIATION:
 Date of enlistment: June 10, 1917.
 Aviation Schools: June 16, 1917, to February, 1918, Avord, Pau, Cazeaux, G.D.E.
 Breveted: October 30, 1917 (Caudron).
 Final Rank: Caporal.

SERVICE IN U.S. AVIATION:
 Commissioned Second Lieutenant: February 21, 1918.
 At the Front: 94th Pursuit Squadron, March 3 to May 3, 1918.
 Killed in combat: (Toul Sector) May 3, 1918.

DECORATIONS:
 Distinguished Service Cross.
 Croix de Guerre, with Palm.

CITATIONS

G.H.Q., A.E.F.

On May 3, 1918, in the region of Autrepierre, France, while on patrol duty, he courageously attacked a group of four monoplanes and one biplane and succeeded in bringing one down before he himself was shot down in flames.

By Command of General PERSHING

Sous-Lieutenant CHAPMAN, CHARLES WESLEY, Pilote Escadrille Américaine N° 94

Glorieusement tombé au cours d'un combat contre un groupe ennemi après avoir abattu un de ses adversaires en flammes.

Charles W. Chapman, Jr.

Those of us who were with Chapman at Pau will always remember an incident that threw light on the determination concealed beneath his modesty and reserve of manner. It was in the acrobatics class, when man after man was sent up alone in the 13-metre Nieuport to do his first spins and aerial summersaults. At last, Chapman's turn came, and up he went to spin and flip with the best of us—but when he landed those who gathered around the machine noticed that his face was white and that he staggered as he walked. That evening he told us—the first spin had made him deathly ill, his head swam, and the sky went black before his eyes. In this condition, expecting every moment to faint, he had finished with honours the full course of acrobatic flying.

We urged him to apply for two-seater work where trick flying is not required, but he persevered and soon overcame his attacks of faintness. On the 3rd of May, 1918, near Autrepierre in Lorraine, Chapman died as he had lived, cleanly and gamely fighting till he was shot down within the enemy lines.

SERVICE RECORD

Victor Chapman, New York City.

Previous Service: August, 1914, to August, 1915
Foreign Legion (Infantry).

Service in French Aviation:
  Date of enlistment: August 1, 1915.
    Esc. V.B. 108 (Mitrailleur), August 10 to
      September 22, 1915.
  Aviation Schools: September 26, 1915, to April
      17, 1916, Avord, Réserve
      Général Aéronautique.
  Breveted: January 9, 1916 (Maurice Farman).
  At the Front: Escadrille Lafayette, April 20 to
      June 23, 1917.
  Final Rank: Sergent.
  Wounded in combat: June 17, 1916.
  Killed in combat: Northeast of Douaumont
      (Verdun Sector), June 23, 1916.

Decorations:
  Médaille Militaire.
  Croix de Guerre, with two Palms.

CITATIONS

October 7, 1916

Citation à l'Ordre de l'Armée:
  Chapman, Victor, Sergent Pilote
    à l'Escadrille 124

Pilote de chasse qui était un modèle d'audace, d'énergie et entrain, et faisait l'admiration de ses camarades d'escadrille. Sérieusement blessé à la tête le 17 juin, a demandé à ne pas interrompre son service. Quelque jours plus tard s'étant lancé à l'attaque de plusieurs avions ennemis, a trouvé une mort glorieuse au cours de la lutte.

Citation à l'Ordre de l'Armée:
  Chapman, Victor, Caporal Pilote à l'Escadrille 124

Citoyen américain, engagé pour la durée de la guerre. Pilote remarquable par son audace s'élançant sur les avions ennemis quelqu'en soit le nombre, et quelque soit l'altitude. Le 24 mai, a attaqué seul trois avions allemands; a livré un combat au cours duquel il a eu ses vêtements traversés de plusieurs balles et a été blessé au bras.

Victor Chapman

No finer obituary of Victor Chapman could be written than the following letter from Kiffin Rockwell to Mrs. John Jay Chapman:

> Escadrille N. 124, Secteur 24
> August 10, 1916

My dear Mrs. Chapman,
I received your letter this morning. I feel mortified that you have had to write me without my having written you before, when Victor was the best friend I ever had. I wanted to write you and his father at once, and tried to a number of times. But I found it impossible to write full justice to Victor or to really express my sympathy with you. Everything I would try to say seemed so weak. So I finally said: "I will just go ahead and work hard, do my best, then if I have accomplished a lot or have been

killed in accomplishing it, they will know that I had not forgotten Victor, and that some of his strength of character still lived. There is nothing that I can say to you or anyone that will do full credit to him. And everyone here that knew him feels the same way. To start with, Victor had such a strong character. I think we all have our ideals, when we begin, but unfortunately there are so very few of us that retain them; and sometimes we lose them at a very early age, and after that, life seems to be spoiled. But Victor was one of the very few who had the strongest of ideals, and then had the character to withstand anything that tried to come into his life and kill them. He was just a large, healthy man, full of life and goodness toward life, and could only see the fine, true points in life and in other people. And he was not of the kind that absorbs from other people, but of the kind that gives out. We all had felt his influence and seeing in him a man, made us feel a little more like trying to be men ourselves.

When I am in Paris, I stay with Mrs. Weeks, whose son was my friend and killed in the Legion. Well, Victor would come around once in a while to dinner with us. Mrs. Weeks used always to say to me: "Bring Victor around, he does me so much good. I like his laugh and the sound of his voice. When he comes into the room it always seems so much brighter." Well, that is the way it was here in the *escadrille*.

For work in the *escadrille*, Victor worked hard, always wanting to fly. And courage! he was too courageous; we all would beg him at times to slow up a little. We speak of him every day here, and we have said sincerely amongst ourselves many a time that Victor had more courage than all the rest of the *escadrille* combined. He would attack the Germans always, no matter what the conditions or what the odds. The day he was wounded four or five of the *escadrille* had been out and come home at the regular hour.

Well, Victor had attacked one machine and seriously crippled it, but the machine had succeeded in regaining the German lines. After that, Victor would not come home with the rest, but stayed looking for another machine. He found five machines inside our lines. None of us like to see a German within our lines, without attacking. So, although Victor was alone, he watched the five and finally one of them came lower and under him. He immediately dived on this one. Result was that

THE ESCADRILLE LAFAYETTE AT LUXEUIL, MAY. 1916

the others dived on him. One of them was a Fokker, painted like the machine of the famous Captain Boelke and may have been him. This Fokker got the position on Victor, and it was a miracle that he was not killed then. He placed bullet after bullet around Victor's head, badly damaging the machine, cutting parts of the commands in two, and one bullet cutting his scalp, as you know. Well, Victor got away, and with one hand held the commands together where they had been cut and landed at Froids where We had friends in a French *escadrille*. There he had dinner and his wound was dressed, and they repaired his machine a little.

That afternoon he came flying home with his head all bound up. Yet he thought nothing of it; only smiled and considered it an interesting event. He immediately wanted to continue his work as if nothing had happened. We tried to get him to a hospital, or to go to Paris for a short while, and rest; but he said "No." Then we said: "Well, you have got to take a rest even if you stay here." The captain told him that he would demand a new and better machine for him, and that he could rest while waiting for it to be ready, and then could see whether or not he should go back to flying. This was the 17th of June.

The following morning Balsley was wounded. The same day or the day after, Uncle Willie came to see Victor and was with us a couple of days. Those first days Victor slept late, a privilege he had not taken before since being in the *escadrille*, always having gotten up at daylight. In the daytime he would be with Uncle Willie, or at the field, seeing about his new machine, or he would take his old one and fly over to see Clyde Balsley. At first Balsley could not eat or drink anything. But after a few days he was allowed a little champagne and oranges. Well, as soon as Victor found that out, he arranged for champagne to be sent to Balsley, and would take oranges over to him. At least once a day, and sometimes twice, he would go over to see Balsley to cheer him up. And in the meantime he wouldn't ever let any one speak of his wound as a wound, and was impatient for his new machine.

On the 21st he got his Nieuport and had it regulated. On the 22nd he regulated the *mitrailleuse*, and the weather being too bad to fly over the lines, he flew it around here a little to get used to it. His head was still bandaged, but he said it was nothing. Late in the afternoon some Germans were signalled and he went up with the rest of us to look for them, but it was a false alarm.

The following morning the weather was good, and he insisted on going out at the regular hour with the rest. There were no enemy planes over the lines, so the *sortie* was uneventful. He came in, and at lunch fixed up a basket of oranges which he said he would take to Balsley. We went up to the field, and Captain Thénault, Prince, and Lufbery got ready to go out on patrol. Victor put the oranges in his machine and said that he would follow the others over the lines for a little trip and then go and land at the hospital.

The captain, Prince, and Lufbery started first. On arriving at the lines they saw the first two German machines, which they dived on. When they arrived in the midst of them, they found that two or three other German machines had arrived also. As the odds were against the three, they did not fight long, but immediately started back into our lines and without seeing Victor.

When they came back we thought that Victor was at the hospital. But later in the afternoon a *pilote* of a Maurice Farman and his passenger sent in a report. The report was that they saw three Nieuports attack five German machines, and at this moment they saw a fourth Nieuport arriving with all speed who dived in the midst of the Germans, that two of the Germans dived toward their field, and that the Nieuport fell through the air no longer controlled by the *pilote*. In a fight, it is practically impossible to tell what the other machines do, as everything happens so fast, and all one can see is the beginning of a fight and then, in a few seconds, the end. That fourth Nieuport was Victor, and, owing to the fact that the motor was going full speed when the machine fell, I think that he was killed instantly.

He died the most glorious death, and at the most glorious time of life to die, especially for him, with his ideals. I have never once regretted it for him, as I know he was willing and satisfied to give his life that way if it was necessary, and that he had no fear of death. It is for you, his father, relatives, myself, and for all who have known him, and all who would have known him, and for the world as a whole, I regret his loss.

Yet he is not dead; he lives forever in every place he has been, and in every one who knew him, and in the future generations little points of his character will be passed along. He is alive every day in this *escadrille* and has a tremendous influence on all our actions. Even the *mécaniciens* do their work better and more conscientiously. And a number of times I have seen Victor's *mécanicien* standing (when there was no work to be done) and gazing off in the direction of where he last saw Victor leaving for the lines.

For promotions and decorations things move slowly in the army, and after it has passed through all the *bureaux*, it takes some time to get back to you. Victor was proposed for *Sergent* and for the *Croix de Guerre*, May 24. This passed through all the *bureaux* and was signed by the general, but the papers did not arrive here until June 25. However, Victor knew on the 23rd, that they had passed, and that it was only a question of a day or so. He had also been promised, after being wounded, the *Médaille Militaire*, which he would have received some time in July. I wish that they could have sent that to you, for he had gained it, and they would have given it to him. But it is against the rules to give the *Médaille Militaire* unless everything has been signed before the *titulaire* is killed.

I must close now. You must not feel sorry, but must feel proud and happy.

Kiffin Rockwell

SERVICE RECORD

LOUIS CHARTON, New York City.

PREVIOUS SERVICE: September 2, 1914, to February 1, 1917, Foreign Legion (Infantry).
Wounded: July 10, 1916.

SERVICE IN FRENCH AVIATION:
Date of enlistment: February 20, 1917.
Aviation Schools: February 28 to August 20, 1917, Chartres, Avord, Pau, G.D.E.
Breveted: May 14, 1917 (Farman).
At the Front: Escadrille Spad 92, August 22 to September 5, 1917.
Final Rank: Sergent.
Prisoner in Germany: September 5, 1917, to Armistice.

DECORATIONS:
Croix de Guerre, with Star.

CITATION

DIVISION DU MAROC,
2ᵉ BRIGADE
8ᵉ RÉGIMENT DE MARCHE DE ZOUAVES
Citation à l'Ordre du Régiment N° 347 du 24 juillet, 1916:

Le Lieutenant Colonel Auroux, Commandant le 8ᵉ Régiment de Marche de Zouaves, cite à l'Ordre du Régiment:

CHARTON, LOUIS, Mˡᵉ 38688

Soldat excellent, a montré un courage remarquable le 10 juillet, 1916. A été blessé en montant à l'assaût d'une tranchée ennemie.

(Signé)   AUROUX

Louis Charton

Louis Charton was born in France of French parents, although he later became a naturalized American subject. At the time of the outbreak of the war he was living temporarily at Toul (Merthe-et-Moselle). He immediately enlisted in the Second Regiment of the Foreign Legion, and went into the trenches with his regiment on the 25th of November, 1914, near Craonne. The following account of his service was written by a fellow *legionnaire* who was with him during the campaigns of 1914-15-16.

> Louis, who was a quiet, modest little chap, had the heart of a lion. He had the spiritual fire which makes the best type of French patriot so superb a soldier. I remember one of our first nights in the trenches when the enemy attacked five times between twilight and dawn. Each time they were repulsed. Louis was one of five men holding a *petit poste* far in advance of the trenches, and it was largely due to the courage of these men that the Germans were unsuccessful in their assaults. On the 25th of September, 1915, the first day of the Champagne offensive, he was one of a patrol of five men and a corporal, all volunteers,

who were selected to destroy or capture a nest of machine guns. They went out in broad daylight, captured four machine guns and one hundred prisoners. On the Somme, in July, 1916, he was severely wounded while marching at the head of his section to the assault of the enemy trenches.

His career as an airman was unfortunately brief. Two weeks after his arrival at Spad 92 he was shot down by anti-aircraft fire from the ground. His motor was badly damaged which compelled him to land in enemy territory on the Verdun sector. The following year he was interned in Switzerland because of ill health, and from there wrote urgent letters to Major Gros asking that he use all of his influence to effect his return to France:

> *Je veux me venger des misères que j'ai subi en captivité, ainsi que venger la mort de mon frère. Je m'ennuie ici, d'être inactive, tandis que tant de mes camarades ont l'honneur de chasser le Boche*

His wishes could not be realised, however, and it was not until the Armistice was signed that he again returned to France.

SERVICE RECORD

Herman Lincoln Chatkoff, Maplewood, Massachusetts.

Previous Service: August 24, 1914, to May 20, 1916, Foreign Legion (Infantry).

Service in French Aviation:
Date of enlistment: May 24, 1916.
Aviation Schools: June 5, 1916, to April 20, 1917. Buc, Chartres, Châteauroux, G.D.E.
Breveted: September, 1916 (Caudron).
At the Front: Escadrille C. 11, April 25 to June 15, 1917.
Final Rank: Sergent.
Seriously injured in line of duty: June 15, 1917, at Chaudun (Aisne).

Decorations:
Croix de Guerre, with two Stars.

CITATION

Q.G. le 15 juin, 1917
Vᵉ Armée, État-Major.
Le Colonel Belhague, Chef d'État-Major de la Vᵉ Armée, cite à l'Ordre du Régiment:

Chatkoff, Lincoln, Caporal Pilote à l'Escadrille C. 11

A livré du 12 mai au 9 juin, 1917, plus de dix combats au cours desquels il a fait preuve de grandes qualités de courage, d'adresse, et de sang-froid. Le 4 juin, a attaqué successivement, au cours d'un même vol, deux groupes de trois et quatre avions ennemis. A eu son avion atteint de six balles et de nombreux éclats d'obus.

Le Chef d'État-Major de la 5ᵉ Armée
(Signé) **Belhague**

Herman Lincoln Chatkoff

The Americans who enlisted in the infantry of the French Foreign Legion all remember H. Lincoln Chatkoff, for he was one of the small group of "Yanks" who volunteered for service in August, 1914, taking an active part in the first trench fighting of the Great War. He transferred to French Aviation as a member of the Franco-American Corps in May, 1916, and received his military brevet in the autumn. But while waiting at the G.D.E. for assignment to a French squadron he became homesick for the Legion, and for a visit with his old comrades there. The result was that he asked for a two months' *permission* to be spent in trenches and billets with his old regiment. Never, perhaps, in the history of the Legion had such an unusual request been made, and it was granted! "Chat" went back to the trenches, where he spent two months fighting cooties and Germans, the renewed experience, as he expressed it in a letter, "doing him a lot of good." At the end of this so-called *permission* he was sent to a French reconnaissance squadron, C. 11, where he made an excellent record. On June 15, 1917, he was seriously injured in a flying accident near Soissons, which incapacitated him for further service.

SERVICE RECORD

ROGER HARVEY CLAPP, New York City.

SERVICE IN FRENCH AVIATION:
Date of enlistment: June 3, 1917.
Aviation Schools: June 13, 1917, to January 12, 1918, Avord, G.D.E.
Breveted: September 16, 1917 (Caudron).
At the Front: Escadrille Br. 120, January 15 to February 28, 1918.
Final Rank: Caporal.

SERVICE IN U.S. AVIATION:
Commissioned First Lieutenant: March 14, 1918.
At the Front: Assigned to the French Squadron Br. 120, March 30 to May 15, 1918.
96th Bombardment Squadron, June 6 to July 6, 1918.
Killed in line of duty: July 6, 1918, at Amanty.

Roger Harvey Clapp

Clapp was a genuine character of the old-fashioned American kind, full of shrewdness, wit, ingenuity, and provincialism. He always refused to make any attempt to learn French, with the thoroughly American idea that all foreigners should be obliged to learn English. It was one of our treats at Avord to listen to a conversation between Clapp and his instructor, who was very fond of him. Roger believed firmly that any Frenchman could understand English if spoken very slowly and loudly, and considered it almost an insult when his carefully enunciated observations missed their mark. We never quite understood how, but he always ended by making himself clear.

He was breveted on Caudron, took the G. 4 training, and went to the Front as pilot of a Bréguet. In Escadrille Br. 120 he earned a reputation for absolute fearlessness, and after a term of exceptionally fine service with the French, was transferred to the American army. On July 6, 1918, while flying near Amanty, Clapp met with a fatal accident. His loss was a heavy one to his comrades, as well as to the Air Service at large, for there were few Americans who had had a broader experience of day-bombing.

SERVICE RECORD

CALEB JAMES COATSWORTH, JR., Buffalo, New York.

PREVIOUS SERVICE: Norton-Harjes Ambulance, 1916.

SERVICE IN FRENCH AVIATION:
Date of enlistment: February 20, 1917.
Aviation Schools: February 24 to July 16, 1917, Avord, Pau, G.D.E.
Breveted: April 25, 1917 (Caudron).
At the Front: Escadrille Spad 80, July 18, 1917, to March 20, 1918.
Final Rank: Sergent.
Slightly wounded in combat: August 16, 1917.

SERVICE IN U.S. NAVAL AVIATION:
Commissioned Ensign: March 20, 1918. Promoted Lieut. (j.g.).
At the Front: U.S. Naval Air Station, Porto Corsini, Italy, summer and autumn of 1918.

DECORATIONS:
Croix de Guerre, with Star (Ambulance).

CITATION

Au G.C., le 7 août, 1916
21ᵉ DIVISION D'INFANTERIE, ÉTAT-MAJOR.

Le Général Commandant la 21ᵉ Division d'Infanterie cite à l'Ordre de la Division:

CALEB COATSWORTH, Volontaire Américain de la Section Sanitaire Automobile Américaine No. 7

Volontaire pour une mission périlleuse, s'en est acquitté avec un sang-froid remarquable, sous un feu intense et continu. A donné, au cours de la campagne, de nombreuses preuves de son mépris du danger et de son esprit de sacrifice.

Le Général commandant la 21ᵉ Division d'Infanterie
(Signé)   DAUVIN

Caleb James Coatsworth

From the day of his arrival at the Front Coatsworth saw a good deal of active service. On August 16, 1917, when still comparatively a novice, he was sent on a "ground-strafing" patrol over the Verdun sector. This is nerve-racking work even to the veteran pilot, the more so when heavy fighting is in progress. The French were attacking, gaining back more of the ground—called the most precious in France because of its cost in human life—which they had lost to the enemy the preceding winter. *Groupe de Combat* 14 was heavily engaged, and Coatsworth's squadron, Spad 80, had the important task of machine-gunning German reserves which were packed in the communication trenches. Great sport, of course, if one enjoys riding in the wake of shells, bursting at the rate of about one hundred per minute, and so close to the ground as to be the easy prey of all enemy *chasse* patrols higher up. He saw for the first time a machine falling in flames, a bi-motor Caudron, and had the satisfaction of knocking into a *vrille* the Albatross which was attacking it.

AMERICAN PILOTS OF THE SPAD 80

But the fun was fast and furious, a give-and-take proposition, the usual thing in a "dog-fight." Two single-seaters attacked him from above at this moment. A bullet struck his radiator, blinding him with water; another shattered his wind-shield; and still another struck his ammunition-box. His life was very probably saved by the timely intervention of another Spad which drove off the tenacious Germans. Coatsworth managed to plane back to French territory, and then, just outside Verdun, crashed his badly damaged Spad, "beautifully and most thoroughly," as he put it. He himself was uninjured in the fall, although he had various minute pieces of radiator in his wrist.

On March 20, 1918, he entered the U.S. Naval Air Service as an ensign and afterward was on service at the Naval Air Station at Porto Corsini, Italy.

SERVICE RECORD

PHELPS COLLINS, Detroit, Michigan.

SERVICE IN FRENCH AVIATION:
Date of enlistment: May 17, 1917.
Aviation Schools: May 22 to September 1, 1917, Avord, Pau, G.D.E.
Breveted: July 28, 1917 (Caudron).
At the Front: Escadrille Spad 313, September 2 to September 18, 1917.
Escadrille Spad 103, September 19, 1917, to January 7, 1918.
Escadrille Lafayette: January 7 to February 18, 1918.
Final Rank: Sergent.

SERVICE IN U.S. AVIATION:
Commissioned Captain: January 9, 1918.
At the Front: 103d Pursuit Squadron, February 18 to March 12, 1918.
Killed in line of duty: March 12, 1918, near Château-Thierry.

DECORATIONS:
Croix de Guerre, with two Palms.

CITATIONS

Au Q.G.A., le 25 octobre, 1917
Ier ARMÉE, ÉTAT-MAJOR.

Le Général Commandant la 1ère Armée, cite à l'Ordre de l'Armée:

COLLINS, PHELPS, M^{le} 12, 385, Caporal au 1er Régiment Étranger, Pilote à l'Escadrille S. 103

Citoyen américain engagé dans l'Armée Française avant la déclaration de guerre des États-Unis. Pilote de chasse d'un courage et d'une adresse exceptionnels. Le 14 octobre, 1917, a abattu en flammes dans nos lignes un avion ennemi.

(Signé) ANTHOINE

IVème ARMÉE, ÉTAT-MAJOR. *Le 25 mars, 1918*
Le Général Commandant la 4ème Armée cite à l'Ordre de l'Armée:

Captain COLLINS, PHELPS, du 1er Régiment de la Légion Étrangère détaché à l'Escadrille Lafayette

Pilote américain engagé dans l'Aviation Française, se révèle de suite comme pilote hors ligne, livrant journellement des combats au cours desquels il abat plusieurs avions ennemis. Au cours d'une patrouille, est tombé mortellement frappé.

Le Général Commandant la 4ème Armée

GOURAUD

Phelps Collins

In October, 1917, while flying with the French in Flanders, Phelps Collins wrote the following letter to Major Gros, of the Lafayette Corps:

> Dear Major,—I brought down my first German this afternoon (one of an enemy patrol of five). I am feeling in good spirits, the

reason being that I can now leave the French Service without having cost the government anything. I have never broken a stick while flying with the French and have knocked down an enemy machine for them.

I have given up my *permission* in order to further prepare myself here before being taken over by the American Army.

This brief letter is characteristic of "Eddie" Collins, who was one of the finest pilots in the Lafayette Corps. No man worked harder to perfect himself in the fine art of aerial combat, and no American who was trained in French schools gained such excellent flying notes from his *moniteurs*. He was a born *chasse* pilot. There are many airmen, both French and American, who remember his wonderful skill at acrobacy and combat. While he was at G.D.E., awaiting orders for the Front, all other flying stopped when Collins climbed into his Spad. Veteran pilots from the Front as well as the *moniteurs* watched him with joy as long as he was in the air. This was an unusual tribute, the highest possible one which could be paid him as a flyer.

COLLINS IN FLANDERS

THEODORE DE KRUIJFF AND PHELPS COLLINS AT PAU

It often happens that a pilot with a good record in the aviation schools makes an indifferent fighter. Not so with Phelps Collins. He was seemingly tireless, going out on voluntary patrols daily between the hours of regular work. Shortly after being sent to the Front, his squadron, Spad 313, was detailed for experimental duties as a night pursuit unit in the Dunkirk sector. Collins was then transferred to Spad 103 which was operating on the same region and used to fly with both squadrons. "*Cest un garçon merveilleux. Il est toujours en l'air*" was the frequent comment of his old French captain in Spad 313.

In this first official victory, of which he speaks in the above letter, he shot down a well-known German ace, who had more than ten Allied planes to his credit.

In the early winter Collins was transferred to the U.S. Air Service and assigned to the 103rd Pursuit Squadron, the old Escadrille Lafayette, which was then operating on the Champagne front.

Here, in a very short time, he shot down two additional enemy planes. Although there was no doubt about the destruction of the German machines, the combats happened so far within the enemy lines that neither of them could be officially confirmed. However, official confirmation mattered little to Collins. So long as he achieved something definite, knowing that he had done so, he was more than satisfied.

On March 12, 1917, he made his last flight. A patrol of German bombing planes was reported by telephone, flying toward Paris. A flight of five machines was sent by the 103rd Squadron to the zone of protection assigned to it by French G.H.Q. This lay between Château-Thierry and Montmirail. Collins had been flying all the morning, but insisted on accompanying this afternoon patrol.

After half an hour of uneventful flying, he was seen to leave the flight, and it was believed by his comrades that he was having motor trouble. A telephone message was received at the aerodrome a few hours later, giving the news of his fall from a great height, and his instant death.

No German machines had been seen either from the air or from the ground, and as the Château-Thierry zone of protection was far from the lines, it is not likely that there were any in that region. (The enemy bombers had passed far to the north and were driven back by a French squadron operating in another zone.) The cause of his death will never be known, but it is likely that it was due to exhaustion after many days of constant flying and fighting. He was buried among French soldiers in the Cemetery of Mont Frenet.

SERVICE RECORD

James A. Connelly, Jr., Philadelphia, Pennsylvania.

Service in French Aviation:
  Date of enlistment: June 15, 1917.
  Aviation Schools: June 20, 1917, to January 12, 1918, Avord, Pau, Cazeaux, G.D.E.
  Breveted: November 1, 1917 (Caudron).
  At the Front: Escadrille Spad 157, January 15 to June 27, 1918.
  Escadrille Spad 163, June 27, 1918, to Armistice.
  Final Rank: Adjudant.

Decorations:
  Distinguished Service Cross.
  Médaille Militaire.
  Croix de Guerre, with five Palms.

CITATIONS

IVe Armée.   7 mai, 1918
Le Général Commandant le 4e C.A., cite à l'Ordre du Corps d'Armée:
  Connelly, James, M^{le} 12246. Caporal à l'Escadrille N. 157 (G.C. 21)

Jeune pilote remarquable d'allant et de hardiesse: avec un camarade a incendié, le 20 avril, 1918, un ballon d'observation ennemi, malgré la présence d'un groupe d'avions auxquels les deux pilotes ont du livrer un dur combat pour regagner les lignes françaises.

6e Armée, État-Major.   Le 22 juin, 1918
Citation à l'Ordre de l'Armée:
  Connelly, James, Sergent à l'Escadrille Spa. 157, G.C. 21. Détaché du 1er Régiment Étranger

Pilote de chasse d'une adresse remarquable. Le ... au cours d'un dur combat, a abattu son deuxième appareil ennemi.
                    (Signé)   Degoutte

Grand Quartier Général des Armées du Nord et du Nord Est, État Major.   Le 4 octobre, 1918
Le Médaille Militaire a été conférée au
  Sergent Connelly, James, (active) du 1er Régiment Étranger, Pilote Aviateur

Engagé volontaire pour la durée de la guerre, s'impose à tous par l'élévation de son caractère, ses qualités de pilote, son mépris absolu du danger. Le 6 septembre, 1918, a remporté sa 5ème victoire en abattant un monoplace ennemi. — Trois citations.
La présente nomination comporte l'attribution de la Croix de Guerre avec Palme.
                    Le Général Commandant en Chef
                                    Pétain

G.H.Q., A.E.F.   17 March, 1919
  Sergeant James A. Connelly, Pilot French Air Service

Distinguished himself by extraordinary heroism in connection with military operations against an armed enemy of the United States at Suippes (France) on 6 September, 1918, and in recognition of his gallant conduct I have awarded him, in the name of the President, the Distinguished Service Cross.
            (Signed)   John J. Pershing
                            Commander-in-Chief

James A. Connelly, Jr.

During the spring of 1917, at Avord, a tall and slender American was to be seen daily, stalking serenely toward the Blériot field. He

109

had little to say, particularly in regard to his own aerial exploits, having little love for what our French comrades called *bourrage de crane*; he abstained from the sensational *sorties* to which the rest of us were involuntary addicts, and in fact did not have a single Blériot confirmation to his credit. His friends will best remember him at this period by a rich Philadelphia accent and the unparalleled splendour of his raiment, which latter was an inspiration to many a budding airman. It was "Jim" Connelly, later to become one of the brilliant fighting pilots of the Lafayette Flying Corps.

Pilots of Spad 163
(Connelly standing sixth from left)

Connelly got to the Front on January 15, 1918, joining the Escadrille N. 157. On June 27 he was transferred to the Spad 163, with which unit he served until the cessation of hostilities. Worn out by constant flying during the heavy fighting of the final summer of the war, and on the point of a nervous breakdown, Connelly hung on with a grim determination to do his duty, and added daily to his brilliant reputation with the French. His skill as pilot, his aggressiveness and reckless courage have placed him among the aces, for he has eight official victories to his credit, as well as many others shot down too far within the enemy lines for confirmation. His devotion to duty has not gone unrecognised. He has won the *Croix de Guerre* and *Médaille Militaire,* and the American D.S.C. Connelly's citations, better than any other form of eulogy, will tell the splendid story of his services to France.

SERVICE RECORD

ALAN A. COOK, Canandaigua, New York.

SERVICE IN FRENCH AVIATION:
Date of enlistment: July 21, 1917.
Aviation Schools: July 31 to December 16, 1917, Avord, Tours, Pau, G.D.E.
Breveted: October 20, 1917 (Caudron).
At the Front: Escadrille Spad 157, December 20, 1917, to July 20, 1918.
Escadrille Spad 163, July 20, 1918, to Armistice.
Final Rank: Adjudant.

DECORATIONS:
Croix de Guerre, with Palm.

CITATION

Le 2 septembre, 1918

Le Général Commandant la IVe Armée cite à l'Ordre de l'Armée:

Le Sergent COOK, ALAN, de l'Escadrille Spa. 163, G.C. 21

Engagé volontaire au 1er Étranger, passé sur sa demande dans l'aviation française, y fait preuve des plus belles qualités d'entrain et de courage. Le 11 août, 1918, a remporté sa première victoire officielle au cours d'un combat très dur où un avion ennemi écrasé dans ses lignes.

Le Général Commandant la IVe Armée
GOURAUD

Alan A. Cook

Cook was one of the little band that went to Tours while the school was still in French hands. He was exceptionally apt at flying and went to Pau before the rest of his class. From Plessis-Belleville he went to Belfort in December, 1917, to join the Escadrille Spad 157. The winter was very severe in the mountain country and little flying was done until the Squadron went to Châlons in February, to form the G.C. 21. From that time on, Cook's hours in the air were many. He went through the Château-Thierry and Champagne battles of 1918, had many combats and one official victory to his credit, and rose to the rank of *Adjudant* in the French Army.

SERVICE RECORD

LINN PALMER COOKSON, Carlinville, Illinois.

SERVICE IN FRENCH AVIATION:
Date of enlistment: June 19, 1917.
Aviation Schools: June 27, 1917, to February, 1918, Avord, Tours, Pau, G.D.E.
Breveted: October 27, 1917 (Caudron).
Final Rank: Caporal.

SERVICE IN U.S. AVIATION:
Commissioned Second Lieutenant: January 26, 1918.
Returned to the United States, June 1, 1918.
Died September 15, 1918.

Linn Palmer Cookson

There are certain men who seem genuinely unlucky, despite the best qualities of energy, good-will, and courage. Linn Cookson was one of these. In the schools he was endlessly delayed by sickness, and at Pau had a bad fall, due to motor trouble. In spite of bad health and worse luck, he was never discouraged, and his dry, satirical wit furnished cheer for all who knew him, during the dreary days of waiting at the G.D.E. At last he transferred to the American Army and joined a newly formed squadron, but Cookson was destined never to reach the Front, for in the summer he was sent home, an invalid, and later on his friends were saddened to hear that he had died on September 15, 1918, as the result of an operation for appendicitis.

SERVICE RECORD

RUSSELL B. COREY, New York City.

SERVICE IN FRENCH AVIATION:
Date of enlistment: July 21, 1917.
Aviation Schools: August 1, 1917, to February, 1918, Avord, G.D.E.
Breveted: October 27, 1917 (Caudron).
Final Rank: Caporal.

SERVICE IN U.S. NAVAL AVIATION:
Commissioned Ensign.

Russell B. Corey

Having lived a good deal in France before the war, Corey had a pleasant time in the schools, where he was able to get along well with the French and to help his comrades by acting as interpreter. At Tours he was made a species of Field-Marshal who mustered the Franco-American Air Forces and marched them to the field with great military precision. Like Bluthenthal and Kyle, Corey took the difficult Schmidt training, and, at the G.D.E., perfected himself in flying a Bréguet. When on the point of going to the Front, he was taken over by the American Navy, and as in the case of so many navy men, the Lafayette Flying Corps has no further record of him.

SERVICE RECORD

EDWARD J. CORSI, Brooklyn, New York.

SERVICE IN FRENCH AVIATION:
 Date of enlistment: May 15, 1917.
 Aviation Schools: June 8, 1917, to May 14, 1918,
  Avord, Pau, Cazeaux, G.D.E.
 Breveted: October 30, 1917 (Caudron).
 At the Front: Escadrille Spad 77, May 30, 1918,
  to Armistice.
 Final Rank: Sergent.

DECORATIONS:
 Croix de Guerre, with Palm and Star.

Edward J. Corsi

Corsi is one of those men who learn slowly, but who learn well. At Avord in the Blériot School he had the usual difficulties in mastering the old *six pattes* and up to the time of his brevet showed no brilliant gift for flying. At Pau, however, he did excellent work and finished by becoming a clever and daring pilot. The French recognised his ability by making him an instructor, so that he did not arrive at the Front until somewhat later than his contemporaries of Avord, but once in the Escadrille Spad 77, he proved that he had mastered his art and possessed fine qualities of initiative and fearlessness.

SERVICE RECORD

JOHN ROWELL COTTON, Chicago, Illinois.

SERVICE IN FRENCH AVIATION:
 Date of enlistment: June 10, 1917.
 Aviation Schools: June 16, 1917, to January 10,
  1918, Avord, G.D.E.
 Breveted: November 30, 1917 (Caudron).
 At the Front: Escadrille Br. 120, January 15
  to June 17, 1918.
 Final Rank: Caporal.

SERVICE IN U.S. AVIATION:
 Commissioned First Lieutenant.
 At the Front: Attached to French Squadron Br.
  120, June to September, 1918.

DECORATIONS:
 Croix de Guerre, with two Stars.

CITATIONS

Le 23 juin, 1918
Le Chef d'Escadron Vuillemin, Commandant l'Escadre de Bombardement N° 12, cite à l'Ordre de l'Escadre les militaires dont les noms suivent: . . .

Le Lieutenant Pilote Américain COTTON,
JOHN, de l'Escadrille 120 (G.B. 5)

Très bon pilote consciencieux et courageux, s'est distingué pendant l'offensive en accomplissant un grand nombre de missions à basse altitude. Le 12 juin, 1918, a soutenu un très dur combat avec des avions ennemis et est rentré avec un avion criblé de balles.

(Signé) VUILLEMIN

G.Q.G., 10 décembre, 1918

1er Lieutenant Pilote JOHN COTTON, à l'Escadrille 12

Officier pilote modèle, d'une conscience et d'un dévouement admirables. A fait toutes les attaques depuis le 28 mars, 1918, s'est particulièrement distingué le 15 juillet, en exécutant un bombardement sur les ponts de la Marne.

John Rowell Cotton

Breveted on Caudron on November 30, 1917, Cotton found himself interested in the day-bombing branch of Aviation, and at his request the French allowed him to specialize in Bréguet work. In addition to being a first-class pilot, he took his bombing seriously, studied every phase of it, and strove to perfect himself in its fine points. Going to the Front in January, 1918, in the Escadrille Br. 120, he did excellent work and won high praise from the French. In June he was transferred to the United States Army with the rank of 1st Lieutenant, but was allowed to continue in the same squadron, where he had become a flight commander in whom high confidence was placed. All through the heavy fighting of the summer, during the German advance and subsequent German retreat, he was constantly in the air, leading his Bréguets across the lines to drop their bombs on enemy bridges, convoys, and munition dumps. Had the war continued, Cotton would have risen to a position of great responsibility, for he was considered by his superiors in the American Army as one of the best day-bombing men we possessed.

SERVICE RECORD

ELLIOT CHRISTOPHER COWDIN, New York City.

SERVICE IN FRENCH AVIATION:
 Date of enlistment: March 5, 1915.
 Aviation Schools: March 9 to May 1, 1915, Pau.
 Breveted: April 29, 1915 (Voisin).
 At the Front: Escadrille V.B. 108, May 3 to August 15, 1915.
  Escadrille N. 38, September 30 to November 10, 1915.
  Escadrille N. 49, November 12, 1915, to January 15, 1916.
  Escadrille N. 65, March 2 to April 18, 1916.
  Escadrille Lafayette, April 28 to June 25, 1916.
 Final Rank: Sergent.

SERVICE IN U.S. AVIATION:
 Commissioned Major: June, 1918.
 Attached to Lockhart Special Mission, Board of Aircraft Production.

DECORATIONS:
 Médaille Militaire.
 Croix de Guerre, with two Palms and Star.

CITATIONS

**GRAND QUARTIER GÉNÉRAL DES ARMÉES DE
L'EST, ÉTAT-MAJOR.** *Le 9 juillet,* 1915

Le Général Commandant en Chef cite à l'Ordre de l'Armée le militaire dont le nom suit:

Caporal COWDIN, Pilote de l'Escadrille V.B. 108

Citoyen américain engagé pour la durée de la guerre, exécute journellement de longues expéditions de bombardement. Excellent pilote qui plusieurs fois a attaqué des avions ennemis. Le 26 juin, 1915, rencontrant simultanément deux avions allemands, les attaque et les force successivement à descendre, l'un d'eux paraissant gravement atteint; a eu lui-même son moteur et son avion gravement endommagés par le tir des avions allemands et plusieurs atteintes dans son casque.

Le Général Commandant en Chef
JOFFRE

**GRAND QUARTIER GÉNÉRAL, ÉTAT-MAJOR
AÉRONAUTIQUE.** *Le* 18 *avril,* 1916

Le Lieutenant-Colonel du Service Aéronautique au G.Q.G. cite à l'Ordre du Service Aéronautique:

Le Maréchal des Logis COWDIN, ELLIOT, de l'Escadrille N. 65

Américain, engagé pour la durée de la guerre, fait preuve journellement d'un dévouement absolu. Pilote énergique et brave, n'a pas hésité à poursuivre dans leurs lignes plusieurs avions ennemis pendant la bataille de Verdun; malgré que son appareil soit en mauvais état, a eu un combat heureux.

(*Signé*) BARRÉS

**GRAND QUARTIER GÉNÉRAL DES ARMÉES
ÉTAT-MAJOR.** *Le* 20 *avril,* 1916

La Médaille Militaire a été conférée au Militaire dont le nom suit:

COWDIN, ELLIOT, M^{le} 11334, Maréchal des Logis, Pilote à l'Escadrille N. 65

Engagé volontaire pour la durée de la guerre, n'a cessé de faire preuve d'un entrain, d'une bravoure et d'un dévouement remarquables. Abattu un avion ennemi au cours de récentes opérations. A attaqué 12 appareils allemands dont l'un d'eux a été détruit. Déjà cité à l'ordre de l'armée.

Le présente nomination comporte l'attribution de la Croix de Guerre avec palme.

(*Signé*) JOFFRE

Elliot Christopher Cowdin

Elliot Cowdin, one of the original seven members of the Escadrille Lafayette, began his war service in the American Ambulance. Meeting Norman Prince in Paris, in February, 1915, he at once caught his enthusiasm and worked with him to further the organisation of the *Escadrille Américaine.*

Prince met with many discouragements and was sometimes almost disheartened. On one of these occasions, Cowdin, on leave in Paris, finding that there were enough breveted American pilots to make up a squadron, talked with Colonel Barrès, then Chief of French Aeronautics in the *Zone des Armées,* who promised him that he would give his active support to the work of assembling the Americans in one unit. Cowdin sent the news to Prince, who immediately regained his enthusiasm for the original plan. In such ways as this, each of the early volunteers played important parts in making the N. 124 a reality.

SERGEANT COWDIN, LIEUTENANT DE LAAGE DE
MEUX, CAPTAIN THÉNAULT, LIEUTENANT THAW

Cowdin received his early training on Voisin, and was sent to the Front as a pilot in the *Groupe de Bombardement* 108. This was nearly a year before the *Escadrille Américaine* was sent to Luxeuil to begin active duty. After three months and a half of bombardment work, he went to Avord for training as a *chasse* pilot, returning to the Front in September, to the Escadrille N. 38. In December, 1915, he went with Thaw and Prince on a month's *permission* to America. This visit is of great historic interest in the history of the Lafayette Corps. Much against their will the three Americans were kept in the public eye. Supporters of the Allied cause urged their example in pleading for America's intervention in the war. German sympathizers, on the other hand, asked for their internment because of their open violation of American neutrality. The French Government was not unmindful of the widespread interest aroused by three Americans who were actually in arms in the French service. Whether intentional or not, the visit to the United States was a piece of excellent diplomacy. It convinced the authorities in Paris that a squadron of American volunteers would have an important influence on opinion in the United States, and a few months later, the N. 124 took its place at the Front.

A week after his arrival at the *Escadrille Américaine*, Cowdin received the *Médaille Militaire* for a combat against a large German patrol, one of which he shot down. He was the first American pilot to receive this much-coveted decoration. He had already been twice cited for his work with the French squadrons, V.B. 108 and N. 65.

One of his most interesting adventures during his service with N. 124, happened while the squadron was operating on the Verdun sector. The account of it comes, strangely enough, from a German source, and is an extract from the diary of Boelke, the great German airman who was killed later in the year:

July 4, 1916

Around Verdun there has not been much aerial activity until today. I had already flown twice and was sitting idly at our aerodrome when I heard the sound of machine-gun fire, and saw one of our German *biplaces* being attacked by a Nieuport. The German soon landed safely in my neighbourhood. 'The devil is loose at the Front,' he declared breathlessly. 'There are six Americans out there. I distinctly saw the flag on the machine! They are very bold and come far on our side of the lines.'

After all, I thought, they can't be so dangerous, and I set out to see for myself. Rightly enough, there they were, flying in a group, back and forth across the lines. I approached, opening fire upon the first one who seemed to be a beginner; at any rate, I was able to approach within a hundred metres and observe him. As he was somewhat in the clouds, I was justified in thinking that I could bring him down; but luck was against me. My machine was fresh from the factory, and after about seventy shots my gun jammed. During this time the other five Americans had come up, and as I was without defence I decided to withdraw. I manoeuvred by sliding down on my left wing, and a few hundred metres lower brought my machine into a normal position. But as they were still chasing me, I repeated the manoeuvre, and at an altitude of 200 metres re-dressed and flew back to camp, little pleased, although untouched, while the Americans continued their flight along the Front.

Boelke's diary [1] was afterward published in Germany, and found its way to France. By examining the records of the Lafayette Squadron, it was possible to identify the pilot whom Boelke attacked. It was Elliot Cowdin who was so nearly ambushed when Boelke dived upon him

---

1. *Richthofen & Böelcke in Their Own Words*, a double edition, *The Red Battle Flyer* by Manfred Freiherr von Richthofen and *An Aviator's Field Book* by Oswald Böelcke is also published by Leonaur.

from under cover of a cloud.

In August, 1916, Cowdin was compelled to retire from active service because of ill health. He spent six weeks in hospital and was then attached to the British Aviation Headquarters in Paris. In January, 1917, he was released from the French Service and returned to America. In June, 1918, he was commissioned Major in the U.S. Air Service and attached to the Lockhart Special Mission, Board of Aircraft Production, with which he served until the close of the war.

Photograph by Campbell Studios, New York

SERVICE RECORD

AUSTEN BALLARD CREHORE, Westfield, New York.

SERVICE IN FRENCH AVIATION:
Date of enlistment: July 16, 1917.
Aviation Schools: July 21 to November 28, 1917, Avord, Tours, Pau, G.D.E.
Breveted: September 29, 1917 (Caudron).
At the Front: Escadrille Spad 94, December 1, 1917, to Armistice.
Final Rank: Sergent.

DECORATIONS:
Croix de Guerre, with two Palms.

CITATIONS

Le 29 janvier, 1918
IVe ARMÉE, ÉTAT-MAJOR.
Le Général Commandant la IVe Armée cite à l'Ordre de l'Armée:

Caporal de la Légion Étrangère, CREHORE, AUSTEN (Américain), M^{le} 12228, de l'Escadrille 94

Jeune pilote de chasse, fin et hardi, attaque ses adversaires dès ses premières sorties, en descend un loin dans ses lignes le 19 janvier, 1918.

Le Général Commandant la IVe Armée
GOURAUD

Le 1 septembre, 1918
Le Général Commandant le Groupe d'Armée de Réserve cite à l'Ordre de l'Armée:

CREHORE, AUSTEN, No. M^{le} 12339. Sergent à la Légion Étrangère, Pilote-Aviateur

Pilote de premier ordre, plein d'allant, d'énergie, et d'audace, à peine remis d'une longue maladie, est revenu à son escadrille où il se bat avec le plus bel entrain, portant le combat même sur les terrains d'aviation ennemis.

Le 9 août a eu des combats très durs au cours desquels son appareil a été criblé de balles.

Austen Ballard Crehore

About the time that active hostilities between Germany and the United States commenced, Austen Crehore tried to enter the Flying Service in the American Army. Refused by the American Examining Board, he came to France, where combat pilots were badly needed, and enlisted in the French Army through the Lafayette Flying Corps.

About four months after arriving in France he had finished aerial acrobacy at Pau, having been breveted at Tours. In spite of physical defects, he completed his training with exceptionally good notes, went to the Front in December, 1917, and gained his first victory a month after joining his *escadrille*. His flying partner at this time was Marinovitch, who later became one of France's leading aces. Crehore deserves a good deal of credit for the later career of Marinovitch, having very probably saved him from being shot down on one occasion. For his work with Spad 94 he was given the *Croix de Guerre* and proposed for the *Médaille Militaire*. Both honours were richly merited, for the quality of his service was unusually fine. He never lost an opportunity for combat, no matter what the odds against him or how small the chance for official recognition of his efforts.

CREHORE AND MARINOVITCH

At another time, far within the enemy lines, he machine-gunned an aviation field, shot down an Albatross which was just taking off, then attacked a German observation balloon, forcing the observers to jump in their parachutes. He forced the balloon to the ground, although his gun was jammed at the time, and he could do no more than dive at it. This exploit was seen from afar by another pilot who reported it at his aerodrome. It was one of many like adventures which accounts for the sincere affection and respect which his comrades, both French and American, had for him. Marinovitch, the Serbian volunteer and his old flying partner, wrote of him as follows:

At the beginning of December, 1917, Crehore arrived in my squadron (Escadrille 94). A few other Americans came about the same time, Putnam, Wally Winter, and Woodward. I got to know Crehore and Winter awfully well, and we were the three best friends in the world. Crehore wanted to get Boches terribly hard; the only trouble was we had Nieuports when nearly every other squadron had Spads, and we were terribly handicapped. Crehore and I were flying every day; never could we find a Boche. December passed and January, and poor old Crehore was nearly wild. By this time, Putnam had got his first, and on the 15th of January, Crehore and I decided we must see one, so we went far into the enemy's lines and waited.

Finally I spied a Boche alone, and a big patrol, but much farther away. I put full motor on, outdistancing Crehore (he had a cylinder off his motor, which, of course, I did not know). I got into a fight with the Boche, but he, having a much superior machine—it was an Albatross—all painted "tango," soon got the better of me, and was just going to bring me down, when Crehore, by very clever manoeuvring caught him, and the Boche fell vertically, losing a bit of his plane. We were twenty kilometres in Germany, and we still had to get home before the big patrol caught us. No matter, Crehore followed him to the ground! This was the first Boche Crehore had ever seen, also his first official victory, and I'll never forget how he saved my life that day with a rotten machine and a motor on the bum!

After the fight I was sure Crehore was going to be the best American flyer and catch up to Lufbery very quick. Unfortunately, just as our squadron got Spads, he fell ill, and the doctor, as soon as he was better, wanted to *reformé* him. He raised such a row at this idea that they sent him home for four months. When he got back, we were having a lot of trouble with our Hispano motors, and Crehore was especially unlucky. However, he had many hard fights bringing back his machine full of holes. On the 15th of July, he saved another pilot attacked by three Boches, and after a big fight got lost in Germany. He found a German aviation field, and a *monoplace* started to get him; he didn't give him time, and just as the Boche was leaving the ground, Crehore jumped on his tail and saw him smash up wonderfully. The clouds were very low, and he could not come home, as we often do, by the sun, so he looked on the aviation field and saw where the wind came from; he knew it was blowing from the west, so made for that direction, following the Forêt de l'Argonne. On his way back he attacked two German sausages and made both observers jump out, but couldn't put them on fire. This Boche was never counted, as he fell too far, and the weather was too bad for him to be seen from our lines. Crehore is one of the finest pilots I know and the best pal I've ever had.

SERVICE RECORD

ARTHUR LAWRENCE CUNNINGHAM, Medford, Massachusetts.

SERVICE IN FRENCH AVIATION:
Date of enlistment: July 7, 1917.
Aviation Schools: July 15, 1917, to February, 1918, Avord, Pau, Cazeaux, G.D.E.
Brevetted: December 1, 1917 (Caudron).
Final Rank: Caporal.

SERVICE IN U.S. AVIATION:
Commissioned Second Lieutenant: January 24, 1918.
Promoted First Lieutenant: August 1, 1918.
At the Front: 94th Pursuit Squadron, March 4, 1918, to Armistice.
Operations Officer, 94th Pursuit Squadron, September 1 to October 1, 1918.
Operations Officer, First Pursuit Group, October 1, 1918, to the Armistice.

CUNNINGHAM AND YORK, AVORD
JULY, 1917

Arthur Lawrence Cunningham

Arthur Cunningham quickly won the distinction of demolishing more Blériots than any one man, except certain Russians, at Avord. This habit vastly amused his fellow students, and gave Cunningham a dash and recklessness which stood him in good stead when he was sent to the Front. He never was hurt in an accident, yet his skill in utterly wrecking the fragile monoplanes was amazing. These smashes were unavoidable and never drew harsh words from the French monitors, but Cunningham persisted, and became a very clever pilot. Before he was sent to the Front he transferred to the American Army, and joined the 94th Pursuit Squadron.

SERVICE RECORD

FRAZIER CURTIS, Boston, Massachusetts.
SERVICE IN FRENCH AVIATION:
Date of enlistment: March 2, 1915.
Aviation Schools: March 2 to August 8, 1915,
Pau.
Released from French Service: August 8, 1915.
Final Rank: Soldat.

Frazier Curtis

In the various accounts of the early history of the Lafayette Flying Corps, Frazier Curtis has not received the credit due him for his really important share in launching the movement. Although well past his thirties, he was learning to fly at Marblehead when the idea of the *Escadrille Américaine* first occurred to Prince, and the two friends discussed the project in all its aspects. In the beginning, Curtis desired to join the British Service, as his French was not fluent, and sailed for England on December 25, 1914, promising to cross to France if his effort to enlist in the R.N.A.S. proved unsuccessful. Refused in England on account of his citizenship, which he was unwilling to give up, he went to Paris on February 9, 1915, and was soon enlisted in the French Aviation.

In Paris, Curtis worked hard, with Prince, the de Lesseps brothers, and other friends, to interest the authorities in the formation of a corps of American flyers. Undaunted by his age—a serious handicap in learning to fly—he went at his training with admirable spirit and energy, but had two bad crashes at Avord during the spring, resulting in a period of hospital and forty-five days' sick-leave. This latter he spent in Paris, recruiting among the Ambulance men, and working toward the organisation of a large corps—always his dream. It was at this period that he got into touch with Dr. Gros, whom he introduced to M. de Sillac: an important service to the future corps. Because of injuries received in flying, Curtis was forced to accept his release from the army but not before he had done valuable pioneer work, which went far toward insuring the future success of the Lafayette Corps.

SERVICE RECORD

ALVIN ALEXANDER CUSHMAN, Brookline, Massachusetts.

SERVICE IN FRENCH AVIATION:
Date of enlistment: June 22, 1917.
Aviation Schools: June 29, 1917, to February, 1918, Avord, Pau, G.D.E
Breveted: December 4, 1918 (Caudron).
Final Rank: Caporal.

SERVICE IN U.S. NAVAL AVIATION:
Commissioned Ensign.

Alvin Alexander Cushman

Cushman was an earnest and hard-working *élève-pilote*, one of the last Americans to take Blériot training. After finishing his perfection work on Nieuport, he transferred to the United States Navy and was sent to England. On May 23, 1918, while flying a B.E. 2, bombing machine, he had a serious accident. A broken thigh kept him in hospital for more than five months. Upon recovering from his injuries he again took up his flying duties, and became a pilot of hydro-aeroplanes. He was stationed at Bolsena, Italy, until the end of the war.

SERVICE RECORD

PHILIP WASHBURN DAVIS, West Newton, Massachusetts.

SERVICE IN FRENCH AVIATION:
Date of enlistment: June 9, 1917.
Aviation Schools: June 15, 1917, to February, 1918, Avord, Pau, Cazeaux, G.D.E.
Breveted: October 28, 1917 (Caudron).
Final Rank: Caporal.

SERVICE IN U.S. AVIATION:
Commissioned Second Lieutenant, February 23, 1918.
At the Front: 94th Pursuit Squadron, April 1 to June 2, 1918.
Killed in combat: June 2, 1918 (Toul Sector).

Philip Washburn Davis

Davis was older than most of those who went through the schools with him, less boisterous and less given to dissertation on his flying prowess. Quiet and pleasant in manner, he was one of the coolest and steadiest of pilots, completing with honour the difficult Blériot training and leaving an excellent record at Pau. He was one of those men who have little to say, but may be counted on in any emergency. After his transfer to the United States Air Service, Davis went to the Front with the 94th Pursuit Squadron, then operating in the Toul Sector. On June 2, 1918, while protecting an English bombing flight, he attacked six German single-seaters and was shot down in flames within the enemy lines.

Philip Davis is mourned by the many friends to whom his fine qualities had endeared him. At his death the Service lost a very gallant officer, under whose serene and quizzical exterior lay a true devotion to duty and the steadfast courage which asks no odds of Fate.

SERVICE RECORD

GEORGE DOCK, JR., St. Louis, Missouri.

PREVIOUS SERVICE: American Ambulance, 1915–16.

SERVICE IN FRENCH AVIATION:
Date of enlistment: June 10, 1917.
Aviation Schools: June 10, 1917, to March 15, 1918, Avord, Pau, Cazeaux, G.D.E.
Breveted: November 14, 1917 (Caudron).
At the Front: Escadrille Spad 12, and Spad 31, March 18, 1918, to Armistice.
Final Rank: Sergent.

DECORATIONS:
Croix de Guerre, with Star (Ambulance Service).
Croix de Guerre, with Star (Aviation).

CITATIONS

Le 28 avril, 1917

Le Directeur du Service de Santé du 31ᵉ Corps d'Armée cite à l'Ordre du Service de Santé du Corps d'Armée:

DOCK, GEORGE, Conducteur Américain, S.S.U. N° 2

Depuis fort longtemps s'est distingué parmi ses camarades par son mépris du danger et son entrain remarquable. Volontaire pour toutes les missions dangereuses; les 18 septembre et 28 décembre, 1916, s'est dépensé pour des évacuations difficiles et particulièrement pénibles sur des routes sans cesse bombardées.
(Signé)   DU BOURGUET

Le 25 mai, 1918

Le Chef d'Escadrons Duseigneur, Commandant le Groupe de Combat N° 11, cite à l'Ordre du Régiment:

Le Caporal DOCK, GEORGE, Pilote à l'Escadrille Spa. 12

Pilote plein d'entrain. S'est dépensé sans compter depuis le début de la bataille, mitraillant les tranchées, attaquant les drachens et livrant de nombreux combats au cours desquels il a obligé l'adversaire à fuir. Est souvent rentré, son appareil atteint par des projectiles ennemis.

(Signé)   DUSEIGNEUR

George Dock, Jr.

Long before our declaration of war, George Dock was driving an ambulance on the Western Front, where, during the great attacks on Verdun, he evacuated wounded under conditions of extreme difficulty. Cited for bravery and coolness under fire while with the Ambulance, he decided in the spring of 1917 that the time had come to take a more active part in the war, and on May 30, he enlisted in the L.F.C. In the schools he took his flying seriously, but had some difficulty in mastering the 18-metre Nieuport. It is a curious fact, that a man who, at one time, almost despaired of successfully handling the small fast machines, developed on the Front into one of the most skilful Spad pilots of the corps.

SAXON. DOCK, READ, AND MILLS AT AVORD, OCTOBER. 1917

In the Escadrille Spad 31, during the fighting on the Marne and in the Argonne, Dock had many thrilling experiences, especially on one occasion when in the midst of a combat, well into the enemy lines, his propeller split, and he only reached friendly territory by a miraculous combination of good luck and skilful handling. Few Lafayette men have seen more of the heavy fighting of 1918 than Dock. On March 15, his squadron arrived at Fère-en-Tardenois, and when, on the 21st, the Germans struck in the north, the Spad 31 patrolled the entire front between the aerodrome and Saint-Quentin, making daily raids far into the enemy lines to shoot up troops and convoys. On May 27, Germany launched her last great attack southward from the Chemin des Dames, and Dock's squadron, as usual, was in the thick of the fighting. His experiences during those long and anxious June days on the Marne, when the air was alive with Pfalz and Fokker scouts, manned by an enemy bitterly *mordant*, will endure in his memory. And so throughout the last summer and autumn of the war, wherever the fighting was heaviest, at Saint-Mihiel and in the Argonne, the Spad 31 was to be found, until at last the strange day came when the news spread from squadron to squadron that the war was over. In years to come, as Dock looks back on his part in the struggle, he should feel a real and lasting satisfaction.

SERVICE RECORD

CHARLES H. DOLAN, JR., Boston, Massachusetts.

SERVICE IN FRENCH AVIATION:
Date of enlistment: August 11, 1916.
Aviation Schools: August 30, 1916, to May 10, 1917, Buc, Avord, Pau, G.D.E.
Breveted: March 10, 1917 (Blériot).
At the Front: Escadrille Lafayette, May 12, 1917, to February 18, 1918.
Final Rank: Sergent.

SERVICE IN U.S. AVIATION:
Commissioned First Lieutenant: January 14, 1918.
At the Front: 103d Pursuit Squadron, February 18, 1918, to October 16, 1918.
On duty in America: October 16, 1918, to Armistice.

Charles H. Dolan, Jr.

Carl Dolan, Irish patriot and stanch follower of John Boyle O'Reilly, is one of the original crowd of old-timers who gave employment to the Annamite wrecking gang at the Blériot school at Buc. With the exception of a forced landing on a shell-wrecked *terrain* near Verdun, his work at the Front was without dramatic incident. His monogrammed Spad was in the midst of many a hotly contested battle, but Fate seemed to be against him. He never succeeded in bringing down an enemy, or, more accurately, he never secured official confirmation of a victory. He gained real distinction, however, by returning from a furlough in America, in the remarkably short period of two months, including travelling time. The average furlough to the States required an actual absence from duty from three to four months, and a few of them, unfortunately, were for the duration of the war. Carl has a fine sense of duty, and did not exceed the limit of his furlough by so much as a day, thus shaming earlier leave-takers, and setting an honourable record for later ones.

At the time of the transfer of the Lafayette Squadron to the American Army, he performed valuable service, as electrician to the unit, and officer in charge of mechanics. With the assistance of a few of the old French *méchaniciens*, loaned by the French Government, he instructed the newly arrived and untried American personnel, in the care and reparation of the intricate Hispano-Suiza motors, and was largely responsible for the success with which they later performed their duties. He did this work in addition to his daily patrols, and with the same painstaking thoroughness. He had a high sense of the importance of the work to be done, and while this gave his fellow pilots irresistible opportunities for boisterous "ragging" every one of them secretly admired him for this very quality. Unlike many Irishmen, Dolan was slow to anger, and could take any amount of chaff with unruffled good nature.

DOLAN AT BUC 1916

The spring of 1918 witnessed the final break-up of the old Lafayette Squadron. It had been the hope of all the men that they might be kept together at the Front as a unit until the close of the war; but the needs of the U.S. Air Service made this impossible. Some of the pilots were sent as flight and squadron commanders to newly formed units; others, as flying instructors, to aviation schools both in France and in America. And so the old, never-to-be-forgotten fellowship came to an end. Carl Dolan is one of the men who did more than his share to make the squadron comradeship bright and happily memorable, and for this service he has the grateful acknowledgment of all of his fellow pilots in Spad 124.

SERVICE RECORD

ROBERT L. DONZÉ, Santa Barbara, California.

SERVICE IN FRENCH AVIATION:
Date of enlistment: November 7, 1916.
Aviation Schools: November 8, 1916, to May 10, 1917, Buc, Avord, Pau, G.D.E.
Breveted: March 19, 1917 (Blériot).
At the Front: Escadrille N. 93, May 20 to June 15, 1917.
Escadrille N. 314, November 28, 1917, to March 22, 1918.
Final Rank: Sergent.

SERVICE IN U.S. AVIATION:
Commissioned First Lieutenant.
On duty at American Acceptance Park, Orly, as Officer in Charge of Motor and Receiving Division and later as Operations Officer, March 25, 1918, to Armistice.

DECORATIONS:
Croix de Guerre, with Star.

Robert L. Donzé

The Great War may have been a call of the blood with Donzé. His forbears were French and some of his remote family connections still live on French soil. It is likely, however, that in common with those of most of the volunteers, his motives in enlisting were mixed. Duty seems all the more duty when it goes arm in arm with adventure. Donzé made no effort to resist the appeal, got his "wings" while flying a Blériot, and was sent to N. 93, a French squadron, where he was the only American representative. A year later there were but few French combat squadrons which did not have at least one Lafayette pilot, but this was not true in the spring of 1917.

Donzé was one of a very small group of "Yanks" who were then laying the foundations for the friendly and sympathetic understanding of one another's qualities which since grew so rapidly among French and American aviators. This broad and firm friendship as it existed in the Air Service became possible because of the early intimacy of the association between French airmen and the Americans of the L.F.C. These latter took to *pinard* as naturally as they did to the air, and, if one may say so, were at home in both elements.

Robert Donzé (right) at a Prise d'Armes, Belfort

Donzé had the misfortune to crash badly after a month of service with N. 93. On June 15, while testing out a new machine, he was forced to land, owing to faulty *réglage*, and ran into a trench hidden by the grass. His Spad turned over, the safety belt broke, and he was pitched out, the tail of the machine coming down on him, breaking two ribs and nearly severing his left arm. The next three months he spent in hospital.

Then he got married, returned to the Front with Escadrille N. 314, where he was on service until his transfer to the United States Air Service. He was then sent to the American Acceptance Park at Orly Field, near Paris, where he served as a flight commander in charge of the fixed motor division, and later as officer in charge of the receiving division. At the end of the war he was still carrying on in this position.

SERVICE RECORD

JAMES RALPH DOOLITTLE, New York City.

PREVIOUS SERVICE: Norton-Harjes Ambulance, 1916.

SERVICE IN FRENCH AVIATION:
Date of enlistment: October 16, 1916.
Aviation Schools: December 21, 1916, to July 1, 1917, Buc, Avord, Pau, G.D.E.
Breveted: March 22, 1917 (Caudron).
At the Front: Escadrille Lafayette, July 2 to July 17, 1917.
Final Rank: Caporal.
Wounded in combat: July 17, 1917.
Released from French Aviation.
Returned to America.
Killed while flying as civilian instructor at Gerstner Field, Lake Charles, Louisiana.

DECORATIONS:
Croix de Guerre, with Palm.

CITATION

Au G.Q.G., le 12 *août,* 1917
Le Général Commandant la 1ère Armée cite à l'Ordre de l'Armée:
DOOLITTLE, JAMES, M^{le} 11994, Caporal Pilote à l'Escadrille N. 124

Citoyen américain. Jeune pilote plein d'entrain. Le 17 juillet, 1917, a livré combat à un avion ennemi qui tentait d'incendier un ballon britannique et l'a mis en fuite. A été blessé de deux balles au cours de ce combat.

(Signé)   ANTHOINE

James Ralph Doolittle

Throughout his career at the Front Doolittle was pursued by hard luck. At G.D.E. while awaiting orders for the Front, he wing-slipped into the ground and was badly cut about the face. After eight weeks in hospital he was sent to the Escadrille Lafayette, two weeks before the squadron was ordered to Dunkirk, for the great British offensive in Flanders. During this move he became lost in the clouds, came out of them over a German aviation field, was machine-gunned from below, changed direction, pulled up into the clouds again, and the next time, saw the ground in the vicinity of a British observation balloon. He was just in time to assist a British pilot who was repulsing an attack upon the balloon. In the battle which followed, Ralph received a flesh wound in the calf of his leg. On landing his machine turned over, and in the crash, an old face wound—the result of his former accident, reopened.

This was his first and last real adventure while at the Front. He passed several weeks in hospital and was then granted his release for the purpose of returning to America. While there he became a civilian instructor at an aviation school at Lake Charles, Louisiana. He met his death in an accident while flying at this school.

SERVICE RECORD

DENNIS DOWD, New York City.

PREVIOUS SERVICE: Foreign Legion (Infantry), 1914-15.

SERVICE IN FRENCH AVIATION:
Date of enlistment: March 28, 1916.
Aviation Schools: April 13 to August 11, 1916, Buc.
Killed in line of duty: August 12, 1916, at Buc.

Dennis Dowd

Dennis Dowd was probably the first American who went to France from the United States for the purpose of enlisting in the French Foreign Legion. Several of his fellow countrymen preceded him by several days in offering their services, but they were either permanently resident in the country or there on business or pleasure at the time war was declared. Dowd, whose love for France came second only to his love for America, sailed immediately after the beginning of hostilities, and enlisted on August 26, 1914. He was not a lover of war and had no illusions as to what the nature of his service was to be. But his former comrades in the Legion and in the 170th Infantry Regiment, to which he afterward transferred, say that he never once complained of hardship or failed in the accomplishment of a duty. He was a keen observer, and wrote of war with a kind of Barbussian touch which made his letters interesting and worthwhile.

> I have never seen the kind of bayonet charge I read about. It is usually the slow amble of a lot of brutally tired men, over ground that has been torn to pieces by big guns, so that when the enemy is reached, there is none of the fancy play with the bayonet as taught at school. Men of both sides have a real distaste for that yard of cold steel, and they just poke dully and rather carefully at one another, until one side or the other runs.

THE AMERICAN BARRACKS AT BUC, 1916

Dowd was wounded in the Champagne offensive of September and October, 1915, and spent the autumn and winter in hospital. When again ready for duty he transferred to the French Air Service, where he made an unusually brilliant record while in training. He had almost completed his *brevet* tests when he was killed by accident while making his altitude flight. He was the second American airman to be killed in France and the first one to meet his death at an aviation school. His loss was an irreparable one to the Franco-American Corps, as it was then called, but coming as it did, at a time when the American attitude toward the Allied cause was still undefined, the news went abroad and did much to enlist American sympathy on the side of liberty-loving nations. And so Dowd served his country in his death as he had served it in life, to splendid purpose.

SERVICE RECORD

MEREDITH L. DOWD, Orange, New York.

PREVIOUS SERVICE: American Ambulance, 1916.

SERVICE IN FRENCH AVIATION:
Date of enlistment: May 14, 1917.
Aviation Schools: June 20 to December 29, 1917, Avord, Pau, G.D.E.
Breveted: November 7, 1917 (Caudron).
At the Front: Escadrille N. 152, January 1 to February 6, 1918.
Final Rank: Caporal.

SERVICE IN U.S. AVIATION:
Commissioned Second Lieutenant: April 8, 1918.
Attached to 471st (French) Squadron at Le Bourget (defense of Paris), April 30 to July 17, 1918.
American Acceptance Park, Orly, July 17 to August 29, 1918.
At the Front: 147th Pursuit Squadron, August 29 to October 26, 1918.
Killed in combat: October 26, 1918, near Dannevoux (Verdun Sector).

DECORATION:
Distinguished Service Cross.

CITATION

The Distinguished Service Cross is awarded to
Second Lieutenant MEREDITH L. DOWD, Air Service

For extraordinary heroism in action near Dannevoux, France, October 26, 1918. Having been unable to overtake and join a patrol, Lieutenant Dowd alone encountered four German planes, which he daringly attacked. He fought with most wonderful skill and bravery, diving into the formation and sending one of the enemy machines to the earth. In the course of the combat his machine was disabled and crashed to the earth, killing him in the fall.

By command of General PERSHING

Meredith L. Dowd

Larry Dowd went to the Front on February 1, 1918, joining the Escadrille N. 152 (the "Crocodiles"), which had the unique distinction of bringing down a Zeppelin at Bourbonne-les-Bains. After receiving his commission in the U.S. Air Service he was sent to a squadron stationed at Le Bourget, then engaged in the defence of Paris. He was a man of action, as he had proved by volunteering in the American Field Service long before our declaration of war, and the life of comparative inactivity at Le Bourget was irksome to him; but his desire for real fighting was soon gratified by his assignment to the 147th Pursuit Squadron. All through the heavy fighting of the autumn of 1918, Dowd played a manful part until he met his death in combat—a combat which exemplifies his splendid qualities of courage and determination.

It was the 26th of October—two o'clock in the afternoon of a hazy autumn day. Motor trouble had forced Dowd to leave the ground a few moments after his patrol and he was flying alone over the Forest of Dannevoux, north of Verdun, when he saw four German scouts crossing the lines. Without an instant's hesitation he attacked the formation, veered off, and attacked again, sending one of the enemy to the earth. As the remaining Germans did not retreat, Dowd continued to attack, and at the third dive was himself shot down by an unlucky burst of machine-gun fire.

SERVICE RECORD

SIDNEY RANKIN DREW, JR., New York City.

PREVIOUS SERVICE: American Ambulance, 1917.

SERVICE IN FRENCH AVIATION:
  Date of enlistment: June 9, 1917.
  Aviation Schools: June 12, 1917, to March 22, 1918, Avord, Pau, Cazeaux, G.D.E.
  Breveted: November 17, 1917 (Caudron).
  At the Front: Escadrille Spad 31, March 25 to May 19, 1918.
  Final Rank: Caporal.
  Killed in combat: May 19, 1918, near Arvilliers.

Sidney Rankin Drew, Jr.

Drew was certainly one of the most interesting men in the Corps. It was not easy at first for him to learn to fly, and during his Blériot training he had moments of bitter discouragement, but under his gentle manners he possessed a determination which surmounted all difficulties and made him, in the end, a very skilful and daring pilot. He had a personality of great individual charm and a kindly thoughtfulness which made him universally liked. Although only twenty-six years of age, he had already won recognition and success in his work, and had given up far more than most of us to fight for the Allied cause. But Fate was to demand of him a still greater sacrifice. Near Arvilliers, on the afternoon of the 19th of May, 1918, he fell, in the midst of a furious combat against five Albatross.

A short and brilliant career, terminated by the most glorious of deaths, leaving a heritage of memories which will be cherished forever by those who loved him—such was the life of Sidney Drew.

SERVICE RECORD

JOHN ARMSTRONG DREXEL, Philadelphia, Pennsylvania.

SERVICE IN FRENCH AVIATION:
Date of enlistment: October 27, 1916.
Aviation Schools: November 15, 1916, to May 10, 1917, Buc, Pau, G.D.E.
Breveted: March 6, 1917 (Blériot).
At the Front: Escadrille Lafayette, May 10 to June 15, 1917.
Final Rank: Caporal.

SERVICE IN U.S. AVIATION:
Commissioned Major: August 14, 1917.
On duty in France, England, and America until the Armistice.

John Armstrong Drexel

Drexel was a Blériot pilot in 1909 in the early days of amateur flying, and once held the world's altitude record for that machine. Nevertheless, when he went to the Blériot school at Buc, as a member of the Lafayette Flying Corps, it was under the status of *élève-pilote*, and he had to begin his training almost at the *penguin* stage. He soon convinced the French *moniteurs* that he was master of the monoplane and was sent to Pau for his work in aerial acrobacy. He went to the Escadrille Lafayette at a time when the United States Air Service had just begun the organisation of its overseas headquarters on the boulevard Haussmann in Paris. After a month at the Front, Drexel was set to Paris to act as *liaison* officer between the French and American services. He was afterward commissioned major, and until the end of the war was on duty connected with the Air Service in France, England, and America.

SERVICE RECORD

NATHANIEL DUFFY, Buffalo, New York.
SERVICE IN FRENCH AVIATION:
  Date of enlistment: May 24, 1917.
  Aviation Schools: June 12, 1917, to April 23, 1918,
    Avord, Pau, Cazeaux, G.D.E.
  Breveted: November 14, 1917 (Caudron).
  At the Front: Escadrille Spad 96, April 25 to
    August 16, 1918.
  Final Rank: Sergent.

Nathaniel Duffy

At Avord, Duffy was one of the aristocrats who resided in the village, whither he and his especial chum, Bob Hanford, repaired for rest and refreshment after sessions at the Blériot field.

When Hanford was killed, everyone's sympathy went out to Duffy, for they had been very close and the loss was a heavy one; Duffy's friends even thought at times that it had affected his health, which troubled him constantly during the fall and winter of 1917. In spite of this he carried on gamely, and was finally assigned to Escadrille Spad 96, where during the severe fighting of the war's final summer, he served bravely and faithfully. Injured in a severe crash, and with his poor health still further undermined by constant ground-*strafing* expeditions during the autumn, Duffy got his release shortly after the Armistice and returned to America.

SERVICE RECORD

WILLIAM E. DUGAN, JR., Rochester, New York.
PREVIOUS SERVICE: Foreign Legion (Infantry),
  1915–16.
  Wounded while serving with
  the Legion.

SERVICE IN FRENCH AVIATION:
Date of enlistment: June 10, 1916.
Aviation Schools: July 9, 1916, to March 26, 1917, Buc, Juvisy, Avord, Cazeaux, Pau, G.D.E.
Breveted: September 20, 1916 (Blériot).
At the Front: Escadrille Lafayette, March 30, 1917, to February 18, 1918.
Final Rank: Sergent.

SERVICE IN U.S. AVIATION:
Commissioned First Lieutenant: January 11, 1918.
At the Front: 103d Pursuit Squadron, February 18 to June 1, 1918.
Officer in Charge of Repair and Testing at American Acceptance Park, Orly, June 1, 1918, to Armistice.

DECORATIONS:
Croix de Guerre, with Star.

CITATION

DUGAN, WILLIAM, soldat de la 1ʳᵉ Cⁱᵉ du 170ᵉ Régiment d'Infanterie
A l'attaque du 1ᵉʳ mai, 1916, s'est porté bravement à l'assaut des tranchées ennemis, et a fait plusieurs prisonniers.

William E. Dugan, Jr.

The noise of the Great War reached Dugan in the tropics of Central America, where he was assistant manager of a banana plantation owned by the United Fruit Company. He immediately gave up his position there and went to France, enlisting in the Foreign Legion. He took part in all of the battles of the Legion, including the great German offensive at Verdun, 1916, and passed unscathed through that horror of mud and shellfire. It was at this period that he gained his intimate knowledge of the courage of men and of their powers of endurance, which was so great an inspiration to him, serving him so well in later emergencies. He was a great admirer of the Legion's old officers, and when asked for a story of infantry experiences, it was never of his own exploits, but of those of the men who commanded his regiment, of their indifference to danger, and their resourcefulness under the most trying conditions. Of his comrades in the ranks, he perhaps most admired Victor Chapman, both for his courage and for his entire lack of those vices which so often fasten themselves upon soldiers in war-time.

One day came Army Rumour, Series 566, Serial Number 9843, to the effect that the 170th Infantry Regiment, called "*Les Hirondelles de la Mort*" was rich in food, honour, and sympathetic officers. Dugan, with several of his American comrades, decided to ask for a transfer. It was granted, but long experience with the new outfit proved that the rumour was greatly exaggerated. Nothing was abundant but the usual body parasites, and the daily ration of hard work. That he did his duty seems apparent from an army citation received for service rendered during the attack of May, 1916. During this battle he investigated a segment of enemy trench line, and returned safely, bringing with him several prisoners.

Dugan had great difficulty in effecting his transfer to Aviation. The officers of the 170th could not be convinced that a corps of American airmen volunteers was in the process of being formed. Finally, a lucky wound sent him to the rear, and while recovering from it at *Hôpital Auxiliaire* 105 at Saint-Étienne, Dr. Gros, working in his interests, arranged for his reenlistment in the Air Service. In March, 1917, he returned to the Front as a pilot, and a month later gave his comrades in Spad 124 considerable anxiety when he failed to return from an early morning patrol far into German territory. There had been a lively battle during which he was attacked by two Albatross who disabled his plane and chased him homeward. He landed at a British aerodrome, and until communication could be established with his squadron, he was mourned as dead.

From 1914 until the 1st of June, 1918, he was constantly in active service, with the exception of a short leave in America, whither he went to be married. He brought his wife with him when he returned and continued flying and fighting as gamely as before. After his transfer to the American Army he was sent to the American Acceptance Park at Orly, as officer in charge of repairs and testing. He held this post until the signing of the Armistice.

SERVICE RECORD

STUART EMMET EDGAR, Nutley, New Jersey.

PREVIOUS SERVICE: Norton-Harjes Ambulance, 1916–17.

SERVICE IN FRENCH AVIATION:
Date of enlistment: May 9, 1917.
Aviation Schools: May 17 to December 8, 1917, Avord, Pau, G.D.E.
Breveted: September 23, 1917 (Caudron).
At the Front: Escadrille N. 158, December 11, 1917, to March 28, 1918.
Final Rank: Caporal.

SERVICE IN U.S. AVIATION:
Commissioned First Lieutenant: March 1, 1918.
On duty at American Acceptance Park, Orly, April 4 to May 30, 1918.
At the Front: 103d Pursuit Squadron, May 30 to August 17, 1918.
Killed in line of duty: August 17, 1918, near Vaucouleurs.

Stuart Emmet Edgar
Edgar came to France six months before our declaration of war

and served in Section 7 of the Norton-Harjes Ambulance. In May, 1917, he enlisted in the Lafayette Flying Corps and took the Blériot training at Avord. With Tucker and Parker, he lived at the Hotel Turco, and every evening the trio were to be seen at dinner, served by Suzanne, the jolly daughter of the house. Their conversations were worthy of the attention of a listener. Tucker and Parker had tramped through the woods of Central America, searched for hidden treasure in the Caribbean Sea, and managed a theatre on Washington Square. Edgar, with his keen mind and unusual powers of observation, had seen many interesting sides of life while doing newspaper work. He left a splendid record, both at Avord and at Pau. His friends saw in him the making of an exceptional combat flyer, but on August 17 he met his death in one of those accidents which seem inevitable in aviation. He was leaving the field to make a patrol, when suddenly, at a height of only four hundred feet, his motor stopped dead, the machine lost speed, and spun to the ground, killing him instantly. The accident cost us a comrade who had won universal liking and respect, and our country a splendid officer. He lies on a hillside in Lorraine— in worthy company, for beside him sleeps Raoul Lufbery.

SERVICE RECORD

DONALD HERBERT ELDREDGE, South Bend, Indiana.

SERVICE IN FRENCH AVIATION:
Date of enlistment: June 13, 1917.
Aviation Schools: June 20, 1917, to February 20, 1918, Avord, Pau, G.D.E.
Brevetted: December 3, 1917 (Caudron).
At the Front: Escadrille Spad 76, February 24 to June 10, 1918.
Final Rank: Sergent.

SERVICE IN U.S. AVIATION:
Commissioned Second Lieutenant, June 17, 1918.
At the Front: Attached to the French Squadron Spad 76, June 17, 1918, to Armistice.
DECORATIONS:
Croix de Guerre, with Star.

CITATION

Au Q.G., le 6 juillet, 1918

Le Général Commandant le 2ᵉ Corps d'Armée cite à l'Ordre du Corps d'Armée:

ELDREDGE, DONALD, Mle 12259, Sergent au 1ᵉʳ Régiment Étranger détaché à l'Escadrille 76

Excellent pilote, adroit et très consciencieux. Le 27 mai, pour porter secours à un de nos avions de réglage, n'a pas hésité à se jeter sur huit monoplaces ennemis. Par son courage et son sang-froid a permis à son chef de patrouille d'abattre l'un d'eux.

(Signé)   PHILIPOT

Donald Herbert Eldredge

Eldredge was one of the last men trained on Blériot at Avord. With his friend Jim McMillen, he belonged to the exclusive Farges set: aristocrats who bicycled back and forth to work at the Blériot *piste*. Beneath his quiet and pleasant manner Eldredge conceals a taut system of nerves, and like many highly strung men, he developed into a skilful and daring pilot. His record throughout the schools was excellent. On February 24, 1918, he went to the Front, assigned to the Escadrille Spad 76. Transferring to the United States Air Service in June, he had the pleasure of being returned to his old French squadron, where he gave a good account of himself through the severe fighting of 1918 until the end of the war.

SERVICE RECORD

DINSMORE ELY, Winnetka, Illinois.

SERVICE IN FRENCH AVIATION:
Date of enlistment: July 13, 1917.
Aviation Schools: July 20, 1917, to February 20, 1918, Avord, Tours, Pau, Cazeaux, G.D.E.
Breveted: October 25, 1917 (Caudron).
At the Front: Escadrille Spad 102, February 24 to April 1, 1918.
Final Rank: Sergent.

SERVICE IN U.S. AVIATION:
Commissioned Second Lieutenant: April 5, 1918.
Killed in line of duty: April 21, 1918.

Dinsmore Ely

At Tours, where he was breveted on August 22, 1917, Ely left behind him the reputation of an excellent pilot and a really brilliant student of the technical side of aviation. Trained in engineering at the Massachusetts Institute of Technology, he found aerodynamics and

the complexities of motors a fascinating study, and often coached his less-gifted comrades in the anxious periods before technical examinations. Unlike the majority of scientific aviators, Ely loved to fly, and at Pau had opportunity to put all his theories to the test. Only the cream of the American pilots were sent to the School of Aerial Gunnery at Cazeaux, and Ely was among these. In spite of old machines fit for nothing but straight flying, he continued to perfect himself in acrobatics; on one occasion, when doing a loop, the wings of his Nieuport were thrown out of adjustment and only the remarkable skill and coolness of the pilot averted a fatal accident.

On February 24, 1918, Ely was sent to the Front, to the Escadrille Spad 102, then operating in the Toul Sector. He served faithfully with this unit until April 3, when he was transferred to the Air Service, with the rank of Second Lieutenant. On April 21, while flying a Spad at Villacoublay, he lost his life in an accident.

SERVICE RECORD

ROBERT GRIMSHAW EOFF, Christiansburg, Virginia.

PREVIOUS SERVICE: American Ambulance, 1917.

SERVICE IN FRENCH AVIATION:
Date of enlistment: July 14, 1917.
Aviation Schools: August 2, 1917, to January 20, 1918, Avord, Tours, Pau, G.D.E.
Breveted: October 27, 1917 (Caudron).
At the Front: Escadrille N. 157, January 24 to March 27, 1918.
Final Rank: Caporal.

SERVICE IN U.S. AVIATION:
Commissioned Second Lieutenant: June 22, 1918.
Promoted First Lieutenant: November 6, 1918.
On duty at American Acceptance Park, Orly, June 29 to August 23, 1918.
At the Front: 95th Pursuit Squadron, August 23, 1918, to Armistice.

DECORATIONS:
Croix de Guerre, with Star.

CITATION

Le 30 *mars*, 1918

Le Général Commandant la IVe Armée cite à l'Ordre de la Division d'Infanterie, le militaire dont le nom suit:

Caporal EOFF, ROBERT, M^{le} 46663, du 1er Régiment de la Légion Étrangère, détaché à l'Escadrille N. 157

Pilote plein d'allant. A engagé de 22 mars, 1918, un combat aérien au cours duquel l'avion qu'il attaquait fut abattu.

GOURAUD

Robert Grimshaw Eoff

Eoff came to the Lafayette Flying Corps from the American Ambulance and was breveted at Tours, October 27, 1917. On January 24, 1918, after passing through Pau with flying colours, he was sent to the Escadrille N. 157, and served faithfully with the French until his transfer to the United States Air Service in the early summer. Of his service with the American Army, let him tell in his own words:

> Since the censorship has been lifted, I can give you a short outline of what I have done since I left Orly. Just as the big drive started (July 18, 1918) I got orders to join the First Pursuit Group and found them in a village near Coulommiers, south of Château-Thierry. It was a hot front, as you can imagine, and

we had heavy odds to face in the Boche Aviation ... a lot of fun all the same, and I'm glad I saw it through. The first of September we were ordered to Rembercourt, fourteen miles north of Bar-le-Duc, on the road to Verdun—to make the attack on the Saint-Mihiel Salient—a walkover, so to speak. On September 26 the attack began between the Meuse and the Argonne— interesting to fly over the same territory I had known so well in Ambulance days. The country is very hilly, resembling our own country (Virginia), and it was a hard push all the way through. Our *groupe* undertook the very low flying—hardly agreeable but exciting at times ... constantly subjected to attack from above. Our efforts were directed against enemy observation planes and balloons.... Now that it is over, the men here expect to be sent home soon.

Eoff's record is one in which those who know him may take pride, a story of quiet devotion to duty, of continuous and faithful service at the Front from the day of his first patrol to the close of hostilities.

SERVICE RECORD

EDWIN BRADLEY FAIRCHILD, Manila, Philippine Islands.

SERVICE IN FRENCH AVIATION:
Date of enlistment: June 27, 1917.
Aviation Schools: August 2, 1917, to January 14, 1918, Avord, Tours, Pau, G.D.E.
Breveted: September 29, 1917 (Caudron).
At the Front: Escadrille Spad 159, January 16, 1918, to Armistice.
Final Rank: Adjudant.

DECORATIONS:
Croix de Guerre, with two Palms and two Stars.

CITATIONS

12 *septembre*, 1918

Le Chef d'Escadrons Duseigneur, Commandant l'Escadre de Combat N° 2, cite à l'Ordre de l'Escadre :

FAIRCHILD, EDWIN BRADLEY, Sergent au 2e Étranger, détaché comme pilote à l'Escadrille, Spa. 159

Engagé volontaire dans l'armée française a toujours fait preuve du plus beau courage. Pilote de chasse depuis huit mois en Escadrille, a accompli avec la plus stricte exactitude et une haute conception du devoir toutes les missions qui lui ont été confiées. A livré de nombreux combats à maintes reprises, a attaqué les troupes à terre.

7 *novembre*, 1918

Le Général Commandant en Chef cite à l'Ordre de l'Armée:

FAIRCHILD, EDWIN BRADLEY (active), Sergent au 1er Régiment de la Légion Étrangère, Pilote Aviateur

Pilote plein d'ardeur, recherchant toute occasion de se battre. Le ... a incendié un Drachen (1ère victoire). Une Citation.

17 *novembre*, 1918

FAIRCHILD, EDWIN BRADLEY, M^{le} 12375, Sergent Pilote à l'Escadrille 159

Engagé volontaire Américain, pilote remarquable, fait montre en toute occasion d'un allant et d'un courage des plus grands éloges. Volontaire pour les missions les plus périlleuses, a pris part à de nombreux engagements de patrouille où par deux fois il a dégagé des camarades.

25 *novembre*, 1918

Le Général Commandant en Chef cite à l'Ordre de l'Armée:

FAIRCHILD, EDWIN BRADLEY (active), Sergent au 1er Régiment de la Légion Étrangère, Pilote Aviateur

Pilote remarquable d'enthousiasme, d'entrain, et de courage. N'a cessé de livrer de durs combats. Le 23 octobre, 1918, a attaqué une patrouille ennemie, descendu désemparé, a réussi par son énergie à ramener son appareil dans nos lignes où il s'est écrasé.

Edwin Bradley Fairchild

The outbreak of the war found Fairchild in Germany. After various adventures, including that of being taken for a spy, he gave up his studies there and went to France where he enlisted as an ambulance driver. In common with many other ambulance men his service gave him the desire for more active duty, and when his period of enlistment had expired he joined the Lafayette Corps. When ready for the Front he was sent to the French Squadron Spad 159, which took an important part in all of the heaviest fighting of 1918, suffering very heavy casualties. Nothing tries a man more than to see his comrades killed on every side of him. Fairchild lost many of his friends in the last summer of the war, but he kept a firm hold on his nerve despite the fact that he himself had several very narrow escapes from death. He gained a wide experience in all phases of pursuit work, and was known throughout his *groupe* as a skilful and daring pilot.

SERVICE RECORD

CLARENCE H. FAITH, Nahant, Massachusetts.
PREVIOUS SERVICE: American Ambulance, 1917.
SERVICE IN FRENCH AVIATION:
 Date of enlistment: May 25, 1917.
 Aviation Schools: July 17, 1917, to May 9, 1918, Avord, Juvisy, Pau, G.D.E.
 Breveted: October 28, 1917 (Caudron).
 Final Rank: Caporal.
SERVICE IN U.S. AVIATION:
 Commissioned Second Lieutenant, May 6, 1918.
 Ferry Pilot, American Acceptance Park, Orly, May 13 to June 9, 1918.
 At the Front: 103d Pursuit Squadron, June 9, 1918, to Armistice.
DECORATIONS:
 Croix de Guerre, with Star (Ambulance).

CITATIONS

17 *mai*, 1917

Le Général Commandant en Chef de la IVe Armée cite à l'Ordre de l'Armée:

CLARENCE H. FAITH

> Ambulancier américain, engagé volontaire, possédant les plus belles qualités de courage et d'esprit de sacrifice. A fait épreuve d'un dévoûment de tout premier ordre dans l'accomplissement de ses missions, pendant un bombardement continuelle de trente heures.
>
> (Signé)   GOURAUD

Clarence H. Faith

Faith enlisted in the Lafayette Flying Corps on May 25, 1917, after a term of service in the Ambulance—service which won him the *Croix de Guerre*. Breveted on Caudron at Juvisy, October 28, he did not get to the G.D.E. until February 28, 1918, when the French were holding Americans there with a view to their transfer to the American army. On May 6, Faith was commissioned Second Lieutenant in the Air Service, and a month later was assigned to the 103rd Pursuit Squadron. With this unit he served honourably until the close of hostilities; it is regrettable that the files of the Lafayette Flying Corps contain no detailed account of his adventures through the heavy fighting of 1918.

SERVICE RECORD

CEDRIC GERALD FAUNT LEROY, Chicago, Illinois.

SERVICE IN FRENCH AVIATION:
Date of enlistment: July 13, 1917.
Aviation Schools: July 20 to November 1, 1917, Avord, Tours, Pau.
Breveted: September 29, 1917 (Caudron).
Final Rank: Caporal.

SERVICE IN U.S. AVIATION:
Commissioned First Lieutenant: February 5, 1918.
Promoted Captain, October 10, 1918.
Promoted Major, March 19, 1919.
Chief *Réceptionnaire* American A.I.C. Issoudun, February 5 to April 2, 1918.
Officer in Charge of Acceptance and Inspection Division, A.A.P., Orly, April 4 to October 24, 1918.
At the Front: 94th Pursuit Squadron, October 25, 1918, to Armistice.

Cedric Gerald Faunt LeRoy

In the days when plotting was the fashion, the old kings of France had in their households an important official known as the "taster," whose duty it was to sample every dish destined for the royal table. The Air Service possessed a similar official, called the "tester," whose occupation was equally precarious. As planes were delivered from the factories it was his duty to take each one up for a trial flight before other pilots, in the schools or at the Front, were allowed to fly it. This was Faunt LeRoy's duty.

With his exceptional mechanical knowledge and delicacy of touch in the air, he made an excellent record in the schools, and his ability was so clearly demonstrated that despite his anxiety to get to the Front after obtaining his *brevet*, the French sent him to Issoudun, where the Americans were in urgent need of a pilot with a thorough knowledge of motors. In January, 1918, he was commissioned in the United States Air Service, and appointed to the post of *Réceptionnaire*, to test all new aeroplanes as received from the factories. While his former comrades were gaining glory in combat over the lines, Faunt LeRoy was forced to remain in the rear, carrying on his monotonous and dangerous task. His record speaks for itself; he has supervised the acceptance of over two thousand French planes, and made more than thirty-five hundred test flights without a serious accident. For the painstaking care and energy with which his work has been performed, Faunt LeRoy has been proposed for the D.S.M., a distinction he has fully earned.

SERVICE RECORD

FEARCHAR IAN FERGUSON, New York City.

SERVICE IN FRENCH AVIATION:
Date of enlistment: June 3, 1917.
Aviation Schools: June 10, 1917, to January 8, 1918, Avord, Pau, G.D.E.
Breveted: October 17, 1917 (Caudron).
At the Front: Escadrille Spad 96, January 10, 1918, to Armistice.
Final Rank: Sergent.

DECORATIONS:
Croix de Guerre, with Palm.

Fearchar Ian Ferguson

Every Lafayette man has known the sorrow of losing comrades in the war, but none perhaps to such an extent as Ferguson. From the beginning at Avord, his special pals were Bob Hanford, Cy Chamberlain, Vernie Booth, and Schuyler Lee. Hanford was killed at Châteauroux while doing his *brevet*; Chamberlain was shot down in combat in June, 1918; Booth and Lee, who were with Ferguson in Escadrille Spad 96, both died heroic deaths during the heaviest fighting of the summer. The only survivor of this group, Ferguson, has left behind him a splendid record and has avenged his comrades in many a bitter combat.

On April 12, near Montdidier, Ferguson had a fight which came very near being his last. He was patrolling about ten kilometres within the German lines, with Booth and several French comrades, when he perceived above his head a flight of eight Albatross. The others did not see the Germans and Ferguson became so interested in watching them that he lost his patrol. There was a battle royal when the eight Boches dove down on him, and it was only by luck and skilful manoeuvring that he escaped with his life. Forty-five minutes later he landed on his aerodrome with twenty-eight bullet holes through his machine. Ferguson was unhurt, but his Spad had made its last flight.

SERVICE RECORD

CHRISTOPHER W. FORD, New York City.

SERVICE IN FRENCH AVIATION:
Date of enlistment: May 9, 1917.
Aviation Schools: May 17 to November 6, 1917, Avord, G.D.E.
Breveted: September 6, 1917 (Caudron).
At the Front: Escadrille, Lafayette, November 8, 1917, to February 18, 1918.
Final Rank: Sergent.

SERVICE IN U.S.AVIATION:
Commissioned First Lieutenant.
Promoted Captain, November 12, 1918.
Promoted Major, May 1, 1919.
At the Front: 103d Pursuit Squadron, February 18 to October 15, 1918.
Prisoner in *Germany:* October 15, 1918, to Armistice.

DECORATIONS:
Distinguished Service Cross.
Croix de Guerre, with Palm and Star.

CITATIONS

The Distinguished Service Cross is awarded to
    Captain CHRISTOPHER W. FORD, A.S., 103d Aero Pursuit Squadron
For repeated acts of extraordinary heroism in action near Rheims, France, March 27, 1918, and near Armentières, France, May 21, 1918. Near Rheims on March 27, Captain Ford, while on patrol duty with two other pilots, led his formation in an attack on eight enemy planes. After twenty minutes of fighting, the American formation shot down three German machines, of which one was destroyed by this officer. Near Armentières, on May 21, he again led a patrol of six planes in attacking twenty enemy aircraft. The attack resulted in ten individual combats. Captain Ford shot down one hostile plane and with his patrol routed the others.
                        By command of General PERSHING

                                                        11 *avril*, 1918
Le Général Commandant la IVe Armée cite à l'Ordre du 3ème Corps d'Armée:
    Lieutenant FORD, CHRISTOPHE WILLIAM, de l'Escadrille Lafayette (G.C. 21)
Jeune pilote nouvellement arrivé sur le front, se révèle comme chasseur courageux et adroit. A abattu avec deux des ses camarades un avion ennemi le 27 mars.

Citation à l'Ordre de l'Armeé :   4 *juin*, 1918
        FORD, CHRISTOPHER W., Pilote à l'Escadrille Américaine 103
A abattu le . . . son deuxième avion ennemi.

Christopher W. Ford

The thirty-eighth and last American to join the Escadrille Lafayette, while it was still a French unit, was Christopher Ford, of New York City. His career as an airman dates from the spring of 1916, when he was flying an old Wright "pusher," Model B, at the Stinson Flying School, San Antonio, Texas. On April 19, 1916, he received civilian *brevet*, 462, and thus equipped, came to France to join the Lafayette Flying Corps. A civilian brevet, however, is of little use to a pilot candidate for military aviation, and Ford had to pass through the regular routine: Blériot, Caudron G. 3, Nieuport, Spad, with a short period of Sopwith training thrown in for good measure. Evidently, the authorities were anxious that he should wholly forget his Wright "pusher" technique. He convinced them that he had, and was sent to Spad 124, which was then on the Aisne Sector, occupying hangars at Chaudun. This was just at the close of the local offensive which resulted in the capture of 11,000 German prisoners and important tactical gains for the French, in the Chemin des Dames area.

Ford, better than most of us, is in a position to speak with knowledge of the importance which paper work plays in the affairs of fledgling aviators; for it was owing to a mistake made in his own paper record at Avord, that he was sent, direct from this school, to G.D.E. without having had the usual course of acrobacy at Pau. He was not able to overcome this really serious handicap at Plessis-Belleville, and so went to the Front only partially equipped for his work as a combat pilot. To make matters worse, he started flying over the lines at once, just after the number of enemy pursuit squadrons had been increased

CHRISTOPHER FORD

to meet the French concentrations. He had never done a *vrille* (spinning nose-dive) and had to submit to a mild hazing at the hands of the other pilots, who told of the ease of falling into one during a combat, and of the difficulty of pulling out with a German sitting on one's tail, firing with annoying deliberation and persistency.

He learned his combat tactics in the best of all schools, although it is sometimes the harshest. During his earliest combats he sometimes practiced acrobacy of weird and unheard-of kinds, and had to level out of it as best he could under very trying circumstances. But he kept at it, and coming home from patrol, he would chase and be chased by imaginary Boches, while losing height over the aerodrome. He made rapid progress, and at last felt justified in adopting, as his individual insignia, a weird device of painted lightning in French tri-colour. This he carried on the wings and fuselage of his Spad, and so boldly displayed that one could recognise his machine in the air, from a distance of a thousand metres.

It is not possible to give here a detailed account of his fine service record. He was first cited by the commandant of the Air Forces of the Fourth French Army for contributing to the destruction of an enemy machine on March 27, 1918. On that date, with two of his comrades, he attacked a formation of three enemy two-seaters and five single-seaters. Although his gun jammed at the beginning of the battle, leaving him helpless to defend himself, he kept directly above his two flying partners, offering them the finest kind of protection, repeatedly diving upon enemy machines and driving them away by making a brave show of aggressiveness. This combat was extraordinary in that it lasted for more than half an hour; and it resulted in the destruction of three German single-seaters. Ford's part in it was of a piece with all of his service in France.

He served with Spad 124 (later the 103rd Pursuit Squadron) on the Aisne, in Champagne, Flanders, at Saint-Mihiel, the Argonne Forest. On October 15, 1918, while leading an offensive patrol, his motor was badly damaged by machine-gun fire from the ground, forcing him to land in enemy territory south of Buzancy. On November 20, he, together with other prisoners in the German prison camp at Villingen, decided to take the matter of transfer into their own hands, and so walked one hundred kilometres to the frontier. They reached Colmar just as the French were entering the town from the other side.

SERVICE RECORD

HENRY FORSTER, Milton, Massachusetts.

SERVICE IN FRENCH AVIATION:
Date of enlistment: June 13, 1917.
Aviation Schools: June 20, 1917, to January 31, 1918, Avord, Pau, G.D.E.
Breveted: October 31, 1917 (Caudron).
At the Front: Escadrille C. 74, February 1 to April 10, 1918.
Escadrille Spad 102, April 10 to April 24, 1918.
Escadrille Br. 224, April 24 to May 3, 1918.
Escadrille Spad 15, June 1 to August 2, 1918.
Final Rank: Sergent.

SERVICE IN U.S. NAVAL AVIATION:
Commissioned Ensign: July 19, 1918.

Henry Forster

As an *élève-pilote* Forster came close to being a genuine *poilu*. Like all of us at Avord, he was a second-class soldier in the French army, but unlike his comrades, it gave him pleasure to act and look and think the part an fond. *Puttees*, fatigue caps, boots, *musettes*, and uniforms were issued to us by the army; our part, according to Forster, was to make use of these articles of equipment. No pilot's swank for him! More than one of us, on arriving at the Quai d'Orsay, has seen trudging sturdily through the crowd ahead, a vaguely familiar figure, clad in faded horizon blue, with frayed *puttees* and hobnailed boots. A disreputable *bonnet de police*, cocked jauntily on one side, and a pair of *musettes*, from which protruded a loaf of war bread and the neck of a bottle of *pinard*, completed the picture. It was Forster, headed in all probability for the Hôtel Maurice.

As a pilot Forster was very steady and reliable; his Blériot work was excellent and he left enviable notes at Pau. From the G.D.E. he was sent with Dudley Tucker to the Spad 74, and did good work through the heavy fighting of the summer of 1918 until his transfer to the American Navy. His experiences as a naval aviator were varied: nearly killed on his first sortie in a Sopwith seaplane, piloting D.H. 9 bombing machines, and ferrying Capronis from Italy.

Eric A. Fowler

SERVICE RECORD

Eric A. Fowler, New York City.

Previous Service: American Ambulance, 1917.

Service in French Aviation:
Date of enlistment: June 9, 1917.
Aviation Schools: June 20 to November 27, 1917, Tours Avord, Pau.
Breveted: October 21, 1917 (Caudron).
Killed in line of duty: At Pau, November 27, 1917.

Volunteering from the ranks of the American Ambulance, Eric Fowler was breveted on Caudron at Tours and went to Avord for advanced training on Nieuport. About the middle of November, 1917, he arrived at Pau, and his anxiety to get to the Front is shown by the fact that in spite of wretched flying weather, he had finished everything but *vol de precision* by the 27th of the month. On the afternoon of that day he was making his last flight preparatory to leaving for the G.D.E. The cause of the accident has never been ascertained—it was one of those mysterious fatalities for which no explanation exists—but suddenly, as he swept over the field at a height of seven hundred feet, his machine faltered, lost speed, and plunged headlong to the ground, killing Fowler instantly. France lost in him a pilot whose only desire was to fly and fight, and his friends were left to mourn a comrade whose brave and modest character had endeared him to both Americans and French. Fowler gave his life in the performance of duty as truly as though he had been shot down in combat over the lines.

SERVICE RECORD

Edmond Charles Clinton Genêt, Ossining, New York.

Previous Service: February 3, 1915, to May 24, 1916, Foreign Legion (Infantry).

Service in French Aviation:
Date of enlistment: May 24, 1916.
Aviation Schools: June 5, 1916, to January 18, 1917, Buc, Pau, Cazeaux, G.D.E.
Brevetted: September 3, 1916 (Caudron).
At the Front: Escadrille Lafayette, January 19 to April 16, 1917.
Final Rank: Sergent.
Wounded in combat: March 19, 1917.
Killed in line of duty: April 16, 1917, north of Montescourt (Aisne).

Decorations:
Croix de Guerre, with two Palms.

CITATIONS

Citation à l'Ordre de l'Armée:

Genêt, Edmond, Caporal à l'Escadrille 124

Citoyen américain engagé au service de la France. A fait preuve des plus belles qualités d'ardeur et de dévoûment, livrant des combats aériens dès son arrivée à l'escadrille, effectuant des reconnaissances à basse altitude, et se dépensant sans compter.

Le 19 mars, 1917, a été blessé au cours d'un combat contre deux avions ennemis et a refusé d'interrompre son service.

Groupe des Armées du Nord.

Genêt, Edmond Charles Clinton, Sergent à l'Escadrille Lafayette, N. 124

Pilote courageux et dévoué, a trouvé, le 16 avril, 1917, une mort glorieuse. A terminé l'énoncé de ses dernières volontés en disant: "Vive la France toujours."

Edmond Charles Clinton Genêt

Edmond Genêt was the great-great-grandson of Citizen Genêt, whom the Revolutionary Government in France sent as Ambassador to America in 1793. It was but natural, therefore, that he should be eager to join with the other American volunteers who had already enlisted in the French Foreign Legion. It was impossible for him to do this in any regular way, for he was already bound to service in the United States Navy.

After much anxious thought he decided upon a bold move. Although he was only eighteen, he went to the French Consul in New York where he gave his age as twenty-one, secured a passport, and without obtaining his release from the navy, sailed for France for the purpose of enlisting in the French army. Technically, perhaps, his act may be called desertion, but it was desertion with a noble purpose, from a safe and easy berth at home to a post of danger in the trenches on the Western Front. He enlisted in the Legion on February 3, 1915, less than a week after his arrival in France, and after two months of training was sent to the Front. Throughout his career as an infantryman he gained the praise both of his officers and of his fellow *légionnaires* by his boyish enthusiasm for the most dangerous tasks, and his disregard for his own safety. Paul Rockwell, himself a former member of the Legion, wrote as follows of Genêt's part in the Champagne offensive of September and October, 1915:

> When his battalion attacked the Germans in the Bois Sabot, he was stunned and thrown into a shell-hole by the explosion of a large-calibre shell. When he recovered his senses, little Genêt, nothing daunted, went bravely on to the assault in the ranks of a regiment of *Zouaves* which had advanced in support of the Legion. Three days later he was able to rejoin his comrades who were mourning him as dead.

Another fellow *légionnaire* spoke of him as "the bravest boy I know." Writing to Genêt's mother of the Champagne battle he said:

> In the advance of September 28 (1915) Genêt kept on until only one man in his company was left beside himself. The others were either shot or had taken refuge in the trenches. It was only then that the two men decided to retreat. His companion got rattled and was killed. Genêt owes his escape to his own coolness and good judgment. As all of their officers were shot, he probably won't be decorated, but the regimental flag receives the *fourragère* of the *Croix de Guerre* for the action in which he took so gallant a part.

Genêt's own account of the battle, written in letters from the trenches, is terribly vivid and gives a clear picture of the reaction of this brave little fellow to the horrors of modern warfare. He was never daunted even when living constantly in the midst of suffering and death, and after fifteen months in the Legion, he was as serious as ever in his purpose to serve France to the end.

From the day of his enlistment, however, his thoughts had turned toward aviation as the branch of war service nearest his heart's desire.

He had sailed for France on January 20, 1915, on the French liner *Rochambeau*. By an odd coincidence, Norman Prince was a passenger on the same boat. Genêt learned from him of his plans, then still very indefinite, for organising a squadron of American volunteers. When at last the consent of the French Government was won and the *Escadrille Américaine* placed on the Front, Genêt was permitted to transfer to the Aviation Service. He was exuberantly happy in his new work. "This is what one can call the real thing!" he said, in writing of it. "This is sport with all the fascination and excitement and sporting chances any live fellow could ever wish for." With his aeroplane he was like a child with a new toy. He marvelled at its speed, its delicate mechanism, and after his first bad crash, its wayward and wilful desire for self-destruction. He made good progress and was sent to the Escadrille Lafayette on January 19, 1917. A few days later he wrote to his mother:

> I've got a Nieuport of my own now, one which is really new, and tomorrow I go over the lines with the *escadrille* for the first time.... We have a very pleasant captain, and our lieutenant, de Laage, is a dandy fellow.... It's a big relief to me to be out here at last, dear mother. The rumble of the big guns this morning which roused me from beneath my warm covering of four big blankets (for it's right cold here and we've snow all over the ground) wasn't new music to my ears. It seemed like old times, the roar of old comrades.... Our living-room, where we are most of the time when off duty, is a mighty attractive little den. We have covered all the walls and ceiling with corrugated cardboard strips (smooth side outside) over the rough boards, and on this in various places I have drawn and painted vivid scenes of aerial combats between French and German machines. We have a huge painting of an Indian head, the symbol of the *escadrille*, which is also painted on each of our machines. The Indian's mouth is open as though he was shouting his terrible war-cry in defiance of his enemies, and he looks very warlike indeed. It's quite an appropriate symbol for the *escadrille*, being something genuinely American.

Several weeks later Genêt was wounded in the face by a bullet during the combat in which James McConnell was killed. And on April 16, 1917, he himself was shot down, probably by anti-aircraft fire, although the precise cause of his death can never be known. The following account of his last flight is taken from a letter written by

Walter Lovell, of the Lafayette Squadron:

> It seems that I am destined always to announce to you bad news. This time it is dear little Genêt who is dead. He has been killed this afternoon flying in the company of Lufbery. On account of the clouds they flew low. The special German batteries were firing at them continuously. Suddenly Lufbery noticed that Genêt had made a half-turn, as if going back. He tried to follow, but lost sight of him in the clouds. He was very much surprised upon his return to the camp to see that Edmond had not returned. A few minutes later we received by telephone the news that Genêt had fallen five kilometres within our lines.
> Lieutenant de Laage, Lufbery, Haviland, and I took the light motor and rushed to the relief station. There we found his body. He had been instantly killed. I saw the machine later and I have never seen so complete a wreck. He had fallen in the middle of the road with the motor at full speed, which proves that the German shell had killed him or rendered him unconscious. I had flown with him in the morning very early, and in the afternoon we were to have flown together, but as he seemed tired I advised him not to fly and went up with Thaw.
> When I returned I learned that he had gone with Lufbery. Haviland, whose *avion* was disabled, had tried to borrow Genêt's Nieuport to fly in his place, but Edmond refused, insisting that he felt all right, and he flew—to his death. For myself, I have lost a very dear friend and a courageous comrade of combat. The squadron has lost one of the most conscientious pilots that it has ever had or ever will have. Edmond fell a few hundred metres from the spot where Mac (James McConnell) fell four weeks ago. He will be buried at Ham tomorrow. I am happy in one thing, and that is that he learned yesterday evening that his citation is now official, and that the German *avion* with which he had fought when McConnell was killed has been compelled to land on French soil and that its crew have been made prisoners.

Genêt was the first American to be killed after the United States declared war upon Germany. He was buried in the little military cemetery at Ham in the midst of a tempest of snow, the ceremony impressive in its simplicity. And so ended the career of this brave-spirited boy whom Captain Thénault called "the Benjamin of the Escadrille

Genêt as a légionnaire, April, 1916

Genêt's funeral at Ham

Lafayette," and who served his own country and France with a purity of purpose which shall never be forgotten.

SERVICE RECORD

JOSEPH FRANCIS GILL, Indianapolis, Indiana.

SERVICE IN FRENCH AVIATION:
Date of enlistment: June 10, 1917.
Aviation Schools: June 15, 1917, to February, 1918, Avord, Pau, G.D.E.
Breveted: December 4, 1917 (Caudron).
Final Rank: Caporal.

SERVICE IN U.S. AVIATION:
Commissioned Second Lieutenant: March 22, 1918.
Assigned to French Squadron Spa. 471 (defense of Paris), June 8 to July 17, 1918.
On duty, American Acceptance Park, Orly, June 17 to August 28, 1918.

Joseph Francis Gill

Gill was breveted on Caudron at Avord, and after taking the *chasse* course at Pau, was detained a long time at the G.D.E., before his transfer to the American army. He was then attached to the French Squadron, Spad 471, on duty at Le Bourget for the defence of Paris, and afterward at the American Acceptance Park at Orly. On August 28 he was injured in an accident which kept him from further service until after the close of the war.

SERVICE RECORD

CLARENCE M. GLOVER, New York City.

SERVICE IN FRENCH AVIATION:
Date of enlistment: June 9, 1917.
Aviation Schools: September 16, 1917, to April, 1918, Avord, Pau, Cazeaux, G.D.E.
Breveted: December 19, 1917 (Caudron).
At the Front: Escadrille Spad 78, July 1, 1918, to Armistice.
Final Rank: Sergent.

Clarence M. Glover

Glover was one of the last, if not the last, of the Lafayette men to be trained in the French schools. He did not get his *brevet* until December 19, 1917, and did not arrive at the G.D.E. until April 2 of the following year. On July 1, 1918, he was assigned to Escadrille Spad 78, where he served honourably until the time of the Armistice.

SERVICE RECORD

CHARLES G. GREY, Chicago, Illinois.

SERVICE IN FRENCH AVIATION:
Date of enlistment: June 17, 1917.
Aviation Schools: July 19 to November 24, 1917, Avord, Juvisy, Pau, G.D.E.
Breveted: September 26, 1917 (Caudron).
At the Front: Escadrille Spad 93, November 26, 1917, to March 13, 1918.
Final Rank: Sergent.

SERVICE IN U.S. AVIATION:
Commissioned First Lieutenant: March 21, 1918.
Promoted Captain: November 6, 1918.
March 21 to August 1, 1918, Aeroplane Tester at Le Bourget and American Acceptance Park, Orly.
At the Front: 213th Pursuit Squadron, August 1, 1918, to Armistice.

DECORATIONS:
Distinguished Service Cross.

CITATION

G.H.Q., A.E.F., *December* 10, 1918

Captain CHARLES G. GREY, A.S. 213th Aero Squadron No. 1961

For extraordinary heroism in action near Montmédy, France, 4 November, 1918. While leading a patrol of three machines, Captain Grey observed a formation of our bombing planes hard-pressed by twelve of the enemy. He attacked the leading enemy machine without hesitation, thereby attracting the enemy's fire and allowing the bombing machines to escape undamaged.

Charles G. Grey

Charles G. Grey went to the old French school at Juvisy and thence the usual route to Plessis. He spent a few months of bad weather with G.C. 12 before being taken into the American Army as First Lieutenant, in March, 1918. He was placed in charge of the Nieuport hangars at the American Acceptance Park at Orly, where he remained until August, 1918. In that month he was assigned to the 213th American Squadron as Flight Commander, and served faithfully during the Saint-Mihiel and Meuse-Argonne drives, for which service he was made a Captain.

Among his exploits was the successful bombing of a German balloon and a German ammunition dump with light Spad bombs. He has four official victories to his credit and has won the D.S.C.

SERVICE RECORD

NORMAN GRIEB, Scarsdale, New York.

SERVICE IN FRENCH AVIATION:
 Date of enlistment: June 13, 1917.
 Aviation Schools: June 19 to August 28, 1917, Avord.
 Died at Bourges: August 28, 1917.
 Final Rank: Soldat de deuxième classe.

Norman Grieb

There are a few Lafayette men, students at Avord in June and July, 1917, who remember a quiet and serious little fellow in the *penguin* class—Norman Grieb. He lived at Farges, came daily to work under the Adjutant Terrier, and returned, alone as often as not, to his lodgings. His keen desire to learn was obvious to everyone, but though he had a friendly smile and a pleasant manner, it was evident that he did not like crowds and preferred to make friends slowly. Then, one day, before we had really had an opportunity to know him, the news came that he had been run over and seriously injured by a motorcar. His comrades visited him as often as possible at the hospital in Bourges, where he lay seemingly on the road to recovery. But the injury to his chest was graver than the doctors had supposed, and on August 28 we were saddened to learn that he was dead—before he could prove his mettle at the Front.

SERVICE RECORD

JAMES MURRAY GRIER, Philadelphia, Pennsylvania.

PREVIOUS SERVICE: American Ambulance, 1917.

SERVICE IN FRENCH AVIATION:
 Date of enlistment: August 1, 1917.
 Aviation Schools: August 2, 1917, to April 10, 1918, Avord, Tours, Pau, G.D.E.
 Breveted: January 6, 1918 (Caudron).
 Final Rank: Caporal.

SERVICE IN U.S. NAVAL AVIATION:
 Commissioned Ensign: April 10, 1918.
 Instructor at Lake Bolsena, Italy, June 19 to September 28, 1918.
 At the Front: U.S. Naval Air Station, Porto Corsini, Italy, September 28 to October 28, 1918.
 Assigned to 341st Royal Marine Air Squadron (Italian), October 28, 1918, to Armistice.

James Murray Grier

Grier was breveted at Tours on January 6, 1918—one of the last American volunteers to go through the schools. Finishing at Pau on February 22, he was transferred to the navy early in April, before he had been assigned to a squadron on the Front. After courses in the naval flying schools, he served for a time as instructor at Lake Bolsena, Italy; was sent to Porto Corsini to join a *chasse* squadron, and later to Venice, where he served in the 341st Italian Squadron, equipped with Henriot Type D. 1 planes. Grier has experienced all the different forms of excitement that naval flying has to offer—escorting convoys, anti-submarine patrols, and daylight bombing raids on Pola, across the Adriatic. Detailed accounts of these adventures would be of great interest, but unfortunately none are at hand.

SERVICE RECORD

ANDRÉ GUNDELACH, Chicago, Illinois.

SERVICE IN FRENCH AVIATION:
Date of enlistment: March 20, 1917.
Aviation Schools: March 24 to July 10, 1917, Avord, Pau, G.D.E.
Breveted: May 31, 1917 (Blériot).
At the Front: Escadrille Spad 95, July 12 to September 8, 1917.
Escadrille Sop. 111, September 24 to December 21, 1917.
Final Rank: Sergent.

SERVICE IN U.S. AVIATION:
Commissioned First Lieutenant: November 9, 1917.
On duty at 7th A.I.C., Clermont-Ferrand, January 3 to May 18, 1918.
At the Front: 96th Day Bombing Squadron, May 23 to September 12, 1918.
Killed in combat: September 12, 1918 (Saint-Mihiel Sector).

DECORATIONS:
Distinguished Service Cross.
Croix de Guerre, with Palm.

CITATIONS

VIe ARMÉE, ÉTAT-MAJOR.   13 *septembre*, 1917
Citation à l'Ordre de l'Armée.

   GUNDELACH, ANDRÉ (sujet américain), Caporal d'Infanterie, Escadrille N. 95

Sujet américain, engagé volontaire dans l'Armée Française depuis mars, 1917.
Pilote plein d'audace et d'entrain. Le 4 septembre, 1917, a abattu en flammes un avion ennemi.

       (*Signé*)   MAISTRE

          G.H.Q., A.E.F., 1918

The Distinguished Service Cross is awarded to

First Lieutenant ANDRÉ GUNDELACH

For extraordinary heroism in action near Buxières, France, September 12, 1918. Lieutenant Gundelach with Second Lieutenant Pennington H. Way, Observer, volunteered for a hazardous mission to bomb concentrations of enemy troops. They successfully bombed their objective, but while returning were attacked by eight enemy planes. Their plane was brought down in flames and both officers killed.

By command of General PERSHING

André Gundelach

Before joining the Lafayette Flying Corps, Gundelach's career had been an adventurous and roving one. While in the American Navy he made the famous cruise around the world and for several years was stationed with the Asiatic Squadron. In March, 1917, he volunteered to fly for France, and was breveted on Blériot at Avord, doing his triangles in weather which made the monitors marvel at his daring. He had always been interested in bombing work, but was sent to the Front on a Nieuport, transferred to a Spad, and shot down a German plane during his second flight on that machine. Shortly after this, a request he had made to be transferred to day bombing was granted, and he joined a famous French bombing squadron, where he soon became known as a pilot of the first order. His broad experience of his chosen work made him a very valuable man, and when the United States Air Service took him over as a First Lieutenant, he instructed for a time at Clermont before being sent to the Front as Flight Commander in the 96th Day Bombing Squadron. Decorated twice and cited while with the French, Gundelach may well be called the ace of American bombardment. He lost his life while returning from an exceptionally perilous mission which he had accomplished alone.

SERVICE RECORD

DAVID W. GUY, St. Louis, Missouri.

PREVIOUS SERVICE: American Ambulance, 1917.

SERVICE IN FRENCH AVIATION:
  Date of enlistment: July 21, 1917.
  Aviation Schools: August 1 to November 28, 1917, Avord, Tours, Pau, G.D.E.
  Breveted: September 22, 1917 (Caudron).
  At the Front: Escadrille Spad 155, December 2, 1917, to January 1, 1918.
    Escadrille Spad 156, January 1 to June 1, 1918.
    Escadrille Spad 38, June 1 to November 7, 1918.
  Final Rank: Sergent.

SERVICE IN U.S. AVIATION:
  Commissioned First Lieutenant: November 7, 1918.

DECORATIONS:
  Croix de Guerre, with Palm.

CITATION

13 *juillet*, 1918

Le Général Commandant la IVe Armée cite à l'Ordre de l'Armée:

Sergent Guy, David, M^{le} 4655, du 1er Régiment Étranger, détaché à l'Escadrille Spa. 38

Pilote de tout premier ordre, courageux et d'un rare sang-froid; recherche toutes les occasions de combattre. Le 1 juillet a abattu dans nos lignes un biplace ennemi.

David W. Guy

Guy went to the Front, to the Escadrille N. 155, on December 2, 1917. On January 1, 1918, he joined Winter, Shaffer, and Putnam in the N. 156, a squadron which changed shortly afterwards to the small Morane monoplanes. Soon after Winter's death these planes were pronounced unsafe, and toward the end of May the squadron was equipped with Spads. In a letter to Colonel Gros, Guy said:

> The evening of May 28 we were all excited by the news that Lieutenant Madon of the Spad 38 had asked for the three Americans (of the 156), and Putnam and I were ordered to take our new Spads and have the guns mounted before morning in order to make an early patrol. We could not get them ready in time, but pushed off later to try to join the formation. I attacked one of two photo Rumplers over Jonchéry and saw the plane pitch over—at the same time I had a water siphon and was forced to land with a dead stick. This Rumpler was confirmed two weeks later, but not officially as I had not seen it wrecked. One afternoon when I was with Putnam we attacked ten Albatross, but I had motor trouble and was forced to quit. It was certainly a revelation to watch Putnam attack. He showed absolutely no fear, and waited until within a few yards of the enemy plane before opening fire. He finally left after driving them nearly twenty kilometres back into their lines. One of Putnam's best fights was when he was left alone to protect two Salmsons. Six Albatross attacked them from above—with every advantage. Putnam saved the Salmsons, and was himself brought down with three bullets in his motor, but not until he had knocked down two of the Albatross. On the 1st of July I chased a *biplace* Rumpler down from 5300 metres, and hit him so that he fell between the lines. He put three bullets in my plane—it was my only official victory.

Guy stayed with the Spad 38 until November 7, four days before the Armistice, when he was transferred to the Air Service, with the rank of First Lieutenant, and assigned to the 1st Aero Squadron. The quality of his service with the French may be judged from the notes given by Madon:

> ... Fait honneur a l'Aviation Française pour laquelle il est une précieuse recrué. Nommé officier dans l'Armée Américaine, pourrait être laissé à l'escadrille 38, où il serait un aide pour ses chefs et un exemple pour ses jeunes camarades.

SERVICE RECORD

BERT HALL, Higginsville, Missouri.

PREVIOUS SERVICE: August to December, 1914, Foreign Legion (Infantry).

SERVICE IN FRENCH AVIATION:
Date of enlistment: December 28, 1914.
Aviation Schools: December, 1914, to March, 1915, Pau, Buc, Réserve Général Aéronautique.
Breveted: August 19, 1915.
At the Front: Escadrille M.S. 38, summer of 1915.
Escadrille Lafayette, April 28 to November 1, 1916.
Escadrille N. 103, November 18 to December 20, 1916.
Final Rank: Adjudant.

DECORATIONS:
Médaille Militaire.
Croix de Guerre, with three Palms.

CITATION

November 26, 1916

BERT HALL, Adjutant Pilot in Escadrille N. 103

Clever, energetic, and courageous pilot, full of spirit. Daily attacking enemy planes at very short distance. On November 26, 1916, shot down a German plane at two hundred meters from our trenches. The following day, after a combat held quite near, returned with his machine hit by several shots, also a shot in his helmet.

(Three additional citations.)

Bert Hall

Bert Hall entered the French Aviation Service from the Foreign Legion (Infantry) in December, 1914. He is one of the original members of the Escadrille Lafayette, and served with it until November, 1916, when he was transferred, at his own request, to the French squadron, N. 103. In January, 1917, he was granted permission to accompany the French Aviation Mission which was sent, at that time, to Roumania, He later asked for, and was granted, permission to return to the United States, supposedly for the purpose of entering the United States Air Service. He remained in America until the close of the war.

SERVICE RECORD

James Norman Hall, Colfax, Iowa.

Previous Service: August 18, 1914, to December 1, 1915, 9th Battalion, Royal Fusiliers (British Army).

Service in French Aviation:
  Date of enlistment: October 11, 1916.
  Aviation Schools: October 16, 1916, to June 14, 1917, Buc, Avord, G.D.E.
  Breveted: April 23, 1917 (Caudron).
  At the Front: Escadrille Lafayette, June 16 to June 26, 1917.
    Escadrille Spad 112, September 22 to October 3, 1917.
    Escadrille Lafayette, October 3, 1917, to February 18, 1918.
  Final Rank: Sergent.

Service in U.S. Aviation:
  Commissioned Captain: February 7, 1918.
  At the Front: 103d Pursuit Squadron, February 18 to March 29, 1918.
    94th Pursuit Squadron, March 29 to May 7, 1918.
  Shot down in combat: May 7, 1918, near Pagny-sur-Moselle (Meurthe-et-Moselle).
  Prisoner in Germany until the Armistice.
  Wounded in combat: June 26, 1917, and May 7, 1918.

Decorations:
  Distinguished Service Cross.
  Légion d'Honneur.
  Médaille Militaire.
  Croix de Guerre, with five Palms.

CITATIONS

Médaille Militaire:

Par Ordre N° 5261 "D" du 9 juillet, 1917, du Général Commandant en Chef, la Médaille Militaire a été conférée:

    Au Caporal Pilote Hall, James Norman (active de l'Escadrille N. 124)

Réformé, après avoir été mitrailleur dans une armé alliée, s'est engagé comme pilote à l'Escadrille Lafayette. Dès son arrivée a montré un courage splendide et le plus pur esprit de sacrifice. Le 26 juin, 1917, a foncé seul sur sept avions ennemis, faisant l'admiration des témoins du combat; blessé grièvement dans la lutte, a réussit a ramener son appareil dans nos lignes.

La présente nomination comporte l'attribution de la Croix de Guerre avec Palme.

    (Signé)   Maistre
    Au G.Q., le 21 janvier, 1918

Le Général Commandant la IVᵉ Armée cite à l'Ordre de l'Armée:

    Le Sergent Hall, James Norman, Mᴸᵉ 11921 de l'Escadrille Lafayette (Groupe de Combat N° 13)

Excellent pilote de chasse, déjà blessé en combat aérien. Revenu au front, y fait preuve des plus belles qualités de hardiesse et d'allant. Le 1 janvier, 1918, a descendu un monoplace ennemi dont une aile s'est détachée et est tombée dans nos lignes (1ᵉʳ avion).

    (Signé)   Gouraud

IVᵉ Armée, État-Major.   *Le 4 avril*, 1918

Le Général Commandant la IVᵉ Armée cite à l'Ordre de l'Armée:

    Capitaine Hall, James Norman, de l'Escadrille Lafayette 103

Pilote d'une grande bravoure, qui livre journellement de nombreux combats. A abattu deux avions ennemis.

    (Signé)   Gouraud

G.H.Q., AMERICAN EXPEDITIONARY FORCES, *April* 10, 1918

The Commander-in-Chief has awarded the Distinguished Service Cross to

JAMES NORMAN HALL, Captain, Air Service, Flight Commander 103d Aero Squadron

On March 26, 1918, while leading a patrol of three, attacked a group of five enemy fighters and three enemy two-seaters, himself destroying one and forcing down two others which were very probably destroyed, the fight lasting more than twenty (20) minutes.

By command of General PERSHING

(*Signed*) FRANK C. BURNETT

Adjutant-General

VIIIe ARMÉE, ÉTAT-MAJOR. *Le* 9 *mai*, 1918

Capitaine HALL, JAMES NORMAN, Pilote à l'Escadrille Américaine

Brillant pilote de chasse, modèle de courage et d'entrain qui a abattu récemment un avion ennemi, a trouvé une mort glorieuse dans un combat contre quatre monoplaces dont un a été descendu en flammes.

(*Signé*) *Le Général Commandant le VIIIe Armée*

GRAND QUARTIER GÉNÉRAL DES ARMÉES
FRANÇAISES DE L'EST ÉTAT-MAJOR. *Le* 17 *mai*, 1919

Après approbation du Général Commandant en Chef les Forces Expéditionnaires Américaines en France, le Maréchal Commandant en Chef les Armées Françaises de l'Est cite à l'Ordre de l'Armée:

Capitaine HALL, JAMES NORMAN

Citoyen américain engagé dans la Légion Étrangère comme pilote à l'Escadrille Lafayette. A fait preuve des plus belles qualités de bravoure et de sang-froid. A abattu 4 avions ennemis.

Le Maréchal Commandant en Chef les Armées de l'Est

PÉTAIN

Par decret du Président de la République en date du 9 avril, 1919, le Capitaine HALL a été promu Chevalier de la Légion d'Honneur.

Cet promotion a été fait avec le motif de ce citation.

James Norman Hall

James N. Hall, after a period of service as an infantryman with Lord Kitchener's first hundred thousand, was honourably discharged from the British Army, and later enlisted in the French Aviation Service and was sent to the Escadrille Lafayette. He was wounded shortly after his arrival at the Front and spent the summer of 1917 in hospital.

HALL NEAR PAGNY-SUR-MOSELLE, MORNING OF MAY 7, 1918
(Snapshot Taken By A German Aviator)

In September, 1917, he returned to the Front as a member of the French Squadron, Spad 112, but was soon permitted to return to his old unit, where he was on duty until after his transfer to the United States Air Service. On March 29, 1918, he was sent as a Flight Commander to the 94th Pursuit Squadron. On May 7, 1918, during a combat near Pont-à-Mousson, while diving on an Albatross single-seater, his upper right plane gave way, the fabric covering it bursting along the leading edge. A moment later an enemy anti-aircraft battery made a direct hit on his motor, and his plane fell out of control near Pagny-sur-Moselle. He was a prisoner in various German hospitals and prison camps until the Armistice.

SERVICE RECORD

EDGAR G. HAMILTON, Newcastle, Pennsylvania.

SERVICE IN FRENCH AVIATION:
Date of enlistment: February 27, 1917.
Aviation Schools: March 3 to July 25, 1917, Avord.
Breveted: June 12, 1917 (Caudron).
Blériot Moniteur at Avord until June 10, 1917.
Technical Instructor at Châteauroux, July 10, 1917, to April 1, 1918.
Chief Technical Instructor at Tours, July 10 to August 20, 1918.
At G.D.E. for training on Sopwith.
Technical Instructor at Châteauroux, August 25, 1918, to Armistice.
Final Rank: Sous-Lieutenant.

Edgar G. Hamilton

Of all the American volunteers in the French Air Service, no one had an experience more disappointing to himself than Edgar Hamilton. After receiving his military *brevet* at Avord, he was made a *moniteur* there, the reason being that he was thoroughly acquainted with motors, spoke French well, and was thus in a position to instruct the American *élève-pilotes*, who because of their lack of French were losing most of the ground-school work. America's entry into the war made this position of Hamilton's a permanent one.

He was anxious to go to the Front, but as his services were badly needed in the rear, his application was refused. He was sent to the American Aviation School at Tours as instructor on motors and aeroplanes, and later to the French training centre at Châteauroux, where he was ground instructor for the American student-pilots. Here he was compelled to remain until the end of the war, doing faithful and conscientious work, all the while longing to get into the fighting and never being given the opportunity. He received no honours in the military sense. His name did not appear in the French list of awards. It was his hard luck to be in the midst of war and yet to see it only from a distance; to say *bonne chance* to pilots on their way to the Front, knowing that he himself could not follow them. It is easy to understand what his own feeling must have been, although he rarely spoke of it. He stuck to his job and he did it well, and all his friends who know the real bitterness of his disappointment, admire and honour him for it.

SERVICE RECORD

ROBERT M. HANFORD, Brooklyn, New York.

SERVICE IN FRENCH AVIATION:
Date of enlistment: May 24, 1917.
Aviation Schools: June 5 to October 15, 1917, Avord.
Killed in line of duty: October 15, 1917, at Châteauroux.
Final Rank: Soldat de deuxième classe.

Robert M. Hanford

Hanford was a fighter, every inch of him; trained on the football field to take punishment and never to give up. Like many of his comrades who since have become famous, he had trouble with the Blériot, but at the time of his death, he had developed into a clever pilot, and he died as a result of one of those fatal mischances which seem unavoidable in aviation.

He was on his *brevet*, flying a Caudron from Avord to Châteauroux, just approaching the latter field where the air was always thick with machines during flying hours. Watching ahead with the intentness of a young pilot, he did not see a Farman approaching straight for his blind spot. A mid-air collision is one of the most terrible of sights to watch: men on the ground turned away in horror.... There was a crash of breaking wood and tearing fabric, and the two machines with their occupants came hurtling to earth.... Death must have been instantaneous. When the news came to Avord it brought grief to every American in the school.

SERVICE RECORD

WILLIS B. HAVILAND, St. Paul, Minnesota.

PREVIOUS SERVICE: American Ambulance, 1915.

SERVICE IN FRENCH AVIATION:
Date of enlistment: January 26, 1916.
Aviation Schools: January 30 to October 20, 1916, Pau, Buc, G.D.E.
Breveted: May 20, 1916 (Caudron).
At the Front: Escadrille Lafayette, October 22, 1916, to September 18, 1917.
Escadrille Spad 102, October 1, 1917, to January 1, 1918.
Final Rank: Adjudant.

SERVICE IN U.S. NAVAL AVIATION:
Commissioned Lieutenant (Senior Grade).
At the Front: Chief Pilot at U.S. Naval Air Station, Dunkirk, February 1 to March 25, 1918.
13th Squadron, R.N.A.S., March 25 to May 1, 1918.
C.O. U.S. Naval Air Station, Porto Corsini, Italy, August 1, 1918, to Armistice.

DECORATIONS:
Croix de Guerre, with Palm.

CITATION

GROUPE D'ARMÉE DU NORD, ÉTAT-MAJOR.   Le 17 mai, 1917
Le Général Franchet d'Esperrey, Commandant le Groupe d'Armées du Nord, cite à l'Ordre de l'Armée:
HAVILAND, WILLIS, Sergent à l'Escadrille N. 124 (N° M¹ᵉ 11731)
Citoyen américain engagé pour la durée de la guerre. Bon pilote courageux et adroit. A attaqué le 26 avril un avion ennemi et l'a abattu dans les premières lignes allemandes.
(Signé)   FRANCHET D'ESPERREY

Willis B. Haviland

From the early days of 1915, when he was driving an ambulance on the Pont-é-Mousson Sector for the American Field Service, until the close of the war, Willis Haviland was continuously on active duty in Europe. By right of faithful and conscientious service, he takes a prominent place in the history of the American volunteers in France. He was one of the earliest of the number to enlist in the Aviation Section of the Foreign Legion and was in training at Paris two months before the *Escadrille Américaine* was first sent to the Front. He joined the squadron at Cachy-sur-Somme and served with it at various parts of the line until his transfer, October 1, 1917, to Spad 102, a French squadron.

It is impossible to give a detailed account of his adventures in French Aviation within the limits of a brief sketch. When he transferred to the United States Naval Air Service after fourteen months of flying at the Front, he was in a position to give valuable assistance to our own Air Service. He was commissioned a Lieutenant and qualified for the naval aviation *brevet* on February 1, 1918. For two months he was detailed as chief pilot and second in command at the United States Naval Air Station at Dunkirk. At the beginning of the German offensive on the Somme he was sent to the 13th Squadron, R.N.A.S. After three weeks of daily combat and reconnaissance flights with this squadron, he was sent on a mission to Italy in connection with the establishment of the U.S.N.A.S. on the Adriatic. Returning to France he selected a personnel of 20 officers and 360 men for the United States Naval Air Station at Porto Corsini, Italy, where he was placed on permanent duty as Commanding Officer.

WILLIS HAVILAND AT CACHY ON THE SOMME

Here they were bombed by the Austrians and in turn bombed the Austrian aerodrome at Pola. Haviland was the first American to make a night bombardment of this enemy station. He also took part in raids, both by night and by day, of the naval base there. In addition to the bombardments, there were daily reconnaissance flights by land and submarine chasing over the Adriatic in single-seater combat machines. Some of the Americans at Porto Corsini were cited for valour by the Italian Government, but up to the present the United States Navy has not permitted its airmen to receive foreign decorations. Haviland himself has been proposed for the silver Medal for Valour, Chevalier of the Crown of Italy, and the Italian War Cross. He already has the French *Croix de Guerre*, with Palm. But better than military awards is the satisfaction which comes from the record, throughout three years of war, of hazardous service faithfully done.

SERVICE RECORD

THOMAS M. HEWITT, JR., Westchester, New York.

PREVIOUS SERVICE: American Ambulance, 1915–16.

SERVICE IN FRENCH AVIATION:
Date of enlistment: April 13, 1916.
Aviation Schools: July 3, 1916, to March 28, 1917, Buc, Juvisy, Avord, Cazeaux, Pau, G.D.E.
Breveted: November 21, 1916 (Caudron).
At the Front: Escadrille Lafayette, March 30 to September 17, 1917.
Final Rank: Sergent.

Thomas M. Hewitt, Jr.

After several months at the Front with the Escadrille Lafayette, Thomas Hewitt was sent back to the depot at G.D.E. for training as a bombardment pilot. Shortly afterward he was released from the French Service and returned to America, November 1, 1917. A few months later he reenlisted in an American infantry regiment and was on duty in the United States until the close of the war.

SERVICE RECORD

DUDLEY LAWRENCE HILL, Peekskill, New York.

PREVIOUS SERVICE: American Ambulance, 1915.

SERVICE IN FRENCH AVIATION:
Date of enlistment: August 3, 1915.
Aviation Schools: September 25, 1915, to May 2, 1916, Pau, Châteauroux, G.D.E.
Breveted: March 17, 1916 (Caudron).
At the Front: Escadrille Lafayette, June 9, 1916, to February 18, 1918.
Final Rank: Adjudant.

SERVICE IN U.S. AVIATION:
Commissioned Captain: January 18, 1918.
At the Front: 103d Pursuit Squadron, February 18 to June 1, 1918.
139th Pursuit Squadron, June 1 to August 1, 1918.
C.O. 138th Pursuit Squadron, August 1 to November 1, 1918.
C.O. 5th Pursuit Group, November 1 to Armistice.

DECORATIONS:
Croix de Guerre, with Star.

CITATION

IIe ARMÉE, ÉTAT-MAJOR. *Le* 8 *octobre,* 1917
Le Chef d'État-Major de la 2ᵐᵉ Armée cite à l'Ordre de l'Aéronautique:
   HILL, DUDLEY, N° Mᵗᵉ 11632, Adjudant Pilote à l'Escadrille N. 124

   Citoyen américain engagé pour la durée de la guerre. Bon pilote de chasse, modèle de dévouement à son devoir. A livré de nombreux combats, particulièrement au cours des dernières attaques de Verdun, et s'est dépensé sans compter, donnant à tous les plus beaux exemples de hardiesse et d'entrain. S'est particulièrement distingué le 18 août au cours de la protection d'un bombardement où il a eu son avion gravement atteint.

Dudley Lawrence Hill

Dudley Lawrence Hill, although not one of the original personnel of the Lafayette Squadron, was one of the first of the immediate followers to transfer from the American Ambulance to the French Aviation Service. Although he had defective vision in one eye, he was passed by Dr. Gros for the French Aviation at a time when applicants were rare, and it was impossible to be too particular. He had additional physical tests to pass at the French *Bureau de Recrutement* in Paris, but hoodwinked the doctor when it came to examining his blind eye, by looking through his fingers with his good one. His imperfect vision did not prevent his making a creditable showing at the schools, but on arrival at Pau he was obliged to submit to another physical examination and the defect of sight was discovered. The captain commanding decided that he could not do acrobatics and proposed his radiation.

French military matters of this kind move with proverbial slowness, and when the papers finally reached Pau, Dudley, with the connivance of his instructors, had so profitably employed his time that he was nearly finished with his acrobatic flying; and having demonstrated his ability notwithstanding his defective vision, he was allowed to continue his training and was sent to the G.D.E. He went to the Front when French combat squadrons were equipped with 15-metre Nieuport biplanes, with Lewis guns mounted on the top planes. From that time until his transfer to the American Air Service, Dudley served constantly as a pilot with N. 124. He has flown with the squadron on every sector of the Western Front. His experience as a *pilote de chasse* is as broad as his length of service indicates. His old French uniform of horizon blue had numberless baptisms of gas and burnt castor oil at a time when the entire American Air Force could have ridden comfortably in one Handley-Page. And yet, to hear him tell of it—but who ever heard "Dud" tell of anything in which he himself was concerned? Unless it was to speak of some headlong flight which he claims to have made from pursuing Germans.

He has a long and enviable record of service which he never mentions, but he is always generous in his praise of the records at the Front of other men. It can be said of him, with absolute certainty, that twenty-five years hence, when most veteran airmen are holding forth garrulously at Memorial Day Celebrations, he will still be the same monosyllabic "Dud" his comrades knew of old. He is poor material for the making of a home-town hero, and in far distant days, when he sits by the chimney corner and his grandchildren clamour for stories about the Great War, "Dud" will stroke his beardless chin and begin: "Well, I remember a little *café* in Bar-le-Duc, where we used to loaf on rainy days. There wasn't a better place on the Western Front for a *vermouth cassis*." After long and futile pleading his grandchildren will go storyless to bed.

SERVICE RECORD

EDWARD F. HINKLE, Cincinnati, Ohio.

SERVICE IN FRENCH AVIATION:
Date of enlistment: July 20, 1916.
Aviation Schools: August 1, 1916, to February 26, 1917, Buc, Avord, Cazeaux, Pau, G.D.E.
Breveted: November 4, 1916 (Blériot).
At the Front: Escadrille Lafayette, March 1 to June 12, 1917.
Final Rank: Sergent.

Edward F. Hinkle

Edward Hinkle, although more than forty years old—far beyond the age limit for candidates in the French Air Service—secured his acceptance through the support of friends and was among the earliest of the American volunteers. He made a creditable record in the aviation schools and was sent to the Front on March 1, 1917. During the next two months he took part in several patrols and was then released from duty on account of illness.

SERVICE RECORD

THOMAS HITCHCOCK, JR., Westbury, New York.

SERVICE IN FRENCH AVIATION:
Date of enlistment: June 25, 1917.
Aviation Schools: June 29 to December 8, 1917, Avord, Pau, G.D.E.
Breveted: September 17, 1917 (Caudron).
At the Front: Escadrille N. 87, December 10, 1917, to March 6, 1918.
Shot down, wounded, in German territory: March 6, 1918.
Escaped into Switzerland: August 28, 1918.
Final Rank: Sous-Lieutenant.

DECORATIONS:
Croix de Guerre, with three Palms.

CITATIONS

Le 2 octobre, 1918

Ordre N⁰ 10372 *"D" G.Q.G.*
Lieutenant THOMAS HITCHCOCK, Pilote
Aviateur

Citoyen américain, a offert spontanément ses services à la France en s'engageant dans une Unite d'Aviation. Blessé et fait prisonnier à la suite d'un combat inégal contre un ennemi supérieur en nombre, s'est évadé de captivité, dans des circonstances périlleuses, pour recommencer à combattre.

Ordre de l'Armée:
Le Caporal HITCHCOCK, THOMAS, sujet américain, N° M^le 12292, du 1er Régiment de la Légion Étrangère, Pilote à l'Escadrille N. 87

Pilote de chasse qui, dès son arrivée, s'est fait remarqué par ses qualités d'allant, de courage, et d'adresse. Le 6 janvier, 1918, après une poursuite hardie et un brillant combat, a abattu un avion ennemi, qui s'est écrasé au sol.
Le 19 janvier, 1918, a abattu son 2ᵉ avion ennemi.

Ordre de l'Armée:
Le Maréchal de Logis HITCHCOCK, THOMAS

Pilote de chasse d'une grande valeur, remarquable de courage et d'adresse, ayant déjà abattu deux ennemis officiellement, le 20 janvier, ayant pris un biplace ennemi en chasse au-dessus de Nancy, le poursuit jusque sur son terrain à plus de 25 kilomètres dans lignes, mitraillant à bout portant les hangars et tuant probablement le pilote.
Le 6 mars, fonçant avec une magnifique ardeur sur un groupe de 3 monoplaces ennemis qu'il forcé à piquer dans leurs lignes, est disparu au cours de cette attaque.

Thomas Hitchcock, Jr.

It was said by the instructors at Avord that Hitchcock was one of the most remarkable Blériot pilots the school had ever turned out. Absolutely at home in the air, he possessed a love of flying, a sureness of touch, and a keenness of eye that made his landings perfect and his air work a pleasure to watch. From Plessis-Belleville, he was sent to a Nieuport Squadron, the N. 87, then stationed at Lunéville. In spite of his antiquated machine and one of the quietest sectors of the Front, Hitchcock distinguished himself in a very short time by bringing down two German *biplaces*. He was always in the air, alone or with Wellman, searching far and wide for Germans. Once he found an enemy he never left him, attacking again and again, until the plane went down or until his ammunition was exhausted.

On one occasion with Wellman he attacked a two-seater over Nancy, following it and shooting burst after burst at point-blank range, until they were over the German airdrome, fifteen miles into the lines.

HITCHCOCK, YORK, WINTER, GUEST, RODGERS, AND SCHREIBER
ON THE WAY TO FRANCE

The enemy pilot dove down and landed with the observer dead in the seat. Flying over the aerodrome, only a few yards off the ground, the two Americans shot their remaining cartridges with deadly effect into barracks and hangars before they rose and headed homeward.

Early in the spring of 1918, when doing patrol, Hitchcock attacked, single-handed, a large patrol of Albatross. Wounded in the back and with his control wires cut, he crashed to the ground and was made prisoner. His escape was one of the cleverest and most sensational of the war. Jumping from a railway carriage full of Germans, travelling by night and hiding by day in the woods, he reached the Swiss frontier at last, and crossed into safety.

SERVICE RECORD

WARREN TUCKER HOBBS, Worcester, Mass.

PREVIOUS SERVICE: American Ambulance, 1917.

SERVICE IN FRENCH AVIATION:
  Date of enlistment: June 10, 1917.
  Aviation Schools: August 2, to December 8, 1917, Avord, Tours, Pau, G.D.E.
  Breveted: September 29, 1917 (Caudron).
  At the Front: Escadrille N. 153, December 11, 1917, to January 15, 1918.
  Escadrille N. 158, January 15 to March 16, 1918.
  Final Rank: Caporal.

SERVICE IN U.S. AVIATION:
  Commissioned First Lieutenant, March 3, 1918.
  At the Front: 103d Pursuit Squadron, May 31 to June 25, 1918.
  Killed by anti-aircraft fire: June 25, 1918 (Flanders).

Warren Tucker Hobbs

Hobbs came to France to drive an ambulance, but wanting more active service he obtained his release immediately upon arrival overseas, and volunteered in the Lafayette Flying Corps. In America he had won fame as an athlete, and the qualities which served him on the track made him a fearless and skilful pilot.

On December 11 he joined the Escadrille N. 153 and served faithfully with that unit until his transfer to the American army, four months later. Hobbs was a man of great personal charm; his ready humour and constant desire to help others endeared him to his comrades, whose confidence he won by his courage and skill in combat. Shortly after his transfer, Hobbs was sent to the 103rd Pursuit Squadron, then operating in Flanders. At seven-thirty on the evening of June 25 he was flying alone—gaining altitude to join his patrol which had left the aerodrome a few minutes before him—over the desolate battle-fields to the southeast of Ypres. Far below and to the north a German anti-aircraft gunner mechanically sighted on the lonely Spad and pulled the lanyard, little dreaming that of all his shells this one was destined to find its mark. Seconds passed—suddenly an angry black puff sprang out close beside the distant plane, which veered and fell flaming in the British lines. Hobbs was buried with full military honours by the British. He lies in worthy company, in one of the quiet cemeteries which consecrate the countryside of Flanders.

SERVICE RECORD

ROBERT B. HOEBER, Nutley, New Jersey.

SERVICE IN FRENCH AVIATION:
Date of enlistment: July 10, 1917.
Aviation Schools: July 10 to December 15, 1917, Avord, Tours, Pau, G.D.E.
Breveted: October 20, 1917 (Caudron).
At the Front: Escadrille Spad 103, December 19, 1917, to Armistice.
Final Rank: Sergent.

DECORATIONS:
Croix de Guerre, with Palm.

CITATIONS

Le 21 juin, 1918
1ʳᵉ ARMÉE, ÉTAT-MAJOR.
Le Général Commandant la 1ʳᵉ Armée cite à l'Ordre de l'Armée:

HOEBER, ROBERT, Mˡᵉ 46607, Sergent du 1ᵉʳ Régiment Étranger, Pilote à l'Escadrille 103

Citoyen américain, pilote de chasse remarquable, joignant à de brillantes qualités de pilotage un courage admirable. Le 2 juin, 1918, à la suite d'un dur combat, a abattu un monoplace ennemi.

(*Signé*) DEBENEY

Robert B. Hoeber

In the aviation schools, Hoeber made an excellent record. In December, 1917, he was sent to the Escadrille Spad 103, of which Fonck, the greatest of French aces, was a member. Hoeber, together with Baylies, Parsons, and Brown, saw service in the most active sectors of the Front, for their *groupe*, *Les Cigognes*, was usually sent to combat the crack German "circuses."

Hoeber took part in many fights, often patrolling with Fonck, whose skill and marvellous eyesight he greatly admired. During the summer of 1918, he shot down one German plane, officially confirmed, and brought down, far beyond the lines, several others which were never counted.

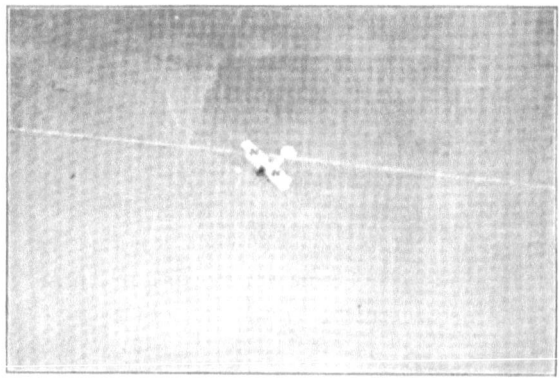

AN ALBATROSS

In March, 1918, when his squadron had been driven from the neighbourhood of Montdidier by the German advance, and had taken refuge at Le Plessis-Belleville, he had an experience of unusual interest. One morning, the commanding officer sent an orderly with an urgent call for an American pilot. Hoeber responded at once and the captain entrusted him with the mission. It appeared that the French had only vague and untrustworthy information regarding the location of the lines in the Montdidier district, and for that reason the *commandant* desired to send an American to get information from the British at Amiens. The weather was very bad, with clouds at three hundred feet and streamers of mist beneath the clouds, but Hoeber made the trip, landed at the British aerodrome, and got all the desired information. While returning he lost his way and did not realise that he was some miles in German territory until a patrol of five Albatross suddenly attacked him. The ensuing combat was bitter, but after he had

had his machine nearly shot to pieces, Hoeber saw that his only hope of escape, with his valuable dispatches, was through the clouds.... He pulled up, lost the Germans in the mist, and finally came out in the clear sunlight above. Not quite sure of his direction, he steered by the sun, and when he finally came in sight of the earth, found himself near one of the Channel ports. As his gasoline was low and the machine in no fit condition to fly, Hoeber landed, had luncheon with the general commanding the R.A.F., borrowed a motorcar and returned to Plessis. His machine never flew again.

SERVICE RECORD

DABNEY D. HORTON, Paris, France.

SERVICE IN FRENCH AVIATION:
 Date of enlistment: August 16, 1916.
 Aviation Schools: August 16, 1916, to July 10, 1917, Buc, Juvisy, Avord, Pau, G.D.E.
 Breveted: March 17, 1917 (Caudron).
 At the Front: Escadrille C. 17, July 13, 1917, to January 5, 1918.
  Escadrille Sop. 255, January 5 to February 18, 1918.
  Escadrille Spad 75, September 15, 1918, to Armistice.
Final Rank: Sergent.

DECORATIONS:
 Croix de Guerre, with Star.

Dabney D. Horton

In the autumn of 1916, Dabney Horton was one of the fifteen or twenty American student-pilots making up the *groupe d'entrainement* of the Lafayette Flying Corps at Buc. The Americans lived in the same barracks with their French comrades, enjoying an intimacy of companionship with them, which was the especial privilege of the early volunteers. In the evenings, when flying for the day was over, everyone went for dinner to M. Ciret's in the village. There, in a tiny room adjoining the *grande salle à manger*, filled with savoury odours and fledgling birdmen, they passed the evenings living in the future, eager for the time when they should go to the Front. That old crowd is now widely scattered. Many of them are dead. Others were spared in some miraculous way and served at the Front until the end of the war. Dabney Horton is among these fortunate few. He remained in French uniform throughout his seventeen months of active service. He piloted Caudrons (G. 4) and Sopwiths in French reconnaissance and bombardment squadrons, doing routine duty of the most dangerous but least spectacular kind.

M CIRET

Photography, reconnaissance artillery *réglage*, trench-strafing,—he has had an enviable share in all kinds of aerial missions, and later became a combat pilot in Spad 75. Between times he wrote verse about his adventures and few men better knew from actual experience of:

The weakened wire,
The tiny bullet of flying fire,
The treacherous wing that would buckle or break—

To quote from one of his own poems.

He knew the joy and the terror of combat from two points of view, the actual and imaginative. But the truest thing one can say of him, was that he undertook a difficult and hazardous job and stuck at it until it was finished.

SERVICE RECORD

RONALD WOOD HOSKIER, South Orange, New Jersey.

PREVIOUS SERVICE: American Ambulance, 1916.

SERVICE IN FRENCH AVIATION:
Date of enlistment: April 5, 1916.
Aviation Schools: May 12 to December 8, 1916, Buc, Avord, Cazeaux, G.D.E.
Breveted: August 13, 1916 (Blériot).
At the Front: Escadrille Lafayette, December 11, 1916, to April 23, 1917.
Final Rank: Sergent.
Killed in combat: April 23, 1917, near Saint-Quentin.

DECORATIONS:
Croix de Guerre, with Palm.

CITATION

Le 1 mai, 1917

Le Général Franchet d'Esperey, Commandant, le G.A.N., cite à l'Ordre de l'Armée:

HOSKIER, RONALD WOOD, Sergent à l'Escadrille N. 124

Citoyen américain engagé au service de la France. Véritable âme d'élite pour sa bravoure et son esprit de sacrifice. Est tombé le 23 avril, 1917, après une héroique défense dans un combat contre trois appareils ennemis.

Ronald Wood Hoskier

Shortly after Ronald Hoskier's transfer from the Ambulance Service to French Aviation, one of his American comrades, in training with him at the Blériot School at Buc, wrote the following letter

> One of our new recruits is Ronald Hoskier whom you may know, for he has been in the American Ambulance Service. He has made a deep impression upon me, and upon the other men as well. His fine, manly face is a clear index of his character, and his eyes are so fearless and honest that one knows with absolute certainty that he is a man to be trusted in any sort of emergency. If all of the later men in the Franco-American Corps are of Hoskier's type, we shall be certain of making a splendid showing at the Front.

This is typical of the high regard in which Ronald Hoskier was held by his comrades in France. Like most young Americans, he had a keen love of adventure, and the life of an airman at the Front gave an outlet which he welcomed. But love of adventure alone would never have prompted him to enlist. His enthusiasm for the cause of France was deep and sincere. He was only twenty, and had a boy's clearness of perception of the issues involved in the war. And so he gave himself without hesitation, and lived only for the time when he should be sent on active duty.

He finished his training in the early winter and was sent to the Escadrille Lafayette when it was operating from the aerodrome at Cachy, on the Somme front. Here he had the privilege of association with

Lieutenant de Laage de Meux, who typified all that is finest in French character. Hoskier found him his ideal Frenchman and lost no opportunity to prove to him his own high devotion to the Allied cause. Paul Rockwell who was in close touch with the Lafayette Squadron wrote of him at this time:

> From the day of his departure for the Front, every time I have met one of the pilots or have received news from the Escadrille Lafayette, Hoskier has been mentioned as one of the most active members of the unit. Since his arrival, the Squadron has not made a single sortie in which he has not taken part. He had innumerable combats and I have heard so much of these that I am always afraid of receiving the news that he has been killed.

It is a common saying among airmen, one too often borne out by facts, that the finest men are the first to go. And so it happened that Ronald Hoskier, one of the men who could least be spared from the Squadron, met his death but four months after joining it. On April 23, 1917, he made his last flight. At that time the Escadrille Lafayette was equipped with Nieuports and Spads, the single-seater *avions de chasse* in use in all French combat squadrons. In addition there was one two-seater Morane Parasol, a monoplane which was often flown by members of the squadron, with Caporal Dressy, the orderly of Lieutenant de Laage de Meux, as machine-gunner in the rear seat. Hoskier made his last patrol in this machine. The following account of his death is taken from a letter written by one of his comrades:

> Three of our finest men lost in one month! The squadron appears to be followed in these days by persistent ill-fortune. This time it is Ronald Hoskier who has been called—one of the best men I have ever known. He was flying a Morane Parasol, and had with him Jean Dressy, a splendid fellow, the old machine-gunner of Lieutenant de Laage. Hoskier went on a reconnaissance accompanied by Thaw, Haviland, and Willis. There were heavy clouds at 2000 metres, so they flew just beneath them. All at once they met an enemy patrol of four or five planes, and a combat began which continued until the Germans disappeared in the clouds. At the same time our *groupe* entered the mist and all of us became separated. None of us ever saw Hoskier or Dressy alive again, but we learned what happened later, from the balloon observers.

Evidently Hoskier saw a German beneath him, and apparently

THE REMAINS OF HOSKIER'S MACHINE

THE FUNERAL OF HOSKIER AND DRESSY

alone. He dove on him, and at the same instant several other enemy machines appeared. They encircled him and opened fire. He hadn't a chance. Suddenly his Morane was seen to dive straight down, full motor. The wings folded up and that was the end. Poor Dressy was thrown clear of the machine in the fall. It is some comfort to us that both men fell within our lines. Their bodies were brought to Ham and buried here, with full military honours, close to little Genêt.

MAJOR HUFFER AT VILLENEUVE

SERVICE RECORD

JEAN HUFFER, Paris, France.

SERVICE IN FRENCH AVIATION:
Date of enlistment: September 28, 1915.
Aviation Schools: January 1 to April 10, 1916, Avord, Cazeaux, Pau.
At the Front: Escadrille N. 95, April 1, 1916.
Escadrille N. 62, June 16, 1916, to March 15, 1917
Escadrille F. 36, July 13 to September 14, 1917.
Escadrille Spad 62, October 4, 1917, to February 18, 1918.
Final Rank: Sous-Lieutenant.

SERVICE IN U.S. AVIATION:
Commissioned Major: November 7, 1917.
At the Front: C.O. 94th Pursuit Squadron, March 17 to June 7, 1918.
Assistant Operations Officer, June 7 to July 25, 1918.
C.O. 93d Pursuit Squadron, July 25, 1918, to Armistice.

DECORATIONS:
Médaille Militaire.
Croix de Guerre, with three Palms and two Stars.

CITATIONS

VIe ARMÉE.   6 *novembre,* 1916
Citation à l'Ordre de l'Aéronautique :

Excellent pilote. Toujours volontaire pour les missions les plus périlleuses. Le 5 novembre, 1916, a fait une longue reconnaissance au-dessus des lignes ennemies, volant pendant plus de deux heures au milieu d'une très forte tempête.

7 *décembre,* 1916
Citation à l'Ordre de l'Armée (VIe):

Dégagé de toute obligation militaire, s'est engagé pour la durée de la guerre. Pilote remarquable d'avions rapides. Modèle de sang-froid et d'allant; n'a cessé de se distinguer au cours de la bataille de la Somme.

Accomplisseur de très nombreuses missions a longue portée. A rapporté chaque fois des documents précieux. Les jours de mauvais temps, a volé dans la tempête au ras du sol au-dessus des lignes ennemies, jusqu'à ce qu'il ait obtenu les renseignements demandés.

Le 24 septembre est rentré avec un appareil criblé de balles.

Le 10 octobre, chargé d'une mission très importante, s'est heurté à un barrage d'avions ennemis, en a abattu un, en a mis un deuxième en fuite. Le groupe d'avions qui devait le protéger s'étant dispersé au cours du combat, n'a pas hésité à pénétrer seul très loin dans les lignes ennemies pour accomplir sa mission et a rapporté d'importants renseignements.

Médaille Militaire:

Ordre N° 4269 "D" du 6 mars, 1917, comportant attribution de la Croix de Guerre avec palme.

Engagé volontaire pour la durée de la guerre, s'est distingué comme pilote pars on adresse, son énergie, son audace, et son sang-froid; a accompli dans des conditions particulièrement difficiles de très nombreuses missions au cours desquelles il a abattu deux avions ennemis. Déjà deux fois cité à l'Ordre.

Citation à l'Ordre de la VIe Armée: *Ordre N°* 45130, *mars*, 1916

Excellent pilote, le 17 mars, 1916, a abattu son troisième avion ennemi.

Le 21 *juin*, 1917

Le Lieutenant Colonel Charrez, Commt. le 1er Groupement A.L.V.F. (Détachement Italie) cite à l'Ordre du Groupement (Ordre du Régiment) l'Escadrille Espinasse appelée apporter son concours aux groupes de la R.G.A.L. détachée en Italie (mai-juin, 1917); s'est particulièrement distinguée dans toutes les missions qui lui ont été confiées.

Sous le commandement éclairé et intrépide de son Chef, Le Capitaine de Fontenilliat, par les brillantes et audacieuses reconnaissances de ses énergiques pilotes et observateurs,

Sous-Lieutenant HUFFER, JEAN

qui ont mis l'ennemi en fuite partout où ils l'ont recontré.

Par la prise de nombreuses photographies des régions montagneuses à battre, par les réglages précis exécutés dans le Trentin au prix de multiples difficultés, cette remarquable escadrille a suscité chez nos alliés l'admiration la plus vive et fait le plus grand honneur au Pays.

Jean Huffer

Enlisting in the Foreign Legion on September 28, 191 5, Huffer was sent at once to the aviation school at Pau, and after training at Pau, Cazeaux, and Avord was sent to the Fronton April 1, 1916. The story of his service in French Aviation is partially told in the text of his army citations. He served in both combat and reconnaissance squadrons on the Western Front and in Italy. After receiving his commission as Major in the United States Air Service he was placed on duty at Villeneuve, where he waited for two months until the first American Pursuit Squadron, the 94th, was ready for active duty. He was made Commanding Officer of the 94th on March 17, 1918, and remained with this unit during its first two months of active duty at the Front. He then became Assistant Operations Officer at Headquarters, First Air Depot, and afterward Commanding Officer of the 93rd Pursuit Squadron, which position he held until the close of the war.

SERVICE RECORD

DANIEL ELLIOTT HUGER, New York City.

SERVICE IN FRENCH AVIATION:
Date of enlistment: January 26, 1917.
Aviation Schools: February 3 to August, 1917, Avord, Pau, G.D.E.
Breveted: June 26, 1917 (Caudron).
Final Rank: Caporal.

SERVICE IN U.S. NAVAL AVIATION:
Commissioned Ensign: March 13, 1918.
In training at Moutchic-Lacanau (France) and Lake Bolsena (Italy).
At the Front: U.S.N.A.S., Porto Corsini, Italy.

Daniel Elliott Huger

Huger began his training in French Aviation early in the winter of 1917. The weather was abominable—cold and raw and wet—and as a result the Avord hospital was filled with ailing aviators, some with pneumonia, some with bronchitis or *grippe*. The men still on duty envied the men who were ill enough to be in bed, for it rained incessantly and flying was almost at a standstill. Huger was one of the men hardest hit by bronchitis, for he did not fully recover from it for more than a year. In August, 1917, while at G.D.E. awaiting assignment to a squadron at the Front, he came down with a second attack, and was compelled to take a long convalescence in the south of France. When again ready for duty, most of the Lafayette Flying Corps men had transferred to the United States Service. Therefore Huger secured his release from French Aviation and enlisted in the U.S.N.A.S. on March 13, 1918.

BOLSENA, ITALY

He trained on flying boats at Moutchic-Lacanau and was sent to Italy in June for further training on Italian machines. On the day before he was to be sent on active duty he went out for final target practice, over Lake Bolsena. When he started to pull out of a dive about twenty feet above the lake, an ammunition magazine fell from a shelf in front of him and became lodged in the controls. He struck the water at terrific speed and would have been drowned had it not been for his life-belt. He was badly injured and spent nearly three months in the U.S. Naval Hospital at Genoa.

Upon his recovery he was sent to the U.S. Naval Air Station at

Porto Corsini, and a few days after his arrival there the Armistice was signed. In aviation one's opportunity for service is largely a matter of chance. Both in France and in Italy, Huger played in continual hard luck. He had far more than his share of it which he accepted with sportsmanlike spirit.

SERVICE RECORD

EARL W. HUGHES, Detroit, Michigan.

SERVICE IN FRENCH AVIATION:
Date of enlistment: June 13, 1917.
Aviation Schools: August 5, 1917, to January 10, 1918, Avord, Tours, G.D.E.
Breveted: October 22, 1917 (Caudron).
At the Front: Escadrille Br. 66, January 14 to June 15, 1918.
Escadrille F. 110, October 6, 1918, to Armistice.
Final Rank: Sergent.

DECORATIONS:
Croix de Guerre, with Star.

Earl W. Hughes

So far as is known, Hughes is the only member of the Lafayette Flying Corps who has done night bombing work, and is the only one who has flown the two-motored Farman. He went to the Front on December 1, 1917, in Escadrille Br. 66. While piloting a Bréguet day bombing machine through the hard fighting in the region of Noyon and Montdidier, Hughes had some thrilling experiences; on one occasion especially, when the patrol leader did not see his objective, and Hughes, with one comrade, left the flight to drop his bombs. Separated from the others, the two started to fight their way back to the lines through a score of Albatross which came diving on them from all directions.

Hughes saw his comrade go down in flames, far beyond the lines, which he himself regained only through the intervention of a friendly cloud.

After a time he found that his health would no longer permit his flying at high altitudes, but instead of giving up aviation, he displayed a fine spirit by asking to be transferred to night bombardment, in which branch of the service he made many thrilling raids during the last months of the war.

SERVICE RECORD

SERENO THORP JACOB, Westport, Connecticut.

PREVIOUS SERVICE: American Ambulance, 1916–17.

SERVICE IN FRENCH AVIATION:
Date of enlistment: March 20, 1917.
Aviation Schools: April 19 to December 24, 1917, Avord, Tours, Pau, G.D.E
Breveted: October 21, 1917 (Caudron).
At the Front: Escadrille N. 157, December 26, 1917, to September 8, 1918.
Final Rank: Sergent.

SERVICE IN U.S. AVIATION:
Commissioned First Lieutenant, September 8, 1918.

CITATION

DECORATIONS:
Croix de Guerre, with Palm.

IVe ARMÉE, ETAT-MAJOR.   Le 25 avril, 1913

JACOB, SERENO, Sergent au 1er Régiment Étranger, M^{le} 12115, attaché à l'Escadrille 157 (sujet américain)

Pilote adroit et audacieux; entrainant une camarade de patrouille est allé incendier un ballon d'observation ennemi malgré une patrouille de cinq Albatros auxquels les deux pilotes ont du livrer un sévère combat avant de régagner les lignes françaises.

Sereno Thorp Jacob

Jacob was already a veteran of the Ambulance Service when he arrived at Tours as an *élève pilote*. He went through Tours, Avord, and Pau without an accident, and joined the Escadrille N. 157 at Belfort. The Squadron was still equipped with the old type 27 Nieuports, and flying this machine, Jacob had many combats and succeeded in burning a German kite balloon.

Most pilots are glad of an occasional rest from flying, but Jacob, according to his comrades, was always *gonflé*—three patrols a day were nothing out of the ordinary for him. The habits of the local Boches formed a study of never-failing interest; it was his delight to lie in wait for the wary Rumpler which so often made its photographic reconnaissance at noon, heralded by a tracery of white shrapnel puffs across the sky. Though he has three official victories to his credit, Jacob has had bad luck in getting confirmations, and among the chalky hills of the Champagne, over which he flew during the attacks of 1918, there are without doubt several fast-disappearing heaps of wreckage which are rightfully his.

SERVICE RECORD

CHARLES CHOUTEAU JOHNSON, St. Louis, Missouri.

PREVIOUS SERVICE: American Ambulance, 1915.

SERVICE IN FRENCH AVIATION:
Date of enlistment: September 2, 1915.
Aviation Schools: September, 1915, to February, 1916, Pau, Ambérieu.
Breveted: January 2, 1916 (Blériot).
Camp retranché de Paris with Escadrille V. 97, February and March, 1916.
R.G.A., April 21 to May 26, 1916.
At the Front: Escadrille Lafayette, May 29, 1916, to October 11, 1917.

Final Rank: *Adjudant.*
Moniteur attached to French Aviation at Second American A.I.C., Tours, November, 1917, to January, 1918.

SERVICE IN U.S. AVIATION:
Commissioned First Lieutenant.
Promoted Captain.
Instructor at Tours.

DECORATIONS:
Croix de Guerre, with Palm.

CITATION

G.A.N., ÉTAT-MAJOR.   *Le* 15 *mai,* 1917

Le Général Franchet-d'Esperey, Commandant 1ᵉ G.A.N., cite à l'Ordre de l'Armée:
    JOHNSON, CHARLES C., Sergent à l'Escadrille N. 124 (N.M. 11627)
    Citoyen américain engagé pour la durée de la guerre. Bon pilote; a rendu à Verdun et sur la Somme d'excellents services à son escadrille. Le 26 avril a attaqué un avion ennemi et l'a abattu.

Charles Chouteau Johnson

Chouteau Johnson has forgotten more Lafayette history than most of us ever knew; for he joined the original Squadron on May 29, 1916, a little more than a month after it was organised for work at the Front. He was a contemporary of Thaw and Lufbery, Victor Chapman, Norman Prince, Kiffin Rockwell, and James McConnell. Many an afternoon of leave in Paris he has spent at the old Chatham rendezvous, surrounded by a flock of fledgling birdmen, entertaining them with stories of the old days when these men first began making history for the corps. Chouteau was always a favourite with the *élèves-pilotes*, who often came to Paris for weekend leave in the hope of finding him there. He was a sort of minor deity to all of the younger men, but a very genial and accessible one with a fund of narrative almost Homeric in its scope and richness.

He liked best, of course, to tell of the adventures of other men. But he himself had a wide experience during the war, first as an ambulance driver and then as an airman. He has flown with N. 124 over the Vosges; at Verdun when the squadron occupied the field on the heights overlooking Bar-le-Duc; from the Chaudun aerodrome south of Soissons; at Cachy and at Ham, on the Somme; at Senard, in the rolling wooded country at the foot of the Argonne Forest. Chouteau could probably make from memory a relief map of the Western Front, marking in all of the aerodromes and the best landing-sites, in case of a *panne de moteur*. Some of these possible landing-fields he chose by experimenting with impossible ones, and others he had the luck to find at the first try; for he had more than his share of motor trouble during his seventeen months at the Front.

He gained his first and last official victory, on April 26, 1917, during a weird and exciting battle among the clouds. A patrol of Lafayette men led by Lieutenant Thaw met an Albatross formation almost directly over the lines, in the most forlorn and desolate region of the Somme battle-fields. The two patrols were at the same height, and with motors wide open both started evenly in the race for the altitude advantage.

The sky was filled with heaped-up masses of April cloud which made it impossible for the machines to keep together. The opposing formations were broken up, and instead of a general battle with the odds about even, there was a series of battles, single machines and groups of two or three meeting suddenly in narrow canons of clear azure, barely avoiding collisions, firing at point-blank, and then disappearing with equal suddenness through towering cliffs of vapour to meet again a moment later, in some distant pool of blue sky. It was like a frontier affair in early Western days, with clouds instead of rocks for cover, and machine guns instead of Winchesters for weapons. Johnson ambushed one of the Albatross and riddled it before the pilot was able to escape. Willis Haviland shot down another. Both victories were confirmed before the patrol had returned to the aerodrome.

After nearly a year and a half of patrol work at the Front, Johnson felt the need of relaxation. He had seen nearly all of his old comrades killed. With the exception of William Thaw, he has probably attended more funeral ceremonies for aviators than any other man in the Lafayette Corps.

A very little of that sort of duty is far more than enough, and but few men could have performed it with Chouteau's stoicism. Finally, having been offered a post as flying instructor at the American Aviation School at Tours, he decided to accept it. He was commissioned First Lieutenant in the United States Army, and in the early summer of 1918, raised to the rank of Captain and sent on duty to the United States.

SERVICE RECORD

HARRY F. JOHNSON, South Bethlehem, Pennsylvania.

SERVICE IN FRENCH AVIATION:
Date of enlistment: June 25, 1917.
Aviation Schools: August 1 to December 10, 1917, Avord, Tours, Pau, G.D.E.
Brevetted: October 1, 1917 (Caudron).
At the Front: Escadrille N. 85, December 12, 1917, to January 9, 1918.
Escadrille N. 98, January 9 to February 16, 1918.
Final Rank: Caporal.
Wounded in combat: January 20, 1918.

SERVICE IN U.S. AVIATION:
Commissioned First Lieutenant: April 12, 1918.
At the Front: Attached to the French Squadron Spad 168, April 12 to May 21, 1918.
Killed in line of duty: May 21, 1918.

DECORATIONS:
Médaille Militaire.
Croix de Guerre, with Palm.

CITATION

Au G.Q.G., le 3 février, 1918

La Médaille Militaire a été conférée au

Caporal JOHNSON, HARRY (active), 1er Groupe d'Aviation, Pilote à l'Escadrille N. 98

De nationalité étrangère, s'est engagé dans l'Armée Française et a été désigné sur sa demande pour servir dans l'aviation. Quoique arrivé depuis peu sur le front, comme pilote dans une escadrille de chasse, s'est déjà fait remarquer par son audace et son entrain. Le 20 janvier, 1918, attaqué par 4 avions ennemis, s'est vaillamment défendu. Grièvement blessé au cours du combat, a eu l'énergie de ramener son appareil dans nos lignes.

La présente nomination comporte l'attribution de la Croix de Guerre avec Palme.

Le Général Commandant en Chef, P.O. le Major-Général

(Signé)   P. ANTHOINE

Harry F. Johnson

Johnson rapidly finished the courses at Tours, Avord, and Pau, and on December 12, 1917, was sent to the Front, first to the N. 85 and later to the N. 98. On January 20, 1918, in a plucky fight against heavy odds, he was shot through the stomach, and exhibited fine courage and coolness by landing his machine undamaged at a French hospital. For this feat he was awarded the *Croix de Guerre* and the *Médaille Militaire*. During his convalescence he was commissioned First Lieutenant in the United States Air Service, and on April 12 he returned to the Front, this time to the Spad 168.

On May 21, at 10.30 in the morning, Johnson was on patrol with Cassady and several others, flying at 4500 metres well into the German lines before Suippes. Cassady was leading the formation, and suddenly he saw Johnson's machine range alongside and give the signal which meant motor trouble. The next moment the Spad banked and planed out of sight toward the lines. His comrades never again saw Johnson alive.

FUNERAL OF HARRY F. JOHNSON

A few moments later some French soldiers in the first-line trenches were astonished to see a Spad about to land, the pilot waving to them to get out of the way. It was Johnson. His machine struck in the midst of a great thicket of barbed wire which sheared off the landing-gear and caused the Spad to turn over end for end. Johnson was thrown out and suffered a fracture of the spine. He never regained consciousness and died a few moments later. Beside Phelps Collins, in the quiet cemetery of Mont Frenet, Johnson sleeps in the soil of France, the soil he died to defend.

SERVICE RECORD

ARCHIBALD JOHNSTON, Pittsburgh, Pennsylvania.

PREVIOUS SERVICE: American Ambulance, 1916.

SERVICE IN FRENCH AVIATION:
  Date of enlistment: July 28, 1916.
  Aviation Schools: August 15, 1916, to April 24, 1917, Buc, Juvisy, Avord, Pau, G.D.E.
  Breveted: January 25, 1917 (Caudron).
  At the Front: Escadrille Spad 83, April 27 to September 12, 1918.
  Final Rank: Sergent.

SERVICE IN U.S. AVIATION:
  Commissioned Captain: December 23, 1917.
  Chief Instructor Aerial Gunnery School, Gerstner Field, Louisiana, and Don Field, Florida.
  Adviser on compilation of textbooks, Wilbur Wright Field, Dayton, Ohio.

DECORATIONS:
  Croix de Guerre, with Palm and Star.

CITATION

Le 18 *octobre,* 1917

Le Chef d'État-Major de la 2ᵐᵉ Armée cite à l'Ordre de l' Aéronautique:

JOHNSTON, ARCHIBALD, Mˡᵉ 11844, Sergent Pilote à l'Escadrille N. 83

Sujet américain, après avoir servi 3 mois dans la Section Sanitaire Américaine N° 3, sur le front de Verdun, s'est ensuite engagé dans l'aviation. Dès son arrivée à l'Escadrille a été volontaire pour toutes les missions et a su faire honneur à son pays en donnant à ses camarades français l'exemple de courage et de l'abnégation.

Archibald Johnston

A happy faculty for getting out of trouble is largely responsible for Archibald Johnston's long and useful career in French and American Aviation. It was a dependable faculty too. It never failed him at critical moments, and there were many of these, both while in training and at the Front. His first real difficulties began at Buc when he had almost finished his brevet flights. There remained but a single long voyage and his altitude test. The weather was abominable, and after vainly waiting for a decent day, he slipped into Paris, as many another man had done, for an afternoon on the *boulevards*. He had never any luck, however, and this occasion was no exception. The weather cleared about two hours after he had left camp. Flying recommenced and before he could return, his absence was noted.

For this breach of discipline he was proposed by the *commandant* for *radiation* from the Air Service, and sent to Dijon for that purpose. After much agonized explaining, he softened the heart of the *commandant* at Dijon who sent him to Juvisy to complete his training. This was during the bitterly cold winter of 1916-17, when flying in all of the aviation schools of northern France was almost at a standstill. Johnston made his altitude test in the worst of it. Twice he came down with a frozen oil pump; the third time, a tail mast on his G. 3 gave way, and the fourth he had a *panne d'essence*. He succeeded at his fifth attempt.

His career at the Front was marked by much hard luck and the same dogged persistency in overcoming it. On May 30, 1917, shortly after his arrival there, he had the worst of an argument with a German, spun a *vrille* half a mile long, and landed in the French lines with a badly damaged radiator. He was next heard of at Verdun, where he and a French flying partner of his squadron gained high praise for a series of raids far into enemy territory, where they disorganised the German motor transport service and machine-gunned troop columns on the roads.

Throughout the war he was the only American pilot in his Squadron Spad 83. He was well liked by his French comrades, and like many other volunteers, did not transfer to the United States Service without many regrets.

His service with the French had well qualified him to be an instructor in aerial gunnery, and after receiving his commission in the U.S.A.S. he was on duty in this capacity at Gerstner Field, Louisiana, and at Don Field, Florida. At the close of the war he was adviser on the compilation of textbooks at Wilbur Wright Field, Dayton, Ohio.

SERVICE RECORD

CHARLES MAURY JONES, Redbank, New Jersey.

SERVICE IN FRENCH AVIATION:
Date of enlistment: March 26, 1917.
Aviation Schools: April 1 to August 12, 1917, Avord, Pau, G.D.E.
Breveted: June 16, 1917 (Blériot).
At the Front: Escadrille Spad 75, August 15, 1917, to January 31, 1918.
Final Rank: Sergent.

SERVICE IN U.S. AVIATION:
Commissioned First Lieutenant: January, 1918.
Promoted Captain: October 5, 1918.
At the Front: 103d Pursuit Squadron, January 22 to June 8, 1918. 13th Pursuit Squadron, June 12 to August 13, 1918. C.O. 28th Pursuit Squadron August 13, 1918, to Armistice.

DECORATIONS:
Croix de Guerre, with Star.

CITATION

G.Q.G., État-Major.   Le 17 novembre, 1918

M. JONES, MAURY, M^le 11550, Lieutenant, Pilote à l'Escadrille Américaine 103

Excellent chef de patrouille. A livré en juin, 1918, de nombreux combats loin dans les lignes ennemies, mettant chaque fois l'ennemi en fuite.

Charles Maury Jones

When Maury Jones first came to the Blériot Division of the *École Militaire* at Avord, French *moniteurs* looked him over sceptically. All of them, from the *Chef de Piste* to the penguin *moniteurs*, gave expression to their despair, one to the other, in those little exclamations which are so eloquent in French. "*Ah! Non!*" "*Mais il est impossible, celuilà!*" and the like. It was not that Jones was thought poor material. But there was too much of him. There wasn't a Blériot in the entire school large enough to fit him. How he ever managed to crowd into a penguin no one but himself knows; and it was not until after his fourth try that he found a *brevet* machine capable of flying with him for an hour at 2000 metres.

MAURY JONES AND CHARLES BIDDLE
AT AVORD—PENGUIN CLASS

Despite his handicap of size, he finished his training in quick time and was sent to the French Escadrille Spad 73. He served at the Front with this squadron until he received his transfer to the U.S.A.S., and was then sent to the 103rd Aero Squadron, the old Escadrille Lafayette, located at La Ferme de la Noblette on the Champagne Front. He took part here in many an historic patrol. He carried no personal insignia on his Spad. It wasn't necessary. He could always be recognised in the air by the height of his head above his windshield. He offered an ample target to enemy *chasse-pilotes*, but the Fates have been mighty kind to Maury. He flew at the Front for more than a year without stopping a bullet, which is an unusual record for a combat pilot. Advanced in rank to a captaincy, he was commanding the 28th Pursuit Squadron at the end of the war.

SERVICE RECORD

CHARLES MAURY JONES, Redbank, New Jersey.

SERVICE IN FRENCH AVIATION:
Date of enlistment: March 26, 1917.
Aviation Schools: April 1 to August 12, 1917.
Avord, Pau, G.D.E.
Breveted: June 16, 1917 (Blériot).
At the Front: Escadrille Spad 73, August 15, 1917, to January 21, 1918.
Final Rank: Sergent.

SERVICE RECORD

HENRY SWEET JONES, Harford, Pennsylvania.

PREVIOUS SERVICE: American Ambulance, 1916.

SERVICE IN FRENCH AVIATION:
Date of enlistment: October 27, 1916.
Aviation Schools: November 28, 1916, to May 10, 1917, Buc, Étampes, Avord, Pau, G.D.E.
Breveted: March 16, 1917 (Maurice Farman).
At the Front: Escadrille Lafayette, May 12, 1917, to February 18, 1918.
Final Rank: Sergent.

SERVICE IN U.S. AVIATION:
Commissioned First Lieutenant: January, 1918.
At the Front: 103d Pursuit Squadron, February 18 to June 1, 1918.
On duty in U.S.A. as Instructor and Experimental Tester, July 1, 1918, until Armistice.

DECORATIONS:
Croix de Guerre, with two Stars.

CITATIONS

Le 14 janvier, 1918
IVe ARMÉE, ÉTAT-MAJOR.
Le Chef d'État-Major de la IVe Armée cite à l'Ordre du Service Aéronautique:

JONES, HENRI, Sergent M^{le} 11969 de l'Escadrille Lafayette (Groupe de Combat 13)
Citoyen américain, engagé dans l'Aéronautique le 27 novembre, 1916. Très bon pilote de chasse, a fait preuve en maintes circonstances de beaucoup d'allant et de sang-froid. Le 1 octobre, 1917, attaqué par plusieurs monoplaces ennemis, est rentré avec son appareil très gravement endommagé. Le 31 octobre, a forcé un appareil ennemi à atterrir désemparé dans ses lignes.

Le Chef d'État-Major de la IVe Armée
PETTELATE

GRAND QUARTIER-GÉNÉRAL DES ARMÉES
DU NORD ET DU NORD-EST.   *Le 17 novembre*, 1918
Après approbation du Général Commandant en Chef les Forces expéditionnaires américaines en France, le Général Commandant en Chef les Armées Françaises du Nord et du Nord-Est cite à l'Ordre du Régiment:

M. JONES, HENRY S., Lieutenant, Pilote à l'Escadrille Américain 103

Excellent pilote qui a livré, en juin, 1918, de nombreux combats victorieux, à l'intérieur des lignes ennemies.

Le Général Commandant en Chef
PÉTAIN

Henry Sweet Jones

A week after his enlistment in the Lafayette Flying Corps, Henry Jones made an exhibition flight in a Blériot which became historic in the annals of the Buc School. For several days he had been making rolling sorties on the ground, tame sport for an *élève-pilote* eager to fly. Henry believed that he could fly, and so giving his six-cylinder Anzani "grasscutter" full gas he came sailing back across the field at about fifty metres altitude. In a two-minute flight he put a Blériot through manoeuvres which would have astonished Pégoud, the old master pilot of that craft.

But when he came down—O! Là! Là! There have been some magnificent crashes on the Buc field, but never a better one than his. He was then sent to the Farman School, and afterward, to the surprise of his old Blériot *moniteurs*, finished his training in a very brilliant manner on Nieuport and Spad.

During his first two months at the Front he spent seventy hours in combat patrols over the lines, an unusually good record even for an old pilot. Some of the best enemy *chasse* squadrons were operating on the sector then, and all the aces of the Imperial German Air Force—as he believed—sat on his tail at one time and another.

Nevertheless, he went blithely through his apprenticeship and the enemy anti-aircraft and machine-gun fire, gaining an experience in combat tactics which was of great value to him during a long period of service with Spad 124.

On rainy days, when life at the Front was a dull sort of business, he was always the liveliest of the crowd in the *popote*. He was never known to have the *cafard*, that "home-sickness-blues" disease, the almost universal plague among flying men in dull weather. Give him a last year's copy of the *Saturday Evening Post* and a bottle of *pinard*, and the world might wag as it would. When the *pinard* gave out he invented substitutes, the one which proved most nearly fatal being bay rum, olive oil, and vinegar.

He loved to hear the rain pattering on the tar-paper roof, and there were but few aviators of any experience to whom that sound was not often most welcome. *Temps aéronautique* it was called. It meant relaxation, and a brief release from the strain of combat patrols. But when the sky cleared again, Henry was always ready for work. He dodged A-A shells from Dunkirk to the Vosges, and at length in the summer of 1918 was sent on duty to the United States. He served as a flying instructor and experimental tester at Carlstrom Field, Arcadia, Florida, and elsewhere until after the close of the war.

SERVICE RECORD

DAVID E. JUDD, Brookline, Massachusetts.

SERVICE IN FRENCH AVIATION:
  Date of enlistment: June 3, 1917.
  Aviation Schools: June 30 to November 26, 1917, Avord, Pau, G.D.E.
  Breveted: October 1, 1917 (Caudron).
  At the Front: Escadrille Spad 73, December 1 to December 18, 1917.
      Escadrille Spad 3, December 18, 1917, to January 22, 1918.
  Final Rank: Sergent.

SERVICE IN U.S. NAVAL AVIATION:
  Commissioned Ensign, January 23, 1918.
  Promoted Lieutenant (Junior Grade).
  At the Front: U.S. Naval Air Station, Dunkirk.
      Attached to 218th Day Bombing Squadron, British R.A.F.
      Northern Bombing Group, U.S.N.A.S.
  On duty in America: September 22, 1918, to Armistice.

David E. Judd

It is a matter of regret that so little detailed information is obtainable regarding the Lafayette men who joined the navy. In bombing squadrons on the Front and piloting hydro-aeroplanes on the Channel and on the Adriatic Sea, they must have had many experiences which would be of interest in the records of the corps. Judd is one of the men concerning whose later service there is little information. Like Wellman and Ovington, he was trained on the double command Blériot, where he developed into an excellent pilot, and at Pau he earned the best of notes.

During the last month of his French service he was a member of the famous Escadrille Spad 3, of the *Cigognes groupe*. He then served at the U.S. Naval Air Station at Dunkirk, with the RAF Day Bombing Squadron No. 218, and with the Northern Bombing Group of the U.S. Navy. He was promoted from ensign to lieutenant, junior grade, and in September was sent to the United States for duty as instructor.

SERGENT JUDD (RIGHT)
AND ADJUDANT DE CURNIEU
AT AVORD

SERVICE RECORD

Hugo N. Kenyon, Peacedale, Rhode Island.

Previous Service: American Ambulance, 1916–17.

Service in French Aviation:
   Date of enlistment: July 5, 1917.
   Aviation Schools: July 19, 1917, to March, 1918, Avord, Juvisy, Pau, G.D.E.
   Breveted: October 16, 1917 (Caudron).
   Final Rank: Caporal.

Service in U.S. Aviation:
   Commissioned Second Lieutenant, April 26, 1918.
   Promoted First Lieutenant November 6, 1918.
   At the Front: 103d Pursuit Squadron, June 1, 1918, to Armistice.

Hugo N. Kenyon

Like many of the Lafayette men, Kenyon is a thorough-going cosmopolitan, the sort of man who is equally at home in Chili or Ceylon, and knows intimately all the prominent citizens of Tierra del Fuego. His adventurous and roving disposition brought him to Europe before our declaration of war, and after a term in the American Ambulance, he enlisted in the Lafayette Flying Corps in July, 1917. While at Pau, Kenyon's Nieuport caught fire at 3000 metres, and he displayed remarkable courage and coolness in landing safely and removing cushion and instruments before beating a retreat from the flames. On the Front, Kenyon's most exciting experiences have been with the 103rd Pursuit Squadron, where he did a great deal of hedge-hopping *chez les Boches* during the heavy fighting on the American sectors.

SERVICE RECORD

Charles W. Kerwood, Bryn Mawr, Pennsylvania.

Service in French Aviation:
   Date of enlistment: February 18, 1917.
   Aviation Schools: February 25 to November 18, 1917, Avord, G.D.E.
   Breveted: August 26, 1917 (Caudron).
   At the Front: Escadrille Br. 117, November 21, 1917, to March 31, 1918.
   Final Rank: Sergent.
   Prisoner in Germany: March 31, 1918, to Armistice. Wounded in attempting escape.

Decorations:
   Croix de Guerre, with Star.

CITATION

Le 26 avril, 1918
G.A.R., Aéronautique Militaire, Escadre 12.
Le Chef d'Escadron Vuillemin, Commandant l'Escadre de Bombardement N° 12, cite à l'Ordre de l'Escadre 12 les militaires dont les noms suivent:

Le Sergent Pilote Kerwood, Charles Wayne (active, Légion Étrangère), détaché à l'Escadrille 117 (G.B. 5)

Très bon pilote, audacieux et courageux. Citoyen américain, engagé volontaire dans la Légion. S'est souvent distingué au cours de missions difficiles, notamment dans la journée du 5 février, 1918, au cours d'une mission lointaine.

(Signé)   VUILLEMIN

Charles W. Kerwood

The most interesting narrative of the life of an American volunteer airman in the French Service which could be compiled would be a stenographic record of the casual conversations in messrooms and barracks of Charles Kerwood. Unfortunately his Boswells were all pilots or observers, and *trop fatigués* after patrol time to write up their diaries. The world is the loser thereby, for Kerwood had many strange adventures and a rare gift for telling of them amusingly.

BAER, PELTON, DE KRUIJFF, AND KERWOOD.
CAFÉ D'AVORD, APRIL, 1917

On March 31, 1918, he was reported killed in combat in the region of Montdidier, and there was deep sorrow throughout the entire Lafayette Corps. Lieutenant Manderson Lehr made the following report on the flight in which Kerwood was brought down:

> Three of us started out on a bombardment expedition. On account of the clouds, we were flying at 800 metres, when upon entering a cloud-bank we separated for fear of running into each other. When we came out of it we were far distant from each other. Again, just before we came to the German lines we entered another cloud. I came out first and looked round for the others, but could not see them, so went on alone to do

work assigned to me. I dropped down to 700 metres, and getting over my objective, bombarded the field. Then I went to the right and saw Kerwood in the distance. I immediately set out and caught up to him. On the way, still at 700 metres, I went through a cloud, and when I came out I saw four Boches come down on him from behind. I immediately became engaged in combat, and when I turned I saw Kerwood below me. He was at about 300 metres, *piquing* for the French lines. I could not see any German immediately upon him; he seemed to have his machine under control, but when I started to catch up to him he suddenly dropped. I think a luminous bullet must have struck him, but cannot ascertain whether he was wounded or forced to land on account of motor trouble. He always said that if he had to die he would like it to be in combat.

A few weeks later some of his friends, prisoners of war in Germany, passing through a civil prison in Landshut, Bavaria, saw the name "Charles Kerwood" scribbled all over the walls of a cell there. This was their first news that he had survived his combat, and was more welcome to them than their first Red Cross food parcels from Berne. While a prisoner he made one attempt to escape, and was shot by a camp guard. The wound healed and he came limping into Paris after the Armistice with the German bullet still in his leg.

Kerwood ought to have fifty-odd years ahead of him and as many annual reunions of the Lafayette Corps. There are some old pilots who will gather there chiefly to hear him tell again of that first memorable bombing raid of his, when, acting as observer and machine-gunner for Manderson Lehr, he dropped all of his bombs at once, and thus, according to his own version of the story, blew up single-handed a whole German village.

SERVICE RECORD

CHARLES M. KINSOLVING, Washington, D.C.

PREVIOUS SERVICE: American Ambulance, 1917.

SERVICE IN FRENCH AVIATION:
  Date of enlistment: June 13, 1917.
  Aviation Schools: July 19 to November 19, 1917, Avord, Tours, G.D.E.
  Breveted: September 25, 1917 (Caudron).
  At the Front: Escadrille Br. 117, November 21, 1917, to February 25, 1918.
  Final Rank: Sergent.

SERVICE IN U.S. AVIATION:
  Commissioned First Lieutenant; February 25, 1918.
  At the Front: Assigned to French Squadron Br. 117, February 25 to June 16, 1918.

At the Front: Assigned to French Squadron Br. 117, February 25 to June 16, 1918.
Instructor at American A.I.C. at Clermont-Ferrand, June 18 to September 28, 1918.
C.O. 163d Day Bombing Squadron, September 30, 1918, to Armistice.

Decorations:
Croix de Guerre, with Star.

CITATION

G.A.R., Aéronautique Militaire, Escadre 12. *Le 2 avril*, 1918

Le Chef d'Escadron Vuillemin, Commandant l'Escadre de Bombardement N° 12, cite à l'Ordre de l'Escadre les militaires dont les noms suivent: ...

Le 1er Lieutenant de l'Armée Américaine Kinsolving, Charles (active, Légion Étrangère), détaché à l'Escadrille 117 (G.B. 5)

Officier américain d'un sang-froid, d'un courage, et d'un allant exemplaires. Engagé volontaire dans la Légion le 17 juillet, 1917. A exécuté en peu de temps de nombreux bombardements dont plusieurs à grande distance.

(*Signé*)   Vuillemin

Charles M. Kinsolving

Kinsolving is one of the few pioneer Bréguet day bombardment pilots still alive, (at time of first publication), and is, incidentally, the only diplomat in the Lafayette Corps. He is equally at home in Washington, Philadelphia, or Brazil. Before enlisting in the Aviation, he had seen service in Section 4 of the American Ambulance. While training at Tours on Caudron he was placed in charge of the American *élèves*, and it is said that he ruled the boys with an iron hand. With his friend Joe Wilson, he went to Plessis-Belleville as an accredited performer on the complex and delicate *manettes* of the G. 4, and in November, 1917, he was assigned to the famous Escadrille Br. 117. While with this squadron, Kinsolving was awarded the *Croix de Guerre*.

To honour the occasion fittingly he exercised a little of his diplomatic skill, borrowed the squadron automobile, and gave his comrades a memorable dinner at a nearby Red Cross hospital. In February, 1918, Kinsolving transferred to the American Army, but continued to serve with his French squadron until June, when he was sent to Clermont-Ferrand as instructor. In September, after many requests, he succeeded in getting to the Front once more—this time as commander of the 163rd Day Bombardment Squadron, with which unit he served until the cessation of hostilities.

SERVICE RECORD

THEODORE DE KRUIJFF, New York City.

SERVICE IN FRENCH AVIATION:
Date of enlistment: March 20, 1917.
Aviation Schools: March 20 to December 4, 1917, Avord, Pau, Cazeaux, G.D.E.
Breveted: August 6, 1917 (Nieuport).
At the Front: Escadrille N. 158, December 6, 1917, to May 21, 1918.
Final Rank: Caporal.

SERVICE IN U.S. AVIATION:
Commissioned Second Lieutenant: May 21, 1918.
American Acceptance Park, Orly, June 6 to July 5, 1918.
American A.I.C. Romorantin, July 5 to November 1, 1918.
Died of pneumonia at Paris, November 6, 1918.

Theodore de Kruijff

Theodore de Kruijff was one of the few Americans who entered the French Aviation Service with previous flying experience. He was breveted on a Curtiss machine, in Buffalo, New York. While flying with a pupil at that place, his machine crashed to the ground, de Kruijff breaking his leg in the fall. On his recovery he continued flying at Newport News until January, 1917, when he came to France and volunteered in the Lafayette Corps. His injured leg gave him much trouble, but he completed his training and was sent with Rufus Rand to the Front to the N. 158, a French squadron.

Randall, Edgar, and Hobbs joined them shortly afterward, and the work of the five Americans won high praise from their French officers. After his transfer to the United States Air Service, de Kruijff was sent to the American Acceptance Park at Orly Field, just outside Paris, where he served as a ferry pilot. On November 6, 1918, he died of pneumonia at the American Military Hospital No. 1 at Paris.

SERVICE RECORD

GEORGE MARION KYLE, Los Angeles, California.

SERVICE IN FRENCH AVIATION:
Date of enlistment: June 27, 1917.
Aviation Schools: July 6 to December 24, 1917, Avord, G.D.E.
Breveted: October 17, 1917 (Caudron).
At the Front: Escadrille Br. 117, December 26, 1917, to February 18, 1918.
Final Rank: Caporal.

SERVICE IN U.S. AVIATION:
Commissioned First Lieutenant: February 19, 1918.
At the Front: Attached to French Squadron Br. 117, February 18 to July 1, 1918.

On duty as Instructor, American A.I.C., Clermont-Ferrand, July 1, 1918, to Armistice.

DECORATIONS:
  Croix de Guerre, with Star.

CITATION

Le 2 avril, 1918

G.A.R., AÉRONAUTIQUE MILITAIRE.
Le Chef d'Escadron Vuillemin, Commandant l'Escadre de Bombardement N° 12, cite à l'Ordre de l'Escadre les militaires dont les noms suivent: ...
Le 1er Lieutenant de l'Armée américaine KYLE, GEORGE MARION (active, Légion Étrangère), détaché à l'Escadrille 117 (G.B. 5)
  Officier américain d'un allant et d'un courage exemplaires. Dès son arrivée à l'escadrille a exécuté plusieurs bombardements de jours dans des circonstances difficiles. S'est particulièrement distingué le 5 février, 1918, au cours d'une expédition comportant le bombardement d'un objectif éloigné.

(*Signé*)   VUILLEMIN

George Marion Kyle

Single-Seater pilots are a clannish lot and apt to make light of other branches of Aviation, not realising the courage and skill of the day bombers, nor the long, intensive training they require. Sometimes when a flight of Bréguets, in beautiful wing-to-wing formation passes over a *chasse* aerodrome, the pilots glance upwards for a moment and murmur a careless compliment; but the fact is that, compared to day bombers, the single-seater men are mere beginners in the art of formation flying.

A BRÉGUET BOMBER

Kyle is one of the small group of Americans who went in for day bombing, a curiously alliterative crew as one runs over the names: Clapp, Kyle, Kerwood, Cotton, and Kinsolving. Ash and Lehr were also bombers, and they like Clapp have given their lives; all have given the best in them with a fine uniformity.

Kyle's first experiences of the Front were in Lorraine, where his squadron was making reprisal raids into Germany, operating with the British Independent Air Force. One of his most interesting *sorties* was a raid on Saarbrück in reply to the German bombardment of Paris on January 21, 1918. His group went over in three flights of ten each and dropped a total of 350 bombs on German territory. Kyle's squadron formed the rear guard. On the way over they could see swarms of German *chasse* planes, rising from their aerodromes to the attack. As the Bréguets were at 17,000 feet, the Germans were unable to rise to their level until the objective had been reached and the bombs dropped, but as they turned to regain the lines, Kyle saw the air thick with Albatross, among which the machines of Richtofen's group, with their red noses and decorated fuselages, were conspicuous. The return flight, over a distance of seventy kilometres must have been epic, though Kyle dismisses it with a simple statement that his squadron shot down three Boches and returned without the loss of a man.

On May 3, while bombing some German aerodromes, Kyle looked over the side of the *carlingue* and witnessed a wonderful single combat between a Spad and an Albatross,—a combat which ended in a spin and fatal crash for the enemy. As the Spad soared upwards victorious, Kyle recognised by the number and insignia on its side that it was Alan Nichols, his old comrade of the Ambulance, and in the aviation schools, who had shot down the German.

SERVICE RECORD

G. DE FREEST LARNER, Washington, D.C.

SERVICE IN FRENCH AVIATION:
  Date of enlistment: July 10, 1917.
  Aviation Schools: July 19 to December 1, 1917,
      Avord, Tours, Pau, G.D.E.
  Breveted: September 28, 1917 (Caudron).
  At the Front: Escadrille Spad 86, December 3,
      1917, to April 1, 1918.
  Final Rank: Caporal.

SERVICE IN U.S. AVIATION:
  Commissioned First Lieutenant: April 24, 1918.
  Promoted Captain: November 8, 1918.
  At the Front: Attached to the French Squadron
      Spad 86, April 24 to June 15,
      1918.
      Flight Commander, 103d Pursuit
      Squadron, June 16, 1918, to
      Armistice.

DECORATIONS:
  Distinguished Service Cross, with Bronze Oak Leaf.
  Croix de Guerre, with two Palms.

CITATIONS

6ᵉ Armée, État-Major.   *Le 1 avril, 1918*

M. Larner, G. de Freest, 1ᵉʳ Lieutenant de l'Armée américaine à l'Escadrille Spa. 86

Entré dans l'Aviation française comme engagé volontaire, y a toujours montré les plus belles qualités de pilote de chasse. Le ... a attaqué seul une patrouille de 3 monoplaces ennemis et abattu l'un d'eux en flammes.

(*Signé*)   Duchêne

Au Q.G.A., le 24 avril, 1918

Le Général Commandant la 3ᵐᵉ Armée cite à l'Ordre de l'Armée:

Le 1ᵉʳ Lieutenant de l'Armée américaine G. de Freest Larner, de l'Escadrille Spa. 86

A triomphé d'un biplace ennemi qui s'est écrasé en flammes dans ses lignes.

(*Signé*)   Humbert

G.H.Q., A.E.F., 4th December, 1918

First Lieutenant, Gorman de Freest Larner, 103d Aero Squadron

For extraordinary heroism in action in the region of Champney, France, 13 September, 1918. Lieutenant Larner attacked an enemy patrol of six machines (Fokker type) and fought against the great odds until he had destroyed one and forced another to retire.

A Bronze Leaf:

For extraordinary heroism in action in the region of Montfaucon, France, 4 October, 1918. While leading a patrol of four *monoplace* planes, Lieutenant Larner led his patrol in an attack on an enemy formation of seven planes. By skillful maneuvering he crashed one of the enemy machines and with the aid of his patrol forced the remainder of the enemy formation to withdraw.

By Order of General Pershing

G. de Freest Larner

Larner enlisted in the Lafayette Flying Corps after the United States Signal Corps had refused him on account of his youth. He arrived at the Front on December 3, 1917, assigned to the Escadrille Spad 86. Except for a few days in the following spring, when transferring to the American Army, he served continuously at the Front until the Armistice—fighting through every important battle of the last year. With the French, and as a Flight Commander in the 103rd Pursuit Squadron, Larner shot down and was officially credited with eight enemy planes, and his friends say that he has many other victories—too far *chez Boches* to be seen by our observers. He has seen the aerial war from every angle, and through it all he never lost his keen aggressiveness, nor missed a chance to fly. His splendid service has not gone unrecognised, for he has been awarded the *Croix de Guerre*, with two Palms, and the D.S.C., with an Oak Leaf. Since the Armistice he has been proposed for an additional French citation to the order of the army, and the Legion of Honour—the highest honour France has to bestow on an officer.

Larner's real baptism of fire was in the German offensive of March 21, 1918. Let him tell of it in his own words:

I feel queer and weak and happy after my experiences of the

LARNER'S SPAD

past few days—especially after this morning's happenings. For three quarters of an hour I was lost in a fog—thirty kilometres behind the German lines. I was never higher than 500 metres, and thought I was surely a goner! Once I found an aviation field and started to land when I saw that it was full of Boche planes ... then I realised where I was. A little later I met a Gotha in the air and found another field where a German sausage was tied to the ground—that meant I was getting close to the lines. Before long I saw the smoke of burning Noyon and the gunners began to shell me. . . .

This offensive is proving the most instructive, the most exhausting, and the most thrilling experience I ever expect to have. . . . The Germans continued their push, demoralizing all the French and English communications. This was serious—they were in a fair way to split the two armies apart before help could arrive. All the French balloons were brought down, making it impossible to tell what was going on behind the enemy lines, and all our aviation fields had to be abandoned. No telephones, no balloons, no observation planes—we did not even know the location of our own lines. Two *escadrilles* of Bréguets and our *groupe* were the only ones available in the first confusion. We have been doing reconnaissance, infantry *liaison*, and machine-gunning troops and convoys, at altitudes ranging from twenty to five hundred metres, and far in the enemy lines. It is all too vast for me to describe—the burning towns; exploding ammunition dumps, abandoned by the French; dead horses and men, scattered along the roads; the hammer-blows of machine guns, shooting up fountains of fiery bullets as you sweep low overhead.

Today the French Front is holding. It does my heart good to see the steady flash of our guns—the firing is a mighty roar by day and by night. . . . .

SERVICE RECORD

SCHUYLER LEE, New London, Connecticut.
PREVIOUS SERVICE: American Ambulance, 1917.
SERVICE IN FRENCH AVIATION:
Date of enlistment: June 1, 1917.
Aviation Schools: August 16, 1917, to January 8, 1918, Avord, G.D.E.
Breveted: October 21, 1917 (Caudron).
At the Front: Escadrille Spad 96, January 10 to April 12, 1918.
Final Rank: Caporal.
Killed in combat: April 12, 1918, east of Montdidier.
DECORATIONS:
Croix de Guerre, with Palm.

CITATION

Le 13 juillet, 1918

LEE, SCHUYLER, M¹ᵉ 12381, Caporal du Régiment de Marche de la Légion Étrangère, pilote à l'Escadrille Spad 96; Pilote Américain, engagé volontaire dans l'Armée Française.

Dès son arrivée en escadrille s'est distingué par son courage et son allant, notamment le 3 février, 1918, où il a contribué à abattre un avion ennemi. A été très grièvement blessé, le 12 avril, 1918, au cours d'un combat aérien.

Schuyler Lee

Quiet and reserved in manner, one had to know Schuyler Lee or to see him in action to realise the dash and audacity that lay concealed under his self-effacement. Once in the north, while flying a Nieuport, he fell in with a large patrol of Fokker triplanes—among the first which appeared on the Front—and after a sensational combat in which his gun jammed hopelessly, he managed by a miracle of skill and luck to extricate himself and return to the field, his machine fairly cut to pieces by bullets. But this *coup dur* merely served to increase his ardour, and among his comrades he became known as a volunteer for every dangerous mission. At last, on the 12th of April, to the east of Montdidier, while Lee was guarding the rear of a Spad patrol, a Fokker triplane stole up behind him unperceived. A short fatal burst, a wild turn, and Schuyler was spinning earthward, killed in his seat, his comrades say.

Had he lived, he would have gone far—there can be no doubt of that—for he had the skill, the courage, and the aggressive spirit which make a great fighting pilot.

SERVICE RECORD

MANDERSON LEHR, Albion, Nebraska.

SERVICE IN FRENCH AVIATION:
 Date of enlistment: June 5, 1917.
 Aviation Schools: June 10 to November 18, 1917, Avord, G.D.E.
 Brevet: September 3, 1917 (Caudron).
 At the Front: Escadrille Br 117, November 21, 1917, to March 15, 1918.
 Final Rank: Sergent.

SERVICE IN U.S. AVIATION:
 Commissioned First Lieutenant: March 15, 1918.
 At the Front: Attached to French Squadron Br 117 March 15 to July 15, 1918.
 Killed in combat: July 15, 1918, near Château-Thierry.

DECORATIONS:
 Croix de Guerre, with Palm and Star.

CITATIONS

G.A.R., AÉRONAUTIQUE MILITAIRE
ESCADRE 12. *Le 4 avril*, 1918

Le Chef d'Escadre Vuillemin, Commandant l'Escadre de Bombardement N° 12, cite à l'Ordre de l'Escadre, les militaires dont les noms suivent: ...

Le Sergent Pilote LEHR, MANDERSON (active, Légion Étrangère), détaché à l'Escadrille Br. 117 (G.B. 5)

Citoyen américain plein d'allant, de courage, et d'adresse. Excellent pilote. A exécuté en peu de temps de nombreux bombardements dont plusieurs à grande distance.

(Signé) VUILLEMIN

G.Q.G., *le* 30 *octobre*, 1918

1er Lieutenant LEHR, MANDERSON, Pilote à l'Escadrille Br. 117

Pilote admirable par son courage et son adresse, son mépris du danger. Affirmé à nouveau ses belles qualités le 15 juillet, 1918, en effectuant une mission de bombardement du champ de bataille à faible altitude. Attaqué par une dizaine d'avions ennemis sur l'objectif a soutenu un combat terrible, et bien que grièvement blessé, a pu grâce à son sang-froid ramener son avion en territoire française, en traversant les premières lignes à moins de 100 mètres d'altitude sous un feu de barrage d'une extrême violence.

Manderson Lehr

Lehr was the old-fashioned type of American boy: full of spirit, cleverness, and dry humour. With him one was never dull. During the long evenings at Avord, he amused a whole barrack-full of comrades with his absurdities, imitations of cows, pigs, roosters, and country dialect. "Bud" was a splendid pilot and one of the most fearless men in the corps. When given a mission to perform, he carried it through at any cost.

Lehr met his death on July 15, 1918, during the heavy fighting along the Marne. Driving a Bréguet, he was on a day-bombing mission, and had dropped his thirty-two bombs on the bridges across which the Germans were making their rush southward. As he turned to make his way back to his aerodrome, he became separated, among the clouds, from the rest of his formation. Suddenly ten Albatross came diving down on the Bréguet, and after a violent combat, during which Lehr's motor was hit, he was heading for the lines when a last unlucky burst gave him a mortal wound. His observer, the French Lieutenant Carles, succeeded in gaining some control over the machine, and managed to cross the lines and land in a rough wooded field. On landing, the machine turned over, the observer was thrown out, and very seriously injured, and Lehr, who by this time was dead, found a funeral pyre in the flaming wreck of his Bréguet. The value of his service and the esteem in which his French comrades held him are shown by the fact that at the time of his death, he was proposed for the Legion of Honour.

SERVICE RECORD

DAVID WILBUR LEWIS, Brooklyn, New York.

PREVIOUS SERVICE: American Ambulance, 1915.

SERVICE IN FRENCH AVIATION:
Date of enlistment: June 21, 1917.
Aviation Schools: June 21, 1917, to February 24, 1918, Avord, Pau, G.D.E.
Breveted: November 13, 1917 (Caudron).
At the Front: Escadrille Spad 79, February 27 to March 29, 1918.
Final Rank: Caporal.

SERVICE IN U.S. AVIATION:
Commissioned Second Lieutenant: March 29, 1918.
At the Front: Attached to the French Squadron Spad 79, April 24 to September 22, 1918.
On duty at Colombey-les-Belles, September 26, 1918, to Armistice.
Slightly wounded in combat: September 7, 1918.

DECORATIONS:
Croix de Guerre, with Star.

CITATION

Le 10 *octobre*, 1918

2me Lieutenant Lewis, David Wilbur, Pilote à l'Escadrille 79

A exécuté de nombreuses reconnaissances à longue portée, a reconnu et mitraillé à très basse altitude les troupes ennemis. A soutenu de nombreux combats, notamment le 1er août, 1918, où, attaqué par trois avions, loin dans les lignes ennemies, il a réussi à ramener son avion criblé de balles.

David Wilbur Lewis

Lewis will always be remembered for having made the most sensational *sortie* on record, in a 45 H.P. Blériot. While monitors paled and comrades held up their hands, he made a complete *tour de piste* at an altitude of three metres. On the Front, in the Escadrille Spad 79, he did good work and went through many exciting experiences. Probably his narrowest escape was on the 7th of September, 1918, near La Fère. His motor was running very badly when suddenly he was attacked by four enemy machines of a new and very fast variety. He brought down the first German in flames and managed to regain our lines with the other three on his tail, riddling his machine with bullets at every burst. Landing in the trenches, he took cover for a few minutes while he rested, and then crawled calmly back to his machine to remove the instruments.

Lewis served with an *escadrille d'armée* which had both Spad single-seaters for fighting, and Bréguets for reconnaissance work. When there were no *chasse* patrols to be made, he amused himself with deep photographic reconnaissances. During the summer of 1918, Lewis and his comic observer were known at every aerodrome between Amiens and the Marne.

SERVICE RECORD

Kenneth Proctor Littauer, New York City.

Service in French Aviation:
Date of enlistment: March 29, 1916.
Aviation Schools: April 1 to October 14, 1916, Pau, Buc, Châteauroux, G.D.E.
Brevetted: July 24, 1916 (Caudron).
At the Front: Escadrille C. 74, October 16, 1916, to January 2, 1918.
Final Rank: Sergent.

Service in U.S. Aviation:
Commissioned Captain: January 1, 1918.
Promoted Major: November 1, 1918.
At the Front: Flight Commander 88th Squadron (Observation), February 15 to July 1, 1918.
C.O. 88th Squadron (Observation), July 1 to September 20, 1918.
Acting Chief of Air Service 3d Army Corps, August 20 to September 20, 1918.
C.O. 3d Corps Observation Group, September 20 to October 24, 1918.

Chief of Air Service, 3d Army Corps, October 24, 1918, to Armistice.

DECORATIONS:
Distinguished Service Cross.
Croix de Guerre, with Palm and Star.
Croix de Guerre (Belgium).
Chevalier de l'Ordre de Léopold.

CITATIONS

G.H.Q., A.E.F.   20 *January*, 1919

The Commander-in-Chief of the American Expeditionary Forces, in the name of the President, has awarded the Distinguished Service Cross for extraordinary heroism in action, to

Major KENNETH P. LITTAUER

For repeated acts of heroism in action near Conflans, France, September 14, 1918, and near Doulcon, France, October 30, 1918.

Major Littauer volunteered on a mission to protect a photographic plane for another squadron on September 14 and continued toward the objective at Conflans even after three other protecting planes had failed to start. In an encounter with five enemy pursuit planes, he completely protected the photographic plane by skillful maneuvering, although his observer was wounded and his machine seriously damaged. On October 30, Major Littauer, on duty as Chief of Air Service of the 3d Corps Army, volunteered and made an important reconnaissance of enemy machine-gun emplacements at a low altitude near Doulcon.

36ᵐᵉ CORPS D'ARMÉE, ÉTAT-MAJOR.   *Le* 25 *février*, 1917

Le Lieutenant-Colonel Chef d'État-Major du 36ᵐᵉ Corps d'Armée cite à l'Ordre de l'Aéronautique les militaires dont les noms suivent: ...

Le Caporal LITTAUER, KENNETH PROCTOR, de l'Escadrille C. 74

Sujet américain, engagé volontaire pour la durée de la guerre, bon pilote, courageux, dévoué, très militaire. A toujours fait preuve d'énergie et de sang-froid, notamment le 8 février, 1917, au cours d'un combat avec un avion allemand, où, bien que son appareil ait été atteint de plusieurs balles, il a forcé son adversaire à la retraite.

                                                                    (*Signé*)   PRUNIER

AVIATION MILITAIRE BELGE, ÉTAT-MAJOR.   *Le* 2 *septembre*, 1917

Personnel. J'ai l'honneur de porter à la connaissance du personnel de l'aviation qu'en témoignage de services rendus à l'Armée Belge, S.M. le Roi a remis hier des distinctions honorifiques aux aviateurs français de l'Escadrille C 74: ...

Chevalier de l'Ordre de Léopold II:

Sergent KENNETH P. LITTAUER

                                                (*Signé*)   PAUL BLOCH

ROYAUME DE BELGIQUE.

Le Ministre de la Guerre a l'honneur de faire savoir au

Sergent LITTAUER, KENNETH, de l'aviation militaire française

Que, par arrête royal du 15 novembre, 1917, N° 4810, la Croix de Guerre lui a été décernée.

Pilote de l'escadrille franco-belge C. 74, ne cesse de faire preuve du plus grand courage et du dévouement le plus absolu. A, pour compte de l'armée belge, plus de 100 heures de vol au-dessus des lignes ennemies.

GRAND QUARTIER-GÉNÉRAL DES ARMÉES FRANÇAISES DE
L'EST, ÉTAT-MAJOR.   *Le* 10 *janvier*, 1919

Après approbation du Général Commandant en Chef les forces expéditionnaires américaines en France, le Maréchal de France, Commandant en Chef les Armées Françaises de l'Est, cité à l'Ordre de l'Armée:

Capitaine LITTAUER, Commandant l'Aéronautique du 3ᵉ C.A.U.S.

Commandant l'aéronautique d'un corps d'armée américain, a obtenu le rendement maximum de ses subordonnés, en leur donnant journellement l'exemple de la plus belle intrépidité. A effectué avec succès de nombreuses liaisons d'infanterie. Le 9 août et le 4 septembre, 1918, a réussi d'importantes missions photographiques que des conditions atmosphériques contraires et le présence de nombreux avions ennemis rendaient très difficiles. Est parvenu le 9 août, par son énergie à ramener au terrain un appareil criblé d'éclats d'obus.

(*Signé*) PÉTAIN

Kenneth Proctor Littauer

Littauer, known to Lafayette men as "Képi," served his apprenticeship at the Front on the old, twin-motor Caudron, and was one of the few men who had actually flown it who could be found to praise this leisurely and vulnerable bird. With the observer and machine-gunner in front, the forward field of fire limited to the space between the propellers, and no protection to the rear worth mentioning, it is a matter for wonder that any pilot should have survived a long experience with this type of craft. Képi did, and accepted with reluctance the newer G. 6 which superseded it. This, too, he flew successfully, although it was a temperamental machine which all pilots hated and which few outlived.

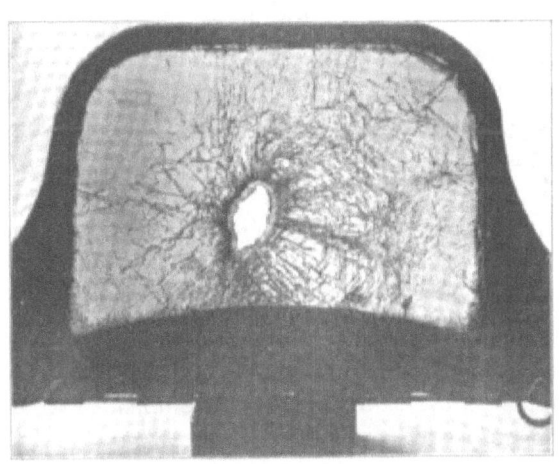

LITTAUER'S WINDSHIELD

His work with C. 74, a Franco-Belgian squadron, was not of a spectacular kind, just the day-in, day-out, routine of photo missions, gun-spotting, and reconnaissance air business which offers little opportunity for brilliant *coups* and far more than a just share of the dangers of war flying.

Képi had phenomenal luck, and in addition was a cool and skilful pilot, so that in more than two years of continuous service he never failed to bring both his observer and his machine back to his aerodrome, although once his gunner was badly wounded, and often his bus resembled those riddled hulks used for targets at the aerial gunnery schools. He cancelled one *bona fide* rendezvous with death by being a fraction of a second ahead of time. While doing artillery *réglage*, he was attacked by several enemy chasse machines. Just as he turned to watch one of them, a bullet from the gun of another passed squarely through the centre of his wind-shield, missing his head by the thickness of a cigarette paper. A narrow margin, but oh! the difference to him!

Adventures of this sort, which age many a young pilot prematurely, gave life a certain zest for him during the fourteen months he spent with C. 74. He was then transferred to the American Air Force with the rank of captain, and, had he wished to do so, might have gone to the rear as an instructor. But Képi was no lover of soft billets. Pilots experienced in *corps d'armée* work were badly needed in the United States Air Service, which was dependent for airmen with actual war experience, in whatever branch, upon the personnel of the Lafayette Corps. Most of these were combat pilots.

The remainder—a mere handful, Littauer, Zinn, Horton, Worthington—had had wide experience in *corps d'armée* work. Kepi was at once placed in command of a squadron equipped with obsolete two-seaters, which the American authorities had purchased from the French. Not discouraged, he organised his *escadrille*, himself instructing both his flying and non-flying personnel, and within a few weeks had developed a genuine working unit. Other squadrons were attached to him, and he was raised to the rank of major. Here again, as always, Képi did his duty and a little more. He never asked his pilots to undertake difficult and important missions without himself leading them, although as a squadron and *groupe* commander it was really his duty to remain on the ground.

This practice, of course, endeared him to all of his men, who gladly followed him anywhere. His squadrons were in the thick of all of the important American actions: at Château-Thierry, the Vesle River, Saint-Mihiel, Argonne-Meuse, and finally with the Army of Occupation at Coblenz bridgehead. The decorations conferred upon him by the French, Belgian, and American Governments partially tell the story of his service to the Allied cause. But more precious than these, surely, is that other award, "Windshield with hole attached," conferred upon him in his old G. 4 days, by Chance, C.A.S. of all the armies of the world, including the Scandinavian.

SERVICE RECORD

RALPH LANE LOOMIS, Bedford, Massachusetts.

SERVICE IN FRENCH AVIATION:
  Date of enlistment: July 21, 1917.
  Aviation Schools: July 26, 1917, to January 1, 1918, Avord, Tours, Cazeaux, G.D.E.
  Breveted: October 21, 1917 (Caudron).
  Final Rank: Caporal.

SERVICE IN U.S. NAVAL AVIATION:
  Commissioned Ensign: January 9, 1918.
  At the Front: U.S. Naval Air Station, Dunkirk, February 14 to August 22, 1918.

Ralph Lane Loomis

Enlisting on July 21, 1917, Loomis was breveted on October 21, and after passing through Pau and Cazeaux, with excellent notes at both places, he was *disponible* at Le Plessis-Belleville, awaiting his turn to go to the Front, when word came that he had been released and transferred to the navy with the rank of Ensign. The adventures of his career as a naval flier are hinted at in a letter to Major Gros:

> My work with the navy consisted in patrols over the North Sea, covering the channels into Zeebrugge and Ostend, and in bombing raids on the same places. We were 'Archied' a good deal by destroyers and land antiaircraft batteries, but were seldom able to catch the enemy seaplanes outside for a scrap—they always flew back to the mole as soon as they sighted us. I arrived at Dunkirk on February 14, 1918, and my last flight and fight combined was on August 22, when we were withdrawn to allow pilots of the Marine Corps to take our places—there being a shortage of machines. At that time we were working with land planes—trusting to our motors 100 miles at sea and often flying as low as 1000 feet.

SERVICE RECORD

WILLIAM F. LOOMIS, Bedford, Massachusetts.

SERVICE IN FRENCH AVIATION:
  Date of enlistment: June 9, 1917.
  Aviation Schools: June 16 to November 20, 1917, Avord, Pau, G.D.E.
  Breveted: September 28, 1917 (Caudron).
  At the Front: Escadrille Spad 153, November 23, 1917, to February 19, 1918.
  Final Rank: Caporal.

SERVICE IN U.S. AVIATION:
Commissioned as First Lieutenant: February 21, 1918.
At the Front: 94th Pursuit Squadron, March 5 to August 18, 1918.
213th Pursuit Squadron, August 18 to October 22, 1918.

DECORATIONS:
Croix de Guerre, with Star.

CITATION

GRAND QUARTIER-GÉNÉRAL DES
ARMÉES FRANÇAISES DE L'EST
ÉTAT-MAJOR.   *Le* 29 *novembre,* 1918

Après approbation du Général Commandant en Chef les forces expéditionnaires américaines en France, le Maréchal de France, Commandant en Chef les Armées Françaises de l'Est, cite à l'Ordre du Corps d'Armée:

Lieutenant Pilote WILLIAM F. LOOMIS, à l'Escadrille Américaine 94

Pilote possédant les plus belles qualités de courage et de sacrifice. Infatigable dans l'accomplissement de son devoir, a livré un grand nombre de combats au cours desquels il a toujours montré un grand courage et un grand sang-froid et justifié la confiance placée en lui comme chef de patrouille.

PÉTAIN

William F. Loomis

Loomis was one of the steadiest pilots among the later group of Americans who took the Blériot training. He crashed no machines, and was never known to make an eccentric or sensational *sortie*. Going to Escadrille N. 153 on November 24, 1917, he did good work for three months with the French, and in February, 1918, transferred to the United States Army, where he served both with the 94th and 213th Pursuit Squadrons. Loomis has had an exceptionally broad experience of the war, in two armies and on many different sections of the Front, and he has always shown himself a fine officer and a first-class pilot.

SERVICE RECORD

EDWARD J. LOUGHRAN, Desoto, Kansas.

SERVICE IN FRENCH AVIATION:
Date of enlistment: March 20, 1917.
Aviation Schools: March 27 to October 26, 1917, Avord, Pau, G.D.E.
Breveted: August 31, 1917 (Caudron).
At the Front: Escadrille Spad 84, October 29, 1917, to February 18, 1918.
Final Rank: Sergent.
Killed in combat: Southeast of Minaucourt, February 18, 1918.

Edward J. Loughran

The latter days of October, 1917, along the Aisne Sector, were trying ones, even for veteran pilots in the French Air Service. At that time the Germans were driven from the last of their high positions, as far as Anizy-le-Château, on the Oise-Aisne Canal, and, farther east, along the Ailette River. There was much hazardous work to be done, trench-strafing at the close of every patrol, machine-gunning enemy reserves in the woods, on roads and in billets, attacking balloons and aerodromes. It was at this period that Edward Loughran was sent to the Front, joining Spad 84, a French squadron in *Groupe de Combat* 13. He was soon given his 180 H.P. Spad and started patrol work over the Chemin des Dames, the Fort de Malmaison, the old reservoir—ground strewn with the wreckage of many *avions*, both French and German. Here he was tested out in a stern school of combat, learned the sound of enemy "105's" and, with his squadron, got on machine-gun terms of intimacy with some of the crack German combat formations then operating in that region.

He passed through his apprenticeship splendidly, with his nerve unimpaired and his love of the excitement and the danger of war flying tremendously increased. During the autumn and early winter he was constantly at the Front, never missing a patrol, learning the work of combat thoroughly, from "the ceiling" down. He refused to accept a leave offered him in January, a three weeks' furlough in America, and remained on duty until his death in combat.

Loughran (in centre) and members of Spad 84

On February 18, 1918, a misty mid-winter morning, he went on early patrol with three members of his squadron. A long reconnaissance of German positions was made, and it was while returning toward the French lines that he had his last combat. He was high and rear man on his patrol, and for some reason lagged far behind the others. Suddenly he was attacked by three enemy *monoplaces* and before his comrades could come to his assistance he was shot down. It was evident that he was only wounded, for the report from the French infantry watching the combat was that he regained control of his Spad, crossed into French territory, and made a normal descent until within 500 metres of the ground. Then suddenly his machine nosed down and crashed with terrific force just back of the French third-line defences south of Minaucourt and a few hundreds metres north and east of Wargemoulin.

He was the second American pilot in Spad 84 to be killed in combat within two months. He is buried in the war cemetery at Mont Frenet, not far from La Ferme de la Noblette, where *Groupe de Combat 13* was then stationed.

SERVICE RECORD

WALTER LOVELL, Concord, Massachusetts.

PREVIOUS SERVICE: American Ambulance, 1915–16.

SERVICE IN FRENCH AVIATION:
Date of enlistment: May 22, 1916.
Aviation Schools: June 29, 1916, to February 24, 1917, Buc, Avord, Pau, G.D.E.
Breveted: October 1, 1916 (Blériot).
At the Front: Escadrille Lafayette, February 26 to October 24, 1917.
Final Rank: Adjudant.

SERVICE IN U.S. AVIATION:
Commissioned Captain: January 1, 1918.
Promoted Major.
Attached to American G.H.Q., Chaumont, October 24, 1917, to July, 1918.
On duty in U.S.A., July, 1918, to Armistice.

DECORATIONS:
Croix de Guerre, with Star (Ambulance).
Croix de Guerre, with Palm (Aviation).

CITATIONS

En Campagne, le 5 octobre, 1915

Par application du decret du 23 avril, 1915, sur la Croix de Guerre, le Médecin Divisionnaire cite à l'Ordre du Jour du Service de Santé de la Division:

Monsieur LOVELL, WALTER, Sous-Chef de Section à la S.S.A.A.

A toujours fait preuve d'un moral remarquable, a toujours été un exemple de courage pour les autres conducteurs, et un précieux auxiliaire pour le Chef de sa Section.
             (*Signé*) D. W. VIELA

2me ARMÉE, G.C. 13.   *Le* 10 *septembre*, 1917
Le Général Commandant la 2me Armée, cite à l'Ordre de l'Armée:
  LOVELL, WALTER, Sergent Pilote à l'Escadrille N. 124 (G.C. 13)
 Citoyen américain engagé au service de la France. Excellent pilote de chasse, plein de sang-froid et de courage. Au cours d'une protection de bombardement a abattu, le 18 août, un avion ennemi qui s'est écrasé en flammes.

Walter Lovell

After six months at the Front as second in command of Section No. 2, American Field Ambulance, Lovell enlisted in the French Air Service. He was among the first of the 1916 volunteers who received all of their early training and were breveted on Blériots at the Buc School. At that early period, the French system for teaching *chasse* pilots was exasperatingly slow. Lovell and the other *élèves* at Buc, spent weeks of their time reading ancient magazines and loafing at Ciret's, the well-remembered restaurant in the village. There was so little flying that all of them lost hope of ever getting to the Front. After three months of actual work, spread over the space of ten, Lovell was sent to the Escadrille Lafayette on the 1st of March, 1917.

He is a natural leader. The same qualities which placed him in a position of responsibility in the Ambulance Service, were called into play in Aviation. There was an even greater need for them at that particular time; for within the next three months Lieutenant de Laage de Meux, James McConnell, Edmond Genêt, and Ronald Hoskier were all killed. It was inevitable that Walter should be chosen as a patrol leader. Throughout his ten months at the Front, he was nearly always at the head of at least one of the daily squadron formations. In addition to this, he did a great deal of lone *chasse*, or made voluntary *sorties* with Harold Willis, his old flying partner in the schools.

They made excursions far into German territory, and shot down enemy planes which could not possibly be confirmed, owing to the distance from French observation posts. Old Lafayette men will remember many an evening at the aerodrome, when both pilots and mechanicians waited anxiously for the return of these two lone birds. Old Sergeant "'Frisco" would look at his watch a dozen times during a quarter of an hour—the last quarter of an hour, when they would have to come home, if at all, because of the limits of their fuel supply.

The rest of us searched the clouds and the bits of blue sky in the direction of the lines, for some sign of them, or listened intently for the faint sound of their motors. At last some one would shout joyfully,

Lovell (on left) as an *élève-pilote* at Buc. September. 1916
L. N. Barclay seventh from left and Harold Willis on right

"'Frisco" (on right) and a *panne de moteur* of Lovell's

"There they are!" pointing out two minute specks, scarcely visible in the gathering twilight; and in a much happier frame of mind, we would watch them planing down from an immense height, until we lost sight of them in the shadows closer to the earth. It was their practice to stay out until the last possible moment. Sometimes they had to come home on *nourrice*, the little emergency gas-tank. Occasionally, with both tanks empty, they reached the field only by planing flatly, and landed with "dead sticks."

Walter Lovell' adventures at the Front would "*fill a book*," if one may use this hackneyed but meaningful phrase; fill it with the use of nothing but essential facts. All of his successful combats were on the German side of the lines, and it is for this reason that he received but one official confirmation of a victory. Even this one would have been unconfirmed—it was miles beyond the French lines—had it not been for unquestionable evidence from other pilots who witnessed the combat. The Escadrille Lafayette accompanied a group of Sopwith bombing planes whose objective was a town well beyond the German frontiers. The formation was attacked, over Dun-sur-Meuse, by a large patrol of Albatross. Lovell shot one of them down in flames. While he was engaged, Willis was attacked by two others, and had his machine so badly riddled that he was compelled to land in Germany. It was a battle royal, one of those hotly contested affairs which thrill the infantrymen watching from below, and cause them to wonder whether, after all, the life of an airman is such a desirable one.

On January 1, 1918, Lovell was commissioned captain in the United States Air Service, and, much to his disappointment, was sent to American G.H.Q. at Chaumont. It was a disappointment felt equally by all of his old fellow pilots, who knew at first hand of his record at the Front. It seemed a great pity that he should have to leave the fighting game, for he was exceptionally well fitted for it, and had he been allowed to remain with the squadron, would have scored a fine list of victories some of them official, but the greater part, doubtless, unofficial, owing to his habit of inconspicuous combat. Evidently he was more badly needed elsewhere. He spent several weeks in visiting French, Belgian, and British squadrons all along the Western Front, flying from one group to another, thus saving a great deal of travelling time. The result of this investigation, which was quickly and thoroughly accomplished, was of great value to the organisation and equipment of our own Air Force. Lovell was afterward promoted major, and served in various capacities in France and America until the signing of the Armistice.

SERVICE RECORD

Gervais Raoul Lufbery, Wallingford, Connecticut.

Previous Service: Foreign Legion (Infantry), August 24 to August 31, 1914.

Service in French Aviation:
  Date of enlistment: August 31, 1914.
  Aviation Schools: May 17 to October 1, 1915, Chartres, Ambérieu, R.G.A.
  Brevet: July 29, 1915 (Maurice Farman).
  At the Front: Escadrille V.B. 106, October 7, 1915, to April 10, 1916.
  At G.D.E. (Division Nieuport) for training as combat pilot, April 10 to May 22, 1916.
    Escadrille Lafayette, May 24, 1916, to January 5, 1918.
  Final Rank: Sous-Lieutenant.

Service in U.S. Aviation:
  Commissioned Major: January 10, 1918.
  At the Front: Attached to 94th Pursuit Squadron and 1st Pursuit Group, January 21 to May 19, 1918.
  Killed in combat: Near Toul, May 19, 1918.

Decorations:
  Légion d'Honneur.
  Médaille Militaire.
  Croix de Guerre, with ten Palms.
  Military Medal (British).

CITATIONS

Grand Quartier-Général des Armées, État-Major. *Le 16 août,* 1916.

La Médaille Militaire a été conférée au Militaire dont le nom suit:

Lufbery, Raoul, Sergent à l'Escadrille N. 124

Modèle d'adresse et de sang-froid et de courage. S'est distingué par de nombreux bombardements à longue portée et par les combats quotidiens qu'il livre aux avions ennemis. Le 31 juillet n'a pas hésité à attaquer à courte distance un groupe de quatre avions ennemis. A abattu l'un d'eux à proximité de nos lignes. A réussi à en abattre un second le 4 août, 1916. La présente nomination comporte l'attribution de la Croix de Guerre, avec Palme.

(*Signé*) Joffre

Au G.Q.G., le 26 septembre, 1916

Le Général Commandant la 2ᵐᵉ Armée, cite à l'Ordre de l'Armée:

L'Adjudant Lufbery, Raoul, Pilote à l'Escadrille N. 124

Pilote d'un allant remarquable. Le 4 août, 1916, a attaqué un avion ennemi qui est venu s'abattre dans ses lignes. Le 8 août a renouvelé le même exploit. L'appareil ennemi est tombé en flammes près de Douaumont.

(*Signé*) Nivelle

G.Q.G., État-Major. *Le 28 octobre,* 1916

Le Général Franchet d'Esperey, Commandant le Groupe d'Armées de l'Est, cite à l'Ordre de l'Armée:

Adjudant Lufbery, de l'Escadrille N. 124

Pilote courageux et adroit. A abattu son 5ᵐᵉ avion le 12 octobre au cours d'une mission importante.

(*Signé*) Franchet d'Esperey

Le 29 janvier, 1917

M. Lufbery, Raoul (active), Adjudant Pilote à l'Escadrille N. 124

A été nommé dans l'Ordre de la Légion d'Honneur au Grade de Chevalier. S'est engagé sous le Drapeau français pour la durée de la guerre. A fait preuve comme pilote de chasse d'une audace remarquable et a abattu jusqu'au 27 décembre, 1916, six avions ennemis.

Déjà deux fois cité à l'Ordre de l'Armée et Médaille Militaire.
La présente nomination comporte l'attribution de la Croix de Guerre, avec Palme.

(*Signé*) Pont

Groupe d'Armées du Nord, État-Major. *Le* 15 *mai*, 1917

Le Général Franchet d'Esperey, Commandant le Groupe d'Armées du Nord, cite à l'Ordre de l'Armée :

Lufbery, Raoul, Adjudant à l'Escadrille N. 124 (N° M^{le} 8217)

Pilote à l'Escadrille Lafayette; adroit et intrépide; véritable modèle pour tous ses camarades. Le 8 avril a obligé un avion ennemi à atterrir. A abattu le 13 avril, 1917, son huitième appareil ennemi, et le 24 avril son neuvième.

(*Signé*) Franchet d'Esperey

Le 19 *mai*, 1917

Par Ordre Général N° 10 "D.E." du 8 mai, 1917, du G.Q.G., S.M. le Roi d'Angleterre a conféré la Médaille Militaire (M.M.) aux pilotes dont les noms suivent, qui se sont signalés par leur bravoure au cours de la campagne : . . .

Adjudant Lufbery, Raoul, de l'Escadrille N. 124

VIe Armée, État-Major. *Au Q.G.A., le* 15 *juin*, 1917

Lufbery, Raoul, Adjudant Pilote à l'Escadrille N. 124 (Aéronautique)

Pilote de chasse merveilleux. Est, pour son Escadrille, un exemple vivant d'audace, de sang-froid, et de dévouement.

A abattu le 12 juin, 1917, son 10e avion ennemi.

(*Signé*) Maistre

Le Général Commandant la 2me Armée cite à l'Ordre de l'Armée :

Le Sous-Lieutenant Lufbery, Raoul, des Troupes Aéronautiques, Pilote à l'Escadrille N. 124

Pilote de chasse qui a livré en deux semaines 16 combats, au cours desquels il a touché et fait tomber désemparés 6 avions ennemis et en a abattu un autre le 4 septembre, 1917 (11me victoire). A eu son appareil 5 fois atteint gravement dans ce combat.

G.Q.G., État-Major. *Le* 29 *octobre*, 1917

M. Lufbery, Raoul, Aviation, Sous-Lieutenant, Pilote à l'Escadrille N. 124

Merveilleux pilote de chasse. Le 22 septembre, 1917, a attaqué deux avions ennemis, en a abattu un (12me avion), et contraint l'autre à atterrir désemparé dans ses lignes. Le 16 octobre a abattu un biplace en flammes en arrière des lignes ennemies. A reçu au cours du combat deux balles dans son moteur (13me avion).

(*Signé*) Maistre

VIe Armée, État-Major. *Le* 9 *novembre*, 1917

M. Lufbery, Raoul, Sous-Lieutenant (Aviation), Pilote à l'Escadrille N. 124

Pilote remarquable. Le plus bel exemple de bravoure, d'énergie, et d'audace. Le 24 octobre, 1917, alors que l'ennemi, battu la veille, essayait de réagir, a fourni un splendide effort, livrant au cours de trois vols successifs, sept combats rapprochés dans lesquels il a battu son quatorzième adversaire et fait tomber désemparés cinq autres avions allemands.

(*Signé*) Maistre

Gervais Raoul Lufbery

From boyhood Raoul Lufbery's life was one of continual adventure. He was born in France of French parents, on March 14, 1885. A year later his mother died, and Raoul was placed by his father in the care of a family in the Auvergne Mountains. In 1890 his father remarried and in 1891 emigrated to the United States. Being uncertain of conditions in America, he left his three boys in the care of their grandmother in France. His second wife died in 1901, leaving him with five small children, the youngest but nine months old. His father being hard-pressed in the care of his family, Raoul, who was still in France, went to work in a chocolate factory at Blois, and during the next three years sent him most of his earnings. This enabled him to establish himself comfortably in America. Then, in 1904, eager for change, with a boy's delight in travel, Raoul set out to see the world.

Leaving Clermont-Ferrand, where he had been employed in a factory, he went to Algiers, to Tunis, and on to Egypt. He then went to Constantinople, where for several weeks he was employed as a waiter in a restaurant. His plan in all his romantic wanderings was to select some city, no matter how far distant if it promised to be interesting, keeping it in mind as an ultimate objective while he worked toward it in leisurely stages. Arriving there he would accept any sort of employment which came to hand, and when he had satisfied his curiosity, move on to new lands. Upon leaving Turkey he went through the Balkan States to Germany, and at Hamburg signed a three months' contract with the Waerman Line, a steamship company whose boats plied between that port and German South Africa. After three years of globe-trotting he went to Wallingford in 1906 for a visit with his father.

But his father, too, was something of a traveller. He was a dealer in stamps and travelled widely in search of specimens which his collection lacked. Knowing little of his son's movements, he sailed for Europe on the day of Raoul's arrival at New York. He had not seen him since he was a lad, and as the event proved, father and son were never to meet again.

Raoul remained at home for nearly two years. Then as his father had not yet returned, he again set out on his travels. He went to Cuba and from there to New Orleans, where he worked in a bakery, and on to San Francisco, where he was a waiter in a hotel. He then enlisted in the United States Army and was sent to the Philippines, where he remained for more than two years. When his period of enlistment had expired, he went on to Japan and from there to China. He wandered through China for months, always insatiably curious, always eager for new adventure. For some time he settled down in a position in the Chinese Customs Service. Then *Wanderlust* carried him to India, where he was employed as a ticket agent at Bombay.

In 1912, while at Calcutta, he made the acquaintance of Marc Pourpe, a French aviator who had just arrived in India with a fellow airman for the purpose of making a series of exhibition flights in Blériot monoplanes. Lufbery had been greatly interested in aviation from the time of the Wright brothers' experiments with gliders. The arrival of the Frenchmen gave him the opportunity for which he had long been waiting. He followed the crowd of curious natives to the field outside Calcutta where the flights were to be made. There he awaited developments, and seeing Pourpe in difficulties with a gang of *coolie* labourers who were erecting his tent hangar, offered to superintend the job. Pourpe gladly accepted the offer, and the following day, thanks to Lufbery's assistance, was ready to begin his flights.

This incident marked the beginning of Lufbery's long and intimate association with Pourpe, and of his own career as an airman which was to continue until his death in combat six years later. Pourpe's flying partner was killed in an accident while they were in India and his own *mécanicien* became ill and returned to France. Lufbery then became a *mécanicien* under Pourpe's instruction and quickly mastered his new calling. Both men were young and adventure-loving and spent more than a year of fascinating travel among the old civilizations of the East. In some places they were looked upon as gods, in others as imposters. Once, in China, the natives, who felt that their reputation as master kite-builders was at stake, after making a careful examination of Pourpe's Blériot, built an exact model of it, of bamboo and gilt paper. It flew beautifully, but was lacking in one essential feature. It had no motor. It would not sing. So they attached a box of bees which made a splendid buzzing sound near at hand. But in the air, much to the disappointment of the Chinamen, they could not compete with the musical box on the man-kite of the foreign devils.

Then came Pourpe's famous flight in Egypt, from Cairo to Khartoum and return. Lufbery followed or preceded him on every stage of the journey, travelling by Nile steamers and cargo boats, on camels or donkeys, by train, and sometimes on foot. In the summer of 1914 they returned to France for a new machine, a Morane Parasol, expecting to return to the Orient for another long tour. War was declared and Pourpe enlisted at once in the Air Service. Lufbery enlisted in the Foreign Legion as an infantryman, transferred a few days later to the Aviation Service, and went with Pourpe to the Front as his mechanic. Pourpe was killed three months later, on December 2, 1914. In writing of the friendship of the two men, Jacques Mortane, editor of the Paris *La Guerre Aérienne*, said:

> I wish that I could give a living picture of these heroes of romance, for I do not think that there exist upon earth two men whose lives have been more extraordinary, more fertile in incident. I loved Marc Pourpe as a brother and I had for Lufbery the most profound affection. Their friendship for each other was a veritable cult, and yet neither ever confided to the other his adventures of former days. In so far as their comradeship was concerned, it began on the day when they first met. Neither knew nor cared what had happened before that time. Lufbery showed an astonishing knowledge of other countries which was very useful to Pourpe in planning his aerial journeys. I remember evenings in Paris when they were studying their maps in preparation for a distant voyage. 'In June,' Lufbery would say, 'there will be heavy rains in this region,' or, 'when you are flying in that country you will be hindered by the prevailing winds.' His conversation was always highly instructive and picturesque.

After Pourpe's death Lufbery was sent to the aviation school at Chartres, where he was breveted on the Maurice Farman and received a later training on the Voisin. His first service at the Front as a pilot was in the Voisin Bombardment Squadron 106. In the spring of 1916 he went to the depot at Le Plessis-Belleville for training as a *pilote de chasse*. He had a good deal of difficulty in learning to fly the Nieuport, and odd though it seems, in the light of his later career, was at first reported by his *moniteurs* as inapt for combat training and more fitted to be a *pilote de bombardement*. Lufbery persevered, overcame his early clumsiness, finished his Nieuport training, and was sent to the Escadrille Lafayette on May 24, 1916.

On July 30 he shot down his first enemy *avion* in a battle to the east of Étain, in the Verdun Sector. The following day he gained his second victory, and on August 4 a third, the enemy machine falling at Abancourt, near Verdun. On August 8 he shot down an *Aviatik*, which fell in flames near the Fort de Douaumont; and during the historic bombardment of the Mauser works, on the 12th of October, 1916, he destroyed a three-passenger *Aviatik*, his fifth official victory. It was in returning from this expedition that Norman Prince was mortally injured. The Lafayette Squadron then went to Cachy on the Somme, and on November 9 and 10, Lufbery destroyed two additional enemy planes, although they were too far back of the enemy lines to be officially credited to him. On December 27, 1916, he had a thrilling singlehanded battle with an *Aviatik* which he finally shot down in the French lines. He himself narrowly escaped death on this occasion, four bullets of his adversary having passed through his Nieuport very close to his body. This was his sixth victory, and henceforth, with every new success his name was mentioned in the official *communiqués*, in accordance with the French practice.

The story of his further victories may be read in part in the list of his army citations. He received official confirmation for seventeen of them, although, at a conservative estimate, this is no more than half the number of planes which he actually destroyed. He had no method of attack, unless absolute fearlessness and a remarkable *finesse* in handling his machine may be called a method. He flew alone a great deal, and waited patiently for his opportunity. He not only waited for it, but he worked for it as well. When he accepted or forced combat, he was always in the most favourable position for attack.

His Spad was really a part of himself, a thing which may be said of but few airmen. He actually flew as a bird flies, without any thought of how it was done. Those of us who were associated with him in the Escadrille Lafayette used to gather at the hangars when not on duty to wait for his return from the lines. We knew where to look for him, always very high, for he kept his altitude on the homeward journey, in the hope of encountering an enemy photographic or reconnaissance machine returning from a mission over French territory. When over the aerodrome he would throttle down and make his descent in beautiful *renversements* without an abrupt movement, so delicately done that there could not be the slightest strain on his machine. Sometimes when in a holiday mood he would give us an exhibition of acrobacy which it was a joy to watch; for he was better than the best of us at stunting.

Finest of all Lufbery's qualities was his simplicity. He knew, of course, that he had become a popular hero. The papers both in France and America were full of his exploits. Children were named after him, scores of silly girls wrote letters to him. Seldom was there a *prise d'armes*

LUFBERY (ON LEFT) RECEIVING THE BRITISH MILITARY MEDAL

LUFBERY, WHISKEY, AND SODA

LUFBERY AND WHISKEY

at the aerodrome when he was not one of the pilots to be decorated. Celebrated Frenchmen were glad to honour him. How we unheroic and unknown airmen envied him the greetings he had from such men as Guynemer, Fonck, Nungesser, and others who had achieved greatly: *"Tiens, Luf! Comment ça va ,mon vieux!"* He never boasted or took credit to himself. He counted his success as three fourths luck, and was always surprised that so much of it should come his way. When foolish people tried to flatter him, he used to say to us after they had gone: "Well, you know, it's funny what things people will say to a man's face. I wonder if they think we like it?" He had to take a lot of it whether he liked it or not; but it had no unfortunate effect upon him. He was always the same old "Luf."

One of his favourite off-duty recreations was hunting for mushrooms. On rainy days when there was no flying, he would go off to the woods with a basket on a long-distance *reconnaissance des champignons*, and often returned with a plentiful supply, enough for the entire squadron. At other times he would spend a whole day romping with Whiskey and Soda, the lion mascots. They were both fond of him, particularly Whiskey, who followed him around the aerodrome like a pet dog. To see his way with the lions, and how readily they acknowledged a master in him, was to understand more clearly the nature of the qualities which had brought him success as a combat pilot.

In January, 1918, he received his commission as major in the United States Air Service. He was a problem to the American authorities, and at first they showed poor judgment in the use which they made of his services. Not knowing what to do with him, they sent him to the American A.I.C. at Issoudun, where they gave him a roll-top desk, a writing-pad and pencil, and absolutely nothing to do. There he sat day after day, whittling his pencil, or making little curlicues on his writing-pad. Any average judge of character could have known after a five-minutes talk with Lufbery that he would never make a paper-work squadron commander. He knew nothing, and wanted to know nothing, about the routine of making reports and of keeping lists and records and indents. His place was at the Front, leading his patrol into combat. One of the men who knew him at Issoudun said that he was pathetically helpless in that den of the more or less typical kind of American officer. In his loneliness he used to confide in his orderly, and ask his advice as to the best means for getting out to the Front!

Relief came when he was sent with the 94th and 95th Pursuit Squadrons to Villeneuve in the Champagne Sector. But no fighting could be done because, although some of the pilots had machines, they had no guns. During the month of waiting for the rest of their equipment, Lufbery taught the men their combat tactics and flew with them to the lines, where they looked longingly across to patrols of enemy planes which they could not attack. Coming back from one of these tantalising patrols, Lufbery would land at the aerodrome of the Lafayette Squadron, then at La Ferme de la Noblette, on the Chalons-Suippes road. "Well," he would say gloomily, "it's nearly a year since the United States declared war, and what do you suppose the 94th is doing? Waiting for machine guns! Six hundred million dollars appropriated for the United States Air Service, and we're loafing around back of the lines because we can't get guns enough to equip a dozen planes!"

The guns came at last, and on April 10, 1918, the 94th started patrol duty on the Toul Sector. There was but little activity in that region then, and the first two months of service was chiefly a hunt for enemy planes which rarely appeared. Lufbery led patrols daily and followed his old practice of lone *chasse*, but without much success. Few Germans were abroad, and when found refused to give battle. The brilliant exception was one plane which came far into the French lines on photographic missions. On May 19 the booming of the French anti-aircraft batteries announced the return of these daring airmen. Lufbery went in pursuit and, as the event proved, to his death. The following account of his last battle is taken from Edward Rickenbacker's story of the action:

> It was about ten o'clock when the anti-aircraft guns on the top of Mont Mihiel began shooting at a very high altitude. An *alerte* came to us immediately that a German photographic plane was coming our way and was at that moment almost directly over our field. The batteries ceased firing and seemed to have scored a hit, for the German machine began a long *vrille*, spinning faster and faster as it neared the ground. Just as the onlookers were sure that it was about to crash, it straightened out and turned back toward the German lines. Lufbery's own machine was out of commission, but another Nieuport was standing on the field apparently ready for use. The mechanicians admitted that it was ready, and without another word Lufbery jumped into the seat and immediately took off. About five minutes after leaving the ground he had reached 2000 feet and was within

MARON (MERTHE-ET-MOSELLE)

Lufbery fell in the garden behind the first house on the right. The tablet bears the inscription: "Raoul Lufbery. Major Air Service, United States Army. Killed in Aerial Combat, May 19, 1918. This tablet is placed here in his memory by his comrades of the United States Air Service."

THE WRECK OF MAJOR LUFBERY'S MACHINE. MAY 19, 1918

range of the German six miles away. The first attack was witnessed by all our watchers. Lufbery fired several short bursts, then swerved away and appeared to busy himself with his gun which seemed to have jammed. Another circle over their heads and he had cleared the jam. Again he attacked from the rear when suddenly his machine was seen to burst into flames. He passed the German and for three or four seconds proceeded on a straight course. Then he jumped. His body fell in the garden of a peasant woman's house in a little town just north of Nancy. There was a small stream about one hundred yards distant and it was thought that Lufbery, seeing a slight chance, had jumped in the hope of falling into the stream. We arrived at the scene less than thirty minutes after he had fallen. Already loving hands had removed his body to the town hall, and there we found it, the charred figure entirely covered with flowers from nearby gardens.

The funeral took place on the following day. General Gérard, Commander of the Sixth French Army, came with his entire staff, and General Edwards, his old commanding officer in the Philippines, and General Liggett and Colonel William Mitchell, of the United States Air Service, together with hundreds of officers, French and American, from all branches of army service on the sector. Lieutenant Kenneth P. Culbert wrote of the funeral to Professor C. T. Copeland of Harvard:

> As we marched to the grave, the sun was just sinking behind the mountain that rises so abruptly in front of Toul; the sky was a faultless blue, and the air heavy with the scent of blossoms. An American and a French general led the procession, followed by a band which played the funeral march and 'Nearer my God to Thee' so beautifully that I for one could hardly keep my eyes dry. Then followed the officers of his squadron and of my own—and after us, a group of Frenchmen famous in the stories of this war, American officers of high rank, and two American companies of infantry separated by a French one. We passed before crowds of American nurses in their clean white uniforms and a throng of patients and French civilians. He was given a full military burial, with the salutes of the firing squad and the repetition of taps, one answering the other from the west. General Edwards made a brief address, one of the finest talks I have ever heard, while French and American planes circled the

field throughout the ceremony. In all my life I have never heard 'taps' blown so beautifully as on that afternoon. Even some of the officers joined the women there in quietly dabbing at their eyes with white handkerchiefs. Truly France and America had assembled to pay a last tribute to one of their bravest soldiers. My only prayer is that somehow, by some means, I may do as much as he for my country before I too go west—if in that direction I am to travel.

Lieutenant Culbert was killed in combat the day after his letter was written. To him Lufbery had been a shining example as he was to thousands of young airmen, French and American; and though the war is over and those heroic days gone for all time, perhaps, they keep his memory bright and follow him still.

SERVICE RECORD
GEORGE A. McCALL, Philadelphia, Pennsylvania.
PREVIOUS SERVICE: American Ambulance, 1916.
SERVICE IN FRENCH AVIATION:
  Date of enlistment: September 1, 1916.
  Aviation Schools: September 14, 1916, to May 28, 1917, Buc, Avord, Pau, G.D.E.
  Breveted: March 16, 1917 (Blériot).
  At the Front: Escadrille Spad 23, May 30 to September 9, 1917.
    Escadrille Spad 86, September 15 to October 22, 1917.
    Escadrille Spad 48, November 6, 1917, to April 23, 1918.
    Escadrille Sal. 30, May 29 to September 30, 1918.
    Escadrille Spad 103, October 24, 1918, to Armistice.
  Final Rank: Sergent.

George A. McCall

George McCall is one of those men who goes his own quiet way at his own leisurely gait. Americans of the essentially gregarious type never understood him, and so they left him to his solitude, much to his satisfaction. Others whose tastes coincided somewhat with his own, admired him for his self-sufficiency—using this term in its original and fine meaning. He was not dependent upon companionship. He had resources within himself which seemed to make it unessential. They admired him, too, for his intense hatred of meddling.

Before joining French Aviation, he was a member of the American Field Ambulance. Once, during his services on the Verdun Sector, an American official connected with the Ambulance found it necessary to make a rather dangerous journey under shell-fire, in the front-line area. He asked for a steady, cool-headed driver, and Mac was chosen by his section commander. He was an ideal man for such a task, for he is not cursed with a vivid imagination. He could no more anticipate the sensation of being killed than he could shine in conversation at a pink tea.

He was the only Blériot pilot of his time who made his flights precisely as they should be made, and while on the ground spent much of his leisure in figuring out how various manoeuvres could best be done. Most of us trusted to instinct or to luck for guidance. Mac never did, with the result that he was the only one of his contemporaries at Buc who carried out to the letter the instructions of the *moniteurs*, and did his spirals and serpentines successfully at the first trial.

At the Front he did his work faithfully and well, serving continuously in French squadrons from May 8, 1917, until the close of the war.

SERVICE RECORD

JAMES R. McCONNELL, Carthage, North Carolina.

PREVIOUS SERVICE: American Ambulance, 1915-

SERVICE IN FRENCH AVIATION:
 Date of enlistment: October 1, 1915.
 Aviation Schools: October 1, 1915, to April 16, 1916, Pau, G.D.E.
 Brevetted: February 6, 1916 (Blériot).
 At the Front: Escadrille Lafayette, April 20, 1916, to March 19, 1917.
 Final Rank: Sergent.
 Killed in combat: Near Jussy (Aisne), March 19, 1917.

DECORATIONS:
 Croix de Guerre, with Star (Ambulance).
 Croix de Guerre, with Palm (Aviation).

CITATIONS

Le 5 octobre, 1915

Citation à l' Ordre du Service de Santé:
McCONNELL, JAMES, de la S.A.A. N° 2

Conducteur engagé de la première heure, animé d'un excellent esprit, a toujours fait preuve d'un courage et d'une hardiesse dignes des plus grands éloges.

Citation à l'Ordre de l'Armée:

McCONNELL, JAMES ROGERS, Sergent Pilote à l'Escadrille N. 124

Citoyen américain engagé au service de la France. Pilote modeste autant que courageux, disait souvent à ses camarades: " Tant mieux si je dois être tué, puisque c'est pour la France." A trouvé une mort glorieuse le 19 mars, 1917, au cours d'un combat contre des avions ennemis.

James R. McConnell

James McConnell's record in the war, and the changes wrought in him by his experiences overseas, epitomize the changing point of view of the great majority of Americans who volunteered to do something for France before our declaration of war. No other member of the old Escadrille Lafayette was so typically American. Some, like Thaw and Lufbery, were "citizens of the world at large"; others, like Rockwell and Victor Chapman, seemed born to an atmosphere of high romance; but McConnell was in the truest sense representative of his country and generation—clever, observant, perfectly balanced, loving sport and adventure, and exceedingly human. He sailed for France in January, 1915, actuated primarily by the spirit of adventure, for he told his friends that the war would not last forever and that he intended to see something of it before it was too late. In the back of his mind was a sense that France was fighting in a just cause, and he said: "I'll be of some use, too, not just a sightseer looking on; that wouldn't be fair."

His friend, Henry M. Suckley, sailed with him on the same steamer, and they joined the American Ambulance Field Service together. During the spring and summer of 1915, McConnell served with Section 2, in the heavy fighting about Pont-à-Mousson and the Bois-le-Prêtre. It is said that no ambulance men, with the possible exception of those at Verdun, went through greater difficulties and dangers than were surmounted by the members of Section 2, and McConnell's letters, some of which were published in the *Outlook* of September, 1915, with a word of introduction by Colonel Roosevelt, were so vivid, humorous, and full of interest that they caused a wide stimulation in contributions and enlistments to the ambulance.

As the summer passed, a change came over McConnell: the daily task of evacuating wounded brought a realisation of what this war meant, the principles at stake, and the spirit in which even the humblest *fantassin* fought for the soil of France and the freedom of the race. He saw middle-aged men, serious, poor, the fathers of families, carried out uncomplaining to the rear, mangled or crippled for life. This was a subject for reflection. He was young and without dependents—and yet these men stood in the first-line trenches at grips with the enemy, while he worked in the rear, in a certain amount of danger, it was true, but still, in his own rapidly crystallizing opinion, an *embusqué*. Many an American has gone through the same stage of realisation and self-examination, and ended, like McConnell, by deciding to play the more active and satisfactory part of a combatant.

On October 1, 1915, McConnell enlisted in the Lafayette Flying Corps, exchanging the khaki of the Ambulance for the horizon blue of France. On February 6, 1916, just one year after his arrival in France, he passed the military *brevet*, and in April he went to the Front as one of the original members of the Escadrille Lafayette. His sunny humanity, close and humorous powers of observation, and knack of vivid description lent an unusual charm to his writings, and his book *Flying for France,* which appeared before our declaration of war, did genuine patriotic service in forming public opinion during the period preliminary to hostilities.

McConnell's career as a pilot at the Front is summed up in the words of his citation to the Order of the Army, "A pilot as modest as he was brave." Flying with Rockwell and Lufbery, men whose element was the air, he became known as a steady and daring companion over the lines, who could be relied upon to do his part in any emergency. In August, 1916, when the Squadron was at Bar-le-Duc, he was on patrol with Rockwell and Prince, over the heavy fighting in the region of Fleury and Thiaumont. Their mission was to prevent the enemy observation machines from doing their work, and they stayed above the lines until darkness began to fall and it was too late for further German activity. The stars were shining when they headed for their field. Prince and Rockwell landed without mishap, but on the way home McConnell had a *panne de moteur*. He wrote:

> I made for a field, but in the darkness I couldn't judge my distance well and went too far. At the edge of the field there were trees, and beyond, a deep cut where a road ran. I was skimming the ground at a hundred miles an hour and heading for the trees. I saw soldiers running to be in at the finish and thought to myself that Jim's hash was cooked, but I went between two trees and ended head-on against the opposite bank of the road. My motor took the shock and my belt held; as my tail went up it was cut in two by some very low telephone wires. I wasn't even bruised.

It was characteristic that in his letter home he made no mention of being injured. As a matter of fact, his back was severely wrenched in the crash, and grew steadily worse, although he continued to fly for several days. Toward the end of the month he and Kiffin Rockwell went to Paris on seven days' leave, and while there the pain grew so intense that night after night he was forced to sit up, unable to sleep.

In the mornings Paul and Kiffin helped him to dress, and he hobbled forth, with the aid of a cane, to the old haunts where comrades were to be found. When the leave was up, he insisted on returning to the Squadron, but by that time he was unable to walk at all, and the captain ordered him off to a hospital. A painful rheumatism settled in the sprained back, and though he returned to the Front in November, it was soon evident that he was in no condition to fly, so he was shipped back to hospital. There he remained until the first week in March, 1917, when news came that the French were about to make an important advance. This was too much for McConnell—already bored and longing to be in the fighting. With a good deal of difficulty he persuaded the *médecin major* to let him go, and returned to the squadron on March 12.

McConnell's grave near Ham

Seven days later he was killed. On the morning of the 19th, he was flying with Genêt over the battlefields of the Somme. Well inside the enemy lines they encountered a pair of German two-seaters. Genêt told of what followed in a letter to his mother:

> I mounted to attack the nearest and left Mac to take care of the second. ... There were plenty of clouds and mist, and after I had finished my scrap, in which I got one of my main upper wing supports cut in half, a guiding-rod cut in half, several bul-

lets through my upper wing, and half an explosive bullet ... in my left cheek, which stunned me for a moment, I went down to look for Mac and help him if he was hard-pressed. Looked all around for fifteen minutes ... but could see neither him nor the German machine which must have attacked him. My upper wing was in great danger of breaking off, my wound was bleeding and pained quite a bit, so I finally headed back for camp, hoping Mac had missed me and gone back. ... When I got to our field I looked in vain for Mac's machine ... my worst fears were confirmed ... we have had absolutely no news of him .. it is terrible.

A few days later the advancing French troops found the wreck of a Nieuport with McConnell's body beside it, so his friends had the sad satisfaction of knowing that he was buried by friendly hands. On the 2nd of April, at the American Church on the avenue de l'Alma, a very beautiful memorial service was held for McConnell and for his old friend Suckley, who was killed—by one of the strange freaks of war—on the day following McConnell's death. Two years before, they had arrived at Bordeaux on the same steamer, and they gave their lives within twenty-four hours of one another—on the Somme, and in distant Macedonia. McConnell's thirtieth birthday was on March 14. In the diary he had kept with scrupulous care ever since his arrival in France, the last sentence written in his twenty-ninth year was:

> This war may kill me, but I have it to thank for much.

SERVICE RECORD

HERSCHEL J. McKEE, Indianapolis, Indiana.
SERVICE IN FRENCH AVIATION:
Date of enlistment: April 12, 1917.
Aviation Schools: April 15 to October 12, 1917; Avord, Pau, G.D.E.
Breveted: August 30, 1917 (Caudron).
At the Front: Escadrille N. 314, October 15, 1917, to February 8, 1918.
Final Rank: Sergent.
Shot down by anti-aircraft fire:
  Near Château-Salins, February 8, 1918.
Prisoner in Germany: Until the Armistice.

Herschel J. McKee

Herschel McKee will always be known, on account of a newspaper clipping, which he probably curses in secret, as "Your Flying Son." It was hard luck that the thing was posted on the Bulletin Board at Avord, but names stick. On October 15, 1917, he went to the Escadrille N. 314. This squadron was engaged in the protection of Nancy, and its machines, of a rather antiquated type, were not supposed to cross the lines. McKee, in his eagerness for combat did not always obey rules, and on the 8th of February, 1918, was shot down by German anti-aircraft guns near Château-Salins, far inside the enemy lines. By good luck he landed unhurt, but was caught by the Germans and made prisoner. In September he made his escape from a prison camp, but was recaptured three days later, and did not succeed in leaving Germany until after the Armistice.

SERVICE RECORD

WILLIAM J. McKERNESS, Wallingford, Connecticut.

SERVICE IN FRENCH AVIATION:
Date of enlistment: June 13, 1917.
Aviation Schools: June 20, 1917, to May 10, 1918, Avord, Cazeaux.
At the Front: Escadrille C. 46 (as observer and machine-gunner), May 12 to August 15, 1918.
Final Rank: Sergent.
Wounded in combat: July 15, 1918.
Killed in combat: August 15, 1918, northeast of Ribécourt.

DECORATIONS:
Croix de Guerre, with Star.

CITATION

DIVISION AÉRIENNE, ÉTAT-MAJOR.

Le 31 *juillet,* 1918

Le Général Commandant la Division Aérienne cite à l'Ordre de la Division:

McKERNESS, WILLIAM, Soldat, Légion Étrangère, Mitrailleur en Avion

Mitrailleur plein de courage, d'adresse, et de sang-froid. Attaqué, le 15 juillet, par une patrouille de 15 monoplaces, a vaillamment engagé la lutte, permettant ainsi aux avions qu'il protégeait de poursuivre leur mission. A été blessé au cours de ce combat, a eu son appareil criblé de balles, un réservoir en feu et son mitrailleur arrière grièvement blessé.

Le Général Commandant la Division Aérienne

(Signé)   M. DUVAL

William J. McKerness

William McKerness was a plucky and determined airman—clean grit all the way through. He had great difficulty in learning to fly and the instructors warned him time after time that if he continued he would infallibly be killed. Whether he believed them or not, he kept on, and none of us will ever forget the cheerful manner in which he used to drag himself out of a nightmare pile of wreckage and ask for just one more chance. As to getting killed, he left his comrades, who were exceedingly fond of him, to do the worrying. It became evident to him at last that Nature had not intended him for a pilot, but instead of accepting his release, which the French offered, McKerness announced that he had come to France to fight in the air, and if he could not be a pilot, he would like to be a machine-gunner. Appreciating the spirit that prompted it, the authorities granted his request, and at the Gunnery School he soon showed his gift for the new work.

On May 12, 1918, McKerness arrived at the Front, assigned to the Escadrille C. 46, and had the pleasure of being ordered to fly with his friend Sitterly, as forward gunner on an R. 11 Caudron. In this three-seater *chasse* work, with Sitterly and Lacassagne, the French rear gunner, McKerness played a splendid part in the bitter fighting along the Marne. His letters, refreshingly free from the taint of "lead swinging," give us glimpses of desperate combat and of a rarely cool and observant combatant:

> There were several Boches *piquing on us*—fifteen—and most of them attacked our machine. . . . One of the first bullets went through the stock of my Winchester and pieces of it went through my combination. Going through the Winchester first is the only thing that saved my leg. Lacassagne was wounded badly in the beginning of the combat, but continued to fire. Bullets were going all through our machine and the next thing I knew, I got a piece of bullet in my back. The (*aileron*) wires were cut by bullets, and when Lacassagne changed his magazines he let one fall on the wires that control the rudder, causing a jam there . . . after this there was no way of turning the machine . . . and one of the motors caught on fire.

The missions of protection, far into the enemy lines, on which McKerness was dispatched, made flying synonymous with fighting, for even the most conservative of German pilots would fight when well *chez lui*. The *triplace* fighting, too, was of a peculiarly desperate character, as the mission of the big Caudron was to stand off the enemy scouts while the Bréguets finished their work or made good their escape.

At length, on August 15, McKerness left the aerodrome, with a French pilot, on his last patrol. Northeast of Ribécourt they were attacked by eight Fokkers, and it is believed that the pilot was killed at the first burst, for the Caudron fell out of control in our lines, between Ribécourt and Saint-Leger. The pilot and both gunners were found dead in their seats.

SERVICE RECORD

JAMES H. MCMILLEN, New York City.

SERVICE IN FRENCH AVIATION:
Date of enlistment: June 25, 1917.
Aviation Schools: June 29, 1917, to February 15, 1918, Avord, Pau, G.D.E.
Breveted: December 3, 1917 (Caudron).
Convoyeur: February 15 to March 12, 1918.
At the Front: Escadrille Spad 38, March 12 to July 10, 1918.
Final Rank: Sergent.

SERVICE IN U.S. AVIATION:
Commissioned First Lieutenant: July 11, 1918.
At the Front: Attached to French Squadron Spad 38, July 11 to September 27, 1918.

James H. McMillen

James McMillen was among the last men to train on Blériot at Avord. One of the aristocratic few who possessed a bicycle, he shared a room with Eldredge at Farges, and pedalled back and forth to the *piste*. He was breveted on December 3, 1917, and arrived at the G.D.E. at a most inauspicious period, when the Americans, many of whom languished in the guard-house, were looked on with a jaundiced eye. Permissions to Paris were unthinkable—unsanctioned visits to the boulevards were fraught with the dangers of a "special mission"—and a cruelly rigorous discipline kept the pilots standing all day in the snow, awaiting the dubious chance of a hop. McMillen's assignment, on March 12, 1918, to the Spad 38 (one of the best squadrons of the French army) made up in part for the trials he had endured at Plessis. The Spad 38 was commanded by Madon, and numbered among its pilots Guy, Shaffer, and Putnam, so McMillen found himself in congenial company.

On July 11 he transferred to the United States Air Service, with the rank of First Lieutenant, and had the pleasure of being sent back to Madon's *escadrille*, where he gave a good account of himself through the heavy fighting of the summer and fall. He has many anecdotes of Madon, with whom he was on the friendliest of terms, and his experiences of flying with the ace will furnish a rich source of memories for days of peace.

SERVICE RECORD

Douglas MacMonagle, San Francisco, California.

Previous Service: American Ambulance, 1916.

Service in French Aviation:
Date of enlistment: October 3, 1916.
Aviation Schools: October 17, 1916, to June 14, 1917, Buc, Avord, G.D.E.
Breveted: April 10, 1917 (Caudron).
At the Front: Escadrille Lafayette, June 16 to September 14, 1917.
Final Rank: Sergent.
Killed in combat: September 14, 1917, near Triaucourt (Meuse).

Decorations:
Cross de Guerre, with Star (American Ambulance).
Cross de Guerre, with Palm (Aviation).

CITATIONS

Au G.Q., le 2 août, 1916

L'automobiliste volontaire Douglas MacMonagle, de la S.S.A. Américaine No. 8.

Un obus étant tombé en plein poste de secours, a conservé toute sa calme et avec le plus grand dévouement, a contribué, sous un bombardement, au chargement de trois blessés dont l'évacuation était urgente.

Le Général Rouguerot
Commandant de la 16ᵉ Division d'Infanterie

G.Q.G., État-Major. *Le 29 octobre, 1917*

Extrait de l'Ordre Général N° 130, portant citation à l'Ordre de l'Armée:

MacMonagle, Douglas, Sergent (1ᵉʳ Régiment Étranger), Pilote à l'Escadrille N. 124

Jeune pilote américain, plein d'audace et de courage. Le 14 septembre s'est porté à la rencontre de huit avions ennemis qui tentaient de survoler nos lignes, a attaqué l'un d'eux résolument, a été tué au cours du combat.

(Signé) Maistre

Douglas MacMonagle

A short while after the death, in combat, of Douglas MacMonagle, the following account was written of him by one of his comrades:

You have doubtless heard, before this, that Mac has gone. It is a terrible loss for me, for all of us. He was one of the truest friends and comrades a man could have. On the morning it happened, L. L. and I flew over to Senard to get some clothing I had left at the Lafayette Squadron, landing at the field just after their patrol had come in from the lines. It was a glorious autumn morning and we were in very gay spirits. But the moment my wheels touched ground, while I was rolling over to the hangars, I knew that something had happened. It was a fearful sort of intuition. Didier Masson walked up to my machine as I was climbing out and said, 'Mac was killed this morning.'

One of the mechanicians was crying and the others standing in groups, doing nothing. I have never seen such a picture of dumb grief. Mac was loved by every one of them. He may have had enemies, nearly every one has; but if so, they were mighty few, and the kind any real man would rather call enemies. than friends. Mac was a man's man, if there ever was one.

"We walked up the hill to the barracks and found all the boys there. The attempts they made at a welcome were pathetic to say the least. Poor old Luf was inconsolable, Bill (Thaw) was pretending to work over squadron business as though nothing had happened. Carl Dolan had just gone with a tractor to get Mac's body which had fallen in the woods near Triaucourt.

Luf told me how it happened. He was leading the patrol when they sighted a flock of enemy single-seaters about 500 metres higher up and not very far distant. They were in the sun, so Luf immediately turned back toward our lines for altitude, hoping to come round them later with the sun in his favour. He saw that the others were all following him, noses up, climbing with him for all they were worth. Well, a moment later, looking back again he found that Mac had turned back and was going straight for the Boches. He was a long way off. Why he did it no one knows. Luf thinks that he may not have seen the Germans at all, for they were right in the sun. But Mac was a man to take chances, even very long ones. Furthermore, I know how keen he was on getting his first victory.

Before the others could help him, two Germans were on his tail, and they got him in the first burst. He received two bullets in the head, so that he couldn't have known what hit him. His body was not mangled, for which we were all profoundly glad, particularly for his mother's sake. She is in France and attended the funeral. I've been transferred back from Spa. 112 and am with 124 again; but with Mac gone, it doesn't seem like the same old crowd...."

So said all of his old comrades of the Escadrille Lafayette. The war was far from being finished at that time, and many fine fellows came later to join the squadron; but Mac's place was never filled, in the hearts of his old friends. He was a man's kind of man, a hater of pretence,

THE FIRING-SQUAD AT DOUGLAS MACMONAGLE'S FUNERAL

and the born enemy of "barracks-flyers." He had a caustic tongue and a formidable wit with which to wield it. To hear him rebuke one of these futile birds who rolled up flying time while on leave in Paris, was a privilege to be grateful for. He was always self-depreciating, but his actions belied his own account of them. After his service with the American Field Ambulance, he went at once into Aviation without the long, pleasant interval of leave in America which many ambulance drivers found necessary before entering another branch of service. He was an excellent combat pilot, and if he had lived, would have been counted among the aces. He is buried at Triaucourt in the Verdun Sector in a little plot of ground which will forever be sacred to all the surviving members of the Lafayette Corps.

SERVICE RECORD

CHARLES T. MALONE, Ossining, New York.

PREVIOUS SERVICE: American Ambulance, 1916–17.

SERVICE IN FRENCH AVIATION:
Date of enlistment: March 21, 1917.
Aviation Schools: April 3 to September 15, 1917. Avord, Pau.
Injured in accident at Pau: September 15, 1917. Released from French Aviation because of injuries received in accident.

Charles T. Malone

Malone is exceedingly lucky to be alive, but in another sense is one of the unluckiest men in the corps. Eager to get to the Front, he gave promise, at Avord, of making a first-class combat pilot. At Pau the instructors had remarked the skill and daring with which he piloted the Nieuport until the day came when he was sent up to do his altitude, on a 120 H.P. machine. Writing to Major Gros of this *sortie*, Malone said:

> A Frenchman and I went up to 5000 metres for an altitude, and while there I ran out of *essence*, which forced me to come down. I was not accustomed to the 120 H.P. motor, which is very heavy, and I overdid the descent a little, coming down so fast that I lost consciousness. I went into a *vrille* while unconscious and the rush of air must have revived me, for I came to in time to make some sort of a landing. I took the chimney off a house and ran into a ditch, turning the machine over and hurting one of my eyes and my head. I think I am about the luckiest man in France to have gotten away with my life.

With keenness undiminished by his accident and a long term in hospital, Malone still hoped to reach the Front, but in July, 1918, the medical authorities declared him unfit for further flying and sent him to Lyons, where he was discharged.

SERVICE RECORD

KENNETH MARR, San Francisco, California.

PREVIOUS SERVICE: American Ambulance, 1915–16.

SERVICE IN FRENCH AVIATION:
Date of enlistment: July 20, 1916.
Aviation Schools: August 8, 1916, to March 26, 1917, Buc, Avord, Cazeaux, Pau, G.D.E.
Brevetted: January 7, 1917 (Blériot).
At the Front: Escadrille Lafayette, March 29, 1917 to February 18, 1918.
Final Rank: Sergent.

SERVICE IN U.S. AVIATION:
Commissioned Captain: January 26, 1918.
Promoted Major: September 17, 1918.
At the Front: 103d Pursuit Squadron, February 18 to March 29, 1918.
94th Pursuit Squadron, April 1 to June, 1918.
(As Flight Commander and later as Commanding Officer.)
On duty in U.S., June, 1918, to Armistice.

DECORATIONS:
Croix de Guerre, with Palm and Star.

CITATION

G.Q.G., État-Major. *Le* 8 *octobre,* 1917

Le Chef d'État-Major de la 2ᵐᵉ Armée cite à l'Ordre de l'Aéronautique:

Marr, Kenneth, N° M^(le) 11843, Sergent Pilote à l'Escadrille N. 124

Citoyen américain engagé au service de la France. Pilote de chasse de valeur. Le 19 septembre a contribué à la chute d'un avion ennemi. Le 22 septembre dans un combat contre plusieurs monoplaces ennemis a eu son avion très gravement endommagé. A réussi par son adresse et son sang-froid à le ramener dans nos lignes.

Ordre N° 12058 "*D*" *G.Q.G.,* 29 *novembre,* 1918

Le Capitaine **Kenneth Marr**, Commandant l'Escadrille Américaine 94

Excellent Commandant d'Escadrille, d'une bravoure légendaire, a été un bel exemple pour toute son unité. Déjà cité.

Kenneth Marr

Kenneth Marr knew intimately half the personnel of the French Air Service from the *commandants* down to the *popote* orderlies. "*Ah! Bonjour, Mar, comment ça va, mon vieux?*" This was the friendly cordial greeting he had from French pilots all along the Western Front. Unofficially and quite unconsciously he did liaison work of the most valuable kind; for knowing him, Frenchmen were bound to feel kindly disposed toward America, whatever their native prejudices against the country may have been. He was a *très bon camarade* with all of them, despite the fact that he spoke French as a Californian, long resident in Alaska, would inevitably speak it. The chief reason for all this was, of course, that he had a gift for friendship.

But in addition, his service record in France dates back to the be-

Marr at Chaudun (Aisne). 1917

ginning of 1916 when he was driving an ambulance for the American Field Service at the time of the great German offensive at Verdun. When his term of enlistment with the ambulance had expired, he at once joined the French Air Service and returned to the Front as a pilot March 29, 1917. He remained with the Escadrille Lafayette until March 29, 1918. Upon this latter date he was sent, with Captains Peterson and Hall, to the 94th Aero Squadron—the first American combat unit, after the Lafayette, to be placed on active duty. A few weeks afterward he was promoted major and placed in command of the 94th, the squadron of Rickenbacker, Campbell, Meissner, Chambers, Winslow, Chapman, and Davis. He was sent on duty to America in the summer of 1918.

SERVICE RECORD

Didier Masson, Los Angeles, California.

Previous Service: 129th and 36th Infantry Regiments (French), August to October, 1914.

Service in French Aviation:
Date of enlistment: October, 1914.
Aviation Schools: Pau, R.G.A.
Brevetted: May 10, 1915 (Caudron).
At the Front: Escadrille C. 18, March to September, 1915.
Escadrille N. 68, September, 1915, to April, 1916.
On duty as moniteur at Cazeaux, April 16 to June 19, 1916.
Escadrille Lafayette, June 19, 1916, to February 15, 1917.
On duty as instructor at Avord, February 15 to June 14, 1917.
Escadrille Lafayette, June 16 to October 8, 1917.
With Escadrille N. 461, Camp Retranché de Paris, October 10 to October 28, 1917.
On duty as Instructor at American A.I.C. (Issoudun), October 28, 1917, to October 1, 1918.
Final Rank: Adjudant.

Decorations:
Médaille Militaire.
Croix de Guerre, with two Palms.

CITATION

Ordre N° 4022 "D," le 8 novembre, 1916

Grand Quartier-Général des Armées, État-Major.

En vertu des pouvoirs qui lui sont conférés par la Décision Ministérielle N° 12285 K du 8 août, 1914, le Général Commandant en Chef a conféré, à la date du 8 novembre, 1916, la Médaille Militaire au Militaire dont le nom suit:

Masson, Didier, Adjudant Pilote à l'Escadrille N. 124

Très ancien pilote; après avoir pris part à de nombreux réglages de tir et reconnaissances, a participé vaillamment aux opérations de chasse du groupe de Verdun. Le 12 octobre, 1916, pendant la protection d'un bombardement, a abattu un avion ennemi. A accompli sa mission jusqu'au bout, malgré une panne d'essence survenue au-dessus des lignes allemandes et qui l'a obligé à revenir en vol plané.

La nomination ci-dessus comporte l'attribution de la Croix de Guerre avec Palme.

Le Général Commandant en Chef

(Signé) Joffre

Didier Masson

The oldest of the American volunteers in the Lafayette Flying Corps, from the point of view of military experience, is Didier Masson, who has been flying almost continually since 1909. In 191 3 he was Chief of Air Service in the army of General Obregon in Mexico. He is, perhaps, the only man in the Lafayette, or any other corps, who has comprised, in his own person, the entire Air Force of a nation. He knows the occidental coast of Mexico, as it is known only to the frigate-birds and pelicans of that desolate and lonely land. While in the service of General Obregon, he often attacked, single-handed, the entire navy of his chief's implacable foe, General Huerta. However, this was not a deed of such reckless daring as might be supposed; for the Huerta navy, in the matter of equipment, was in a class with the Obregon Air Force. One ancient gunboat, with engines developing about four knots per hour, manned by beach-combers and other nautical soldiers of fortune, kept the sea lanes open, after a fashion, for the Huerta gun-runners. Didier's first appearance above this antique tin pot caused an immense stir. He was flying a Curtiss of a now forgotten model and carried a load of tin cans—filled with explosive and tied up with pieces of wire. Time after time he dropped these missiles on the tin-pot gunboat with no appreciable result in so far as he could determine.

At the time of the outbreak of the other great war in 1914, Didier resigned his Mexican commission and offered his experience as a military aviator to the French Government. At that time he held two brevets: one from the Aero Club of California and one from the Aero Club of America. He received his third one in the French Service, in February, 1915, and went to the Front, first, as a pilot in the French Squadron C. 18. Later, taking pursuit training, he was transferred to the Combat Squadron N. 68, in September, 1915, and in July, 1916, to the Escadrille Lafayette. Didier was long *chef de popote* of this latter unit. While this was by no means his most distinguished service at the Front, it was a very useful one. Under his management, the squadron mess became famous all along the Western Front, and many distinguished guests, both French and British, gladly acknowledged the excellence of his dinners.

In the latter days of the war he was sent to Avord as an instructor in the French aviation school there. A good many of the later volunteers received their Nieuport training at his hands, and splendid training it was. Natural aptitude and a long apprenticeship in flying made him one of the most skilful pilots in the French Service. Old warrior that he was, he found the work more suited to his years than the strain of combat patrols. In this position he served France, and America, the country of his adoption, until the close of the war.

SERVICE RECORD
WILLIAM HENRY MEEKER, New York City.
SERVICE IN FRENCH AVIATION:
Date of enlistment: June 3, 1917.
Aviation Schools: June 13 to September 11, 1917, Avord, Pau.
Breveted: July 26, 1917 (Caudron).
Final Rank: Caporal.
Killed in line of duty: September 11, 1917, at Pau.

William Henry Meeker

Serious, determined, and intensely patriotic, Meeker was a young American of the very highest type; had he lived he would have done splendid work at the Front, and his death at Pau is particularly sad on this account. Meeker took the Caudron training and made a most brilliant record at Avord; few men have been breveted in a shorter time. He was all anxiety to get to the Front, and once his Nieuport training was finished, he took the train for Pau without the loss of an hour. There, while doing a vertical spiral in an 18-metre Nieuport, he fell into a wing slip, as any young pilot is apt to do, failed to pull out of it in time, and crashed into the ground, killing himself instantly. At his funeral the whole school turned out to do him honour; the coffin-bearers were five comrades of the Lafayette Corps, and Lieutenant Chevalier, of the United States Navy.

SERVICE RECORD
WALTER B. MILLER, New York City.
PREVIOUS SERVICE: American Ambulance, 1916–17.
SERVICE IN FRENCH AVIATION:
Date of enlistment: June 10, 1917.
Aviation Schools: June 16, 1917, to March, 1918, Avord, Juvisy, G.D.E.
Breveted: October 10, 1917 (Caudron).
Final Rank: Caporal.
SERVICE IN U.S. AVIATION:
Commissioned Second Lieutenant: April 1, 1918.
At the Front: With First Observation Group, April 1 to August 3, 1918.
Killed in combat: Near Château-Thierry, August 3, 1918.

Walter B. Miller

Walter Miller was a genuine original, the oddest, drollest, and most likable of men. His life was a kaleidoscopic succession of adventures by land and by sea; surveying the coast of Central America, running shells through the submarine blockade to Archangel, driving an ambulance on the Western Front, piloting an aeroplane in some of the heaviest fighting of the war, and meeting death in an epic combat against thirty enemy machines. Those of us who lived in the same barrack with Miller will never forget him, his gayety, his optimism, his generosity, his fine careless courage.

LEFT TO RIGHT: MILLER. BULLEN, SITTERLY. RODGERS, (UNIDENTIFIED), WINSLOW, MACKE, AVORD, SUMMER OF 1917

On dreary evenings when the rain dripped outside, it was Miller who cheered us with his inexhaustible repertory of songs and stories. Half Irish, he had the true story-teller's gift; we followed the incidents of his career, weak with laughter or breathless in suspense. On the Front he earned the reputation of an indefatigable flyer, aggressive, determined, and brave as a lion. On August 3, above the battle raging to the north of Château-Thierry, Miller fought his last fight and went down, overwhelmed by swarming Fokkers.

SERVICE RECORD

BENNETT A. MOLTER, Wausau, Wisconsin.

SERVICE IN FRENCH AVIATION:
Date of enlistment: November 2, 1916.
Aviation Schools: November 8, 1916, to July 16, 1917. Buc, Avord, Pau, G.D.E.
Breveted: May 12, 1917 (Blériot).
At the Front: Escadrille Spad 102, July 20 to August 1, 1917.
Final Rank: Caporal.

SERVICE IN U.S. AVIATION:
Commissioned Captain.
On service in U.S., summer of 1917 to Armistice.

Bennett A. Molter

Bennett Molter was sent to the French Squadron N. 102, in July, 1917, and soon afterward was injured in a flying accident at his aerodrome. In August, 1917, he was granted permission to return to America, and while there transferred to the United States Air Service. He was commissioned captain and remained on duty in the United States until the close of the war.

SERVICE RECORD

ROBERT L. MOORE, Denison, Texas.

PREVIOUS SERVICE: Norton-Harjes Ambulance, 1917.

SERVICE IN FRENCH AVIATION:
Date of enlistment: May 24, 1917.
Aviation Schools: June 9 to November, 1917, Avord, G.D.E.
Breveted: September 26, 1917 (Caudron).
At the Front: Escadrille C. 305, November, 1917, to January 1, 1918.
Escadrille Spad 96, January 6 to May 1, 1918.
Final Rank: Sergent.

Robert L. Moore

Moore went to the G.D.E. without the single-seater training the majority of Lafayette men had at Avord and at Pau, and was sent, November, 1917, to fly a Caudron in the Escadrille C. 305. His ambition was to pilot a scout machine, and he was allowed to return to Plessis-Belleville for Nieuport training. This alleged training consisted in giving the pilot, accustomed only to flying the slow and steady Caudron, a 15-metre Nieuport, and telling him to fly; and it is to Moore's credit that he went to the dubious task without hesitation and finished without wrecking a machine. On January 1, 1918, he was sent to the Escadrille N. 96, and after four months of service at the Front, was released from the army on account of ill health.

SERVICE RECORD

GEORGE CLARK MOSELEY, Highland Park, Illinois.

SERVICE IN FRENCH AVIATION:
Date of enlistment: July 10, 1917.
Aviation Schools: July 18 to December 25, 1917, Avord, Tours, Pau, G.D.E.
Breveted: October 20, 1917 (Caudron).
At the Front: Escadrille Spad 150, December 27, 1917, to February 4, 1918.
Final Rank: Caporal.

SERVICE IN U.S. NAVAL AVIATION:
Commissioned Ensign: February 4, 1918.
Promoted Lieutenant (Junior Grade).
Naval Aviation School: February 6, to March 10, 1918, Moutchic-Lacanau (Gironde)
At the Front: U.S. Naval Seaplane Station, Dunkirk, March 15 to June 20, 1918.
U.S. Army Bombing School: June 25, to July 20, 1918, Clermont-Ferrand.
Attached to English Bombing Squadron 218, July 25 to September 10, 1918.
Attached to French Squadron, Escadrille de Saint-Pol, September 25 to November 5, 1918.

George Clark Moseley

Before he took to flying, Moseley was a famous football player at Yale, an All-American end. Big, bluff, and breezy, his usual salutation was a tremendous slap on the back, a slap which rendered speech impossible for several minutes. One imagined him in the air, piloting his machine with a series of careless and powerful jerks.

With his friend Spencer he went through the schools at Tours, Avord, and Pau, leaving the record of a fearless and skilful pilot. Still with Spencer, he was sent to the Escadrille N. 150 on December 27, 1917, and served faithfully with that unit until his transfer to the navy in February, 1918. The death of Spencer, his dearest friend, in January, was a terrible loss to Moseley, but he carried on with no outward sign of the lasting grief he must have felt.

After his transfer to the navy, Moseley was stationed at Dunkirk, in a squadron of hydro-aeroplanes—small, fast machines doing *chasse* work in the North Sea. The harbour of Dunkirk was one of the most dangerous seaplane bases in use by the Allies during the war—a long, narrow fairway, whose sides bristled with cranes, wireless poles, and the masts of ships. It was necessary to take off lengthwise along the basin no matter what the direction of the wind, and on his first "hop" in a hydro Moseley had a crash from which he was fortunate to escape alive. The wind was strong and across the fairway. He made a perfect get-away, but the wind caught him as he passed the point of the *quai*, drifting him toward two battleships which were moored side by side, filling half the narrow basin.

In spite of his efforts to pull up and over, the wireless rigging of one of these vessels caught his pontoons, and after a moment of acrobatics as sensational as they were involuntary, his plane crashed head first onto the deck of the second ship. After half an hour of dreamless sleep, Moseley limped back to his quarters, sore all over, and with a deep cut on his forehead, but ready for another *sortie*. He was stationed at Dunkirk until the close of the war.

SERVICE RECORD

ALAN H. NICHOLS, Palo Alto, California.

PREVIOUS SERVICE: American Ambulance, 1917.

SERVICE IN FRENCH AVIATION:
Date of enlistment: July 1, 1917.
Aviation Schools: July 26 to December 17, 1917, Avord, Tours, Pau, G.D.E.
Breveted: October 18, 1917 (Caudron).
At the Front: Escadrille Spad 85, December 19, 1917, to June 2, 1918.
Final Rank: Sergent.
Killed in combat: June 2, 1918, near Montdidier.

DECORATIONS:
Croix de Guerre, with two Palms.

CITATIONS

Citation à l'Ordre de l'Armée:
Le 13 *juin*, 1918

NICHOLS, ALAN, du 1ᵉʳ Régiment Étranger, Pilote à l'Escadrille Spad 85

Excellent pilote américain engagé dans l'armée française. A toujours montré de grandes qualités de sang-froid et d'énergie. Attaqué par deux monoplaces ennemis, en a abattu un en flammes.

Le 13 *juillet*, 1918

Citation à l'Ordre de l'Armée:

NICHOLS, ALAN, Sergent du 1ᵉʳ Régiment, Étranger, Pilote à l'Escadrille Spad 85
Citoyen américain engagé dans l'armée française pour la durée de la guerre, pilote énergique, brave, et plein d'entrain, modèle de calme et de devoir. Très grièvement blessé en attaquant un avion ennemi, a gardé cependant assez de calme et de présence d'esprit pour pouvoir ramener son avion dans nos lignes.

Alan H. Nichols

Nichols was a quiet and rather serious boy, who showed little interest in the *cafés* and *boulevards*, and made almost a cult of his flying. His comrades at Tours, where he was breveted on October 18, 1917, recognised in him a natural flyer, with a genuine love for the air. Pau was a memorable stage in his progress; a step nearer the Front, and the first opportunity to do unlimited flying of the kind he liked.

He wrote his family:

I finished *vol de groupe* this morning, the most fascinating thing imaginable. One learns to fly in formation, exactly as they patrol the lines at the Front. Each man has a big number on the side of his plane, and a position in the *groupe*, which he must keep and still follow the leader. The *moniteur* gives a meeting-place, such as '1000 metres above the *château*,' or, '1500 metres over the square wood,' and the first to arrive circles over the spot until the others come up. When they see each other's numbers, the leader starts off—it is up to him where. That is the value of it; they turn you loose to experiment and you learn a lot by yourself. We got some wonderful views of the sparkling, snowy Pyrenees, rough like the Sierras and solidly snow-covered. As for grand-stand seats, we have them! At the end, I spiralled down—right-hand, too—and hit the *piste* and landed without turning the engine on again, which pleased me very much.

Nichols reached the Front on December 19, 1917, assigned to the Escadrille Spad 85, and soon proved his mettle by shooting down a German *monoplace* in flames—the combat witnessed by his friend, George Kyle. On June 2, 1918, he made his last patrol. Over the German lines, beyond Soissons, he saw two enemy machines above him and became detached from his patrol while getting into position to attack. As he opened fire, a third German, whom he had not seen, dove on him from behind and shot him through the stomach. In spite of the shock and loss of blood, Nichols disengaged himself with characteristic coolness and managed to make a landing in the French lines.

NICHOLS'S COMRADES: ROLL-CALL AT TOURS

At 2.30 in the afternoon he was brought in an ambulance to the Royallieu Hospital, near Compiègne, where American nurses did everything possible for him and sat at the bedside while he rallied enough to tell of the combat. From the first it was evident that there was no hope for him; through the afternoon and evening he sank gradually, without suffering, and died just before midnight.

SERVICE RECORD

Charles B. Nordhoff, Los Angeles, California.

Previous Service: American Ambulance, 1916-17.

Service in French Aviation:
Date of enlistment: June 3, 1917.
Aviation Schools: June 14, 1917, to January 12, 1918, Avord, Pau, G.D.E.
Breveted: October 30, 1917 (Caudron).
At the Front: Escadrille N. 99, January 15 to February 19, 1918.
Final Rank: Caporal.

Service in U.S. Aviation:
Commissioned Second Lieutenant: February 19, 1918.
Promoted First Lieutenant: February 20, 1919.
At the Front: Assigned to French Squadron N. 99, February 19 to July 11, 1918.
On executive Staff, U.S. Air Service, July 11 to Armistice.

Decorations:
Croix de Guerre, with Star.

CITATION

Citation à l'Ordre de l'Aéronautique:
Engagé volontaire dans l'aviation française, où il a servi pendant six mois. A fait preuve de courage et de décision en livrant de nombreux combats, notamment le 29 mai, 1918, où il a, avec sa patrouille, abattu un avion ennemi.

Charles B. Nordhoff

Breveted at Avord on October 30, 1917, Nordhoff got to the Front on January 15 of the following year, assigned to the Escadrille N. 99, then stationed at Lunéville. In March the N. 99 went to Manoncourt, near Nancy, as one of the squadrons forming the new *Groupe de Combat 20*, which numbered among its pilots Thompson, Shoninger, Fairchild, Bullen, and Sinclaire. The *groupe* led the dreamy life of the Lorraine Front until the German attack in the Champagne, when it was sent successively to Villeseneux, Lormaison, and Villiers Saint-Georges. On July 11, Nordhoff (who had transferred to the Air Service and was flying as an American officer attached to the French) was ordered to report to the Executive Staff of the Air Service, where he spent the balance of the war in removing split infinitives from military reports—a task for which the training of a *chasse* pilot fitted him perfectly.

SERVICE RECORD

CARTER LANDRAM OVINGTON, Paris, France.

SERVICE IN FRENCH AVIATION:
Date of enlistment: April 20, 1917.
Aviation Schools: May 8 to December 10, 1917. Avord, Pau, Cazeaux, G.D.E.
Breveted: August 31, 1917 (Caudron).
At the Front: Escadrille Spad 85, December 2, 1917, to January 9, 1918.
Escadrille Spad 98, January 9 to April 1, 1918.
Final Rank: Sergent.

SERVICE IN U.S. AVIATION:
Commissioned First Lieutenant: April 1, 1918.
At the Front: Attached to the French Squadron Spad 98, April 1 to May 29, 1918.
Killed in combat: May 29, 1918, near Fismes.

DECORATIONS:
Croix de Guerre, with Palm.

CITATION

Le 16 *juin*, 1918

Le Général Commandant la 4ᵉ Armée cite à l'Ordre de l'Armée:

Le Lieutenant OVINGTON, CARTER LANDRAM, Armée Américaine, Escadrille Spa. 98

Officier américain, détaché sur sa demande dans une escadrille de chasse française. Jeune pilote d'élite qui s'est imposée à l'estime de tous. Pilote brave, ne demandant qu'à aller de l'avant. Tombé à l'ennemi le 29 mai, 1918.

(*Signé*)   GOURAUD

Carter Landram Ovington

Though born and bred in Europe, Ovington preserved his American characteristics and in all his actions showed the good stock he sprang from. He was the only son of the late Edward J. and Mrs. Georgia Ovington, the devoted Secretary of the Lafayette Flying Corps. The families of both his father and mother were warm-hearted friends of France. Curiously enough his grandfather, H. A. Ovington, of Brooklyn, New York, was Colonel of the Lafayette Guard on the occasion of General Lafayette's last visit to America in 1824.

Long before America declared war, Ovington, though barely nineteen, became restless and talked of nothing but his desire to enter Aviation. His mother with true Spartan courage made no attempt to dissuade him from the course which his sense of duty dictated, though she was terrified at the thought of the dangers which her boy would run. Ovington had the nature of a born aviator. He was proficient in all sports, and never happier than when rushing his motorcycle at full speed around dangerous corners.

He took to aviation training readily and left a remarkable record at the schools, with no breakage. His perfect knowledge of French and his understanding of the people made him very popular with his French officers, and when assigned to the French Escadrille N. 98, he quickly won their respect and admiration. He was eager for patrol, handled his machine delicately and skilfully, and loved the air as his element. When commissioned as First Lieutenant in the United States Air Service in April, 1918, he was assigned to the American Acceptance Park at Orly. But he was eager to return to the Front. His squadron commander made a strong request to have him reassigned to his squadron, where, a little more than a month later, he was doomed to fall under particularly dramatic circumstances.

LANDRAM OVINGTON AND AUSTIN PARKER

May 29, the day of his death, will always remain in the memory of those who were in France as one of the most dreary and discouraging of the whole war. The weather was atrocious, dark and cold with low-lying clouds enveloping the earth like a wet blanket. The Germans had succeeded in their surprise drive west of Rheims, in front of Château-Thierry, and it looked as though they would push their lines to the gates of Paris. Their offensive in this sector was so unexpected that few French squadrons were before them. The 98th was called upon to help offset this deficiency and Ovington with his comrades rose to the occasion. He was in the air many times that day, meeting the onrushing German machines, attacking enemy patrols at four different times during a single *sortie*. Once, when his gun jammed, he landed in a field, repaired it, and flew off again.

Upon returning to camp, about 12.45, he found other patrols ready to start and immediately volunteered. His commanding officer, Captain Cauboue, who was leading the first one, gave him the direction of the second, consisting of two other French machines. Their mission took them far behind the German lines in an attack on German balloons. It was on the homeward journey, that, owing to the low-lying clouds, which the machines were obliged to penetrate, Ovington collided head on with a French machine, piloted by Sergent L. Hoor. The pilot of the third machine, who witnessed the collision, reported that the wings of both Spads were torn asunder by the terrific impact, and that the wreckage fell upon the German troops in the region of Lagéry, north of Château-Thierry. This region was the scene of fierce fighting, the Germans being finally thrown back by the French and American troops. Neither his grave nor that of his comrade, nor the remains of their machines, have ever been found.

SERVICE RECORD

DAVID SHELDON PADEN, Evanston, Illinois.

PREVIOUS SERVICE: American Ambulance, 1917.

SERVICE IN FRENCH AVIATION:
Date of enlistment: July 14, 1917.
Aviation Schools: August 1, 1917, to September 4, 1918, Avord, Tours, Châteauroux, Pau, G.D.E.
Breveted: May 26, 1918 (Caudron).
At the Front: Escadrille Spad 163, September 6, 1918, to Armistice.
Final Rank: Sergent.

DECORATIONS:
Croix de Guerre, with Palm.

CITATION

IVe ARMÉE.   27 octobre, 1918
Citation à l'Ordre de l'Armée:

Sergent PADEN, DAVID SHELDON

Excellent pilote recherchant toutes les occasions de combat. À le 30 septembre, 1918, remporte sa première victoire en abattant un biplace ennemi.

David Sheldon Paden

Paden was one of the last men to enlist in the Lafayette Flying Corps. He arrived at Avord on August 1, 1917; was breveted at Châteauroux in May of the following year, and reached the Front in September. His squadron at that time was flying over the sector between Rheims and the Argonne, and Paden as a beginner was thrown into some of the heaviest fighting of the summer. He has had many interesting experiences, one of which he describes in the following passage from a letter to Major Gros:

We were flying at about 1000 metres, just under a heavy bank of clouds, which we dodged into from time to time to get away from the Boche A.A. gunners. Almost under us, at about 200 metres from the ground, four Spads and four Fokkers mysteriously appeared and started a scrap. From our altitude they looked like a bunch of gnats flying around in a little tight circle. We dove into the mess and climbed on the merry-go-round, as it were. Everybody was chasing around in a circle trying to get directly behind an enemy plane and not daring to leave the circle for fear another plane would line up and start business. About half the machines were simply firing off into space as far as I could figure. Every time I got a Boche in front of me lined up in my sights, I got a bit nervous about the one behind me, took a look at him, and lost the man in front. Finally, as if by mutual consent, the circle broke up. I saw one Spad leave in a fairly steep dive with a Fokker right behind him. I saw them only for a moment, as I was busy watching several unpleasant neighbours who seemed to have intentions of giving me lead poison. When we got back to our field we lacked one *pilote*, Sergent Féry; he was the one I had seen with the Boche, diving for our lines. He landed in the midst of an old trench, with two bullets in his legs and one that passed through his neck.

SERVICE RECORD

HENRY BREWSTER PALMER, New York City.

PREVIOUS SERVICE: American Ambulance, 1916–17.

SERVICE IN FRENCH AVIATION:
Date of enlistment: May 25, 1917.
Aviation Schools: June 9 to November 12, 1917, Avord, Pau.
Breveted: September 30, 1917 (Caudron).
Final Rank: Caporal.
Died of pneumonia at Pau, November 12, 1917.

DECORATIONS:
Croix de Guerre, with Star (Ambulance).

CITATION

Citation à l'Ordre du Brigade:
The Commander-in-Chief of the Armies of the Orient, cites to the Order of the Brigade:
PALMER, HENRY BREWSTER
Volunteer in the American Ambulance, Section No. 3, before the entry of the United States into the war. For courageous action in removing wounded in the region of Monastir between October and December, 1916.

Henry Brewster Palmer

Henry Palmer's death was particularly sad. Long before our declaration of war, impelled by a genuine sense of the justice of the Allied cause, he was in active service as an ambulance driver on the Western Front and in Macedonia. But the part of a non-combatant was not to his liking, and on May 16, 1917, he applied for enlistment in the Lafayette Flying Corps. Even at Avord he chafed under the delays due to bad weather, yearning always to do a man's work at the Front. Palmer was considered one of the most brilliant Blériot pilots among the later group at Avord. A flyer by instinct, he had a delicacy of touch and precision of eye that were wonderful, and his landings, light as eiderdown, were a delight to watch. At last the day came when he finished his *brevet* and Nieuport training at Avord and took the train for Pau, overjoyed to be a step nearer the Front. Those of us who stayed behind never saw him again. Struck down by swift pneumonia, he died shortly afterward. His body lies on a sunny hillside near Pau.

SERVICE RECORD

AUSTIN GILLETTE PARKER, Helena, Montana.

SERVICE IN FRENCH AVIATION:
Date of enlistment: May 2, 1917.
Aviation School: May 8 to December 15, 1917, Avord, Pau, G.D.E.
Breveted: September 24, 1917 (Caudron).
At the Front: Escadrille Spad 85, December 19, 1917, to January 9, 1918.
Escadrille Spad 98, January 9 to April 13, 1918.
Final Rank: Sergent.

SERVICE IN U.S. NAVAL AVIATION:
Commissioned Ensign: May 24, 1918.
U.S. Naval Air Station, Lake Bolsena, Italy.
At the Front: U.S. Naval Air Station, Porto Corsini, Italy.
Attached, 241st (Italian) Combat Squadron.

DECORATION:
Italian War Cross.

Austin Gillette Parker

It is impossible to think of Parker without thinking of Dudley Tucker, for they were inseparable companions; together they adventured through the jungles of Central America, made the voyage to France, enlisted in the Lafayette Flying Corps, and went through the Blériot School at Avord. With Bluthenthal, they lived at the Hotel Turco, and after dinner, when the smiling Suzanne brought coffee and *liqueurs* to the little table in the corner, the conversation was always worthy of a listener's ear. While Bluie puffed at his pipe, with an occasional nod or grunt of approval, Tucker told of the curious sides of life he had seen as business manager of the Washington Square Theatre, and Parker spoke of newspapers and their making. Never again in this world can the pleasant trio meet, for both Tucker and Bluthenthal were killed in combat on the Marne.

Parker went at his flying methodically and conscientiously, but he had the old newspaper man's contempt for thrills and took no part in the usual *bourrage de crâne*. He was breveted on September 24, 191 7, and arrived at the Front on December 19, assigned to the Escadrille N. 85. He made an excellent record with his unit and transferred to the Navy on May 24, 1918. After a period of instruction on naval planes at Lake Bolsena, Italy, he was placed on active duty at the U.S. Naval Air Station at Porto Corsini. During the last offensive on the Italian Front he was attached to the 241st Combat Squadron of the Royal Italian Naval Air Service. For his service here and at Porto Corsini he was awarded the Italian War Cross.

SERVICE RECORD

Edwin Charles Parsons, Springfield, Massachusetts.

Previous Service: American Ambulance, 1915–16.

Service in French Aviation:
Date of enlistment: April 13, 1916.
Aviation Schools: May 15, 1916, to January 20, 1917, Buc, Avord, Cazeaux, Pau, G.D.E.
Breveted: August 23, 1916 (Caudron).
At the Front: Escadrille Lafayette, January 25, 1917, to February 26, 1918. Escadrille Spad 3, April 24, 1918, to Armistice.
Final Rank: Sous-Lieutenant.

Decorations:
Médaille Militaire.
Croix de Guerre, with eight Palms.
Croix de Guerre (Belgian).
Croix de Léopold (Belgian).

CITATIONS

IIe Armée.   3 *octobre*, 1917

Le Général Commandant la 2me Armée cite à l'Ordre de l'Armée:

Parsons, Edwin, Sergent au 1er Régiment Étranger, Pilote à l'Escadrille N. 124

Bon pilote de chasse qui exécute avec entrain les missions qui lui sont confiées. Le 4 septembre a attaqué et abattu un avion ennemi en pièces sur Neuvilly (1er avion).

Ière Armée.   25 mai, 1918
  Citoyen américain fait preuve depuis deux ans déjà comme pilote de chasse d'un dévouement absolu, d'une joyeuse bravoure. Le 6 mai, 1918, a abattu seul son 2e avion ennemi.

Ière Armée.   4 juin, 1918
  Excellent pilote de chasse. A abattu seul le 17 mai, 1918, son 3e avion ennemi.

Citation à l'Ordre de l'Armée:
  Excellent pilote de chasse. Exécute avec intelligence toute mission. A abattu le 19 mai, 1918, son 4me avion ennemi.

Citation à l'Ordre de l'Armée:
  Pilote très énergique, plein de courage et d'entrain. Le 20 mai, 1918, a abattu son 5ème avion ennemi.

Médaille Militaire:
  Citoyen américain pilote, d'élite, exécutant avec crânerie et bonne humeur les missions les plus ingrates. A abattu le —— son sixième avion ennemi. Cinq citations.

Citation à l'Ordre de l'Armée:
  Excellent pilote de chasse, remarquable pour son audace, bravoure, et dévouement. A abattu le 26 *septembre*, 1918, son septième avion ennemi.

Citation à l'Ordre de l'Armée:
  Pilote de chasse exceptionnel pour son courage; un vrai modèle pour ses camarades. Le 1er octobre a descendu très bas dans les lignes ennemies et abattu son huitième avion ennemi dan les très durs circonstances.

Edwin Charles Parsons

Parsons is one of the American volunteers who was referred to by the French Pilots in G.C. 13 as *un chic type*. This is about as far as Frenchmen can go in the matter of compliment. One must have been born to the distinction, and then, in war-time, to have earned it all over again at the Front. Parsons was and did. Seeing him on leave one might easily have thought him an *aviateur des boulevards* who had never been nearer the Front than the *Camp Rentranché de Paris*. The resemblance was only superficial, for his eyes were never turned toward that promised land of all *aviateurs embusqués. Permission* over, he got into his well-worn flying clothes and a pair of *sabots*, and could always be seen, ten minutes before patrol time, clopping briskly out to the aerodrome.

Many an aeroplane engine has grown tired in his service, for he worked them hard. His old "E.C.P." bus was a well-ridden and frequently a well-riddled bird. His year of service at the Front with Spad 124 came at a time when the battle for supremacy between French and German airmen was the most keenly contested, and the odds in numbers of combat machines if anything on the side of the latter. Ted could always be counted to hold up his end of a combat. Doubtless there were plenty of times when he was badly frightened. But he had a way of concealing his emotions of whatever kind, so that no one could ever be certain that he was anything but bored or highly amused at the results of his adventures. He remained with Spad 124 until February, 1918, when it became the 103rd Aero Squadron of the United States Air Service. Realising the chaotic condition of American Aviation at that time, and profiting by the experience of other American volunteers who were being transferred, and losing weeks and even months of flying duty in the process, he decided to remain with the French.

He liked the French Service and hoped to organise a second Escadrille Lafayette among those Americans who were remaining in French squadrons. This plan was not feasible, however, so he was transferred to Spad 3, the old *escadrille* of Guynemer of the famous *Cigognes* group. During the spring and summer of 1918 he brought down seven more enemy planes, all of them officially confirmed. While with the *Cigognes*, he was given the rank of *Sous-Lieutenant*, the *Médaille Militaire*, the Belgian *Croix de Léopold*, and added seven more palms to his *Croix de Guerre*. He has been generously honoured by the French, in return for three years of gallant and faithful service for that country and for America.

SERVICE RECORD

PAUL PAVELKA, Madison, Connecticut.

PREVIOUS SERVICE: Foreign Legion (Infantry), November 28, 1914, to October 10, 1915.
Wounded while serving with Legion.

SERVICE IN FRENCH AVIATION:
Date of enlistment: October 18, 1915.
Aviation Schools: December 10, 1915, to August 8, 1916; Pau, Cazeaux, G.D.E.
Breveted: February 23, 1916 (Blériot).
At the Front: Escadrille Lafayette, August 11, 1916, to January 24, 1917.
Escadrille N. 391, February 8 to June 15, 1917.
Escadrille N. 507, June 15 to November 11, 1917.
Final Rank: Sergent.
Killed in line of duty: Near Salonica, November 12, 1917.

DECORATIONS:
Croix de Guerre, with Palm.

CITATION

Citation to the Order of the Army:
PAVELKA, PAUL, Sergeant, Aviation Pilot with the Army of the Orient

An American volunteer, he enlisted for the duration of the war; was badly wounded while an infantryman, in June, 1916; was transferred to the Aviation and became a keen fighting pilot, being tenacious and very conscientious. While in the Near East he has always been on the go, giving untiring proof of devotion to duty. Fought numerous air duels, following which he frequently returned with his machine riddled by bullets.

Paul Pavelka

Paul Pavelka went to France in October, 1914, as a member of the Army of Counani, obtained his release from this corps and joined the Foreign Legion. On the 9th of May, 1915, when the Legion attacked the German positions north of Arras, it was Pavelka who gave first-aid to Kiffin Rockwell who was wounded in the leg during the advance. Five weeks later, on the 16th of June, Pavelka himself received a bayonet wound in the leg during the bitter hand-to-hand fighting in the enemy trenches around Givenchy. He returned to duty before the Champagne offensive of September and October, 1915, and took part in all of the fighting in which his regiment was engaged throughout this battle.

In December, 1915, he was transferred to French Aviation, and joined the Escadrille Lafayette at Verdun in August, 1916. One of his earliest experiences at the Front as an airman was that of falling in flames, a more terrible one, as he afterward said, than any he had known in the infantry. By wing-slipping, he was able to keep the flames away from the *carlingue* of his Nieuport, and fell unhurt into a swamp.

PAVELKA'S FUNERAL IN SALONICA IN NOVEMBER, 1917

Pavelka was a great lover of adventure and wanted an experience of war as widely diversified as possible. Therefore, in December, 1916, he asked that he be sent to the Army of the Orient. He was attached first to the Escadrille N. 391 and later to N. 507, operating on the Salonica front. After his three years of fighting as an infantryman and aviator, it was the irony of fate that he should be killed by an accident related to neither of these branches of service. He was an enthusiastic horseman, and one day while off duty undertook to ride a vicious animal belonging to an officer of a British cavalry regiment stationed near his aerodrome. The horse fell with him and he received internal injuries from which he died on November 12, 1917. Pavelka was widely known throughout the Allied armies stationed at Salonica. He had made a splendid record for himself there, and all of his airmen comrades together with many British and French officers of other branches of service were at his grave. The *piquet d'honneur* was furnished by a battalion of the Foreign Legion and there was also an armed guard of Serbian soldiers. He was one of the few survivors of the famous American Section of the *2ᵉ Régiment du Marche* of the Foreign Legion, and one of the earliest of the volunteers of the Lafayette Corps. Pavelka's name stands high among those who joined the service of France when the need was greatest.

SERVICE RECORD

ALFRED D. PELTON, Montreal, Canada.
SERVICE IN FRENCH AVIATION:
Date of enlistment: February 19, 1917.
Aviation Schools: February 27 to September 25, 1917, Avord, Pau, G.D.E.
Breveted: July 15, 1917 (Caudron).
At the Front: Escadrille N. 151, September 27 to December 1, 1917.
Escadrille N. 97, March 5 to May 31, 1918.
Final Rank: Sergent.
Killed in combat: May 31, 1918, near Soissons.

Alfred D. Pelton

Although he was a Canadian both in birth and residence, Alfred Pelton was so eager for service in France that the executive committee of the Lafayette Corps decided to make an exception in his case and to admit him to membership. Pelton was as much at home with the Americans in the French

Air Service as were the scores of Americans who enlisted in the Canadian Air Force. He was sent to the French Squadron N. 151, where he was the only Lafayette Corps representative. Throughout the autumn and early winter of 1917, he acted as host to every American pilot who landed at his aerodrome at Chaux, near Belfort, on the Vosges Sector, and many of them who landed there for fuel or food will long remember his friendly, cordial greeting and his warm-hearted hospitality.

He was granted a three months' furlough in the winter, and upon his return to the Front in March, 1918, was sent to N. 97, where he did faithful and excellent work during the great German offensive of that spring. He was in the thick of heavy fighting, the most severe of all of it coming at the end of May, when the enemy crossed the Chemin des Dames and pushed on to Château-Thierry. For a time Allied pilots were greatly outnumbered, and many of them were shot down during battles in which the odds were all against them. Alfred Pelton was killed on the 31st of May, when his squadron was bravely carrying the fight into enemy territory. He fell within the German lines in the region of Soissons, and was at first thought to have been made prisoner. It was not until four months later that news of his death was received through the International Red Cross.

SERVICE RECORD

DAVID MCKELVY PETERSON, Honesdale, Pennsylvania.

SERVICE IN FRENCH AVIATION:
  Date of enlistment: October 9, 1916.
  Aviation Schools: October 16, 1916, to June 14, 1917, Buc, Avord, Pau, G.D.E.
  Breveted: April 16, 1917 (Blériot).
  At the Front: Escadrille Lafayette, June 16, 1917, to February 18, 1918.
  Final Rank: Sergent.

SERVICE IN U.S. AVIATION:
  Commissioned Captain: January 19, 1918.
  Promoted Major: August 29, 1918.
  At the Front: 103d Pursuit Squadron, February 18 to March 29, 1918.
  94th Pursuit Squadron, April 1 to May 25, 1918.
  C.O. 95th Pursuit Squadron, May 25 to October 8, 1918.
  On duty in America from October 8, 1918, to Armistice.
  Killed in line of duty: March 16, 1919, at Daytona Beach, Florida.

DECORATIONS:
  Distinguished Service Cross, with Bronze Oak Leaf.
  Croix de Guerre, with Palms.

CITATIONS

G.H.Q., A.E.F.

Captain DAVID MCK. PETERSON, A.S., Aero Squadron

For extraordinary heroism in action near Lunéville, France, on May 3, 1918. Leading a patrol of three, Captain Peterson encountered five enemy planes at an altitude of 3500 meters and immediately gave battle. Notwithstanding the fact that he was attacked from all sides, this officer, by skillful maneuvering, succeeded in shooting down one of the enemy planes and dispersing the remaining four.

The Bronze Oak Leaf is awarded to Captain Peterson for extraordinary heroism in action near Thiaucourt, France, on May 15, 1918. While on a patrol alone, Captain Peterson encountered two enemy planes at an altitude of 5200 meters. He promptly attacked despite the odds and shot down one of the enemy planes in flames. While thus engaged he was attacked from above by the second enemy plane, but by skillful maneuvering he succeeded in shooting it down also.

By command of General PERSHING

VIe ARMÉE. 9 novembre, 1917

Le Général Maistre, Commandant la VIe Armée, cite à l'Ordre de l'Armée:

PETERSON, DAVID MCKELVY, Sergent (Légion Étrangère), Pilote à l'Escadrille 124

Excellent pilote de chasse à l'Escadrille Lafayette. D'un crâne et d'une conscience admirables. Le 19 septembre, 1917, a abattu un avion ennemi, le poursuivant dans sa chute jusqu'à moins de 500 mètres d'altitude, malgré les canons et mitrailleuses ennemis (1er avion).

Le 24 octobre, 1917, s'est dépensé sans compter attaquant à très faible altitude, les réserves ennemies qu'il a mitraillées à plusieurs reprises.

Citation à l'Ordre de l'Armée: 29 novembre, 1918

Excellent officier et pilote audacieux, d'une habileté et d'un courage exceptionnel. Le 15 mai, 1918, a battu deux avions ennemis dans le secteur de Saint-Mihiel. Déjà deux fois cité.

David McKelvy Peterson

There are two Lafayette men, beside himself, who remember well the day when David Peterson walked into the *Bureau de Recrutement* at the Invalides to sign his papers for admission to French Aviation. He came down the hallway whistling "The Girl I Left Behind Me," a horribly tuneless execution of the air. These other recruits thought this an evidence of natural excitement upon a very great occasion. But they didn't know Peterson. They soon learned of their mistake and kept on learning better of it throughout two years of association with him in French aviation schools and at the Front.

It may be said without any exaggeration that he is the only American who has never had a thrill from his adventures as an airman. No event of the war ever stirred the tranquil depths of his nature. He simply couldn't be elated or depressed, frightened or overjoyed. The first *tour de piste*, the first *brevet* flight with the inevitable *panne de château*, the first *vrille* at the *École d'Acrobacy* at Pau, the first patrol over the lines, the first official victory—these events, so memorable in the lives of most pilots, he accepted with admirable placidity. For him, red-letter days had no existence.

As a patrol leader, he was without an equal, and he led more patrols than any other pilot of the Lafayette Squadron. With his blue-pennanted Spad in front, dodging its way among the *éclatements*, pilots in the machines following were in no danger of a surprise attack from enemy *chasse* planes. He saw everything while in the air. Often those of us who were with him received our first intimation that there were Germans in the neighbourhood when he "waggled" his warning, tipped up and dove. We had only to follow him down to be led to the enemy in quick time.

When the air was quiet, with not a white shell-burst on the sector to announce a foe, he would edge over, farther and farther into Germany, looking for something exciting to do. Suddenly he would "point" and hold a straight course, motor wide open; and we thinking, "Now, what is he up to?" Sometimes it would be a balloon, and although in those days the French had no incendiary bullets capable of igniting one, we shot at the bag for the sport of seeing the Germans haul it down. Sometimes it was a train, or motor transport on the roads. Coming back to the aerodrome the rest of us would be greatly excited over the events of the patrol, one pilot cursing a jammed gun, another jubilant because the old Vickers had worked perfectly. The mechanicians crowded around eager to hear all about it, examining the planes for holes. Peterson would jump out of his bus, stretch his legs, wiggle the kinks out of his neck, and walk over to the *Bureau du Groupe* to make out the *Compte Rendu*—the pilot's report of the events of the patrol. Then, in the "Remarks" column he would write in a firm clear hand, "*Rien à signaler*"—nothing to report!

Some of us thought his idea of nothing to report a rather strange one. When the weather was bad he was busy in his room in barracks, building shelves, making a table or a washstand. His quarters were always the most comfortable in the place—excepting only Thaw's, and

PETERSON AT AVORD,
APRIL, 1917

he had Percy, his old *légionnaire* orderly, to work for him. As *Groupe* 13 was continually on the move, following the offensives, either Allied or enemy, we had constantly to make new homes for ourselves in old, draughty Adrien barracks. For most of us this was a hopeless task. After tacking a few strips of tar paper over the larger cracks and knot-holes, we would give it up, and adjourn to Pete's room, always snug and cosy, with a fire and a neat pile of fuel in the wood-box.

Nothing ever worried him, and that is the inscription we would have put over his grave if he had been killed. The sentiment is neither original nor sentimental. But it would have been very applicable in his case. It still is, if one changes the tense of the verb, for luckily there has been no change in him. He is still living. (N.B. While the *History of the Lafayette Corps* was in preparation for the printers, it was learned that Major Peterson was killed on March 16, 1919, while flying at Daytona Beach, Florida.)

The number of his combats is among the largest of those of Lafayette pilots. Enemy airmen never succeeded in reaching him with their bullets, although his Spad was frequently badly damaged. On the 1st of April, 1918, he joined the 94th Squadron as Flight Commander and was soon placed in command of the 95th, in which position he completed a splendid record of war service. A month before the Armistice was signed he was sent on duty to America.

SERVICE RECORD

GRANVILLE A. POLLOCK, New Orleans, Louisiana.

PREVIOUS SERVICE: British Royal Marine Artillery, January 10, 1915, to February 23, 1916.

SERVICE IN FRENCH AVIATION:
Date of enlistment: December 24, 1916.
Aviation Schools: January 1 to July 14, 1917, Buc, Avord, Pau, G.D.E.
Breveted: May 12, 1917 (Blériot).
At the Front: Escadrille Spad 102, July 15 to October 14, 1917.
Escadrille Spad 65, October 16, 1917, to January 8, 1918.
Final Rank: Sergent.

SERVICE IN U.S. AVIATION:
Commissioned First Lieutenant, January 18, 1918.
Attached to Instrument Division, Technical Dept. U.S.A.S. Washington, D.C.
Officer in Charge of Flying, American Acceptance Park, Orly.

DECORATIONS:
Croix de Guerre, with Star.

CITATION

Iᵉ ARMÉE, AÉRONAUTIQUE. *Le 19 octobre, 1917*

Le Général Commandant la Iᵉ Armée, cite à l'Ordre de l'Aéronautique:

POLLOCK, GRANVILLE, Nᵒ Mˡᵉ 12006, Caporal du 1ᵉʳ Régiment de la Légion Étrangère, Pilote à l'Escadrille N. 102

Pilote énergique et courageux, s'est spécialement distingué le 15 août, 1917, dans une protection de mission photographique, au cours de laquelle il est sorti victorieux d'un combat. Rentré avec de nombreuses balles dans son appareil.

Granville A. Pollock

Pollock's war service has been an unusually varied one. In September, 1914, he went to England—hoping that he might be permitted to enlist in the Royal Naval Air Service. But at that time Americans were not accepted for British Aviation. He then offered his services to the Belgian Minister of War. Being again refused, he arranged with a representative of the Pierce-Arrow Motor Car Company, to take charge of a number of trucks which had been sold to the British Admiralty. This gave him the entering wedge. He was permitted to enlist in the Royal Marine Artillery, was given the rank of Staff Sergeant, and placed in charge of all mechanical work for this brigade of Admiralty cars which mounted anti-aircraft guns. He served in France until February, 1916, taking part in the Battles of Neuve Chapelle, the second Battle of Ypres, Hill 60, and Loos. This antiaircraft and siege brigade was then transferred from the Admiralty to the War Office, and Pollock was honourably discharged.

AMERICANS AT AVORD
Standing (left to right): Wells, Rheno, Kerwood. Huger, Pollock.
Kneeling: Stehlin. Molter, Rounds

Returning to France, he enlisted in the Lafayette Corps, and on July 15, 1917, was sent to the French Squadron, Spad 102. While with this unit, he particularly distinguished himself for his photo missions far back of the German lines. Pollock made a specialty of this work, using for it a single-seater photo Spad. He was afterward transferred to Spad 65, of *Groupe de Combat* 13, a welcome change to him, for here he met again old friends of the Lafayette Squadron.

On January 18, 1918, he was commissioned First Lieutenant in the United States Air Service, and granted leave to return to America before taking up his new duties. In March following, he was attached to the Instrument Division, Technical Department, U.S.A.S., at Washington, D.C. He was again sent to France in July, 1918, as Pilot in Charge of Flying, at the American Acceptance Park at Orly Field, near Paris. He held that position until the close of the war.

Eager for further adventure, after the Armistice, Pollock planned a lone trans-Atlantic flight *via* the Azores in a two-seater Sampson. He was given permission by the C.A.S., A.E.F., made his arrangements with the Sampson Company, and, although it was mid-winter, was ready to take a chance, even though the hope of succeeding seemed a faint one. Fortunately or unfortunately, General Pershing, hearing of the forlorn hope, refused his sanction. It was a sad blow to Pollock. He had set his heart upon making the trial, cost what it might. General Pershing's veto probably saved his life and with this comfort he has had to be content.

SERVICE RECORD

WILLIAM THOMAS PONDER, Maugum, Oklahoma.

SERVICE IN FRENCH AVIATION:
  Date of enlistment: June 4, 1917.
  Aviation Schools: June 19, 1917, to February 1, 1918, Avord, Pau, Cazeaux, G.D.E.
  Breveted: November 7, 1917 (Caudron).
  At the Front: Escadrille Spad 67, February 3 to February 17, 1918.
  Final Rank: Caporal.

SERVICE IN U.S. AVIATION:
  Commissioned Second Lieutenant, February 27, 1918.
  Ferry Pilot, American Acceptance Park, Orly, March 22 to May 12, 1918.
  Promoted First Lieutenant, November 2, 1918.
  Promoted Captain, May 14, 1919.
  At the Front: Attached to French Squadron Spad 163, May 12 to September 1, 1918.
  103d Pursuit Squadron, September 7, 1918, to Armistice.

DECORATIONS:
  Distinguished Service Cross.
  Croix de Guerre, with four Palms.

CITATIONS

Ordre N° 1294 " E." IV° Armée, 5 *juin*, 1918
2° Lieutenant PONDER, WILLIAM THOMAS, de l'Armée Américaine, détaché à l'Escadrille Spa. 163
2° Lieutenant de l'Armée Américaine, venu sur sa demande dans l'aviation française, y fait preuve des plus belles qualités de combat et de sang-froid. A, le ——, à la tête de sa patrouille, abattu un avion ennemi.

Order N° 11054 " D," G.Q.G., le 30 octobre, 1918
Lieutenant PONDER, WILLIAM, Pilote à l'Escadrille Spa. 163
Venu sur sa demande à servir dans l'aviation française, y fait preuve des plus belles qualités de chasseur. À la tête de sa patrouille a livré un combat au cours duquel un avion ennemi a été abattu.

G.H.Q., A.E.F.   *December* 10, 1918
First Lieutenant WILLIAM T. PONDER, A.S, 103d Aero Squadron, No. 1951
For extraordinary heroism in action near Fontaines, France, 23 October, 1918. Having been separated from his patrol, Lieutenant Ponder observed and went to the assistance of an Allied plane, which was being attacked by thirteen of the enemy. Against great odds, Lieutenant Ponder destroyed one enemy plane, and so demoralized the rest that both he and his comrade were able to return to their lines.

By Command of General PERSHING

William Thomas Ponder

Dartmouth College has been well represented in the Lafayette Flying Corps by such men as Thompson, Whitmore, York, Dock, and Ponder—all good fellows in the best sense of the word. In the Blériot School at Avord, during the occasional *sorties* obtained between spells of bad weather, picking up stones, and installing gasoline storage systems, Ponder showed himself a steady and reliable pilot, but none of us realised the brilliant future that lay ahead of him; probably because he talked so little of his own flying prowess. Ponder is the ideal Westerner, large, good-natured, and laconic. He is essentially a man of action, and it needed the setting of the Front to throw into relief his splendid qualities of daring and aggressive skill.

He arrived at the Front on February 3, 1918, going to the Escadrille Spad 67. On February 27 he was transferred to the American army, with the rank of Second Lieutenant, and was soon sent to the Front again, at his own request, this time to the Spad 163, *Groupe de Combat* 21.

With this *groupe*, in company with Cassady and Larner, Ponder took part in some of the heaviest fighting of the war, and made a name for himself as a rarely valuable combat pilot. On September 1 he was called to an American squadron, the 103rd Pursuit, with which he served until the war was over.

The curt words of his citations tell the story of Ponder's achievements better than anything which might be written here. He has seven official victories to his credit, four French citations to the Order of the Army, and the American D.S.C.

SERVICE RECORD

FREDERICK H. PRINCE, JR., Boston, Massachusetts.

SERVICE IN FRENCH AVIATION:
 Date of enlistment: January 29, 1916.
 Aviation Schools: February 2 to October 20, 1916, Pau, Buc, Cazeaux, G.D.E.
 Breveted: May 21, 1916 (Caudron).
 At the Front: Escadrille Lafayette, October 22, 1916, to February 15, 1917.
 Final Rank: Adjudant.

SERVICE IN U.S. ARMY:
 Commissioned First Lieutenant, Q.M. Corps. C.O., M.T.C. 549 (in U.S.A.).
 Attached to Brigade Staff, 16th Infantry Brigade, 8th Division, at Brest.

Frederick H. Prince, Jr.

Frederick Prince joined the French Service at a time when all prospective aviators were sent to Dijon to receive their uniforms and equipment as *soldats de deuxième classe*. He started training at Pau in February, 1916, was then sent to Buc, where he completed his *brevet* tests on Caudron; returned to Pau for further work on the Morane Parasol, went to Cazeaux for machine-gun practice, and returned to Pau for his work in acrobacy and combat.

He was sent to the Front, to the Escadrille Lafayette, on October 22, 1916, a few days after the death of his brother, Norman, and remained until February when he was sent to Pau as an instructor. In the spring of 1917 he received orders to report to the French Military Mission at Washington, D.C., and did not return to France until the end of September.

While at G.D.E. at Le Plessis-Belleville, awaiting reassignment to a squadron, he was ordered to report to the *Chef de Liaison* attached to the 26th U.S. Division at Neufchâteau, and remained there until the end of January, 1918, when he was sent to Le Bourget as a *convoyeur*. He was finally released from the French Service on April 10, 1918, and failing to meet the requirements for the United States Air Service, he returned to America, where he was commissioned as a First Lieutenant in the Quartermaster Corps. He commanded the M.T.C. 549 and was afterward sent to Brest, where he was attached to the staff of General R. E. Bradley, commanding the 16th Infantry Brigade, 8th Division. He held this position until the close of hostilities.

SERVICE RECORD

NORMAN PRINCE, Boston, Massachusetts.

SERVICE IN FRENCH AVIATION:
 Date of enlistment: March 4, 1915.
 Aviation Schools: Pau, R.G.A., G.D.E.
 Brevetted: May 1, 1915 (Voisin).
 At the Front: Escadrille V.B. 108 and V.B. 113,
  May 20, 1915, to February 15,
  1916.
  Escadrille Lafayette, April 20 to
  October 12, 1916.
 Injured in line of duty: October 12, 1916.
 Died of injuries: October 15, 1916.
 Final Rank: Sous-Lieutenant.

DECORATIONS:
 Légion d'Honneur.
 Médaille Militaire.
 Croix de Guerre, with three Palms and Star.

CITATIONS

Au G.Q.G., 15 août, 1915

Le Chef du Service Aéronautique cite à l'Ordre du 3ᵉ Groupe d'Escadrille de Bombardement:

NORMAN PRINCE, Sergent Pilote à l'Escadrille V.B. 108

Citoyen américain, engagé volontaire pour la durée de la guerre. Excellent pilote militaire, qui a toujours fait preuve de la plus grande audace et de présence d'esprit; toujours impatient à partir, a pris à de nombreuses expéditions de bombardements, particulièrement heureuses dans une région où l'artillerie ennemie, par laquelle son avion fut maintes fois atteint, rendait la tâche difficile.

(Signé) BARRÈS

PRINCE AT PAU, MARCH, 1915

Médaille Militaire: 26 septembre, 1916 (J.O. du 3 novembre, 1916)

PRINCE, NORMAN, Adjudant à l'Escadrille N. 124

Engagé volontaire pour la durée de la guerre, a fait preuve en toutes circonstances, des plus belles qualités de bravoure et d'audace, livrant journellement de multiples combats dans les lignes allemandes; le 23 août, 1916, a forcé un appareil ennemi à atterrir et a abattu un deuxième le 9. Déjà blessé et cité à l'Ordre.

Légion d'Honneur (Chevalier): Au G.Q.G., le 30 novembre, 1916

PRINCE, NORMAN, Mle 919, Adjudant Pilote à l'Escadrille N. 124

En escadrille depuis dix-neuf mois, s'est signalé par une bravoure et un dévouement hors de pair dans l'exécution de nombreuses expéditions de bombardement et de chasse. A été très grièvement blessé le 12 octobre, 1916, après avoir abattu un avion allemand. Déjà Médaille Militaire.

Norman Prince

Before the war, Norman Prince had spent many pleasant hunting-seasons at Pau, where he made friends among the French and learned to speak the language fluently. When war broke out in 1914 it was natural that his thoughts should turn to France, the country he had grown to love and admire almost as his own. He might have gone overseas as an ambulance driver or to enlist in the infantry, but—like many other horsemen and polo-players—he had become interested in flying, and it occurred to him that if he became a pilot before offering his services to France, he might be received as a member of the Flying Corps—a possibility which appealed to all his instincts as a sportsman. November found him, in company with Frazier Curtis, at the Burgess flying school at Marblehead, Massachusetts, learning to pilot hydro-aeroplanes, and it was here that he conceived the idea of organising a squadron of American volunteer airmen to serve with the French. Curtis, also a sportsman and a sincere believer in the Allied cause, gave the project his encouragement from the first, although he confessed that before agreeing to offer his services to France, where he felt that ignorance of the language might prove a serious handicap, he planned to attempt enlistment in the British Royal Naval Air Service.

On January 20, 1915, Prince sailed for France on the *Rochambeau*, and on March 4 he signed his enlistment papers and was sent to be trained at Pau. During the five weeks that elapsed between his arrival in Paris and his enlistment, he worked day and night to interest the French in his project. He obtained the active cooperation of the de Lesseps brothers; he arranged for introductions and interviews through the kind offices of Mr. Robert Chanler; he laid his plans before Mr. Robert Bliss, who introduced Prince to M. de Sillac. His enthusiasm and energy were irresistible; before his departure for Pau he had fairly launched the movement which resulted in the formation of the *Escadrille Américaine*.

Prince was not a man to linger in the schools. On May 1 he was breveted and was soon at the Front, piloting a Voisin with the Escadrille V.B. 108, where his exploits and adventures are too well known to need description here. In the autumn he was transferred to the Squadron V.B. 113 equipped with Voisin-Cannon planes—an innovation of which great things were expected. But the life of comparative inactivity irritated Prince, who had the restless and aggressive temperament of a genuine *pilote de chasse*. On October 30, 1915, he wrote to M. de Sillac:

> The squadron with which I am at present is *en repos*. I dislike to stay in such a situation and would prefer to be a member of a unit more active than the *Escadrille* of *Avions-Canons*, which works rarely except during attacks.

In December, 1915, Prince was given leave, with Cowdin and Thaw, to spend three weeks in the United States—a visit which aroused a vast amount of public interest. All three were sons of families well known at home, and there was a wide appeal in the thought of these young men in French uniform, all of whom had seen action on the Western Front and who were members of a branch of the service which still attracted a certain romantic interest. The newspapers gave entire columns to the subject, and when Germany protested that the visiting pilots should be interned, the question was discussed from one end of the country to the other.

On his return to France, Prince was sent to the R.G.A., at Le Bourget, for *perfectionment* on Nieuport, and on April 20, 1916, he reached the Front again—this time as a fighting pilot of the newly formed *Escadrille Américaine*, the realisation of his old dream. His career with the squadron—as brilliant as it was brief—has been described so fully in a score of magazine articles and books that nothing remains to be said. Like Rockwell and Chapman, he was a pilot of the first order, a real combatant, who would have gone far had he been spared. The *Croix de Guerre*, the *Médaille Militaire*, and the *Legion d'Honneur* (awarded him as he lay dying of his wounds) are evidence of the esteem in which his French chiefs held him.

He made his last *sortie* on October 12, 1916, the day of the great raid on the Mauser Works at Oberndorf. Lufbery, de Laage, Masson, and Prince had accompanied the bombers as far as their fuel capacity permitted, and returned to a friendly aerodrome to fill their tanks, taking the air once more to protect the returning raiders. Darkness was drawing on; the bombers were straggling home, harried by determined and aggressive Fokkers. Prince shot down one of the enemy, and when the last of the Allied machines had crossed the lines and it was nearly dark, he made for the field at Corcieux, in the Vosges. Let his friend McConnell tell the rest of the story:

> He spiralled down through the night air and skimmed rapidly over the trees bordering the field. In the dark he did not see a high-tension electric cable that was stretched just above the tree-tops. The landing-gear of his aeroplane struck it. The machine snapped forward on its nose. It turned over and over. The belt holding Prince broke and he was thrown far from the wrecked plane. Both of his legs were broken and he naturally suffered internal injuries. In spite of the terrific shock and his intense pain Prince did not lose consciousness. He even kept his presence of mind and gave orders to the men who had run to pick him up. Hearing the hum of a motor and realising that

NORMAN PRINCE

GRAVE OF NORMAN PRINCE, LUXEUIL

a machine was in the air, Prince told them to light gasoline fires on the field. 'You don't want another fellow to come down and break himself up the way I've done,' he said. Lufbery went with him to the hospital in Gérardmer.

As the ambulance rolled along Prince sang to keep up his spirits. He spoke of getting well soon and returning to service. It was like Norman. He was always energetic about his flying... No one thought that Prince as mortally injured, but next day he went into a coma. Captain Happe ... accompanied by our officers, hastened to Gérardmer. Lying unconscious on his bed, Prince was named a second lieutenant and decorated with the Legion of Honour.... He died on the 15th of October ... was brought back to Luxeuil and given a funeral similar to Rockwell's. It was hard to realise that poor old Norman was gone.... He never let his own spirits drop and was always on hand with encouragement for others. I do not think Prince minded going. He wanted to do his part before being killed and he had more than done it. Day after day he had freed the lines of Germans, making it impossible for them to do their work, and three of them he had shot to earth.

SERVICE RECORD

DAVID E. PUTNAM, Brookline, Massachusetts.

SERVICE IN FRENCH AVIATION:
Date of enlistment: May 31, 1917.
Aviation Schools: June 10 to December 10, 1917, Avord, Pau, G.D.E.
Breveted: October 17, 1917 (Caudron).
At the Front: Escadrille Spad 94, December 12, 1917, to January 1, 1918.
Escadrille Spad (and M.S.P.) 156, February 7 to June 1, 1918.
Escadrille Spad 38, June 1 to June 14, 1918.
Final Rank: Sergent.

SERVICE IN U.S. AVIATION:
Commissioned First Lieutenant: June 8, 1918.
At the Front: C.O. 134th Pursuit Squadron, June 24 to September 13, 1918.
Killed in combat: September 13, 1918, near Saint-Mihiel.

DECORATIONS:
Distinguished Service Cross.
Légion d'Honneur.
Médaille Militaire.
Croix de Guerre, with Palms.

CITATIONS

36ᵉ Division, État-Major.   *G.Q.G., le 10 février, 1918*

Le Général Paquette, Commandant la 36ᵉ Division d'Infanterie, cite à l'Ordre de la Division: ...

    Le Caporal Putnam, David, de l'Escadrille M.S.P. 156

Étant en patrouille de chasse, a attaqué un groupe d'avions ennemis et a abattu un de ces appareils.

IVᵉ Armée, État-Major.   *Le 21 février, 1918*

Le Général Commandant la IVᵉ Armée cite à l'Ordre de l'Armée: ...

    Caporal de la Légion Étrangère Putnam, David, Mˡᵉ 12214, de l'Escadrille M.S.P. 156

Étant en patrouille le 19 janvier, 1918, a livré un combat très vif à deux biplaces ennemis, les a poursuivis jusqu'à très faible altitude dans leurs lignes, abattant l'un d'entre eux qui est tombé en flammes.

Le Général Commandant la IVᵉ Armée
GOURAUD

IVᵉ Armée, Aéronautique.   *21 mars, 1918*
Citation à l'Ordre de l'Armée:

    Sergent Putnam, David, du 1ᵉʳ Régiment de la Légion Étrangère, détaché a l'Escadrille M.S.P. 156

Pilote adroit et audacieux, recherche toutes les occasions de combattre. A attaqué deux avions ennemis et a abattu l'un d'eux en vue de nos tranchées.

Citation à l'Ordre de l'Armée: *20 juin, 1918*

    Putnam, David, Mˡᵉ 12214, Sergent à 1ᵉʳ Régiment de la Légion Étrangère, détaché à l'Escadrille M.S.P. 156

Pilote de chasse de tout premier ordre. Attaquant une patrouille de dix monoplaces ennemis, a abattu l'un d'eux pendant que quatre autres tombait désemparés et a mis en fuite le reste de la patrouille ennemie (septième victoire).

Citation Médaille Militaire:

    Putnam, David, Pilote Aviateur, du 1ᵉʳ Régiment de la Légion Étrangère

Par son entrain, son adresse, son mépris du danger, se révèle comme un pilote de tout premier ordre. Attaquant récemment une patrouille de neuf avions ennemis, a abattu l'un d'eux. Le lendemain, au cours d'une mission de protection, a résolument attaqué une patrouille de huit appareils et a abattu deux de ses adversaires, remportant ainsi ses 5ᵉ et 6ᵉ victoires. Trois citations.

    1ᵉʳ Lieutenant Putnam, David, Pilote à l'Escadrille Spa. 38

A été nommé dans l'Ordre de la Légion d'Honneur en Grade de Chevalier. Pilote admirable de dévouement, d'une endurance, d'une volonté, et d'un courage exemplaire. En escadrille, depuis 6 mois seulement, s'est de suite révèle comme un pilote exceptionnel, d'une adresse et d'une habileté hors de pair. Infatigable, recherchant toutes les occasions de combattre, pousse la hardiesse jusqu'à la témérité, allant attaquer l'ennemi jusqu'à 20 kilomètres dans ses lignes. En moins d'un mois a abattu officiellement 6 avions ennemis, portant ainsi à 9 le nombre de ses victoires. Déjà quatre fois cité à l'Ordre.

David E. Putnam

Among the Americans who have fought for France, there was no more inspiring figure than that of Dave Putnam. He was a splendid type of young American, a keen sportsman, a loyal friend, a fervent patriot. There is not a Lafayette man who is not better for having known Putnam, whose splendid example was always before the eyes of his comrades. Even during the period of training we realised that here was a man out of the ordinary, for his life held but one object: to get to the Front. The only occasions on which we saw him gloomy or depressed were when the weather prevented him from flying. His constant anxiety to complete his training made him always the first to arrive at the field and the last to leave it.

Putnam came to France in the spring of 1917—a tall, athletic youngster of twenty, fresh from Harvard, where he was a student in his sophomore year. On May 31 he enlisted in the Lafayette Flying Corps and was sent to Avord, where he took the slow Blériot training. Breveted in October, 1917, he made a brilliant record at Pau and arrived at the Front in the Escadrille N. 156 on December 12. From the first he showed the qualities which were to make him famous: the skill in piloting, the devotion to duty, and the aggressiveness of a true fighting man. A comrade writes about him at this period:

> Our sector was a very quiet one when we went out to the 156; German planes were scarce, and if we wanted to fight we had to go a long way hunting behind the lines. This was especially forbidden by our *commandant*; you know how cautious the French are in giving young pilots permission to do any *chasse libre*. When we were fortunate enough to get this permission you could rely on Putnam to stretch the privilege to the limit. I speak from experience, remembering that it was he who led me into my first scrap, when we were twenty-five kilometres in German territory.

In the spring of 1918, the squadron exchanged their Nieuports for the tiny Morane Parasols—smallest, fastest, and trickiest of all *chasse* planes. In piloting this little hornet, Putnam's art reached a perfection which astonished even his veteran comrades. On one occasion, while hunting alone over the lines, Putnam attacked eighteen German single-seaters, shot down the leader, and got clean away! His formidable little plane, swift as a hawk, almost invisible, and piloted by a man to whom the appearance of a Black Cross was a signal for immediate combat, became the terror of the local Boches.

Early in the summer, Putnam was transferred to the Escadrille Spad 38, commanded by Madon, one of France's greatest fighting pilots. It was here that the American attained the summit of his skill, for Madon took a great liking to him and showed him all the tricks which spell success in the air. As he developed a style of his own, it became evident that Putnam would make one of the really great fighting flyers, for in addition to the headlong aggressiveness which was his leading characteristic, he had wonderful eyes, could shoot straight, and acquired rare skill in combat manoeuvres.

His greatest feat was performed on June 5, above the Second Battle of the Marne, when he shot down five Germans in five minutes. Owing to the difficulty of French confirmations, only one of these Germans was counted officially, but there can be no doubt about the other four, as several eye-witnesses saw them go down.

On June 24, Putnam, now a First Lieutenant in the United States Air Service, was given command of the 134th Pursuit Squadron, and from then up to the time of his death, he brought down five official enemy planes as well as several others, too far within the German lines to be confirmed. His conduct of the Squadron won the warmest praise of his superiors, and yet, unlike many Squadron Commanders, his additional duties were never allowed to diminish the number of his flights or combats.

The end came on September 13, when Putnam and another pilot were attacked by eight Fokkers. Putnam shot down one enemy, but as he attacked, a brace of Germans got into position behind him and he fell mortally wounded, probably dead before he reached the earth. It was a splendid death in the midst of combat, certainly the ending he would have chosen for himself, but the loss was a bitter one to every member of the Lafayette Flying Corps.

Putnam was credited with thirteen official victories, but he had certainly shot down an equal number of German planes which fell too far within their lines to be confirmed; that was the penalty for his offensive spirit. For his services with the French, he was decorated with the *Croix de Guerre*, the *Médaille Militaire*, and the *Légion d'Honneur*, and after his transfer to the American Army, General Pershing conferred upon him the D.S.C., as well as proposing him for the Congressional Medal of Honour.

SERVICE RECORD

RUFUS R. RAND, JR., Minneapolis, Minnesota.

PREVIOUS SERVICE: Norton-Harjes Ambulance, 1917.

SERVICE IN FRENCH AVIATION:
Date of enlistment: July 26, 1917.
Aviation Schools: July 28 to December 4, 1917, Avord, Tours, Pau, G.D.E.
Breveted: September 14, 1917 (Caudron).
At the Front: Escadrille Spad 158, December 6, 1917, to Armistice.
Final Rank: Adjudant.
DECORATIONS:
Croix de Guerre, with Palm and Star.

CITATIONS

13 *septembre*, 1918

IIIe Armée, État-Major.
Le Général Commandant la 3e Armée cite
 à l'Ordre du 34e Corps d'Armée :
Le Sergent Rand, Rufus Randall, du 1er
 Régiment Étranger, Pilote à l'Escadrille
 Spa. 158, M^{le} 12355

 Pilote de chasse. Le 21 août, 1918, au cours
d'une patrouille a attaqué un biplace ennemi
qu'il a abattu en flammes.
  (*Signé*)   Humbert

IIIe Armée, État-Major.   9 *juillet*, 1918
Le Général Commandant la 3e Armée cite à l'Ordre de l'Armée :
 Le Sergent Rand, Rufus Randall, du 1er Régiment Étranger, Pilote américain
         à l'Escadrille Spa. 158

 Pilote américain. Le 6 juin, 1918, a probablement abattu un avion allemand qui n'a pu
être homologué à cause de l'éloignement dans les lignes. Le 9 juin, au cours d'une lutte inégale
de deux avions français contre neuf ennemis, a fait preuve d'une remarquable sang-froid
en dégageant son chef de patrouille quoiqu'il soit lui-même poursuivi par plusieurs avions
ennemis. A ramené son appareil criblé de balles.
                    (*Signé*)   Humbert

Rufus R. Rand, Jr.

Rand is an example of the scientific aviator; he knows all about motors, all about rigging, and all about aerodynamics—the wonderful thing is that he still flies, (1920). At the Front he not only flew, but knocked down his share of Germans with the same scientific precision he used in tuning up a motor. Rand is one of the few Americans who have piloted the small Morane *monocoque* over the lines, and he was convinced that with a few trifling alterations the Morane would be the best of *chasse* machines.

He has an endearing weakness for *explication des coups,* and many an hour of leave has been spent in the old Crillon while Rufe went into details of these same trifling alterations.

Rand has had some of the hardest fights and narrowest escapes that a man can go through and survive. Once his *nourrice,* the small auxiliary gasoline tank in the upper wing, was pierced by a stream of bullets, some of which missed the pilot's head by a hair's-breadth—only remarkable luck saved the Spad from being set afire.

One had only to look at his machine, with bits of fabric plastered over the wings and fuselage, to know that he fought at close quarters.

THE LITTLE MORANE (DAVID GUY)

The French recognised his fine qualities of courage and skill, cited him twice in army orders, and promoted him to the rank of *Adjudant*.

SERVICE RECORD

JOHN F. RANDALL, Meriden, Connecticut.
PREVIOUS SERVICE: American Ambulance, 1917.
SERVICE IN FRENCH AVIATION:
  Date of enlistment: July 20, 1917.
  Aviation Schools: July 28 to December 8, 1917, Avord, Tours, Pau, G.D.E.
  Breveted: October 1, 1917 (Caudron).
  At the Front: Escadrille Spad 158, December 11, 1917, to April 18, 1918.
  Final Rank: Sergent.
SERVICE IN U.S. AVIATION:
  Commissioned First Lieutenant: March 23, 1918.
  At the Front: 103d Pursuit Squadron, June 6 to June 14, 1918.
  Injured in line of duty: June 14, 1918.
  On duty at American A.I.C., Issoudun, October 13, 1918, to Armistice.

John F. Randall

Randall's progress through the schools was uneventful and his record excellent, but shortly after his arrival at the Front he became the victim of a series of misfortunes calculated to destroy one's faith in the ultimate goodness of Providence. On December 11, 1917, he was sent to the Escadrille Spad 158. After a brief period of service with this unit, he was severely scalded when a large vat of boiling water turned over on him, and was forced to undergo a long and painful treatment in hospital. In March, 1918, while still a convalescent, he transferred to the American army with the rank of First Lieutenant, and after serving for a time as a ferry pilot, was sent out to the 103rd Pursuit Squadron, then stationed at Dunkirk. Overjoyed to be again on the Front, Randall's bad luck still followed him. Eight days after his arrival at Dunkirk he was severely injured in a landing accident— one leg crushed, with a dangerous fracture of the bone. Owing to the seriousness of the injury, he was sent to England for convalescence, and up to the time of the Armistice he had not recovered sufficiently to be able to fly.

SERVICE RECORD

ROBERT E. READ, Franklin, Pennsylvania.

PREVIOUS SERVICE: American Ambulance, 1917.

SERVICE IN FRENCH AVIATION:
Date of enlistment: June 13, 1917.
Aviation Schools: June 23, 1917, to January 20, 1918, Avord, Pau, Cazeaux, G.D.E.
Breveted: November 18, 1917 (Caudron).
Final Rank: Caporal.

SERVICE IN U.S. NAVAL AVIATION:
Commissioned Ensign: January 24, 1918.
Promoted Lieutenant (Junior Grade).
At the Front: U.S. Naval Air Station, Dunkirk, as pilot and later as commanding officer.

DECORATIONS:
Légion d'Honneur.
Croix de Guerre, with Palm.

CUSHMAN, DOCK, AND READ
AVORD, JULY. 1917

Robert E. Read

Read was among the last of the Blériot students at Avord. Breveted on November 18, 1917, he did well at the schools of Pau and Cazeaux, and was taken over as an Ensign in the United States Naval Air Service before he had been assigned to a squadron at the Front. Sent to Dunkirk as a member of one of the squadrons using that port as a base,

Read was soon promoted to a lieutenancy and made Commanding Officer of the Station.

Before the war he had been in the Naval Reserve and acquired a lasting taste for nautical life, so his superiors had no difficulty in recognising the jolly tar under the aviator's uniform. As commander of an important station, Read enjoyed all the perquisites of his high office; the phonograph, the cinema, the large touring-car, and the specially imported African *chef* of surpassing excellence.

SERVICE RECORD

LEONARD M. RENO, Chicago, Illinois.

SERVICE IN FRENCH AVIATION:
Date of enlistment: March 20, 1917.
Aviation Schools: March 23 to July 20, 1917, Avord, Pau, G.D.E.
Brevetted: May 10, 1917 (Blériot).
At the Front: Escadrille Spad 103, July 23 to September 18, 1917.
Escadrille Bréguet 134, June 4 to July 18, 1918.
Final Rank: Sergent.

SERVICE IN U.S. NAVAL AVIATION:
Commissioned Ensign: July 18, 1918.
At the Front: U.S. Naval Air Station, Porto Corsini, Italy, October, 1918.

DECORATIONS:
Croix de Guerre, with Palm.

CITATION

Citation à l'Ordre de l'Armée:
Excellent pilote plein d'entrain et très ardent. Toujours volontaire pour toutes les missions qu'il ne cesse d'accomplir d'une manière parfaite. Demande constamment à être employé et donne à tous l'exemple du courage, du sang-froid, et de l'énergie.
Vient d'abattre le 18 juillet, 1918, un avion ennemi au cours d'un combat très dur contre des forces supérieures au retour d'un bombardement.

Leonard M. Reno

Leonard Reno was one of six Lafayette pilots who during 1917-18 belonged to Spad 103, the *escadrille* of Fonck. After two months at the Front he was injured in a fall in Belgium when his machine was disabled by anti-aircraft fire. After undergoing two operations at a hospital at Dunkirk he went to America on convalescent leave, and upon his return to France in the spring of 1918, he was transferred from *chasse* to day bombardment. His second period of service at the Front was with the French Squadron Bréguet 134.

Reno took part in the heavy aerial battles in the vicinity of Montdidier and Noyon. The importance of day bombing was then fully recognised, and all of the squadrons detailed for this service were heavily engaged. During June and the early part of July Bréguet 134 was operating in the Montdidier-Noyon Sector. When the fighting had quieted down there, it was sent to the Marne in anticipation of the attack on Château-Thierry. It was at this time that Reno had some of the most exciting adventures of his career as an airman. While the Germans were crossing the Marne, the French day bombers practically lived in their machines. They took the air time after time, returning to the aerodrome only long enough for additional loads of bombs and fuel.

Reno brought down a German on his last day of service with the French. He was to go to Paris on July 18, 1918, to receive his commission as Ensign in the United States Naval Air Service. On the morning of that day he made a farewell raid with his squadron upon Oulchy-le-Château, then twenty kilometres within the enemy lines. The objective was bombed, and upon the return journey the formation had to fight their way through a large patrol of enemy *chasse* planes.

There were but four French Bréguets and two of these were shot down, one in flames and the other *en vrille,* leaving only Reno and his captain plugging away homeward for dear life. It was a wild race, with each Bréguet manoeuvring desperately against a tenacious little swarm of Albatross.

Just before reaching the French lines Reno's observer pounded him on the shoulder indicating a German diving to attack from three quarters front, the blind spot.

He pulled up perpendicularly with the one thought of getting his motor in line with the enemy's fire. The German did the same thing in order to avoid collision, making an excellent target at close range. A burst of fire from squarely underneath brought him down. Reno's observer pounded him on the back with joy, and performed absurd pantomimes all the way to the ground indicative of the reception they would receive at the aerodrome.

They were unable to reach their own field, however, because of their damaged machine. Both tires had been punctured by bullets; the wings were in tatters; five clean holes had been made through the propeller without otherwise damaging it, and one control wire was shot away.

When Reno transferred to the Naval Air Service he had to take the complete ground-school course at Moutchic-Lacanau, where he learned to fly all boats used by the United States Navy. He was then sent to Italy, where he completed another course in acrobacy, this time on Italian pursuit boats. He arrived at the United States Naval Air Station at Porto Corsini in time to make only one offensive patrol before the Austrian armistice.

SERVICE RECORD

WALTER D. RHENO, Vineyard Haven, Massachusetts.

SERVICE IN FRENCH AVIATION:
Date of enlistment: December 24, 1916.
Aviation Schools: January 31 to July 16, 1917, Buc, Avord, Pau, G.D.E.
Breveted: May 10, 1917 (Blériot).
At the Front: Escadrille Spad 80, July 18 to September 15, 1917.
Returned to America, October 19, 1917.
Final Rank: Sergent.
Died of pneumonia in Paris, October 10, 1918.

DECORATIONS:
Croix de Guerre, with two Palms.

CITATIONS

Le 16 *septembre,* 1917

Le Général Commandant la IIe Armée cite à l'Ordre de l'Armée:

Le Caporal RHENO, WALTER DAVIS, Pilote à l'Escadrille N. 80

Très bon pilote américain; montre de grandes qualités d'audace et d'entrain; le 18 août a abattu un biplace ennemi qui s'est écrasé dans ses lignes.

IIe ARMÉE. 13 *octobre,* 1917
Citation à l'Ordre de l'Armée:

Le Caporal RHENO, WALTER D., Pilote à l'Escadrille N. 80

Excellent pilote américain, beaucoup d'entrain et d'audace. Nombreux combats. Le 6 septembre, 1917, a attaqué un avion ennemi loin dans les lignes allemands et l'abattu.
(*Signé*) GUILLAUMAT

Walter D. Rheno

Walter Rheno did good work at the Front during his two months of service there. On August 18, 1917, he and a French Lieutenant belonging to his squadron brought down a two-seater Albatross, and on September 6, he alone shot down a *monoplace.* On October 17, 1917, he was granted a three weeks *permission* to go to America, and while at home he was asked to transfer to the United States Air Service.

For some reason the transfer did not take place, and after waiting nearly a year for his commission, he returned to France in October, 1918, hoping to be reassigned to duty in French Aviation. His desire was not to be realised, however. He became ill with pneumonia a few days after his arrival in Paris, and died in an American hospital there on October 10, 1918.

SERVICE RECORD

KIFFIN YATES ROCKWELL, Asheville, North Carolina.

PREVIOUS SERVICE: Foreign Legion (Infantry), August 11, 1914, to September 2, 1915 (wounded while serving with the Legion).

SERVICE IN FRENCH AVIATION:
Date of enlistment: September 2, 1915.
Aviation Schools: September 2, 1915, to April 16, 1916, Avord, Pau, R.G.A.
Brevet: October 22, 1915 (Maurice Farman).
At the Front: Escadrille Lafayette, April 20 to September 23, 1916.
Final Rank: Sergent.
Wounded in combat: May 24, 1916.
Killed in combat: September 23, 1916 (near Rodern, Alsace).

DECORATIONS:
Médaille Militaire
Croix de Guerre, with four Palms

CITATIONS

Paris, le 7 juillet, 1916
Médaille Militaire

ROCKWELL, KIFFIN YATES, Mⁱ 34805, Caporal à l'Escadrille N. 124

Engagé pour la durée de la guerre, a été blessé une première fois le 9 mai, 1915, au cours d'une charge à la baïonnette. Passé dans l'Aviation, s'est montré pilote adroit et courageux. Le 18 mai, 1916, a attaqué et descendu un avion allemand. Le 24 mai n'a pas hésité à livrer à plusieurs appareils ennemis un combat au cours duquel il a été atteint d'une grave blessure à la face.

Les promotions et nominations ci-dessus comportent l'attribution de la Croix de Guerre avec Palme.

(Signé) ROQUES

Citation à l'Ordre de l'Armée août, 1916
ROCKWELL, KIFFIN YATES, Pilote à l'Escadrille 124

Engagé pour la durée de la guerre. Entré dans l'aviation de chasse, s'y est classé immédiatement comme pilote de tout premier ordre, d'une audace et d'une bravoure admirables. N'hésite jamais à attaquer l'ennemi quelque soit le nombre des adversaires qu'il rencontre, l'obligeant le plus souvent, par sa maîtrise, son mordant, à abandonner la lutte. A abattu deux avions ennemis. A rendu les plus grands services à l'aviation de chasse de l'armée en se dépensant pendant quatre mois sans compter devant Verdun.

Citation à l'Ordre de l'Armée:
ROCKWELL, KIFFIN YATES

Pilote américain qui n'a cessé de faire l'admiration de ses camarades par son sang-froid, son courage, et son audace. A été tué au cours d'un combat aérien le 23 septembre, 1916.

Kiffin Yates Rockwell

It is probable that Kiffin Rockwell was the first American to offer his services to France against the German aggressors, for on August 3, 1914, he wrote to the French Consul at New Orleans:

> I desire to offer my services to the French Government in case of actual warfare between France and Germany, and wish to know whether I can report to you at New Orleans and go over with the French reservists ... or must go to France before enlisting. I am twenty-one years old and have had military

training at the Virginia Military Institute. I am very anxious to see military service, and had rather fight under the French Flag than any other, as I greatly admire your Nation. If my services can be used by your Country, I will bring my brother, who also desires to fight under the French Flag.

Rockwell was a born soldier. Both his grandfathers, Captain Henry Rockwell, of North Carolina, and Major Enoch Shaw Ayres, of South Carolina, were officers of the Confederate Army, and a more remote ancestor was a captain on General Washington's staff during the Revolution. His nature was made up of the simple virtues of a mediaeval warrior—pride amounting almost to sensitiveness, energy, determination, dauntless courage, and unbounded faith in the justice of his cause. Such men are rare and unmistakable when met; they stand a little aloof from the rest of the world and radiate a sense of great things—an atmosphere which shames the cynic and stills the voice of the doubter. It is not difficult to imagine the train of reasoning which led him to enlist: a great war was about to overwhelm Europe; France was preparing to defend her frontiers and republican ideals against an aggression which menaced all human liberty; one's course was clear— one must enlist to fight for France. And the flame of his idealism never for an instant flickered. Long afterward, when he had come to know all the squalor and disillusion of war, he wrote to his mother:

> If I die, you will know that I died as every man should—in fighting for the right. I do not consider that I am fighting for France alone, but for the cause of humanity, the most noble of all causes.

In August, 1914, accompanied by his brother Paul, Rockwell crossed to France and enlisted in the Foreign Legion. From the beginning, his record of service was a splendid one—months of dreary trench life with the infantry did nothing to diminish his enthusiasm or fighting spirit. On May 9, 1915, when the Legion stormed La Targette, he was severely wounded in the thigh, and transferred to the Aviation after a long period of convalescence. In the autumn, Victor Chapman wrote from Avord:

> I find a compatriot I am proud to own . . . called Rockwell. He got his transfer about a month ago from the legion. He was wounded on the 9th of May, like Kisling; in fact half of the *Deuxième de Marche* were wounded that day, not counting the

killed and missing. He gives the best account I have heard. Having charged with the Third Battalion and being wounded in the leg in the last *bouck*, he crawled back across the entire field in the afternoon. At this moment I have mixed feelings of pride, envy, and sorrow, for he has just received a postal from a friend who has returned to the regiment. They were given a banner and three days ago were up where the big advance took place. On account of their reputation and the general understanding that they were reserved for attack, the regiment must have been in the very thick of it and has enormous losses.... Rockwell is chafing because he changed too soon. 'There is nothing like it' (he says); 'you float across the field, you drop, you rise again ... the *sac*, the 325 extra rounds, the gun—have no weight.'

On the Alsatian Front (May 18, 1916) Kiffin Rockwell shot down the first enemy plane credited to the Escadrille Lafayette. The combat was characteristic of the man and his method of attack. He told of it in a letter to his brother Paul:

> This morning I went out over the lines to make a little tour. I was somewhat the other side of our lines when my motor began to miss a bit, and I turned back. Just as I started ... I saw a Boche machine about seven hundred metres under me and a little inside our lines. I reduced my motor and dove on him; he saw me at the same time and began to dive toward home. It was a machine with a pilot and a machine-gunner, carrying two rapid-fire guns, one facing the front, and one facing the rear, turning on a pivot so that it could be fired in any direction. The gunner immediately opened fire on me and my machine was hit, but I didn't pay any attention to that and kept going straight for him until I got within twenty-five or thirty metres of his machine. Then, just as I was afraid of running into him, I fired four shots, and swerved my machine to the right to avoid having a collision... I saw the gunner fall back dead on the pilot, his machine gun fall from its position and point straight up in the air, and the pilot fall to one side of the machine as if he too were done for. The machine fell off to one side—then dove vertically toward the ground with a lot of smoke coming from the rear. I circled around, and three or four minutes later saw smoke coming up from the ground, just behind the German trenches.

It was his first combat—the first time he had encountered an enemy machine in the air—the first time he had fired his gun at a German plane! And with four shots (afterwards verified by the squadron armourer) he killed both pilot and observer, and sent the machine down in flames!

In discussing men, the French used a phrase which described admirably a keen and bitter fighter—*Il en veut, il fait la guerre.* Rockwell had come to France to fight; not to loaf, "swing the lead," or pose as a hero—and when he went over the lines it was *la guerre à outrance.* He shot down several Germans so far in their own lines that even the combats were invisible to friendly observers. On the Verdun Front, in July, 1916, he took part in forty officially daily reported combats; in August he fought thirty-four aerial duels. Wounded in the face by an explosive bullet, he refused Captain Thénault's offer to send him to a hospital for treatment, and after twenty-four hours in Paris to reassure his brother, he hurried to the Front to fight and fly again. His letters to Paul Rockwell give us glimpses of an extraordinary driving energy and determination:

> I had thought beforehand that yesterday and today I would try my damnedest to kill one or two Germans for the boys (comrades in the Legion) who got it this time last year—but I had no luck. Am tired out now; have been out four different times today, all the time going up and down. Once I dropped straight down from 4000 metres to 1800 on a Boche, but he got away. It tires one a lot—the change in heights and the manoeuvring.

The day after Victor Chapman's death he wrote:

> He and I had roomed together and flown together a great deal, and I had grown very fond of him. I am afraid it is going to rain tomorrow, but if not, Prince and I are going to fly about ten hours and will do our best to kill one or two Germans for Victor.

Rockwell's brief and splendid life was ended by the most glorious of deaths—struck down in the heat of combat, twelve thousand feet above the earth. Flying with Lufbery over the Vosges, on the 23rd of September, 1916, Rockwell became separated from his companion, and attacked a German two-seater well inside the French lines.

In his daring and headlong fashion, he plunged straight at the enemy, paying no attention to a stream of bullets from the observer. He did not open fire until at such close quarters that watchers on the ground thought a collision inevitable—his gun stammered faintly, and the Nieuport turned its nose down, losing one wing as it hurtled toward the earth. A great wound, where an explosive bullet had passed through his chest at the base of the throat, must have caused instant death.

His loss was an irreparable one to the Escadrille Lafayette—for he was a rare combat pilot, and his chivalrous and romantic example brought out the finest qualities of his companions.

ROCKWELL'S GRAVE

His funeral was worthy of his life and death. Fifty English pilots and eight hundred R.F.C. mechanics, a regiment of French Territorials, a battalion of Colonials, and hundreds of French pilots and mechanics, marched behind his bier. At the grave, Captain Thénault said:

> When Rockwell was in the air, no German passed ... and he was in the air most of the time.... The best and bravest of us all is no more.

SERVICE RECORD

ROBERT LOCKERBIE ROCKWELL, Cincinnati, Ohio.

PREVIOUS SERVICE: Interne Anglo-American Hospital and Hôpital Auxiliaire (Saint-Valéry-en-Caux), February 29, 1915, to February 3, 1916.

SERVICE IN FRENCH AVIATION:
Date of enlistment: February 7, 1916.
Aviation Schools: February 15 to September 15, 1916, Buc, Cazeaux, Pau, G.D.E.
Breveted: May 20, 1916 (Blériot).
At the Front: Escadrille Lafayette, September 17, 1916, to February 18, 1918.
Final Rank: Adjudant.

SERVICE IN U.S. AVIATION:
Commissioned Captain: January 31, 1918.
At the Front: 103d Pursuit Squadron, February 18, 1918, to Armistice (as Flight Commander and Commanding Officer).

DECORATIONS:
Légion d'Honneur.
Croix de Guerre, with two Palms.

CITATIONS

VIe ARMÉE, ÉTAT-MAJOR.   29 octobre, 1917
Citation à l'Ordre de l'Armée:

ROCKWELL, ROBERT, Sergent 1er Régiment Étranger, Pilote à l'Escadrille N. 124

Citoyen américain engagé dans l'Aéronautique. Pilote de chasse plein d'allant et d'entrain. A livré de nombreux combats.

Le 6 mai, 1917, a eu son avion gravement endommagé au cours d'un combat contre deux monoplaces ennemis.

Le 24 septembre, dans une rencontre avec une patrouille ennemie bien supérieure en nombre, a contraint l'un de ses adversaires à atterrir désemparé dans ses lignes.

                                            (Signé)   MAISTRE

GRAND QUARTIER GÉNÉRAL DES ARMÉES FRANÇAISES
DE L'EST, ÉTAT-MAJOR.   Le 17 mai, 1919

Après approbation du Général Commandant en Chef les Forces Expéditionnaires Américaines en France, le Maréchal Commandant en Chef les Armées Françaises de l'Est cite à l'Ordre de l'Armée:

Capitaine ROCKWELL, ROBERT L.

Citoyen américain engagé dès le début de la guerre dans la Légion Étrangère. S'est distingué dans toutes les opérations auxquelles il a pris part, a fait preuve des plus belles qualités comme pilote à l'Escadrille Lafayette.

Par décret du Président de la République en date du 9 avril, 1919, le Capitaine Rockwell a été promu Chevalier de la Légion d'Honneur.

Cette promotion a été faite avec le motif de ce citation.

Robert Lockerbie Rockwell

When Rockwell offered his services to French Aviation, he carried with him to the recruiting *bureau* a letter from his old *Médecin Chef* of Hôpital Auxiliare 3 Bis. It was a masterpiece of eulogy which closed as follows:

My dear Rockwell, excellent driver of automobiles whose skilful mastery of motors I have so often had occasion to admire; splendid *pilote-aviateur*—accustomed as you are to the dangers of aerial navigation, I have no doubt that you will render to my Country the greatest and most fruitful services.

Rockwell presented the letter when asked for his credentials at the recruiting office in Paris, modestly admitted his proficiency as a pilot, and was sent at once to Pau. There he worked hard to perfect himself, so that, in so far as is known, no reference was ever made to the too flattering peroration in his letter of recommendation. It may be that only M. de Sillac and Dr. Gros knew of it, but they of course were both warm friends of all the volunteers and did everything possible to further their interests.

Rockwell received some of the most fearful drubbings at the hands of German patrols which have been experienced by any pilot in the Lafayette Flying Corps. Memorable among these is one of the 6th of May, 1917, when he was making a solitary hunt. He met an enemy formation of seven single-seaters coming into the sun, and attacked the rear man, counting upon his advantage of position to offset the odds in numbers. The other six manoeuvred into position and pounced upon him *en masse*. He escaped by some freak of chance, and landed at the aerodrome, half an hour later, with tires punctured, his *aileron* controls more than half shot away, the braces of his landing-gear badly holed, and his wings pierced in many places.

During another combat his motor failed him at a critical moment, and he had to dive through a large enemy flight of *monoplaces*. His oil radiator burst during the plunge, drenching him with thick castor oil, coating his windshield, and so blinding him that he was completely at the mercy of the pursuing Germans. He fell in a nose-dive for a long distance, and the enemy, thinking him killed, gave up the pursuit. He pulled out of the *vrille* at 300 metres, and contour-chased back to the aerodrome.

Despite many really nerve-racking adventures of this kind, he kept his grip upon himself through more than two years of service at the Front. He spent a good deal of his leisure, answering in kind, letters from unknown female correspondents in America. Many of these were from silly girls. When a photograph was requested, he would send a shamefully idealized portrait of himself, and then ignore further notes, letting his distant admirers pine away in hopeless longing as a punishment for their unwomanly boldness.

Meanwhile, he carried on with his more necessary duty, and after the Armistice, was made C.O. of the 93rd Pursuit Squadron. Accustomed as he assuredly was, before the close of the war, to the dangers of aerial navigation, there is no doubt that he fully justified the confidence of his old *Médecin Chef.*

SERVICE RECORD

MARIUS ROMAIN ROCLE, New York City.

PREVIOUS SERVICE: Foreign Legion (Infantry), September 26, 1914, to June 5, 1916. Wounded while with the Legion.

SERVICE IN FRENCH AVIATION:
Date of enlistment: June 5, 1916.
Aviation Schools: June 5, 1916, to January 28, 1917, Buc, Cazeaux, Pau.
At the Front: Escadrille N. 84.
Escadrille C. 46.
Escadrille Br. 213.
As observer and machine-gunner, February 1, 1917, to February 19, 1918.
Final Rank: Caporal.

SERVICE IN U.S. AVIATION:
Commissioned Second Lieutenant: February 19, 1918.
13th Aero Squadron, February 19 to March 15, 1918.
644th Aero Squadron. April 15 to Armistice.

DECORATIONS:
Croix de Guerre, with Star (Foreign Legion).

CITATION

Le 9 octobre, 1915

Le Lieutenant Colonel Commandant le Régiment de Marche de la Légion Étrangère cite à l'Ordre du Régiment:

MARIUS ROCLE, M^{le} N° 33652

Excellent soldat courageux; le 28 septembre, 1915, s'est offert spontanément pour faire partie d'une patrouille envoyée sous le feu violent à la reconnaissance des tranchées allemandes.

(*Signé*) COT
Lieutenant-Colonel Commandant le Régiment de Marche de la Légion Étrangère

Marius Romain Rocle

After a year and eight months of service with the Foreign Legion, during which time he was wounded, Marius Rocle was transferred to Aviation and became one of the three members of the Lafayette Corps who served at the Front as machine-gunner and observer. Throughout his entire period of service in French Aviation he played a lone hand, in that he was always the sole American member of his unit; but Rocle was always *persona grata* with French pilots and was never at a loss for good companionship. He has served his guns in practically every type of French two-seater *avion* and knows intimately all sectors of the Western Front. When America entered the war he and Frederick Zinn were the only two Americans with actual war experience as observers and machine-gunners. Zinn was placed on duty at the American G.H.Q. Rocle was attached to the 13th and later to the 644th Aero Squadron. At the time of the Armistice he had been on active duty for more than four years. The record speaks for itself, and is one of which any soldier may well be proud.

SERVICE RECORD

WILLIAM B. RODGERS, JR., Pittsburgh, Pennsylvania.

SERVICE IN FRENCH AVIATION:
Date of enlistment: June 25, 1917.
Aviation Schools: June 29, 1917, to 1918, Avord, Juvisy, Châteauroux, G.D.E.
Breveted: October 1, 1917 (Caudron).
Final Rank: Caporal.

SERVICE IN U.S. NAVAL AVIATION:
Commissioned Ensign April 10, 1918.
U.S. Naval Instructional Center, Moutchic-Lacanau, April 10 to June 1, 1918.
U.S. Naval Air Station, Lake Bolsena, Italy, June 1, 1918, to Armistice.

William B. Rodgers, Jr.

In the schools Rodgers and Walter Miller were inseparable friends. At Juvisy, where they took the Caudron training, both earned the reputation of very daring pilots. From the G.D.E., Miller was sent to a Bréguet Squadron, where he remained until he met his death in July, and Rodgers was transferred to the navy and assigned to the United States Naval School at Moutchic-Lacanau, and later to the Naval Air Station at Lake Bolsena, Italy, where his skill in handling flying-boats won him the place of Chief Pilot. Had the fortunes of war permitted Rodgers to fight, as he had hoped, on the Western Front, those who know him are convinced that he would have made a name for himself in combat.

Clifford de Roode

No Lafayette man who came to Avord after March, 1917, will fail to remember de Roode, our interpreter, drillmaster, and intermediary in dealings with the authorities.

His position was a difficult one, which carried with it enough unpopularity to make it a matter of congratulation that he has survived the war. Some of the harder and more suspicious among us even accused de Roode of suggesting the abhorred drill, but this was never verified. At any rate, his was the martial figure which paraded before our outraged ranks, ejaculating from time to time that unpleasant word: *Fixe!*

One thing we owe to de Roode: he taught us (by example) to salute with all the grace of a Saumur cavalryman and the precision of the Prussian Guard. To watch him was a lesson in military etiquette. We stood in line, de Roode in front. The captain approached. De Roode snapped about-face—a stiff bow from the waist, and up went the right arm, elbow high, and hand bent back gracefully from the wrist. Then, *"Bonjour, mon capitaine"*

These displays of military ardour found favour in high places, favour which expressed itself in providing de Roode with a gold-braided hat and the *galons* of a *sous-lieutenant*. Encouraged by this signal honour, he learned to fly, in intervals when military and diplomatic duties were not too pressing, and finally appeared in all the glory of wings.

Note: Service record not available.

SERVICE RECORD

Kenneth Albert Rotharmel, Miami, Florida.

Previous Service: American Ambulance, 1916–17.

Service in French Aviation:
Date of enlistment: July 10, 1917.
Aviation Schools: July 12, 1917, to February 24, 1918, Avord, Tours, Pau, Cazeaux, G.D.E.
Breveted: October 23, 1917 (Caudron).
At the Front: Escadrille Spad 112, February 25 to April 26, 1918.
Final Rank: Caporal.

Service in U.S. Aviation:
Commissioned Second Lieutenant: April 4, 1918.
At the Front: Attached to French Squadron Spad 112, April 26, 1918, to Armistice.

Decorations:
Croix de Guerre, with Star.

CITATION

GRAND QUARTIER GÉNÉRAL DES
ARMÉES FRANÇAISES DE L'EST
ÉTAT-MAJOR.   26 *janvier*, 1919

Le Maréchal de France Commandant en Chef les Armées Françaises de l'Est cite à l'Ordre du Régiment:

Lieutenant ROTHARMEL, KENNETH, de l'Armée Américaine au 16me Groupe de Combat

Américain engagé volontaire dans l'aviation française en juillet, 1917, n'a cessé d'être au groupe un exemple de volonté, de courage, et d'abnégation. Pilote adroit, a pris part à de nombreux combats au cours des opérations de mars-novembre, 1918.

Le Maréchal Commandant en Chef les Armées Françaises de l'Est

PÉTAIN

Kenneth Albert Rotharmel

Rotharmel was assigned to the Escadrille Spad 112 on February 17, 1918. His joyful antics, the evening of his departure from the G.D.E., will long be legendary among the natives of that mournful hamlet, Plessis-Belleville.

With the Spad 112 Rotharmel has had a broad experience of *chasse* work in all of the important operations of 1918. Like most of us, he had a certain amount of hard luck, especially on one occasion when he found a German two-seater lost far behind our lines. The observer was leaning forward in his cockpit, doubtless poring over his map, and it looked like "cold meat" to Rotharmel, in whose mind the unfortunate Rumpler was already *homologué*. Getting into beautiful position without being seen, he pulled trigger—the guns stuttered for an instant and then hopelessly jammed!

During the latter part of the war, Rotharmel acted as liaison officer between the G.C. 16 and the American Air Service, and his duties were performed with a zeal and efficiency which won hearty praise from the authorities of both.

SERVICE RECORD

LELAND L. ROUNDS, New York City.

SERVICE IN FRENCH AVIATION:
Date of enlistment: October 16, 1916.
Aviation Schools: October 16, 1916, to August 1, 1917, Avord, Pau, G.D.E.
Breveted: May 8, 1917 (Blériot).
At the Front: Escadrille Spad 112, August 3 to December 22, 1917.
Final Rank: Sergent.

SERVICE IN U.S. AVIATION:
Commissioned First Lieutenant: January 3, 1918.
Chief Pilot, American A.I.C., Tours, January 1 to May 1, 1918.
On duty U.S. Aviation, H.Q. Paris, May 1, 1918, to Armistice.

DECORATIONS:
Croix de Guerre, with Palm.

CITATION

Q.G. 2ᵐᵉ Armée.   13 *octobre*, 1917
Le Général Commandant la 2ᵐᵉ Armée cite
  à l'Ordre de l'Armée:

Rounds, Leland Laselle, Mˡᵉ 11918, Caporal des Troupes Aéronautiques, Pilote
  à l'Escadrille N. 112

Sujet américain, engagé dans l'Armée Française le 16 octobre, 1916, s'est signalé son arrivé en escadrille comme excellent pilote, énergique et courageux. Le 5 septembre, a abattu un avion ennemi.

Leland L. Rounds

The most interesting and the most satisfying of aerial experiences came to Leland Rounds very soon after his arrival at the Front—Verdun Sector—when he gained a victory in his first combat. During his earlier patrols over the lines, he was mystified, as new pilots often are, at the apparent, occasional uneventfulness of war-time flying. Nothing happened—at least, nothing that he had been able to see. He was air-blind for a week or two. Then came second sight and a terrific scare, both at the same moment. What he first saw were the pencilled lines of smoke stabbing through the air from the muzzle of an enemy machine gun.

In the excitement of the moment, he fell into a *vrille*. The German pilot was close on his tail and, as luck would have it, passed him in a vertical dive without having registered a hit. Coming out of his nose-spin, Rounds found the enemy single-seater directly in front of him. He disclaims any credit for having bagged him. All that he had to do, he said, was to crook his index finger at his Vickers. There was no chance for a miss. However that may be, he shot down the enemy plane and its destruction was immediately confirmed from infantry observation posts.

Another adventure, when his Spad caught fire at 3500 metres, is perhaps equally interesting to him in retrospect; for, strange though it seems, he lived to have a retrospect of that terrifying experience. He landed somehow, in a marsh near Verdun, in a sea of cool, delicious, wet mud, and in one sense was none the worse for the bath.

During all his flying experience Rounds had constantly to fight against attacks of faintness when above 3500 metres. As a great deal of pursuit work takes place above that altitude, these attacks came quite often. Everything went black before his eyes, and once he fainted, regaining consciousness just in time to prevent a crash. After his transfer to the United States Air Service, he was sent to the American Aviation

School at Tours, where he guided many young birdmen through the period of their solo flights. He called it an *"embusqué* job."

ROUNDS AND HIS MECHANO

Perhaps he should have remained at the Front, flying and fainting and recovering consciousness just before splashing on the ruins of some shell-wrecked village. Perhaps, in the end, he might have died for France, an heroic, but not always a useful sacrifice. The American Air Force in France was the gainer because he was denied this privilege.

SERVICE RECORD

LAWRENCE RUMSEY, Buffalo, New York.
PREVIOUS SERVICE: American Ambulance, 1915.
SERVICE IN FRENCH AVIATION:
   Date of enlistment: September 9, 1915.
   Aviation Schools: September 11, 1915, to June 1, 1916, Pau, Avord, G.D.E.
   Breveted: February 2, 1916 (Caudron).
   At the Front: Escadrille Lafayette, June 4 to November 25, 1916.
   Final Rank: Sergent.

Lawrence Rumsey

Lawrence Rumsey, one of the earlier members of the Escadrille Lafayette, was prevented by ill health from taking any very active part in patrol work at the Front. He spent a good deal of time in hospital and was finally released from French Aviation as physically unfit for further service.

SERVICE RECORD

HAROLD YOUNG SAXON, Washington, D.C.

SERVICE IN FRENCH AVIATION:
Date of enlistment: June 10, 1917.
Aviation Schools: June 21, 1917, to January 18, 1918, Avord, Pau, G.D.E.
Breveted: November 14, 1917 (Caudron).
At the Front: Escadrille Spad 31, January 21 to June 17, 1918.
Escadrille Spad 12, June 17, 1918, to Armistice.
Final Rank: Sergent.

DECORATIONS:
Croix de Guerre, with two Palms.

CITATION

Q.G., le 4 septembre, 1918

Ve ARMÉE, ÉTAT-MAJOR.

Le Général Commandant la Ve Armée cite à l'Ordre de l'Armée:

SAXON, HAROLD, Sergent, du 2e Groupe d'Aviation, Pilote à l'Escadrille Spad 12

Très bon pilote qui fait preuve du plus bel esprit de sacrifice, de discipline, et de mordant. A incendié un drachen le 22 août, 1918.

Le Général Commandant la Ve Armée
BERTHELOT

Harold Young Saxon

Saxon is one of the most amusing and original of men; to know him is to like him, and he is known and spoken of wherever Lafayette men meet. At Avord, where he studied the eccentricities of the Blériot, we used to pass the hours between *sorties* in games of "Duck on the Rock" and hockey. Saxon's amazing skill and activity at these pastimes earned him the title of the "Human Flea." Like many others, who believed in adopting the customs of the country, he cultivated a moustache during his months of training—a moustache which flourished richly at the ends, but was discouragingly sparse in the middle section. These drooping sprouts, long and tenderly trained, lent to their cultivator a strongly Oriental air, which, taken with the fact that he spoke the language of Annam with fluency and perfect accent, made the title of "King of the Annamites" fall to him naturally. It was often noticed that Jim, the slant-eyed orderly, when he shook Saxon's foot, preparatory to administering the morning coffee, did so with the air of one approaching royalty.

In the Spad 31 and later in the Spad 12, George Dock and Saxon were a pair which upheld the best of American traditions. A very clever and reliable Spad pilot, Saxon was in the air at every opportunity, and fought through every important battle on the Western Front during 1918. With the natural desire of an American to fight under his own flag, he applied for transfer to the United States Air Service, but an enlarged tonsil prevented his passing the physical tests. It took nearly a year and a number of victories in the air to persuade the army medical authorities that the modern scout machine is able to carry an enlarged tonsil in addition to the pilot.

SERVICE RECORD

LAWRENCE SCANLON, Cedarhurst, Long Island.

PREVIOUS SERVICE: Foreign Legion (Infantry), November 26, 1914, to January 1, 1917. Wounded, June 16, 1915.

SERVICE IN FRENCH AVIATION:
Date of enlistment: February 8, 1917.
Aviation Schools: February 24 to September 1, 1917, Avord, Châteauroux.
Reformé from French Aviation, September, 1917.
Final Rank: Soldat de deuxième classe.

DECORATIONS:
Croix de Guerre, with Star (Infantry).

Lawrence Scanlon

Late in the winter of 1916-17, when the number of American student pilots at Avord had increased from twenty to forty or thereabouts, the most observing of the older men noticed among the newcomers a slightly built, red-haired chap in a well-worn *poilu* uniform. No one knew his name. No one had seen him come. He merely appeared, one day, sitting on a cot in the American barracks presided over by Jim, the Annamite orderly.

We all learned in time that this was Scanlon; but not until a month later when Charles Trinkard arrived, did we know that he was "Red" Scanlon of the Legion. For Scanlon invented the art of self-effacement. Once, when he was being discussed by some of the crowd at barracks, one man promised to buy a dinner for the crowd if "Red" could innocently be tricked into the well-known prelude, "When I was in the Legion..." which some of the old volunteers were so fond of playing. He was quite safe in making the offer, which is still outstanding.

Charles Trinkard, an old foot-soldiering comrade of his, told us of Scanlon's enlistment in the Legion on November 26, 1914; how he first went over the top with the Legion near Carrency on the 9th of May, 1915, when the regiment lost three quarters of its effectives;

and a second time on June 16 near Souchez, when he was severely wounded in the right leg. After thirteen months in the hospital of Passy near Veron, he was discharged with the bad leg shortened several inches. *Reformé* from the infantry (for he was no longer fit for service) he enlisted in the Lafayette Corps.

SCANLON'S CRASH INTO THE BAKERY

While in training at the Avord School he had a series of extraordinary flying accidents. Accidents at an aviation school are so common that most of them are forgotten before the day has passed. Not so with Scanlon's crashes. They are still remembered, and will be talked about years hence wherever his contemporaries at Avord gather for reunions. The most remarkable one happened in the spring of 1917 when he dove through the bakery roof at the Artillery School, creating panic among the *boulangers* and a *crise de pain* throughout a whole regiment of young artillerymen. He crawled out of the ruin of the bakery, and thereafter was much bothered by pilots and instructors who wanted to know what marvellous kind of "*porte-bonheur*" he carried.

His wounded leg gave him a great deal of trouble, and after three more fearful crashes, he was released from the service, greatly to his own disappointment and to that of every man in the corps. For Scanlon is one of those men who may be called, in all truth, the salt of the earth.

SERVICE RECORD

WALTER JOHN SHAFFER, Dauphin, Pennsylvania.

SERVICE IN FRENCH AVIATION:
  Date of enlistment: August 1, 1917.
  Aviation Schools: August 1 to December 28, 1917, Avord, Tours, Pau, G.D.E.
  Breveted: October 7, 1917 (Caudron).
  At the Front: Escadrille Spad 156, January 1 to June 1, 1918.
    Escadrille Spad 38, June 1 to October 3, 1918.
  Final Rank: Sergent.
  Shot down southeast of Laon, October 3, 1918.
  Prisoner in Germany until the Armistice.

DECORATIONS:
  Médaille Militaire.
  Croix de Guerre, with three Palms.

CITATIONS

4ᵉ ARMÉE.   18 août, 1918
Citation à l'Ordre de l'Armée:
Le Sergent SHAFFER, WALTER JOHN, Mle 12367, du 2ᵉ Groupe d'Aviation, Escadrille Spa. 38

Sous-officier plein d'allant et d'entrain, recherchant toujours les occasions de combattre. A fait preuve d'un ténacité rare et d'une endurance extraordinaire, dans les missions contre drachens, revenant souvent avec son avion criblé de balles. Le 4 août, 1918, a abattu en flammes un drachen ennemi.

                 Le Général Commandant la 4ᵉ Armée
                                          GOURAUD

VIᵉ ARMÉE, ÉTAT-MAJOR.   20 septembre, 1918
Citation à l'Ordre de l'Armée:
     SHAFFER, WALTER, Sergent à l'Escadrille Spa. 38, G.C. 22 détaché du
                1ᵉʳ Régiment Étranger

Pilote hardi et plein de hardiesse. Le 26 août, 1918, a abattu son 1ᵉʳᵉ avion ennemi après un combat mené avec un allant qui fit l'admiration de tous.

                 Le Général Commandant la 6ᵉ Armée
                          (Signé)   DEGOUTTE

Citation Médaille Militaire:
     Sergent SHAFFER, WALTER, Pilote à l'Escadrille Spa. 38

Sous-officier pilote de tout premier ordre. A donné des preuves d'allant et d'énergie au cours de nombreux combats. A abattu un avion et incendié un drachen. Le 3 octobre, 1918, à acharnant à mitrailler un drachen au sol, a eu son appareil criblé de balles et a été contraint d'atterrir dans les lignes ennemies — légèrement blessé. Capturé, s'est évadé peu de temps après. A été repris avant d'avoir pu atteindre nos lignes et traité durement en représailles. Deux victoires. Deux citations.

Walter John Shaffer

Shaffer has had an exceptionally interesting experience of the war. He has flown over the lines on the Nieuport, the Morane Parasol, and the Spad. He served in the same squadron with the "aces," Putnam and Madon, and on October 3, 1918, was shot down and taken prisoner by the Germans.

His first Boche was shot down while on patrol with Madon. They were flying over the Marne Sector when the "ace," who was leading the patrol, made out a Boche *biplace* below them; he dove, but his guns jammed just as he got into position. A second man then dove, filling the air with the smoke of his incendiary bullets, but missing the German. Shaffer dove next, and shot a burst of nearly a hundred cartridges before he was so blinded by the smoke that he lost sight of the enemy.

On returning to the aerodrome, he found Madon in conversation with the group commander. "Who was the third to attack the Boche?" asked Madon, and when Shaffer admitted that he was the man, the "ace" held out his hand. "You got him," he announced.

On another occasion, near Rheims, while flying with one comrade, Shaffer had a narrow escape. He had seen a patrol of four *monoplaces*, which he took to be Spads, overhead, and the next moment he attacked an Iron-Crossed two-seater which was doing *réglage* five hundred metres below him. The German observer must have been a champion shot, for in three or four bursts he shot off Shaffer's *béquille* and put several bullets through the top plane, so close to the pilot's head that they fairly grazed the skin. At this moment, to cap the climax, the four innocent-looking *monoplaces* upstairs, which were in reality Fokkers, took a hand in the fight, and only the courage and skill of Shaffer's comrade disengaged him from a very bad situation.

On October 3, while diving on a *saucisse* twelve kilometres behind the German lines, Shaffer had his motor ruined by bullets from the ground, and was forced to land. His own account of the adventure follows:

> A dead stick, six hundred metres high, and ten miles behind the Boche lines—I was out of luck all right; I would be a prisoner. The question was, would it be a live or a dead one, for the ground beneath was nothing but barbed wire, trenches, and shell-holes. As I planed down, the thought occurred to me that when an aviator lands in enemy territory, he has explicit orders to burn or destroy his plane. As I felt sure I would not have time to burn my plane, I decided to destroy it, a simple matter considering the ground ahead. All I had to do was to throw her over on one wing and my speed and the rough ground would do the rest. I did not have long to wait. With a splintering of struts and stays, and a ripping of cloth as the lowered wing touched the earth, the plane buried its nose in the ground, crushing the landing-gear and propeller. Considering the fact that it was the first time I had deliberately smashed a plane, I

had not done badly, for the wreck would have pleased the most critical squadron commander. The only useful things left were the tail and the two guns, and the latter were not working, as I found when I attacked the balloon.

SERVICE RECORD

CLARENCE BERNARD SHONINGER, New York City.

PREVIOUS SERVICE: American Ambulance, 1916–17.

SERVICE IN FRENCH AVIATION:
Date of enlistment: May 24, 1917.
Aviation Schools: June 5, 1917, to February 20, 1918, Avord, Juvisy, Pau, G.D.E.
Breveted: November 26, 1917 (Caudron).
At the Front: Escadrille N. 99, February 22 to May 29, 1918.
Final Rank: Caporal.
Shot down in combat: Near Fismes, May 29, 1918. Prisoner in Germany until the Armistice.

Clarence B. Shoninger

On May 29, the third day of the great German advance south from the Chemin des Dames, a patrol of the Spad 99 was ordered to reconnoitre the rapidly shifting front and drive back any Germans who might be doing *réglage* between Rheims and La Fère-en-Tardenois. Shoninger's machine was not running properly, and to his bitter disappointment the captain told him that he could not go. While the *mécaniciens* were starting the other machines, Shoninger worked frantically with his man in a desperate hope of getting the motor to run. As the last of the patrol took off, it seemed to run satisfactorily, so he rushed to the captain and begged permission to follow. A grudging nod was sufficient for Shoninger; he dashed to his machine, strapped himself in, and next moment was following the patrol toward the lines. Between Rheims and Fismes he became separated from the patrol, and at that moment was attacked by a gang of Albatross, one of which he forced to land in the ensuing fight. But either the Albatross or the *mitrailleuses* on the ground riddled Shoninger's machine with bullets and cut his controls, sending him crashing down into a German anti-aircraft battery near Crugny.

It was long believed that Shoninger had been killed, until one day it was learned that he was a prisoner. The tale of his captivity is long and interesting as his friends learned when, shortly after the Armistice, he returned safely to Paris.

SERVICE RECORD

REGINALD SINCLAIRE, Corning, New York.

SERVICE IN FRENCH AVIATION:
Date of enlistment: June 15, 1917.
Aviation Schools: June 20 to December 2, 1917,
Avord, Pau, G.D.E.
Brevetted: October 2, 1917 (Caudron).
At the Front: Escadrille Spad 68, December 4,
1917, to October 4, 1918.
Final Rank: Adjudant.

DECORATIONS:
Croix de Guerre, with three Palms.

CITATIONS

Le 7 mars, 1918

I^{èr} ARMÉE, ÉTAT-MAJOR.

Le Général Commandant la 1ère Armée cite à l'Ordre de l'Armée:

SINCLAIRE, REGINALD, M^{le} 12254, Caporal du 1er Régiment Étranger, Pilote à l'Escadrille Spad 68

Pilote américain, engagé volontaire, d'une ardeur et d'une bravoure au-dessus de tout éloge. Le 17 février, 1918, par sa maitrise et son attitude résolue, a tenu en respect une protection de trois avions de chasse, permettant ainsi à son camarade d'abattre un avion.

Citation à l'Ordre de l'Armée:

SINCLAIRE, REGINALD, M^{le} 12254, Adjudant au 1er Régiment Étranger, Pilote à l'Escadrille Spad 68

Remarquable pilote de chasse, possédant des qualités supérieures de sang-froid, de décision, et d'audace réfléchies. A livré de nombreux combats au cours desquels 2 avions ennemis sont tombés désemparés. Le 17 juin, 1918, a abattu en flammes un avion allemand à plusieurs kilomètres à l'intérieur des lignes ennemis.

Le 17 septembre, 1918

Reginald Sinclaire

Sinclaire, in his day, was one of the steadiest Blériot pilots at Avord. He broke nothing in the schools, and after his arrival at the Front, in the Spad 68, he became widely known for his brilliant and aggressive work over the lines. Through the thickest of the fighting in 1918, he was constantly with his squadron, flying often three times a day in company with a French comrade, Gauderman. They were a formidable pair, but through all their work they were followed by ill luck in getting confirmations. Once at the G.C. 20, a number of Lafayette men were seated at the bar when Sinclaire came rushing in all smiles, and ordered champagne for the crowd.

Gauderman and I just shot down three Boches, we were fifteen miles into their lines beyond Soissons when we ran across a patrol of four Pfalz. It was just a case of keep above them—*pique* and *chandelle*; in three dives we had three of them dropping, two in flames. We had to hand it to the other fellow, he was so plucky. He would not leave, but stuck around trying to get into a position to shoot—poor devil, we could have got him, but he was too nervy, we didn't have the heart.

Like many others that Sinclaire shot down, these Germans were so far in their lines that no one of them was ever confirmed.

In addition to his fine military qualities, Sinclaire's good-fellowship has made him equally popular with his French and American comrades, and he will be one of the leaders in all future reunions of the Lafayette Flying Corps.

SERVICE RECORD

GLENN SITTERLY, Spring Valley, Illinois.
PREVIOUS SERVICE: American Ambulance, 1917.
SERVICE IN FRENCH AVIATION:
Date of enlistment: May 31, 1917.
Aviation Schools: June 12, 1917, to March 24, 1918, Avord, G.D.E.
Breveted: September 22, 1917 (Caudron).
At the Front: Escadrille C. 46, March 26 to August 20, 1918.
Escadrille Spad 38, October 15, 1918, to Armistice.
Final Rank: Adjudant.

DECORATIONS:
Croix de Guerre, with Palm.

Glenn Sitterly

Glenn Sitterly was one of the pioneers in the *triplace* pursuit work which developed in the spring of 1918. A pilot of unusual cleverness, he had need of all his skill in this branch of the service, for it proved to be a hazardous duty.

Sitterly was assigned to the Caudron 46, one of the frequently cited *escadrilles* of the French Army. From March until the middle of August, he took part in the work of shooting up trenches and communications at low altitude, protecting day bombardments far beyond the lines, and effecting ordinary barrage patrols. In July, his machine was brought down in flames, near Villers-Cotterets, but by a miracle he and his *mitrailleurs* escaped injury. In August, Sitterly transferred to *monoplace chasse* work, and was sent to the *escadrille* of Madon. There he brought down his second official enemy plane, a two-seater which was distributing sheets of propaganda over French territory. Sitterly is reticent about recounting his experiences, and it is only by seeing his uniform, torn by shrapnel and bullets, that one can realise the narrow escapes he has had.

SERVICE RECORD

ROBERT SOUBIRAN, New York City.

PREVIOUS SERVICE: Foreign Legion (Infantry), August 28, 1914, to February 25, 1916. Wounded, October 19, 1915.

SERVICE IN FRENCH AVIATION:
Date of enlistment: February 27, 1916.
Aviation Schools: February 27 to October 20, 1916, Pau, Buc, G.D.E.
Breveted: May 22, 1916 (Caudron).
At the Front: Escadrille Lafayette, October 22, 1916, to February 18, 1918.
Final Rank: Adjudant.

SERVICE IN U.S. AVIATION:
Commissioned Captain: January 26, 1918.
Promoted Major: February 18, 1919.
At the Front: 103d Pursuit Squadron, as Flight Commander and later as Commanding Officer, February 18, 1918, to Armistice.

DECORATIONS:
Légion d'Honneur.
Croix de Guerre, with two Palms.

CITATIONS

VIme ARMÉE.   9 *novembre*, 1917

SOUBIRAN, ROBERT (Légion Étrangère), Pilote à l'Escadrille Spa. 124

Américain engagé dès le début de la guerre dans la Légion Étrangère, où il prit part aux combats de l'Aisne en 1914 et aux attaques de Champagne en 1915. Blessé le 19 octobre, 1915. Passé dans l'Aviation, s'est montré excellent pilote, remplissant avec une ardeur remarquable les missions qui lui ont été confiées. Le 17 octobre, au cours d'une protection d'attaque de drachens, a forcé un appareil ennemi à atterrir désemparé.   (*Signé*)   MAISTRE

GRAND QUARTIER GÉNÉRAL DES ARMÉES FRANÇAISES
DE L'EST, ÉTAT-MAJOR.   *Le* 17 *mai*, 1919

Après approbation du Général Commandant en Chef les Forces Expéditionnaires Américaines en France, le Maréchal Commandant en Chef les Armées Françaises de l'Est, cite à l'Ordre de l'Armée:

Capitaine SOUBIRAN, ROBERT

Citoyen américain engagé en août, 1914, dans la Légion Étrangère. S'est distingué dans l'Infanterie (blessé en septembre, 1915), puis comme pilote à l'Escadrille Lafayette, où il a montré les plus belles qualités de courage et d'audace.

Le Maréchal Commandant en Chef les Armées de l'Est
                                                                    PÉTAIN

Par décret du Président de la République en date du 9 avril, 1919, le Capitaine Soubiran a été promu Chevalier de la Légion d'Honneur.
Cet promotion a été fait avec le motif de ce citation.

Robert Soubiran

There are towns and villages all along the battle area in France where the name of Robert Soubiran will be remembered long after those of most of us have been forgotten. In point of experience he is one of the oldest of the American volunteers, having enlisted in August, 1914, with Thaw, Kiffin Rockwell, Dennis Dowd, Alan Seeger, Chatkoff, Zinn, Bach, and Trinkard. Of French descent, and speaking the language fluently, he made friends among the inhabitants of scores of villages where the Legion was stationed when on repos. He whittled his bread with the natural ease of an old *poilu* reservist; then sticking his open clasp-knife upright in the deal table, he would drink *pinard* from his *bidon* with audible zest. Old French housewives hearing him speak English were astonished. "*Mais c'est un Français, celui-là!*" High praise, reserved to Soubiran alone of all his compatriots in the Legion.

He served as an infantryman until the close of the Champagne offensive of 1915, when he was wounded in the knee. After four months in hospital he was again ready for active duty, and was transferred to the Aviation Corps. Learning to fly cost him no more than the usual amount of effort, although he found it hard to adapt himself to the genteel ways of living common to this chic branch of war service. His infantry practices clung to him, and many an old *commandant*, the occasional guest of the squadron, detecting the former *fantassin*, became his friend at once and would warm to the theme of the *engagés volontaires* in the Legion.

The pilots in the Escadrille Lafayette have Soubiran to thank for the only complete photographic record which they have of their life at the Front. He was present with his camera at every ceremonial in which the Squadron took part. He snapped every crash, every bizarre accident at the aerodrome, and filled memory books with photographs of all of their goings and comings from one sector to another, squadron parties in Bar-le-Duc, Villers-Cotterets, Nancy, Soissons, Dunkirk, Châlons, Épernay—photographs which are priceless to them now.

One could talk at great length of his service in France. Like William Thaw's and Frederick Zinn's, it is, in itself, a history in miniature of the Great War. Eighteen months in the Legion as an infantryman, twenty-three months in French Aviation, and on November 11, 1918, nearly ten months in the United States Air Service with more than four hundred hours of combat flying, is a record of which to be proud. On January 3, 1919, he was mentioned as follows in General Orders No. 2 of the First United States Army Air Service Commander:

> Captain Robert Soubiran, A.S.U.S.A., Commanding Officer of the 103rd Aero Squadron, rendered meritorious service particularly while preparing and during the Saint-Mihiel and Argonne-Meuse attacks. He has courageously and ably fulfilled the duties of Flight Commander, Squadron and Group Operations Officer, and Commanding Officer of the 103rd Aero Squadron. He has been daily noticeable for his energetic ability, materially assist-

ing in the early organisation, equipment, and operation of that squadron and subsequently of the 3rd Pursuit Group.

SOUBIRAN AND HIS SPAD

He had earlier been proposed for the rank of major, but instructions from the War Department discontinued all promotions from the date of the nth of November, 1918, so that he did not receive his well-earned advance until many months later. Long after the signing of the Armistice he was still on duty in France. He was one of the first Americans to take part in the war and one of the last to leave the country which had been his home for nearly five years.

SERVICE RECORD

DUMARESQ SPENCER, Highland Park, Illinois.

SERVICE IN FRENCH AVIATION:
Date of enlistment: July 10, 1917.
Aviation Schools: July 18 to December 24, 1917, Avord, Tours, Pau, G.D.E.
Breveted: October 21, 1917 (Caudron).
At the Front: Escadrille N. 150, December 27, 1917, to January 22, 1918.
Final Rank: Caporal.
Killed in line of duty: January 22, 1918, near Belfort.

DECORATIONS:
Croix de Guerre, with Star.

CITATION

Le Lieutenant Colonel. Chef d'État-Major de la 7ème Armée, cite à l'Ordre du Service Aéronautique de la 7ème Armée:

Le Brigadier SPENCER, DUMARESQ (active) Pilote à l'Escadrille Spad 150

Jeune pilote courageux et rempli d'allant, le 19 janvier a attaqué un groupe de monoplaces ennemis et est rentré avec son appareils atteint de balles. S'est tué le 22 janvier, 1918, en revenant atterrir au terrain.

Dumaresq Spencer

Spencer's keenness to fly and constant anxiety to get to the Front were noticeable all through his period of training. At Tours, at Avord, and at Pau, he was impatient of every delay which retarded, even for a few hours, his progress toward active duty. On December 27, 1917, he arrived at Belfort, assigned to the N. 150, a squadron which was at that time equipped with the Type 27 Nieuports. On his first patrol over the lines he found occasion to show his daring and aggressive spirit, for he became lost from the formation and flew alone into the enemy lines on the lookout for trouble. At Mulhouse, ten miles into German territory, he found a lone Albatross practicing acrobacy over the city. Spencer plunged headlong to the attack and a point-blank combat ensued, watched, no doubt, by hundreds of Germans in the town below. Several times both pilots went into *vrilles* with full motor, pulled out and renewed the combat, until at last Spencer lost his opponent and returned to his aerodrome, the Nieuport bearing many scars of battle.

During his short life at the Front, Spencer became known as the keenest man in his squadron, flying whenever possible, no matter how cold or windy the day. He was possessed of but one idea: to shoot down German machines. His one complaint was the difficulty of getting a combat on the quiet Alsatian Front.

On January 22, 1918, Spencer made his last patrol. Returning from the lines, he left his formation and flew to a target near the aerodrome, where the pilots were encouraged to try their skill in shooting. While making a sharp turn over the target, his machine lost speed and fell in

SPENCER'S GRAVE, BELFORT

a spin, crashing to the ground and killing Spencer instantly. His loss was a bitter one, for he had endeared himself to many friends, and would have gone far had he been spared.

SERVICE RECORD

ALFRED HOLT STANLEY, Elmira, New York.

PREVIOUS SERVICE: American Ambulance, 1916–17.

SERVICE IN FRENCH AVIATION:
Date of enlistment: April 12, 1917.
Aviation Schools: June 2, 1917, to February 22, 1918, Avord, Pau, Cazeaux, G.D.E.
Breveted: November 13, 1917 (Caudron).
At the Front: Escadrille Spad 23, February 24, 1918, to Armistice.
Final Rank: Adjudant.

DECORATIONS:
Médaille Militaire.
Croix de Guerre, with four Palms and two Stars.

CITATIONS

Le 19 *mai*, 1918

Citation à l'Ordre de l'Aéronautique:

STANLEY, ALFRED HOLT, Caporal Pilote de l'Escadrille Spa. 23

Le 4 mai, a permis, par sa très vigilante protection, qu'un drachen fut incendié malgré la présence d'un avion ennemi.

Citation à l'Ordre de l'Armée:

STANLEY, ALFRED HOLT, Sergent-Pilote de l'Escadrille Spa. 23

Le 24 juin, 1918, malgré la pluie, les nuages très bas, et les violents tirs des mitrailleuses de terre, a exécuté par ordre une reconnaissance à 700 mètres d'altitude, et 30 kilomètres à l'intérieur des lignes ennemies.

IIe ARMÉE.

Très brillant pilote de chasse, audacieux et toujours intrépide. Le 30 octobre, 1918, a abattu un avion ennemi.

Engagé volontaire pour la durée de la guerre dans l'armée française, de nationalité américaine, malgré les avantages qui lui ont été offerts dans l'armée de sa nation a resté dans l'aviation française. Pilote d'une énergie et d'une hardiesse incomparables, réunissant toutes les qualités de chasseur, volontaire pour toutes les missions périlleuses. Dans de nombreux combats a prouvé son très grand mépris du danger, donnant à tous ses camarades le plus bel exemple du devoir et de sacrifice. Quatre citations.

Cinquième citation et Médaille Militaire.

2e ARMÉE. *Le* 13 *octobre*, 1918

Le Général Commandant la 2e Armée cite à l'Ordre de l'Armée:

Le Sergent STANLEY, ALFRED HOLT, M^{le} 12218, du 1er Régiment de la Légion Étrangère, Pilote à l'Escadrille Spa. 23

Pilote d'une audace remarquable, prouve journellement son très grand mépris du danger. Le 18 septembre, au cours d'un dur combat, a eu son avion détérioré par les balles. Chasseur d'élite, s'est distingué dans maints combats par son adresse et sa résolution. Le 18 septembre, 1918, a attaqué et abattu un biplace ennemi. Deux citations antérieures.

Le Général Commandant la 2ème*Armée:*

(Signé) HIRSCHAUER

Alfred Holt Stanley

Stanley is a fine example of the quiet determination which pushes deliberately ahead through all obstacles to success. In the schools he never boasted about his flying. On the contrary, he was doubtful of his skill. At Pau he said frankly that he disliked acrobatics, which made him ill. But it was noticeable that he did not ask to go on a two-seater type of machine. After leaving Pau, he flew for a time in the squadron which protected Paris, constantly perfecting himself in the fine points of chasse work, and at length, in February, 1918, when he felt that he had thoroughly mastered combat flying, he went to the Front in Escadrille Spad 23, commanded by the "ace," Pinsard. Once in the thick of the fighting, it was clear that his long preparation had made him a pilot of the first order.

During the battles of 1918 he won several victories. He has the distinction of coming out alive from an adventure such as few men have known. On the 23rd of September, in the region of Étain, near Verdun, he was attacking a German *biplace*, when suddenly the pilot manoeuvred in such a way as to bring Stanley directly under the observer's gun, at a range of only twenty yards. A stream of incendiary bullets poured into his fuselage and upper plane, setting fire to the small *nourrice* gasoline tank, ruining the motor, and cutting the oil and water connections. With great presence of mind, after dropping three thousand feet, Stanley succeeded in extinguishing the fire. As he was then quite low, and at a distance of eight kilometres in the German lines, it was a question of starting the motor or being taken prisoner. With a pierced crank case, a broken connection rod, and no oil or water, he managed to make the motor stagger along sufficiently to cross the first line and land within a few metres of the second-line trenches.

SERVICE RECORD

FRANK ELMER STARRETT, Athol, Massachusetts.

PREVIOUS SERVICE: American Ambulance, 1917.

SERVICE IN FRENCH AVIATION:
Date of enlistment: July 19, 1917.
Aviation Schools: August 1, 1917, to January 3, 1918, Avord, Tours.
Final Rank: Soldat de deuxième classe.
Killed in line of duty: January 3, 1918, at Tours.

Frank Elmer Starrett

Almost from the time of his enlistment in the Lafayette Corps, luck was against Starrett. His training was seriously retarded by the transfer of his detachment from Avord to Tours, and shortly after his arrival at the latter school he was taken ill with bronchial pneumonia and forced to spend two months in hospital. Chafing with impatience to get to the Front, he refused the convalescent leave offered him on his discharge from the hospital and resumed training before he had fully recovered his strength.

Keen, intelligent, and quick to master the principles of flying, Starrett gave promise of fine service at the Front; but he was destined never to reach it. On January 3, 1918, while on a brevet flight, he was killed in one of those accidents which remain forever unexplained. His Caudron fell near Pontlevoy, and he was buried, with full military honours, in the American cemetery at Tours.

SERVICE RECORD

RUSSELL F. STEARNS, Pawtucket, Rhode Island.

PREVIOUS SERVICE: American Ambulance, 1917.

SERVICE IN FRENCH AVIATION:
Date of enlistment: April 12, 1917.
Aviation Schools: April 26 to December 24, 1917, Avord, Juvisy, Pau, G.D.E.
Breveted: October 21, 1917 (Caudron).
At the Front: Escadrille Spad 150, December 27, 1917, to February 24, 1918.
Final Rank: Caporal.

SERVICE IN U.S. MARINE AVIATION:
Commissioned Second Lieutenant.
Served two months in U.S.M.A. Discharged on account of ill-health.

Russell F. Stearns

Stearns enlisted in the corps after a term of faithful service in the American Ambulance, and arrived at Avord on April 26, 1917. He was one of the few who took the double-command Blériot training, was transferred later on to Juvisy, and breveted on Caudron there. The fact that he became a pilot and went through the school of acrobacy at Pau speaks well for his determination and pluck, for he hated flying from the beginning, and often told his friends that he dreaded the thought of going into the air and disliked the very sight of a flying machine.

On December 27, 1917, Stearns was sent to the Escadrille N. 150, with which he served until February 24, when he went to America on leave. While at home he obtained his release from the French army and transferred to the United States Marine Air Service, but ill health, which had hindered him in France, forced him to obtain his discharge after serving two months.

SERVICE RECORD

JOSEPH CHARLES STEHLIN, Brooklyn, New York.

SERVICE IN FRENCH AVIATION:
  Date of enlistment: February 19, 1917.
  Aviation Schools: March 1 to August 16, 1917,
      Avord, Pau, G.D.E
  Breveted: June 23, 1917 (Blériot).
  At the Front: Escadrille Spad 95, August 18 to
      October 2, 1917.
  Final Rank: Sergent.

DECORATIONS:
  Croix de Guerre, with Palm.

CITATIONS

VI⁰ ARMÉE, ÉTAT-MAJOR.
Citation à l'Ordre de l'Armée:
  STEHLIN, JOSEPH CHARLES (Infanterie),
    Pilote à l'Escadrille No. 95
  Jeune pilote plein d'entrain; a attaqué, le 7 septembre, 1917, un avion qui est tombé en flammes dans ses lignes.

Joseph Charles Stehlin

Joseph Stehlin made an excellent beginning as a combat pilot, shooting down a German plane soon after his arrival at the Front. In January, 1918, when he was about to be released from French Aviation for the purpose of accepting a commission in the United States Air Service, he took advantage of this opportunity, and notwithstanding urgent orders from the American authorities that he should remain in France so that his transfer might be effected, he secured a French *permission*, and returned to America.

A considerable correspondence then took place between the French Embassy in Washington and the Ministry of War in Paris, relative to his status. The Military *Attaché* of the French Embassy in Washington wrote to the French Ministry of War, asking that Stehlin's engagement with the French Army be cancelled, stating that the United States Air Service would take him over with the rank of Lieutenant if he could be cleared from his French Army obligations. This correspondence covered a period of several months. Stehlin, meanwhile, uncertain of his rating, and in doubt as to what he should do, accepted employment as a speaker for Liberty loans. He did very good work and was instrumental in raising large sums of money. In this way he served his country to good advantage. Still in doubt as to his status, he returned to France on October 30, 1918, reaching Paris after the Armistice was signed.

SERVICE RECORD

HENRY ELMER STICKNEY, Rutland, Vermont.

SERVICE IN FRENCH AVIATION:
Date of enlistment: July 21, 1917.
Aviation Schools: July 31 to December 2, 1917, Avord, Tours, Pau, G.D.E.
Breveted: October 3, 1917 (Caudron).
At the Front: Escadrille Spad 150, December 4, 1917, to June 20, 1918.
Final Rank: Sergent.

SERVICE IN U.S. AVIATION:
Commissioned First Lieutenant: June 3, 1918.
At the Front: Attached to French Squadron Spad 150, June 21, 1918, to Armistice.

DECORATIONS:
Croix de Guerre, with Palm.

CITATION

G.Q.G., 3 *novembre*, 1918

Lieutenant HENRY STICKNEY, de l'Armée Américaine, Pilote à l'Escadrille Spa. 150

Officier pilote d'un grand courage, s'est signalé dans de nombreux combats. Le 1ᵉʳ septembre, 1918, au cours de l'un d'eux a abattu un avion ennemi.

Henry Elmer Stickney

Stickney is probably the smallest man in the Lafayette Flying Corps. In a Spad, in order to bring his gun-sights in line with his eye, he had to bolster himself up with cushions and to sit on the very edge of the seat that he might be able to reach the rudder bar. He comes from Vermont, and had his first aerial experience while touring his native mountains on a motorcycle, when, for some reason, the throttle became stuck in the wide-open position. He sped up a hill at breakneck speed and down the other side with a velocity nearly equal to that of a Spad. Seeing a large ditch looming ahead in the valley, he was debating what he should do, when the front wheel struck—and Stickney made a prolonged but wingless flight. He survived this accident and was none the worse for it afterward. His first experiences as an aviator were in Vermont where he built and tested gliders. These machines, according to Stickney, worked splendidly in the air, but were always destroyed upon reaching the ground. Therefore the amateur accepted the French Government's invitation to fly free of charge and to fight on the Western Front.

On June 14, 1918, while patrolling the lines between Soissons and

Noyon, Stickney had a combat which came near being his last. He had left his patrol to attack a German too far in to catch, and was flying alone near Soissons when he saw two enemy *réglage* machines heading for their lines. Seeing no protection, he allowed the first one. to pass and was attacking the second from above when suddenly he heard the stutter of guns behind him and saw tracer bullets streaking past. The adventure as he told of it in a letter, follows:

> Looking around I found three Fokker triplanes had joined the party and seemed to be taking turns shooting at me. I made one attack on the *biplace*, shooting both guns at point-blank range and redressing just in time to avoid a smash; then, without looking for the result of my shots, I turned to attack the nearest triplane, which was now pretty close and making a lot of noise. When I pulled the triggers to open fire, my guns jammed and left me feeling rather simple in the midst of the Germans, who were setting up a Roman-candle effect with the tracer bullets from their guns. Deciding to leave such company, I pointed the nose of my machine toward the ground and let it have all its motor. It fell like a plummet for more than 2000 metres, and finally I nursed it out of its dive into *ligne de vol,* only 150 metres from the ground; but whose ground? Fritz's, for they soon announced it with a little machine-gun work.
>
> Evidently they did not allow enough for my speed, for their tracers passed just behind my tail, and as they continued to miss me I began to feel more comfortable. Just at this moment I heard a machine gun behind me, and looking back, found the triplanes were still in the game, having come down at a more gentle angle. I bet on my old Spad for speed and turned her nose toward the friendly French 'sausages.' Eventually I reached our lines, and then the shooting was turned on the Germans, but they still followed. Then a curious thing happened: I seemed to be climbing again, mounting to the height of the 'sausages.' This was not what I wanted, as I needed all my speed to keep ahead of Fritz. I looked at the altimeter and found that my altitude had not changed, and then it dawned upon me that the 'sausages' were being pulled down, as the Germans were still on my tail and dangerously near. When at last I passed over the 'sausage' line, all the balloons were on the ground. I finally reached my field and landed. The machine was hit in nine places, three or four just missing my gas tank.

SERVICE RECORD

DONALD E. STONE, New York City.

PREVIOUS SERVICE: Norton-Harjes Ambulance, 1916–17.

SERVICE IN FRENCH AVIATION:
Date of enlistment: April 8, 1917.
Aviation Schools: June 15, 1917, to March 16, 1918, Avord, Pau, Cazeaux, G.D.E.
Breveted: October 22, 1917 (Caudron).
At the Front: Escadrille Spad 12, March 18 to April 21, 1918.
Final Rank: Caporal.
Killed in combat: April 21, 1918.

DECORATIONS:
Croix de Guerre, with Star (Ambulance).
Croix de Guerre, with Star (Aviation).

CITATION

Groupe de Combat 11, le 27 avril, 1918
Caporal STONE, DONALD, Pilote à l'Escadrille Spa. 12

Engagé volontaire de nationalité américain. Jeune pilote qui pendant son court séjour à l'Escadrille a fait preuve d'une audace, d'un dévouement, et d'une ardeur remarquable. S'est particulièrement distingué le 21 avril au cours d'un violent engagement, y a fait preuve de la plus belle œuvre.

Donald E. Stone

As one looks back on former comrades of the Lafayette Flying Corps, it is remarkable how each individual stands out, for most of them were unusual men, of imagination and adventurous spirit. Stone had travelled much, worked at widely different things, and known people of the racial and social extremes. Cattle-rancher in Mexico, ambulance driver before our declaration of war, and a fighting pilot on the Western Front, Stone's adventurous life ended on April 21, 1918, when he was shot down in a stirring combat against thirteen Germans.

He was a thoughtful, silent, rather serious chap who in rare moods talked well of interesting places and people, a man respected by his acquaintances and loved by his friends. His sincerely patriotic character is illustrated by the following passage from a letter written by him to Major Gros on May 15, 1917:

> As it is my good fortune to be in France, serving with the American Ambulance, I have learned something of the needs of the Allied Powers. Now that my country is at war for the same cause ... I am anxious to contribute a greater service than by driving an ambulance ... and after studying our needs and my own fitness, I have chosen Aviation.

SERVICE RECORD

UPTON SULLIVAN, Philadelphia, Pennsylvania.

SERVICE IN FRENCH AVIATION:
Date of enlistment: June 13, 1917.
Aviation Schools: June 25, 1917, to January 6, 1918, Avord, Pau, G.D.E.
Breveted: November 16, 1917 (Caudron).
At the Front: Escadrille N. 90, January 8 to April 8, 1918.
Final Rank: Sergent.

SERVICE IN U.S. NAVAL AVIATION:
Commissioned Ensign: April 12, 1918.
At the Front: With Northern Bombing Group, U.S.N.A.S., until the Armistice.

Upton Sullivan

Sullivan always got on well with the French and was very much at home in his squadron, the N. 90, then stationed at Nancy. His captain, in the spring of 1918, offered to propose him for a Lieutenancy, but Sullivan had already applied for a commission in the United States Navy. During the summer he transferred to the United States Naval Air Service. He had a very severe crash in a Handley-Page and was injured, but was able to continue flying after his release from hospital, and served with the Northern Bombing Group, U.S.N.A.S., until the signing of the Armistice. It is regrettable that we have no account of his adventures after transferring from the French Service, for the bombing work undertaken by the navy was often of the most interesting character.

SERVICE RECORD

LESLIE R. TABER, Auburn, New York.

PREVIOUS SERVICE: American Ambulance, 1917.

SERVICE IN FRENCH AVIATION:
Date of enlistment: June 25, 1917.
Aviation Schools: July 19, 1917, to March 9, 1918, Avord, Tours, G.D.E.
Breveted: October 26, 1917 (Caudron).
At the Front: Escadrille Br. 29, March 11 to March 17, 1918.
Final Rank: Caporal.

SERVICE IN U.S. NAVAL AVIATION:
Commissioned Ensign: March 19, 1918.
At the Front: Attached to the British Handley-Page Night Bombing Squadron No. 214. First U.S. Naval Night Bombing Squadron.

Leslie R. Taber

Taber was trained at Avord, at Tours, and at the French bombing school of Sacy-le-Grand. On March 11, 1918, he joined the Escadrille Br. 29, then operating in the Vosges, and saw active service with that unit until March 17, when he transferred to the United States Naval Air Service with the rank of Ensign. Since that time he has had an exceptionally broad experience of aviation, having flown many types of planes in France, Italy, England, and Belgium. On one occasion he ferried a 600 H.P. Caproni from Milan, Italy, to Calais. From July, 1918, to the close of hostilities, he piloted a Handley-Page as a member of the Northern Bombing Group, and made repeated raids on Zeebrugge and other German bases on the Belgian coast. Altogether, Taber's experience of the war is one to be envied, for he has enjoyed a rare amount of travel and a large share of adventure.

SERVICE RECORD

WILLIAM HALLET TAILER, Roslyn, New York.

SERVICE IN FRENCH AVIATION:
Date of enlistment: July 21, 1917.
Aviation Schools: July 31 to December 12, 1917
                Avord, Tours, Pau, G D.E.
Breveted: October 10, 1917 (Caudron).
At the Front: Escadrille Spad 67, December 14
              1917, to February 5, 1918.
Final Rank: Sergent.
Killed in line of duty: February 5, 1918, nea Verdun.

William Hallet Tailer

Tailer's progress through the schools was brilliant, and when, on December 14, 1917, he was sent to the Escadrille Spad 67, of the famous *Groupe of Cigognes*, he seemed assured of an equally brilliant future. Less than two months later he was buried at the Front.

A friend, writing in the columns of the Paris *Herald*, said of Tailer:

> He was as fine a type of the rising generation of Americans as you could wish to meet ... endowed with one of the rarest natures, a cheerful spirituality which looked only on the bright side of life. Billy ... was a member of the ... 7th Regiment, passed some time on the Mexican Border, and afterwards passed into the Aviation Service, where he made extraordinary

progress. It seems but yesterday that he left his home to take his first lessons in the new art.... He was one of many in the village of Roslyn to volunteer for service ... and is, I think, the first of these to go.

On February 6, 1918, the day after Tailer's death, another Lafayette man, attached to the *Cigognes*, wrote:

> Yesterday William H. Tailer of Spad 67 was killed while flying patrol over the lines. As the captain made a *virage* he saw Tailer's machine fall nose down and go into a *vrille* from which he never pulled out. Some officers on the ground saw him fall. At about a thousand metres he lost both wings and the plane crashed about three kilometres back of the lines. No one can say definitely what happened ... they were being shelled by German anti-aircraft. The consensus of opinion is that he must have been hit. I am trying to have a firing squad of U.S. Regulars to render the last military honours. First Phil Benney and now Bill Tailer ... two of my best friends and two of the finest boys who ever lived.

MONUMENT ERECTED TO THE MEMORY OF
WILLIAM H. TAILER BY THE CITIZENS OF ROSLYN

SERVICE RECORD

ELMER B. TAYLOR, Cedar Grove, New Jersey.

SERVICE IN FRENCH AVIATION:
 Date of enlistment: July 21, 1917.
 Aviation Schools: July 31, 1917, to January 31, 1918, Avord, Tours, Pau, G.D.E.
 Breveted: November 2, 1917 (Caudron).
 At the Front: Escadrille C. 74, February 1 to April 1, 1918.
  Escadrille Spad 102, April 1 to April 6, 1918.
 Final Rank: Sergent.

SERVICE IN U.S. NAVAL AVIATION:
 Commissioned Ensign: June 12, 1918.
 At the Front: 9th Squadron, Northern Bombing Group, June 15 to October 27, 1918.
 Died of pneumonia: October 27, 1918, at Calais.

Elmer B. Taylor

Enlisting on July 21, 1917, Taylor made exceptionally fast progress through the schools and arrived at the G.D.E. with men who had enlisted three months before him. While at Plessis he was taken seriously ill. After two months of hospital and convalescence he arrived at the Front. He was assigned to the Escadrille C. 74, and then to the Spad 102, only to be transferred to the navy six days later. In the Naval Air Service he was a member of the 9th Squadron, Northern Bombing Group, where he made an excellent record. The hardships of the previous winter had undermined his health and he was finally compelled to go to hospital with a severe attack of bronchial trouble. This developed into pneumonia from which he died, on October 27, 1918.

SERVICE RECORD

HUGH TERRES, Kensington, London, S.W., England.

SERVICE IN FRENCH AVIATION:
 Date of enlistment: May 15, 1917.
 Aviation Schools: May 26, 1917, to March 30, 1918, Avord, Crotoy, G.D.E.
 Breveted: November 20, 1917 (Caudron).
 Final Rank: Caporal.

SERVICE IN U.S. NAVAL AVIATION:
 Commissioned Ensign: April, 1918.
 Killed in line of duty: Near Milan, Italy, August 17, 1918.

Hugh Terres

All the Lafayette men who were *élèves* at Avord during the spring and summer of 1917 will remember Terres, the pleasant, dark-eyed fellow, blessed with perfect French and English of the Oxford variety, who acted for a time as our interpreter. His position, as intermediary between American *élèves* and French authorities, was not an easy one, but his tact and good-breeding smoothed over many a difficult situation and made him liked and respected by all of his comrades. Terres had accepted the work of interpreter with the idea of becoming a student-pilot, for it was not in him to stand back when there was difficult or dangerous work to be done, and none of his friends were surprised when he announced, in the middle of the summer, that he was to begin flying. He took the Caudron training, was breveted on November 20, 1917, and, as he had decided to specialize in bombing, was sent to Le Crotoy before going to the G.D.E. Commissioned Ensign in the United States Navy before he had been assigned to a squadron on the Front, Terres was sent to Italy, where he met his death on August 17, 1918. While flying a Caproni near Milan, the huge plane ran out of petrol at a very low altitude over bad ground, and in the ensuing crash Terres was killed, with the two pilots accompanying him. His death cost the navy a skilful and courageous officer, and brought sadness to all who had known and admired his fine qualities.

SERVICE RECORD

WILLIAM THAW, Pittsburgh, Pennsylvania.

PREVIOUS SERVICE: Foreign Legion (Infantry). August 21 to December 24, 1914.

SERVICE IN FRENCH AVIATION:
Date of enlistment: December 24, 1914.
Aviation Schools: February 1 to March 20, 1915. Saint-Cyr, Buc, R.G.A.
Breveted: March 15, 1915 (Caudron).
At the Front: Escadrille D. 6 (as observer and machine-gunner), December 24, 1914, to February 1, 1915.
Escadrille C. 42, March 26, 1915, to January 29, 1916.
Escadrille N. 65, March 28 to April 15, 1916.
Escadrille Lafayette, April 21, 1916, to February 18, 1918.
Final Rank: Lieutenant.
Wounded in combat: May 24, 1916.

SERVICE IN U.S. AVIATION:
Commissioned Major: January 26, 1918.
Promoted Lieutenant-Colonel, November 12, 1918.
At the Front: C.O. 103d Pursuit Squadron, February 18 to August 10, 1918.
C.O. 3d Pursuit Group, August 10, 1918, to Armistice.

DECORATIONS:
  Distinguished Service Cross, with Bronze Oak Leaf.
  Légion d'Honneur (Rosette).
  Croix de Guerre, with four Palms and two Stars.

CITATIONS

Le 3 mai, 1915

Citation à l'Ordre de la 2ᵉ Division de Cavalerie:
  Le Caporal THAW, Pilote de l'Escadrille C. 42

A effectué, les 8, 11, 12, mai, 1915, des réglages dans des circonstances particulièrement difficiles, pilotant son appareil avec une maîtrise et un sang-froid remarquables, revenant six fois de suite au-dessus de son objectif, malgré un feu violent de l'artillerie ennemie.

Le 9 mai, 1915

Citation particulière pour le Service Aéronautique:
  Un avion chargé de régler le tir d'une pièce d'artillerie a été pendant ce réglage canonné d'une façon intense et précise par des canons ennemis de tous calibres.
  Cet avion était conduit par le Pilote Thaw, et avait à son bord le Lieutenant Félix, observateur. Sans se laisser détourner de sa mission, cet avion a évolué pendant plus d'une demi-heure au-dessus de son objectif, au milieu des éclatements, les évitant pour revenir sans cesse à son point d'observation. Il a montré une volonté, dans la poursuite du but, une ténacité sans peur, dignes d'éloges.
  Le Général Commandant le D.A.L. félicite le Lieutenant Observateur Félix et le Pilote Thaw.

Le 17 mai, 1915

Ordre de l'Armée de Lorraine Nᵒ 48:
  Le Général Humbert, Commandant de Détachement d'Armée de Lorraine, cite à l'Ordre de l'Armée:
  Le Lieutenant FÉLIX, Observateur; Le Caporal THAW, Pilote de l'Escadrille C. 42

Ont toujours fait preuve des plus belles qualités de bravoure et de sang-froid. À deux reprises, au cours de voyages d'observation, ont eu leur avion violemment canonné et atteint par des éclats d'obus causant de gros dommages. Ont néanmoins continué à observer les positions ennemies et ne sont rentrés qu'après l'accomplissement intégral de leur mission.

LE MINISTRE DE LA GUERRE, PARIS.   *Le 6 juillet, 1916*
                                       Vu le Décret du 13 août, 1914

Sont inscrits aux tableaux spéciaux de la Légion d'Honneur et de la Médaille Militaire les militaires dont les noms suivent: Pour prendre rang du 18 juin, 1916 . . .

Légion d'Honneur pour Chevalier
  THAW, WILLIAM, Mˡᵉ 5503, Lieutenant à l'Escadrille N. 124

Engagé volontaire pour la durée de la guerre. Pilote remarquable par son adresse, son entrain, et son mépris du danger. A livré récemment dix-huit combats aériens à courte distance. Le 26 mai au matin a attaqué et abattu un avion ennemi. Le soir même a de nouveau attaqué un groupe de trois appareils allemands et les a poursuivis de 4000 à 1000 mètres d'altitude. Grièvement blessé au cours du combat, a réussi grace à son énergie et son audace à ramener dans nos lignes son avion gravement atteint et à atterrir normalement. Déjà deux fois cité à l'Ordre.
  Les promotions et nominations ci-dessus comportent l'attribution de la Croix de Guerre, avec Palme.

                      (*Signé*)   ROQUES

Ordre Nᵒ 36 du 3 mai, 1917

Le Général Franchet d'Esperey, Commandant le G.A.N., cite à l'Ordre de l'Armée:
  THAW, WILLIAM, Lieutenant à l'Escadrille N. 124

Excellent pilote. Revenu sur le front après guérison d'une blessure grave. N'a cessé de donner l'exemple du courage et de l'entrain. Pendant la retraite allemande, a fait preuve d'initiative intelligente en atterrissant près d'éléments en marche, pour leur communiquer des renseignements sur l'ennemi qu'il avait recueillis en volant à basse altitude et grâce auxquels des surprises ont pu être évitées. Le 28 avril a abattu un avion ennemi. (2ᵐᵉ avion.)

G.H.Q., A.E.F.

  Major WILLIAM THAW, Commanding Officer, 103d Pursuit Squadron

For extraordinary heroism in action near Rheims, France, March 26, 1918. Major Thaw was the leader of a patrol of three planes which attacked five enemy *monoplaces* and three *biplaces*. He and another member of the patrol brought down one enemy plane, and the three drove out of control two others and dispersed the remainder.

The Bronze Oak Leaf is awarded to Major Thaw for extraordinary heroism in action near Montaigne, France, April 20, 1918. In the region of Montaigne, Major Thaw attacked and brought down burning an enemy balloon. While returning to his own lines the same day he attacked two enemy *monoplaces*, one of which he shot down in flames.

By command of General PERSHING

IVe ARMÉE. 13 *avril*, 1918

Le Général Commandant la IVème Armée cite à l'Ordre de l'Armée:

>Commandant Major THAW, WILLIAM, de l'Escadrille Lafayette (G.C. 21)

Commandant une escadrille qui à l'exemple de son Chef se fait remarquer par son audace et son succès. Pilote ardent qui à la tête d'une patrouille a abattu un avion ennemi après un dur combat.

(Signé) GOURAUD

VIe ARMÉE, ÉTAT-MAJOR. *Le* 30 *avril*, 1918
Citation à l'Ordre de l'Armée:

>M. THAW, WILLIAM, Major, Chef de l'Escadrille Américaine N° 103 (Lafayette)

Chef d'escadrille absolument remarquable. Donne à ses pilotes le plus bel exemple de courage et d'entrain, faisant de son escadrille une unité de premier ordre. Le 20 avril, au cours du même vol, abattu un avion ennemi et incendié un drachen.

(Signé) DUCHÊNE

GRAND QUARTIER GÉNÉRAL DES ARMÉES FRANÇAISES
DE L'EST, ÉTAT-MAJOR. *Le* 17 *mai*, 1919

Le Maréchal Commandant en Chef les Armées Françaises de l'Est cite à l'Ordre de l'Armée:

>Lieutenant-Colonel THAW, WILLIAM

Citoyen américain, engagé dès le début de la campagne dans la Légion Étrangère. A fait preuve des plus remarquable qualités de soldat et de chef. S'est distingué à l'Escadrille Lafayette, d'abord comme pilote et ensuite comme commandant de cette unité.

PÉTAIN

Par décret du Président de la République en date du . . . avril, 1919, le Colonel Thaw a été promu Officier de la Légion d'Honneur.

Ce promotion a été fait avec le motif de ce citation.

William Thaw

The record of William Thaw's service in the Allied cause is in itself a history of the Great War. To one acquainted with the development of military aviation, it reads like romance of the most unusual kind. One has only to remember the aerial setting of his adventures and the sweep of events through four long years; then, giving the imagination free play, allowing it to transform a series of dry biographical facts, it is possible to construct a tale of those adventures which, even with such an aid, will fail far short of the truth.

In August, 1914, Thaw was a soldier of the second class, an infantryman in the French Foreign Legion. At the close of the war he was a Lieutenant-Colonel in the United States Air Service. Between times, and at all times, he was "Bill" to his old comrades in the Legion and to his old pilots in the Escadrille Lafayette.

He enlisted in the Foreign Legion on August 7, 1914, and on August 21 was officially accepted as a member of that regiment. In company with twenty-nine other American volunteers he was sent to Rouen. After six weeks of drill there and at Toulouse and the Camp de Mailly, a six days' march to Craônne was made, and on October 16, the American volunteers saw their first service with the Legion in the front-line trenches. All this while Thaw, having been an airman in civilian days, was planning and working to effect a transfer to the French Air Service. He had tried to enlist as a pilot in the beginning, and was told that he must first join the Legion as an infantryman. James Bach and Bert Hall were also interested in this project, and the three men discussed their chances daily and nightly, in trenches and billets. Finally, early in October, they were granted permission to visit the aerodrome of the Escadrille D. 6 (Captain de Gorges commanding). This was a squadron of Deperdussins, two-seater monoplanes with 80 H.P. Gnome motors, long since suppressed as a military *avion*.

There the Americans met Lieutenant Brocard (then senior pilot of D. 6, later Commandant Brocard of the *Bureau du Sous-Secrétaire d'État de l'Aéronautique*). They pressed their case earnestly and enlisted Lieutenant Brocard's help. The result was that in November, 1914, Bach's orders for transfer to the Air Service were received, and on the 15th he left for Saint-Cyr to begin his training. Thaw was worried, so back he went to the Escadrille D. 6, a thirty-two kilometre hike. That he actually walked this distance is, to those who know Thaw's love of less exhausting modes of travel, sufficient comment on his determination to become a military aviator. He again talked with Lieutenant Brocard, a courteous gentleman and always a loyal friend of the American volunteers, who assured him that the orders for his own transfer to Aviation were on the way. They came on December 24, 1914, together with a message from Lieutenant Brocard saying that Thaw was to be attached to the Squadron D. 6, where he was to begin his war-time flying as a *soldat-mitrailleur*. In those days, however, "machine-gunner" was a misnomer. The weapons carried were carbines and automatic pistols, and the fighting, although tremendously exciting, was nothing like so deadly as it became later on.

Raids and reconnaissances over enemy territory were interesting enough as observer and gunner; but Thaw was eager to become a pilot. His pre-war experience had been only with Curtiss hydroplanes, but he succeeded in convincing the French *Service Aéronautique* that he could pilot any kind of machine. He was sent to Saint-Cyr where French *élèves-pilotes* were learning to fly the old Caudron, type G. 2. Although he had never before seen this craft, he was put on solo flying at once. He trained at Saint-Cyr, Buc, and later at Le Bourget, which was then a modest school of four hangars and a couple of Adrien barracks. Having mastered the G. 2, which was the fastest combat machine the French had, he spent his time in making flights with officers who were training to be aeroplane observers.

It was about the 20th of March, 1915, that he learned from Norman Prince of the plans for the formation of a squadron of American pilots. French squadrons then had a flying personnel of six and there were already more than that number of Americans available. Thaw disclaims any credit for having furthered the project. On the contrary, according to his own testimony, he was very lukewarm, for he had already finished his training and was about to return to the Front, this time as a pilot. He received orders to join the other Americans at Pau, but, instead, he went to the French Ministry of War and requested that he be sent to the Front at once. The request was granted, and on March 26, 1915, he was ordered to the French Squadron C. 42 (Captain Delaney commanding) operating from Nancy and later from Lunéville. He was made a *Sergent* on May 18 and in the same month was cited once in divisional and twice in army orders.

Norman Prince and Elliot Cowdin were sent to the Front as pilots in a Voisin squadron. Other Americans were either at the Front or in training and the plans for an *Escadrille Américaine* were well under way. While the last formalities were being arranged, Thaw, who of course approved of the idea, and had later given it his active support, was transferred to the Escadrille N. 65 with Cowdin, and served with this squadron while awaiting the other Americans. On April 15, 1916, orders came for all the Americans to proceed to Luxeuil, and on April 20, the pilots of the *Escadrille Américaine* assembled for active duty.

These are the facts, in briefest outline, of William Thaw's service previous to the formation of the Escadrille Lafayette. No airman of whatever nationality has had a broader experience in the Great War than he. He is the only member of the original squadron of volunteers who served with it throughout the entire period of its existence. He has flown and fought in every type of aircraft which has been used for combat in the French Service and was probably the first pilot in that Service to fly the twin-motor Caudron at the Front. He has potted at enemy machines with rifles, revolvers, rockets, and machine guns, and lost count long ago of his combats and his total hours of flight *au-dessus des lignes ennemies*. It is no exaggeration to say that he has had, at least once, every conceivable kind of aerial experience, including that

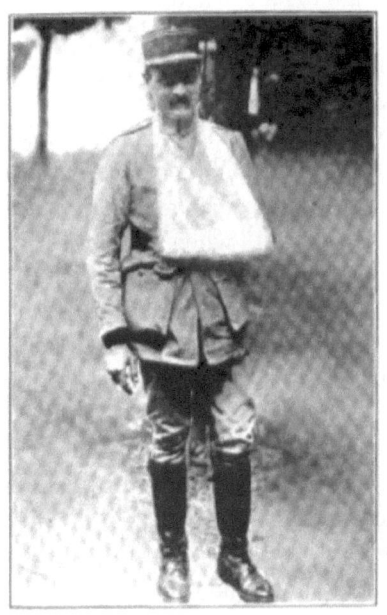 

WILLIAM THAW AFTER HIS COMBAT OF MAY 24. 1916

THAW WITH THE ESCADRILLE C. 42 AT LUNÉVILLE, JUNE. 1915, WATCHING A GERMAN PLANE

THAW BUILDING A BOAT FROM AN AEROPLANE FUSELAGE, DUNKIRK. 1918

of being wounded. He was shot through the forearm during a combat on May 24, 1916.

His record of service is not to be estimated by his score of official victories. Creditable as this is, it is nothing like so great as those of some other Allied airmen with fewer service stripes. William Thaw's first interest was always in the victories of his pilots, and he worked harder for their successes than for his own. As a Squadron Commander, he was without a peer. Even as "Major Bill," when he might have rested "*tranquille*" as the French say, he still led his pilots on patrol. Patrol, under his leadership, meant combat, and under the most favourable conditions for victory. He fought with his head as well as with his nerve. Few men knew better how to manoeuvre for position and the precise second when to attack.

Lufbery and Thaw—"Luf" and "Bill"—one thinks of them together, for they were the soul of the Escadrille Lafayette. Many a green pilot had his first combat in company with one or the other of them. To see Thaw's big "T" or Lufbery's Swastika on the wings of a neighbouring plane was always a heartening sight when there were enemy machines in the vicinity. And how those young airmen kept the insignia in view until they had mastered their combat tactics! On the ground and in the mess, during times of great nerve-strain, Thaw was a tonic for all his pilots. He was never flustered, never frightened, never excited. And when, as frequently happened, the squadron was lying opposite the Richtofen crowd, and getting as good as it sent in the matter of machine-gun fire in combat, he was always cheery and cool and made his men believe, often against their better judgment, that, as a squadron, they could give "the circus" odds in engine power and altitude, and still fight it to a standstill.

SERVICE RECORD

CLIFTON B. THOMPSON, Hyde Park, Massachusetts.

SERVICE IN FRENCH AVIATION:
Date of enlistment: June 10, 1917.
Aviation Schools: June 18, 1917, to January 13, 1918, Avord, Pau, G.D.E.
Brevetted: October 30, 1917 (Caudron).
At the Front: Escadrille Spad 99, January 15 to May 28, 1918.
Final Rank: Caporal.

SERVICE IN U.S. AVIATION:
Commissioned Second Lieutenant, May 28, 1918.
At the Front: Attached to the French Squadron, Spad 99, May 28, 1918, to Armistice.

DECORATIONS:
Croix de Guerre, with Star.

CITATION

Le 22 février, 1919

Le Colonel Commandant la 1ère Division Aérienne cite à l'Ordre de la Division:

THOMPSON, CLIFTON, M^{le} 12252, Sous-Lieutenant de l'Armée Américaine, Pilote Aviateur

Excellent pilote, consciencieux et discipliné. Engagé volontaire dans l'Armée française. Depuis plus d'un an dans l'aviation, y fait preuve d'un courage toujours égal et du plus bel esprit du devoir. Volontaire pour toutes les missions périlleuses et toujours plein d'allant au combat, s'est distingué notamment le 5 novembre, 1918, au cours d'une reconnaissance au ras du sol en attaquant successivement à la mitrailleuse deux convois d'artillerie ennemie.

(*Signé*)   VAULGRENANT

Clifton B. Thompson

No American was ever more loved by his French comrades than "Tommy" Thompson. His twinkling eyes, his infectious grin, and constant readiness for a joke were always irresistible; officers with many rows of stripes round their hats, before whom squadron commanders paled and trembled, have been known to clap Thompson familiarly on the back, saying, with a chuckle: "*Allons, mon vieux Thompson, ça gaze?*"

Before the war Thompson was an intercollegiate cross-country runner of the first order. On one occasion at the Front his speed and endurance won him fame. It was after dinner at the *popote*, and as the Armistice was being celebrated, every one had consumed more than the ordinary quantity of *pinard*. Talk turned to cross-country running, and Captain Rougevin, who commanded the Spad 99, began to brag of Thompson's attainments. An argument ensued which ended in an officer from another squadron offering to bet fifty louis that Thompson could not run some phenomenal number of kilometres in an hour. Thompson's comrades took him outside the tent and inquired earnestly if he really believed he could win the bet. Tommy was confident, and the officers of Spad 99 staked every *sou* they could scrape together on the result. It was a moonlight night and half of *Groupe de Combat* 20 followed the running on bicycles and in motorcars. Needless to say, "Tommy" won easily: a valuable member of the Squadron in more senses than one.

The Americans of *Groupe* 20 will never forget his first ground-strafing expedition. It was in June, 1918, in the small French attack at Ressons-sur-Matz. After an hour of shooting up everything German in sight, Thompson returned to find that he had a hole through the *fuselage* of his machine, which looked as though a dinner plate had been thrown through it. The huge *éclat* had missed the pilot's back by the thickness of a cigarette paper.

On another occasion, in the early part of July, he was on patrol over Soissons, when suddenly, above him, appeared two large patrols of the Richtofen group. The Spads immediately began to take altitude; but the red-nosed Fokkers hung above them. Suddenly a German *piqued* alone—shot two quick bursts, and two Spads, piloted by comrades of Thompson, went plunging down in flames. Manoeuvring wildly and with his plane riddled with bullets, Thompson finally managed to extricate himself from a very bad situation. On looking around he discovered that he was twenty-five miles into German territory, and perceived, just ahead of him and following the course he was forced to take toward the lines, a patrol of Fokker triplanes. Flying behind and beneath them, his gun hopelessly jammed, Thompson said that the next two minutes were the longest of his life, but the enemy did not notice him, and he regained our lines in safety.

His record at the Front is a story of faithful and courageous service—of unabated keenness to fly and to fight, of the moral courage which refuses to give way to the grief occasioned by the constant loss of comrades-in-arms.

SERVICE RECORD

CHARLES TRINKARD, Ozone Park, New York.

PREVIOUS SERVICE: Foreign Legion (Infantry), August 24, 1914, to March 1, 1917. Wounded, 1915.

SERVICE IN FRENCH AVIATION:
Date of enlistment: March 13, 1917.
Aviation Schools: March 20 to August 30, 1917, Avord, Pau, G.D.E.
Breveted: July 24, 1917 (Caudron).
At the Front: Escadrille N. 68, September 1 to November 29, 1917.
Final Rank: Caporal.
Killed in line of duty: November 29, 1917, near Toul.

DECORATIONS:
Croix de Guerre, with Star.

Charles Trinkard

In the summer of 1914, Charles Trinkard, later known to scores of American volunteers as "Tiny Trink," worked his way to France on a cattle-boat, and joined the Second Battalion, Foreign Legion. After almost a year in the trenches, he took part in the first Champagne offensive, in September, 1915, where he was twice wounded in the right shoulder by machine-gun fire. After months in hospital he rejoined the Legion in time for the battle of the Somme, coming through this campaign unscathed.

He was transferred to the Lafayette Corps in March, 1917, and started his training in French Aviation at Avord. The other American *élèves-pilotes* there welcomed him with great joy, for Trinkard's reputation had preceded him. He was a rare *raconteur*, and made life in the Legion real to many an American boy eager to know of it at first hand. No dinner at Farges, or the *Café des Aviateurs*, was complete without "Trink," and when in addition we had Australian Red Luks, ordinary seaman and soldier of fortune, to sing his sea chanties and recite original poetry, rainy afternoons passed happily enough.

WAINWRIGHT ABBOTT (LEFT)
AND CHARLES TRINKARD

After completing his training, Trinkard was sent to the French Squadron, N. 68, then on the Lorraine Front. He had applied for and had been granted a month's leave of absence in America, but he delayed accepting it until he had had further experience at the Front as an airman.

He was killed on Thanksgiving Day, 1917, while doing acrobacy over a village where his old regiment of *Légionnaires* were billeted while on *repos*. He had just returned from a patrol over the lines with two pilots of his squadron, and knowing that his old comrades were stationed nearby, he said *Bonjour* in loops and nose-dives, after the common practice of airmen. He wing-slipped while making a vertical turn, and being at a low altitude, crashed into the ground before he could regain flying speed, and was instantly killed. His former comrades were the first to reach the wrecked machine. One of them wrote later:

> We did not know who had fallen, but when we saw the khaki uniform and the red *fourragère* of the Legion, we were mightily grieved, and the Americans were especially sad, for we all knew Trink and the splendid work he had done as an infantryman. He did more than his duty in this war and did it cheerfully.

SERVICE RECORD

DUDLEY G. TUCKER, New York City.

SERVICE IN FRENCH AVIATION:
Date of enlistment: May 9, 1917.
Aviation Schools: May 22, 1917, to January 26, 1918, Avord, Pau, G.D.E.
Breveted: September 30, 1917 (Caudron).
At the Front: Escadrilles Spad 74 and Spad 15, January 28 to July 8, 1918.
Final Rank: Sergent.
Killed in combat: July 8, 1918.

Dudley G. Tucker

Tucker's life, previous to his enlistment in the Lafayette Flying Corps, was of exceptional interest. He was business manager of the Washington Square Players, and in the winter of 1917 was on his way to China and Japan to study the theatre in the Orient. Travelling by way of Panama with Austen Parker, it was decided to stop over a steamer at that place in order to visit the ancient mines and ruins of Darien. In their wanderings through the jungles of the coast the two Americans became hopelessly lost and finally emerged at the plantation of a mysterious German, who, for reasons which were never made clear, kept them practically as prisoners for several weeks. Unknown to his unpleasant host, Tucker succeeded in buying a dugout canoe from some Indians who lived near by in the forest, and hugging the shore in their fragile vessel he and Parker made the one hundred and fifty mile voyage to Panama.

As war seemed imminent and they had personal reasons for disapproving of the German race, they decided to give up the trip to the Orient, took passage to Bordeaux in a Brazilian steamer, and enlisted in the Lafayette Flying Corps.

At Avord, Tucker inhabited the Hotel Turco, with Parker, Edgar, and Bluthenthal. They were an interesting lot and their evening conversations covered many phases of life—sport, travel, journalism, literature, and the theatre.

Tucker left the record, at Avord and at Pau, of a skilful and courageous pilot and went to the Front on January 28, 1918, assigned to the Escadrille Spad 74. Transferring later to the Spad 15, he found himself with Harry Forster in the *Groupe de Combat* 13, the famous unit of which the Escadrille Lafayette formed part. There was heavy fighting to be done on those memorable summer days of 1918—all the way from Rheims to Montdidier the enemy was strong in the air—and the Spad 15 was always in the thick of it: ground-strafing, infantry *liaison*, balloon attacks, and constant offensive patrols.

On July 8 Tucker, with four French comrades, was patrolling the Marne Salient. They were well into the enemy lines in the region of Fismes, and had noticed German scouts above them, when they saw a strong patrol of a dozen or more Fokkers diving to attack a pair of French reconnaissance machines below. Plunging down to the rescue, the pilots of the Spad 15 engaged in a fast and desperate combat, and when the formation reassembled, ten minutes later, Tucker had disappeared.

Several months afterward the Red Cross at Berne received word from Germany that he was wounded and a prisoner, and repeated messages to the same effect caused his many friends to expect him in Paris when the prisoners were released after the Armistice. But those who awaited his appearance became increasingly anxious, for he was not among the returning *kriegsgefangenen*. No further word of Tucker has come out of Germany—one can only hope that he is alive, prevented from communicating with his family by one of those illogical and unaccountable webs of circumstance which distinguish real from imaginary life.

SERVICE RECORD

GEORGE EVANS TURNURE, JR., Lenox, Massachusetts.

SERVICE IN FRENCH AVIATION:
Date of enlistment: February 16, 1917.
Aviation Schools: February 25 to July 25, 1917, Avord, Pau, G.D.E.
Breveted: June 16, 1917 (Blériot).
At the Front: Escadrille Spad 103, July 27 to December 16, 1917.
Escadrille Lafayette, February 12 to February 18, 1918.
Final Rank: Sergent.

SERVICE IN U.S. AVIATION:
Commissioned First Lieutenant: January 2, 1918.
At the Front: 103d Pursuit Squadron, February 18 to August 28, 1918.
Flight Commander, 28th Pursuit Squadron, August 28, 1918, to Armistice.

DECORATIONS:
Légion d'Honneur.
Croix de Guerre, with two Palms and a Star.

CITATIONS

1ère ARMÉE, ÉTAT-MAJOR.   *Au Q.G.A., le 6 novembre,* 1917
Le Général Commandant la 1ère Armée cite à l'Ordre de l'Armée:
TURNURE, GEORGE, Mle 41132, Sergent au 1er Régiment Étranger, Pilote à l'Escadrille S. 103

Citoyen américain engagé dans l'aviation avant la déclaration de guerre des États-Unis. Pilote de chasse d'un courage et d'un sang-froid remarquables. Le 17 octobre, 1917, a abattu un avion ennemi.

(*Signé*)   ANTHOINE

VIe ARMÉE, COMMANDANT DE L'AÉRONAUTIQUE.   *Q.G., le* 29 *avril,* 1918
Citation à l'Ordre de l'Aéronautique de l'Armée:
TURNURE, GEORGE EVANS, Lieutenant Pilote, Escadrille Américaine N° 103 (Lafayette)

Officier pilote remarquable par son entrain et son audace. Toujours prêt à accomplir les missions les plus périlleuses.
Le 20 avril, a contribué à abattre un avion ennemi.

Le Chef de Bataillon Commandant l'Aéronautique de l'Armée

DÉTACHEMENT D'ARMÉE DU NORD, ÉTAT-MAJOR.   *Q.G., le* 7 *juin,* 1918
Le Général de Mitry, Commandant le Détachement d'Armée du Nord, cite à l'Ordre de l'Armée:
Le Lieutenant TURNURE, GEORGE EVANS, Pilote à l'Escadrille Lafayette

Pilote d'une ténacité admirable. Sans se laisser rebuter par l'insuccès de trois tentatives, a abattu un drachen en flammes, remportant ainsi sa troisième victoire.

(*Signé*)   DE MITRY

GRAND QUARTIER GÉNÉRAL DES ARMÉES FRANCAISES
DE L'EST, ÉTAT-MAJOR.   *Le* 17 *mai,* 1919
Le Maréchal Commandant en Chef les Armées Françaises de l'Est cite à l' Ordredel' Armée:
Lieutenant TURNURE, GEORGE EVANS

Citoyen américain engagé dans la Légion Étrangère. S'est fait remarquer comme pilote à l'Escadrille Lafayette, par son courage, son audace donnant un très bel exemple à tous. A abattu trois appareils ennemis.

(*Signé*)   PÉTAIN

Par décret du Président de la République en date du 9 avril, 1919, le Lieutenant TURNURE a été promu Chevalier de la Légion d'Honneur.
Cet promotion a été fait avec le motif de ce citation.

George Evans Turnure, Jr.

The following letter, written to Dr. Gros, is taken from the files of the Lafayette Flying Corps:

> Escadrille Lafayette
> La Ferme de la Noblette, Champagne
> February, 1918

Dear Major Gros:

It seems to me very important that you should have for your records of the Lafayette Corps an account of a combat in which George Turnure of Spad 103 took part. It was only by chance that I learned of it, and upon meeting Turnure recently I asked for details. After an endless amount of persuasion, I learned the following:

On September 30 (1917) George went on patrol with Adjudant Fonck, the great French "ace." There were four or five in the patrol at first, but because of motor trouble the others were compelled to return to the aerodrome, leaving only Adjudant Fonck and Turnure to continue.

They were at an altitude of 6200 metres when they met a German two-seater which they immediately attacked. Turnure denies having played any effective part in the combat, although in my opinion there is no doubt that he kept his Vickers warm.

TURNURE AND JIM THE ANNAMITE ORDERLY AT AVORD

However, he insists that his role was only that of an admiring spectator of Fonck's superb attack.

Well, Fonck got under the tail of the enemy, gave the pilot the *coup de grâce*, whereupon the machine turned clean over and started falling out of control. It crumpled up in the air, most of the wreckage falling near Poperinghe in the French lines. The *mitrailleur* either fell out or jumped, for his body was found some distance from the remains of the machine.

Both Turnure and Fonck landed nearby, and upon examining the papers in the pockets of the dead Germans they found that the pilot was Captain Weissmann, the man who had brought down Captain Guynemer about two weeks before. This German pilot's name had, of course, been heralded throughout Germany, and every French and American airman on the Flanders Front, where he was supposed to be flying, was longing to bring him down.

It is a fact worth recording that an American pilot, a Lafayette man, took an active part in this famous combat. The rest of us Americans are happy that one of our number has had such good fortune. Turnure himself will not give you this information, I am afraid, so I have taken it upon myself to do so.

A great deal more might be said of George Turnure's record at the Front, which was excellent throughout. About two weeks before his combat while flying with Fonck, he himself shot down a German two-seater near Ypres. After his transfer to the United States Air Service, he was sent to the Escadrille Lafayette, which was about to become the 103rd Pursuit Squadron. On April 20, 1918, in company with Major Thaw, he shot down a German *saucisse*, and on June 1, while flying alone, he destroyed another. From August 20 until the Armistice he was a flight commander with the 28th Pursuit Squadron.

SERVICE RECORD

STEPHEN MITCHELL TYSON, Princeton, New Jersey.

PREVIOUS SERVICE: American Ambulance, 1917.

SERVICE IN FRENCH AVIATION:
Date of enlistment: May 25, 1917.
Aviation Schools: June 6 to December 17, 1917, Avord, Pau, G.D.E.
Breveted: October 16, 1917 (Caudron).
At the Front: Escadrille Spad 85, December 19, 1917, to July 19, 1918.
Final Rank: Sergent.
Killed in combat: July 19, 1918, near Chassins-Dormans.

DECORATIONS:
Croix de Guerre, with Palm.

CITATION

Le 13 *juin*, 1918

Citation à l'Ordre de l'Armée:

TYSON, STEPHEN MITCHELL, M^{le} 12221, Caporal du 1er Régiment Étranger, Pilote
à l'Escadrille Spad 85

Pilote américain engagé dans l'armée française, toujours volontaire pour les missions difficiles. A abattu récemment un avion ennemi, le poursuivant jusqu'au sol dans ses lignes.

Stephen Mitchell Tyson

Tyson went to France at seventeen years of age, and served honourably for six months as an ambulance driver; but disliking the part of a non-combatant, he applied to enter the Lafayette Flying Corps as soon as his term of ambulance service was up. Flatly refused because his weight was fifteen pounds over the maximum, he went to work with determination to reduce, and though it was extremely irksome to his temperament, he succeeded, after a month of Turkish baths and exercise, in making the weight. There was a strain of seriousness underlying his irresponsibility; he wanted to be a fighting pilot and he became one. Tyson was a born flyer; the air was his element and he loved it as a sailor loves the sea. He flew carelessly and naturally as a hawk, man and machine welded into a single swift and intelligent creature of the skies. Supremely confident, always on the offensive, and with the born fighter's love of desperate odds, his last combat was a thing to make every American thrill with pride.

It was the 19th of July, 1918, and at last the Germans had begun their historic second retreat from the Marne. At five-thirty in the long summer afternoon Tyson was beating back and forth at 15,000 feet between Dormans and Château-Thierry, with a small patrol of Spads, detailed to protect some photographic two-seaters. Suddenly, to the northwest of Dormans, they perceived a flight of eight enemy single-seaters and dove to the attack. As the Germans would not give battle and headed back into their lines, the French leader turned to resume his mission of protection, and at that instant Tyson was seen to detach himself from the patrol and head swiftly after the retreating Germans. It was over in an instant. As the enemy turned at bay he attacked them from beneath, one against eight, both guns spitting fire and lead. Next moment, caught in the concentrated fire of the enemy at point-blank range, the Spad was seen to veer wildly, whirl downward in a *vrille*, burst into flames and explode while still 6000 feet above the earth.

SERVICE RECORD

WILLIAM CAREY VAN FLEET, JR., San Francisco, California.

SERVICE IN FRENCH AVIATION:
Date of enlistment: July 21, 1917.
Aviation Schools: July 31, 1917, to June 30, 1918. Avord, Tours, Pau, Cazeaux, G.D.E.
Breveted: October 7, 1917 (Caudron).
At the Front: Escadrille Spad 78, July 1 to August 26, 1918.
Final Rank: Sergent.

SERVICE IN U.S. NAVAL AVIATION:
Commissioned Ensign: August 28, 1918.
At the Front: U.S. Naval Air Station, Dunkirk, September 1 to 15, 1918.
Escadrille de Saint-Pol, September 15 to October 30, 1918.
U.S.S. Texas, 6th Battle Squadron, November 4, 1918, to Armistice.

DECORATIONS:
Croix de Guerre, with Palm.

CITATION

GENERAL HEADQUARTERS OF THE FRENCH ARMIES OF THE EAST.   January 15, 1919

With the approbation of the Commander-in-Chief of the American Expeditionary Forces in France, the Marshall of France, Commander-in-Chief of the French Armies of the East, cites to the Order of the Army:

Airplane Pilot WILLIAM VAN FLEET, Ensign in the U.S. Navy

Displayed a great initiative and courage during numerous pursuit patrols and during numerous combats which took place inside the enemy lines. On October 14, 1918, he attacked a battery of heavy artillery, in retreat, and thus contributed to its capture.

PÉTAIN
Commander-in-Chief of the French Armies of the East

William Carey Van Fleet, Jr.

Breveted at Tours on October 7, 1917, Van Fleet's course through Pau was delayed by illness and he was later a victim of the cold and living conditions at Le Plessis-Belleville. He did not get to the Front until July 1, 1918, but while with his squadron, the Spad 78, he showed himself a skilful and aggressive pilot. In the short time that elapsed before his transfer to the navy he had numerous combats and a total of more than thirty hours over the lines, and when he left, his captain declared that the squadron had lost a future "ace."

Before the war Van Fleet had conducted a series of experiments with one-man submarines and it was natural that he should choose to be a Naval pilot. He was fortunate after his transfer in being detached to the Escadrille de Saint-Pol which was equipped with *chasse* planes and operated in the always active sector at the northern end of the lines. While with this unit, Van Fleet was the first American pilot to enter Lille after its delivery by the Allied forces. He will never forget his welcome by the civilian population.

On November 4 Van Fleet was sent with two other pilots to the U.S.S. *Texas* of the Grand Fleet, to introduce the English method of flying land scout machines from the decks of the ship. They practiced this method of taking off, from both American and British vessels, until after the signing of the Armistice, and witnessed the surrender of the German fleet.

SERVICE RECORD

CHARLES HERBERT VEIL, East Palestine, Ohio.

SERVICE IN FRENCH AVIATION:
Date of enlistment: April 12, 1917.
Aviation Schools: May 17 to December 16, 1917, Avord, Pau, G.D.E.
Breveted: October 20, 1917 (Caudron).
At the Front: Escadrille Spad 150, December 18, 1917, to October 9, 1918.
Final Rank: Sergent.

SERVICE IN U.S. AVIATION:
Commissioned First Lieutenant: October 9,

Le Général Commandant la IIIe Armée cite à l'Ordre de l'Armée:

Le Sergent VEIL, CHARLES HERBERT, M^{le} 12173, du Groupe d'Aviation, Pilote à l'Escadrille Spa. 150

Pilote de chasse. A remporté le 1er septembre, 1918, sa deuxième victoire en abattant 1 monoplace ennemi faisant partie d'une forte patrouille.

VIIIe ARMÉE, ÉTAT-MAJOR. *Au Q.G.A., le 4 novembre,* 1918
Le Général Commandant la VIIIe Armée cite à l'Ordre de l'Armée:

Le Sergent VEIL, CHARLES HERBERT, M^{le} 12173, du Groupe de Combat 16, Escadrille Spa. 150

A abattu le 19 septembre, 1918, un biplace ennemi aux abords de Metz.
Le Général Commandant la VIIIe Armée
(Signé) GERARD

Charles Herbert Veil

Veil's career illustrates well the fallacy of making prophecies based on a man's performance in the schools. During the Blériot training he told his comrades frequently that he disliked flying and found it extremely difficult to learn, but at Pau he seemed to have gotten the knack of handling the Nieuport, and once on the Front, in Escadrille Spad 150, he developed into a very skilful combat pilot. Veil served the French well through most of the heavy fighting of 1918, and was one of the last Lafayette men to transfer to the American army. On June 10, near Noyon, he made a *sortie* which came very near to being his last.

The weather was cloudy, and while flying alone, Veil perceived a German who appeared suddenly beneath him through a hole in the clouds; he dove without hesitation and had shot one burst, when a patrol of nine Fokkers, which he had taken for English Dolphins, attacked him, taking him completely by surprise.

> Nothing remained to do. I entered into their formation; they immediately scattered and fired on me from all angles. I shot at one which crossed in front of me as I was making a hurried retreat; he fell to the ground out of control on the German front lines. The others followed me down to a very low altitude, twenty or thirty feet, and continued firing. I regained our own lines and had to pull up to make it over the trees, with the machine guns on me both from the ground and from above. I received five bullets in my propeller, an explosive bullet in the wing, and my machine was so damaged that it could not be flown again.

SERVICE RECORD

BENJAMIN STUART WALCOTT, Washington, D.C.
SERVICE IN FRENCH AVIATION:
Date of enlistment: June 3, 1917.
Aviation Schools: June 3 to October 27, 1917, Avord, Pau, G.D.E.
Breveted: September 6, 1917 (Caudron).
At the Front: Escadrille Spad 84, October 29 to December 12, 1917.
Final Rank: Caporal.
Killed in combat: December 12, 1917 (Champagne Sector).
Commissioned First Lieutenant: U.S. Air Service. (Commission arrived after his death.)

DECORATIONS:
Croix de Guerre, with Palm.

CITATION

4ᵐᵉ Armée. 23 décembre, 1917
Citation à l'Ordre de l'Armée:

Le Caporal Pilote WALCOTT, STUART, Mlᵉ 12200, de l'Escadrille Spa. 84
(13ᵉ Groupe de Combat)

Américain engagé pour la durée de la guerre. Jeune pilote d'un courage et d'un esprit admirables. Le 12 décembre, 1917, attaque un appareil ennemi et le poursuit jusqu'à 1500 mètres de hauteur et à 4 kilomètres dans ses lignes où il l'abat. Attaqué à son tour par trois monoplaces ennemis, est descendu désemparé.

Le Général Commandant la 4ᵐᵉ Armée
GOURAUD

Délivré par le Maréchal de France, Commandant en Chef les Armées de l'Est.
PÉTAIN

Benjamin Stuart Walcott

Walcott arrived at Avord, at a time when the Blériot School was so crowded with Russians and Americans that progress for most of us was interminably slow. But he was capable and eager and his early *sorties* in *pingouin* and *rouleur* convinced the instructors that he could drive a machine straight on the ground and was ready to begin real flying. Keen to get to the Front and always ready to do a little more than was asked of him, he finished the Blériot training and was breveted six weeks ahead of his contemporaries—a splendid record. The story was the same at Pau—Walcott was a man to hold back rather than to push; the instructors in formation-flying, acrobatics, and combat declared that he was a pilot with a brilliant future before him.

On October 29, 1917, he was sent to the Front, to the Escadrille Spad 84, in the same *groupe* with the Escadrille Lafayette. It was some time before he was given a machine and allowed to fly over the lines, for the French took all possible care of their young pilots, and his letters written home at this period are full of impatience to get into action. In his first and last combat, on December 12, he exhibited a coolness, a daring, and a determination which, had he been spared, would have taken him far. Walcott was flying, with a single French comrade, over the lines to the right of Rheims, when a German twoseater crossed to do some reglage. The Frenchman attacked at once, but found that his guns were not working and turned away. The enemy machine took flight and as the French pilot headed for the aerodrome, he saw Walcott, who had followed him down to the attack, taking altitude as rapidly as possible—already 3000 feet above him.

The final combat was seen by observers on the ground. Six minutes later the German returned to complete his mission, unaware of the Spad waiting high above. Walcott made a swift attack; the German fled with the Spad in hot pursuit. After a chase of four kilometres into enemy territory, the two-seater was seen to go down in flames,

Stuart Walcott (left) and Edward Loughran (right) at le Plessis-Belleville

Stuart Walcott's grave at Leffin Court, Ardennes

and the American soared up victoriously, turning to regain his lines. At that moment three Albatross single-seaters, which had approached unseen, dove down with a prolonged rattle of machine-gun fire—the Spad wavered, fell out of control, and crashed to the ground near Saint-Souplet. Walcott was killed, in the exultation of combat and victory—an heroic end, worthy of a soldier.

SERVICE RECORD

WILLIAM E. WASS, Brunswick, Maine.

PREVIOUS SERVICE: American Ambulance, 1917.

SERVICE IN FRENCH AVIATION:
  Date of enlistment: June 3, 1917.
  Aviation Schools: June 3, 1917, to February 12, 1918, Avord, Pau, Cazeaux, G.D.E.
  Breveted: October 30, 1917 (Caudron).
  At the Front: Escadrille Spad 91, February 15 to November 4, 1918.
  Final Rank: Sergent.

SERVICE IN U.S. AVIATION:
  Commissioned First Lieutenant: November 5, 1918.

DECORATIONS:
  Croix de Guerre, with Palm and Star.

CITATION

Le 24 avril, 1918

Citation à l'Ordre de l'Armée:

Caporal WASS, WILLIAM, engagé dans l'aviation française

Pilote nouvellement venu à l'Escadrille. Fait preuve des plus grandes qualités de courage et de mordant. Faisant partie d'une patrouille attaquée par des avions ennemis en nombre supérieur, a dégagé un de ses camarades, en attaquant avec rapidité et décision un appareil ennemi qui a été vu tombant en vrille.

William E. Wass

It was at Savigny—the *piqué* class presided over by Sergent Moses, that cautious Peruvian. The Americans loafed disconsolately beneath the wings of the Blériots, engaged in the usual afternoon pastime of waiting for the wind to drop. On the field across the road, the "aces" of Bergada's advanced *piqué* class were in the air, buzzing up and down the *piste* at dizzy altitudes. The *manche à vent* hung limply from its pole.

Suddenly Wass rose from his place in the shade, strolled over to where Moses sat and spoke earnestly to the monitor, who began by shaking his head, and ended with a nod signifying grudging assent. It was enough. Authorized to try the air, Wass strapped on his helmet and climbed into one of the ancient *six-pattes.* Next moment he was off: on a *sortie* which became almost legendary among students of the Blériot. Leaving the ground in a superb *cheval de bois*, he banked to the left so steeply that his wing brushed the grass. By this time the whole class was on its feet—Moses wringing his hands and eloquent in three languages. Wass now nosed down to gain speed and pulled up into a formidable *chandelle*; almost stalled, slipped on his right wing, did a quarter turn of a spiral, and came out with his wheels within a yard of the ground, headed at right angles to his former course.

WRAPPED GRACEFULLY
AROUND A TREE

It was magnificent acrobacy, but a terrible thing to watch. Even Charlot, the living proof of Darwin's theory, who turned tails at the far end of the field, was said to have muttered the Annamite equivalent for O *la, la!* The remainder of the flight is a blurred memory, like a nightmare; at length Wass landed and announced that the air was excellent—not a bump! "*Mon vieux*" said Moses, very solemnly, "go at once to Bergada's class; I will not have you killed in mine. You others—*rentrez les appareils!*"

Although he developed into a first-class pilot, his friends thought that a special Providence watched over Wass. Once at the Front, with his guns jammed and hemmed in by a large patrol of Fokkers, his engine failed only a few hundred feet above a forest.

Redressing high over the trees, he folded his arms and waited. Five minutes later he awoke from a refreshing sleep—some distance from his machine, which was wrapped gracefully around a tree. Needless to say that he survived the war and shot down his share of enemy machines.

SERVICE RECORD

WILLIAM A. WELLMAN, Cambridge, Massachusetts.

SERVICE IN FRENCH AVIATION:
Date of enlistment: June 13, 1917.
Aviation Schools: June 29 to December 1, 1917, Avord, Pau, G.D.E.
Breveted: September 29, 1917 (Caudron).
At the Front: Escadrille Spad 87, December 3, 1917, to March 14, 1918.
Final Rank: Sergent.

DECORATIONS:
Croix de Guerre, with two Palms.

CITATIONS

Le 6 *mars,* 1918
Citations à l'Ordre de l'Armée:

Le Caporal WELLMAN, WILLIAM AUGUSTUS, M^{le} 12274, du 1er Régiment de la Légion Étrangère, Pilote à l'Escadrille N. 87

Américain engagé à la Légion Étrangère, se distingué comme un pilote de chasse remarquable par son ardeur et son courage. Le 19 janvier abattu un avion ennemi qui s'est écrasé au sol, près du Bois du Mant de la Croix.

Le 23 *mars,* 1918

Le pilote américain, M. de Logis, WELLMAN, WILLIAM AUGUSTUS

Pilote de chasse, montrant les plus belles qualités d'audace. Le 20 janvier, ayant pris un biplace ennemi en chasse au-dessus Nancy, le poursuivit jusqu'à sur son terrain à plus de 25 kilomètres dans les lignes, mitraillant à bout portant les hangars et tuant le pilote.
Le 10 février mitraille à faible altitude un terrain d'aviation ennemi. Le 9 mars abat un biplace ennemi de réglage dans la région de P—— (2 avions ennemi, homologué) et presque immédiatement après abat un des monoplaces ennemis d'escorte.

William Augustus Wellman

Wellman, with Hitchcock, was sent from the G.D.E. to Spad 87, then stationed at Lunéville. They were a wild pair, and within a few weeks had shattered the dreamy life of the German squadrons stationed opposite. The sector covered by the N. 87 extended from the Vosges to Pont-à-Mousson, and since the beginning of the war it had been one of the quietest portions of the Front. When a French machine crossed the lines to do a little *réglage*, the Germans took great care not to be in the vicinity, and when occasionally a Rumpler came over very high to photograph, the French, having nothing to conceal, paid little attention. But Wellman and Hitchcock loved fighting for the sport of it, flew constantly, and used their wits in every possible way to get near the enemy.

WELLMAN AND JUDD AT AVORD

Their most sensational exploit became proverbial among American pilots; for they chased a German two-seater to its aerodrome, many miles behind the lines, followed it to the ground, through a storm of bullets from protecting machine guns, and circled the field *en rasemotte*, sending soldiers, mechanics, and pilots in a mad scramble for shelter.

Wellman was a fearless and clever pilot and an excellent shot. In the short time he was at the Front he gained three official victories. When finally his health gave way and he was invalided out of the army, his squadron lost a valuable pilot, and a comrade of whom everyone had grown fond.

SERVICE RECORD

FRANK W. WELLS, Syracuse, New York.

SERVICE IN FRENCH AVIATION:
 Date of enlistment: January 6, 1917.
 Aviation Schools: January 12 to August 4, 1917, Buc, Avord, Pau, G.D.E.
 Breveted: May 10, 1917 (Caudron).
 At the Front: Escadrille Spad 93, August 6 to December 23, 1917.
 Final Rank: Sergent.

SERVICE IN U.S. AVIATION:
 Commissioned First Lieutenant: January 3, 1918.
 Brevet Monitor, American A.I.C., Tours, January 10 to June 17, 1918.
 Supply Officer and Test Pilot, Wilbur Wright Field, Dayton, Ohio, July 15, to Armistice.

Frank W. Wells

Frank Wells proved to many of the less confident men how easy it was to deal with a voluble French *moniteur* on a strictly English-speaking basis. Many an instructor in the aviation schools has been wearied into silence or flattered into liking by his assumption that they understood perfectly his explanations in English of wild *sorties* or breaches of *discipline de piste*. Without a word of their language, he made innumerable friends among his French comrades wherever he went. He was always entirely at home with them, wholly unconscious of the language barrier, and as warmly liked by the *mécaniciens* of his squadron as by the pilots themselves.

The adventure at the Front most nearly fatal to him happened during the late summer of 1917, when Spad 93 was at the aerodrome at Souilly on the Verdun Sector. Reprisal and counter-reprisal raids were being made on aviation fields all along that part of the Front. Wells scorned bomb-proof shelters until once, during a night bombardment, a German pilot made a direct hit upon an Adrien barrack at Souilly, killing and wounding a dozen or more men. Wells himself was slightly wounded by flying splinters, but carried on with patrol work as usual the following day.

Upon his transfer to United States Aviation he was sent to the American Training Centre at Tours as *brevet* pilot. He loved discipline and became a semi-benevolent despot to the American cadets who were under his eye during their final flying tests. Stern of aspect and with a dry and somewhat caustic humour, he was openly feared and secretly liked by all of them. On June 25, he was sent on duty to the United States, acting as Supply Officer and Test Pilot at Wilbur Wright Field until after the Armistice.

SERVICE RECORD

Herman Whitmore, Haverhill, Massachusetts.

Service in French Aviation:
Date of enlistment: June 13, 1917.
Aviation Schools: June 21, 1917, to March 22, 1918, Avord, Pau, Cazeaux, G.D.E.
Brevetted: October 30, 1917 (Caudron).
At the Front: Escadrille Spad 77, March 24 to April 6, 1918.
Final Rank: Caporal.
Shot down in combat: April 6, 1918, near Montdidier.
Prisoner in Germany until the Armistice.

Herman Whitmore

When Whitmore was shot down and captured only a short time after his arrival at the Front, the Lafayette Flying Corps lost a man who certainly would have added to its laurels. All through the schools he gave promise of a brilliant future, handling a machine as though the air were his proper element. Shot down in one of his first combats, he showed his mettle by bringing down an Albatross in flames before his own machine fell out of control.

While in Germany he made several attempts to escape, but his luck was bad, and he did not return to France until after the Armistice.

SERVICE RECORD

JOHN JOYCE WHITMORE, New York City.

SERVICE IN FRENCH AVIATION:
 Date of enlistment: February 8, 1917.
 Aviation Schools: February 25 to November 22, 1917, Avord, Pau, G.D.E.
 Breveted: September 3, 1917 (Caudron).
 At the Front: Escadrille Spad 315, November 24, 1917, to February 5, 1918.
  Escadrille Spad 314, May 13 to May 23, 1918.
 Released: June 19, 1918, because of injuries received in service.
 Final Rank: Sergent.

John Joyce Whitmore

Whitmore was seriously injured in an accident soon after beginning his training at the Blériot School, and was compelled to spend many weeks in hospital at the best season for flying of the year. When he returned to duty, Blériot training had been discontinued, so that he had to begin again at the beginning, and learn to fly a Caudron. During his three months at the Front he was severely handicapped by his old injuries, and at last found it necessary to accept his release from French Aviation. His career as a combat pilot, which was cut short through no fault of his own, illustrates the haphazardness of aerial fortune which has prevented a large number of Lafayette Corps men from fulfilling their expectations of service in the war.

SERVICE RECORD

CHARLES HERBERT WILCOX, Pasadena, California.

SERVICE IN FRENCH AVIATION:
 Date of enlistment: February 8, 1917.
 Aviation Schools: February 10 to July 16, 1917, Avord, Pau, G.D.E.
 Breveted: May 31, 1917 (Blériot).
 At the Front: Escadrille Spad 80, July 18, 1917, to January 18, 1918.
  Escadrille Lafayette, January 25 to February 18, 1918.
 Final Rank: Sergent.

SERVICE IN U.S. AVIATION:
Commissioned First Lieutenant: January 9, 1918.
At the Front: 103d Pursuit Squadron, February 18 to June 18, 1918.
On duty in America: June 25, 1918, to Armistice.

DECORATIONS:
Croix de Guerre, with two Palms and Star.

CITATIONS

Q.G.A., le 30 *avril,* 1918
6ᵉ ARMÉE, ÉTAT-MAJOR.
Citation à l'Ordre de l'Armée:

M. WILCOX, CHARLES HERBERT, Lieutenant, Pilote à l'Escadrille Américaine N° 103 (Lafayette)

Officier pilote remarquable par son audace et son entrain. Le 23 avril, a abattu un avion ennemi.
(*Signé*) DUCHÊNE

D.A.N. COMMANDEMENT DE L'AÉRONAUTIQUE.

En vertu des pouvoirs qu'il tient de l'instruction du 11 février, 1918, le Chef d'Escadron Commandant l'Aéronautique du D.A.N. cite à l'Ordre de l'Aéronautique les militaires dont les noms suivent: ...

WILCOX, CHARLES HERBERT, Lieutenant, Pilote à l'Escadrille Américaine N° 103 (Lafayette)

Faisant partie d'une patrouille qui a abattu un avion ennemi, le 21 mai, 1918.

Le Chef d'Escadron Commandant l'Aéronautique
MORISSON

GRAND QUARTIER GÉNÉRAL DES ARMÉES DU NORD ET DU NORD-EST, ÉTAT-MAJOR.   *Le* 30 *octobre,* 1918

Après approbation du Général Commandant en Chef les Forces Expéditionnaires Américaines en France, le Général Commandant en Chef les Armées Françaises du Nord et du Nord-Est cite à l'Ordre de l'Armée:

Lieutenant WILCOX, CHARLES HERBERT, Pilote à l'Escadrille 103

Officier remarquable par son audace et sa ténacité. Le 9 juin, 1918, a abattu son troisième avion ennemi.

Le Général Commandant en Chef
(*Signé*) PÉTAIN

Charles Herbert Wilcox

Charles H. Wilcox, who was among the earliest of the 1917 volunteers, completed his period of training without any of those bizarre accidents which happened to so many inexperienced flyers. Steady nerves and an even temperament served him well and gained for him good notes from all of his *moniteurs*. He was sent to the Front as a pilot of the French Squadron, Spad 80, the *escadrille* of Paul Baer, C. J. Coatsworth, and Walter Rheno. The four Americans who flew together frequently had many exciting adventures over the Verdun Sector during the summer of 1917, and a hard race for the first official victory which fell to Rheno. Wilcox and Baer, old flying partners in the schools, had an odd similarity of experience at the Front, so that they are always spoken of together at the gatherings of Lafayette men. Both were keen pilots, eager to get results. Both did their work well, taking much more than their allotted share of patrol duty for the sake of the experience which it brought; and for more than six months both fought battles without the fine incentive which an actual verified success brings to a pilot. Americans who met them occasionally at Bar-le-Duc, the old rendezvous for airmen on the Verdun Front, will remember their disgust at their ill-fortune. All of the Germans they attacked carried sky-hooks. They declined to fall even though riddled with bullets. Their motors were armour-plated and their gas tanks indestructible, in so far as the experience of Pilots Wilcox and Baer was concerned.

Evidently all that was needed was transfer to the United States Air Service. Both men were sent to the 103rd Pursuit Squadron, formerly the Escadrille Lafayette. They were in fact sent to this unit while it was still under French orders. By May 22, Baer had become an "ace" and on June 9, Wilcox shot down his third enemy plane. He, too, would undoubtedly have been counted among the "aces" had he been permitted to remain on active duty in France. He had thoroughly mastered his combat tactics, and had become a flight leader of first-rate ability. Unfortunately, and to his own bitter disappointment, he was sent to America at a time when he was best qualified for service at the Front, and from July 1 until the Armistice, he was employed as a flying instructor at various aviation schools in the United States.

SERVICE RECORD

MARCELLUS EDWARD WILD, Rochester, New York.

PREVIOUS SERVICE: Norton-Harjes Ambulance, 1916–17.

SERVICE IN FRENCH AVIATION:
Date of enlistment: March 29, 1917.
Aviation Schools: April 13 to October 18, 1917, Avord, Pau, G.D.E.
Brevetted: August 24, 1917 (Caudron).
At the Front: Escadrille Spad 15, October 20, 1917, to March 30, 1918.
Final Rank: Sergent.

SERVICE IN U.S. NAVAL AVIATION:
Commissioned Ensign: May, 1918.
Instructor at U.S.N.A.S., Pensacola, Florida, until the Armistice.

DECORATIONS:
Croix de Guerre, with Star.

Marcellus Edward Wild

Wild was one of the hundred and more Americans who joined the Lafayette Corps in the spring and early summer of 1917. The Avord School was internationalized in those days. Beside the Frenchmen and the Americans, there were Russians, Portuguese, Montenegrins, Belgians—*élèves-pilotes* from all Allied countries with the exception of Great Britain and her colonies. The Blériot was then being discarded for the more practical and rapid double-command Caudron, and Wild was one of the fortunate ones who served his early apprenticeship on both types of machines. He went on active duty as a member of the famous French Squadron, Spad 15, of *Groupe de Combat* 13, under the command of Commandant Féquant, and gained his first knowledge of actual war flying during the French offensive, along the Chemin des Dames, of October, 1917. He spent the winter on the Champagne Front, patrolling the lines from Rheims to the Argonne Forest, preparing himself in the most practical way for his later service with the United States Naval Air Forces. In the spring of 1918 he was sent home on sick-leave, and while in the United States was assigned to duty at the U.S.N.A.S. at Pensacola, Florida. He remained at this station as an instructor until the close of the war.

SERVICE RECORD

GEORGE GALE WILLARD, Chicago, Illinois.

SERVICE IN FRENCH AVIATION:
Date of enlistment: May 26, 1917.
Aviation Schools: June 12 to December 24, 1917, Avord, Juvisy, Pau, G.D.E.
Breveted: November 1, 1917 (Caudron).
At the Front: Escadrille Spad 157, December 26, 1917, to January 13, 1918.
Final Rank: Caporal.

SERVICE IN U.S. AVIATION:
Commissioned Second Lieutenant: March 19, 1918.
Air Guard of Paris: March 19 to July 2, 1918.
At the Front: 147th Pursuit Squadron, July 2, 1918, to Armistice.

George Gale Willard

Breveted on Caudron at Juvisy, Willard got to the Front on December 26, 1917, when he was sent to the Escadrille N. 157. Eighteen days later he was taken seriously ill and, much to his disgust, it was necessary to sent him to hospital. On March 19, 1918, he was transferred to the United States Air Service, and assigned to an American squadron engaged in the defence of Paris. His friends, who dropped in at Le Bourget at this period, will remember Willard's impatience in being detained at what he considered an *embusqué* job, and his fear that the war might be over before he could get to the Front again. On July 2, when he was sent to join the 147th Pursuit Squadron, there was still plenty of fighting left to be done, and Willard has had all the adventures the air has to offer—ground-strafing, balloon attacks, aerial editions of the "Philadelphia Free for All"—at Château-Thierry, Saint-Mihiel, and in the Argonne.

SERVICE RECORD

HAROLD BUCKLEY WILLIS, Boston, Massachusetts.

PREVIOUS SERVICE: American Ambulance, 1915-16.

SERVICE IN FRENCH AVIATION:
Date of enlistment: May 22, 1916.
Aviation Schools: June 30, 1916, to February 28, 1917, Buc, Avord, Cazeaux, Pau, G.D.E.
Brevetted: October 20, 1916 (Blériot).
At the Front: Escadrille Lafayette, March 1 to August 18, 1917.
Shot down in combat: Near Dun-sur-Meuse, August 18, 1917.
Prisoner in Germany until October 13, 1918.
Escaped into Switzerland, October 13, 1918.
Final Rank: Sergent.

DECORATIONS:
Médaille Militaire.
Croix de Guerre, with two Palms and Star.

CITATIONS

En Campagne le 5 octobre, 1918
Citation à l'Ordre du Service de Santé de la 73ᵉ Division:
WILLIS, HAROLD B., Conducteur à la S.S.A.A.

A toujours fait preuve d'un courage et d'une hardiesse dignes des plus grands éloges; notamment pendant l'attaque du 4 juillet s'offrit pour aller chercher des blessés dans un endroit très périlleux, et eut sa voiture criblée d'obus.

Le Médecin Principal de 2ᵐᵉ Classe
(*Signé*)   VIELO

2ᵉ ARMÉE, ÉTAT-MAJOR.
Le Général Commandant la 2ᵉ Armée cite à l'Ordre de l'Armée:
WILLIS, HAROLD BUCKLEY, Sergent-Pilote de L'Escadrille N. 124, G.C. 13
(mort en combat)

Citoyen américain, engagé au service de la France. Véritable modèle pour ses camarades d'escadrille par son courage et sa haute conception du devoir. A fourni par ses reconnaissances de nombreux et utiles renseignements. Est tombé le 18 août au cours d'un combat contre deux avions ennemis qui venaient attaquer des avions de bombardement qu'il escortait.

Harold Buckley Willis

The names of Harold Willis and James Bach are linked together in Lafayette Corps history. It was Bach's unsought-for distinction to be the first man in the Corps to be taken prisoner, and Willis's to be the first in the Escadrille Lafayette. Bach's was the greater misfortune, for he was a captive from September 23, 1915, until the close of the war, after having served at the Front less than a month. Willis was not captured until three years later, and at that time he had behind him six months of ambulance service, and more than five months of combat patrols with Spad 124. The story of the battle which ended his career as an airman may best be told in his own words, which are copied from a letter written from a Westphalian prison camp:

> This is the first chance I have had to write you a long letter. I have heard nothing from the outside yet, but am hopeful. Hope is all that keeps us going. I will tell you how I happened to be the first in the *escadrille* to be taken alive—a dubious distinction. We were protecting a group of bombing planes on a daylight raid some distance in enemy territory. Suddenly we were attacked by a rather energetic patrol of *monoplaces*, and a general mix-up ensued. One of our planes in front of me was attacked, and I was able to 'crock' the German—short-lived satisfaction. The *monoplace* was protected by two others, which in turn attacked me from behind, riddling my machine. To continue in a straight line was fatal. So I did a *renversement* and attacked—my only defence.
> Immediately, of course, I was separated from our group, which continued. It would not have been so bad had my motor not been touched at the first volley. It worked only intermittently, causing loss of height. We had a wild fight almost to the ground. I did all sorts of stunts to avoid fire on the line of flight. The enemy flew well. We missed collision twice by inches. I was badly raked by cross-fire; music of bullets striking motor and cables. Toward the end my windshield was shattered and my goggles broken by a ball, which slightly stunned me. I had an awful feeling of despair at the thought of the inevitable landing in Germany. As I neared the ground, I had an instant's desire to dive into it—saw a wood in front of me, jumped it, and landed instinctively on the crest of a hill. One of the Germans flew over me, waved his hand, turned, and landed, followed by his

two comrades.

All saluted very politely as they came up—young chaps, perfectly correct. My machine was a wreck; thirty bullets in the fuselage, motor, and radiator, exactly half of the cables cut, tires punctured, and wings riddled. It was a beautiful machine and had always served me well. Too bad!

The aviators took me to lunch at their quarters, where I awaited a motor which took me to a prison in a fortress. One always expects to be either killed or wounded—never taken. So I had left the ground in two sweaters, no coat, and with no money. Confess I cried like a baby when I was finally alone in my cell. The first three days were terrible. One is not glad to be alive, especially when one wakes, forgets for a moment where one is, and then remembers. Pleasantest are the nights, for one always has vivid dreams of home or the Front. You can understand how wearing it is, to be helpless—a sort of living corpse—when there is need of everyone. I try not to think of it.

OFFICERS' PRISON CAMP, KARLSRUHE, BADEN

His chief occupation, like that of all prisoners, was in hoarding and concealing food from an all-too-limited ration supply, making compasses, transcribing maps from some priceless original, smuggled in, perhaps, under a piece of adhesive tape, stuck on the bottom of some fellow prisoner's foot. He was transferred from Karlsruhe, in Baden, to Landshut, in Bavaria, to Gutersleh, in Westphalia—other camps too numerous to mention.

He was confined in ancient fortresses with walls yards thick, and windows checkered with iron bars, almost fly-proof in mesh; in open camps of wooden barracks, surrounded by alternate defences of barbed wire and too watchful sentries. Wherever they went, monomaniacs of Willis's restless, liberty-loving nature, plotted incessantly. They nursed their fixed idea under the most adverse of circumstances, and brought plot after plot to the proof of trial. Some of these plans failed; others were successfully carried out, and the prisoners recaptured on the long tramp to the border. This was Willis's fate on three occasions.

His last attempt gained him his freedom. The escape was made from the camp at Villingen, Baden, the nearest to the Swiss border of all German prisons. The large arc lamps which flooded the prison grounds with brilliant light were short-circuited, just as the guard was changing. Willis and his fellow prisoners crossed the inner barriers of the camp by various means: one group on a flimsy bridge made of the small pine boards of Red Cross food boxes; another on scaling ladders. Willis, dressed like a camp guard and carrying a wooden gun, rushed out with the sentinels when the alarm was sounded, and escaped in the darkness under a heavy but widely scattered rifle fire. In company with Lieutenant Isaacs, U.S.N., he reached the Rhine, swam it at night, and arrived at Paris in good time to witness the wild demonstration of Armistice night. One can realise, in a measure, what his happiness must have been during that last month of the war, his pleasure in the simple comforts of life, the zest with which he ate his food, the pure joy of breathing free air.

Those of us who saw him in Paris at that time will not forget how supremely content he was with everything. A walk along the *boulevards* from the Place de la Concorde to the Opera was, for him, a magnificent treat. He saw everything with unaccustomed eyes. We envied him his fresh viewpoint; and now that he was safely home, we envied him his experience as well.

To be sure, being a prisoner of war, he missed some of the outward rewards of service. At the time when he fell within the German lines, he had just been proposed by Commandant Féquant, of *Groupe de Combat* 13, for the rank of *Sous-Lieutenant* in the French army—no mean distinction and one rarely awarded to foreigners. And in view of his prospective transfer to the American Service, he had likewise been proposed for the rank of major in the U.S.A.S. Both of these honours would have been his had he not been captured. But a new, keenly active sense of the joy of personal liberty, is far more than compensation for all the braid, gold or black, in Paris.

SERVICE RECORD

JOSEPH VOLNEY WILSON, Wheeling, West Virginia.

PREVIOUS SERVICE: Norton-Harjes Ambulance, 1917.

SERVICE IN FRENCH AVIATION:
Date of enlistment: July 21, 1917.
Aviation Schools: August 3 to November 19, 1917, Avord, Tours, G.D.E.
Breveted: September 25, 1917 (Caudron).
At the Front: Escadrille Br. 117, November 21, 1917, to January 16, 1918.
Final Rank: Caporal.

SERVICE IN U.S. AVIATION:
Commissioned First Lieutenant: January 16, 1918.
At the Front: Attached to French Squadron, Br. 117, January 16 to July 1, 1918.
Instructor at American A.I.C., Clermont-Ferrand, July 1 to September 30, 1918.
163d Day Bombing Squadron, September 30 to October 23, 1918.
Killed in line of duty: October 23, 1918, at Delouze.

DECORATIONS:
Croix de Guerre, with Star.

CITATION

G.A.R. AÉRONAUTIQUE MILITAIRE, ESCADRE 12.   Le 2 avril, 1918.

Le Chef d'Escadron, Vuillemin, Commandant de l'Escadre de Bombardement N° 12, cite à l'Ordre de l'Escadre les militaires dont les noms suivent: . . .

Le 1ᵉʳ Lieutenant, Pilote de l'Armée Américaine, WILSON, JOSEPH VOLNEY (Active Légion Étrangère), détaché à l'Escadrille Br. 117

Officier américain d'un courage remarquable. Dans la journée du 5 février, 1918, a contribué à abattre un avion ennemi, lors d'une expédition de bombardement sur un objectif éloigné.
(Signé)   VUILLEMIN

Joseph Volney Wilson

Wilson, leaving the Ambulance Service in the spring of 1917, immediately joined the Lafayette Flying Corps, and was breveted at Tours in September. His varied training included Blériot, G. 4 and G. 3 Caudron, Nieuport, and Bréguet. He went to the Front in November with but thirty hours of school flying registered in his *carnet de vol*.

Being assigned to Escadrille 117, of Day-Bombing Group 5, Wilson was given for an observer a *sous-officier* who thought his mission in life was to shoot down Germans. Wilson being in sympathy with the idea, these two were always in trouble, and never a scrap but they managed to be about somewhere. Twice Wilson came back over his lines with a motor badly damaged by bullets. He and his observer could not understand the use of defensive formations. Few battles were to be had by following such tactics. In March, 191 8, Wilson had a *panne* in, or rather over, Germany, and started for home with a dead motor.

On the way, two Albatross single-seaters appeared.

One of them was shot down by Wilson's observer, and the other, Wilson, with no motor, dodged all the way back to the lines. Later in the spring he was cited for more low bombing over Château-Thierry when it was the business of the Air Force to destroy bridges over the Marne. For this work he was also proposed for the American D.S.C. and a Squadron Commander's duty. About this time he was sent back to Clermont-Ferrand as an instructor in bombing, and remained there until September, when he went back to the Front with Charles Kinsolving to organise the 163rd American Squadron.

During the German advance upon Amiens, he participated in a great deal of the "strafing" work on the advancing German troops, flying low along the roads, scattering troop columns and transport. After this experience, he came back to Paris with a well-thought-out plan for armouring the Bréguet plane. He presented his scheme to the Technical Section of the Air Service, and was perfecting his armoured seat at the time of his death. In October he fell while testing a D.H. 4, and was instantly killed. One of the oldest American pilots, and with Kinsolving the oldest American bomber, his loss was greatly felt. He is buried at Gondrécourt, near Roger Clapp, who was his flying partner in the old days of French Aviation.

SERVICE RECORD

ALAN F. WINSLOW, River Forest, Illinois.

SERVICE IN FRENCH AVIATION:
Date of enlistment: July 10, 1917.
Aviation Schools: July 19 to December 24, 1917,
                        Avord, Juvisy, Pau, G.D.E.
Breveted: October 12, 1917 (Caudron).
At the Front: Escadrille Spad 152, December 24,
              1917, to February 12, 1918.
Final Rank: Sergent.

SERVICE IN U.S. AVIATION:
    Commissioned Second Lieutenant: February 20,
        1918.
At the Front: 94th Pursuit Squadron, April 1 to
        July 31, 1918.
Wounded in combat: July 31, 1918.
Prisoner in Germany until the Armistice

DECORATIONS:
    Distinguished Service Cross.
    Croix de Guerre, with Palm.

CITATIONS

The Distinguished Service Cross is awarded to
Second Lieutenant ALAN F. WINSLOW, 94th Aero Squadron, A.S.
For extraordinary heroism in action in the Toul Sector on June 6, 1918. While on a patrol consisting of himself and two other pilots, he encountered a *biplace* enemy plane at an altitude of 5000 meters, near Saint-Mihiel. He promptly and vigorously attacked, and after a running fight extending far beyond the German lines, shot his foe down in flames near Thiaucourt.

VIIIe ARMÉE. *Le* 16 *avril*, 1918
Citation à l'Ordre de l'Armée:

Sous-Lieutenant ALAN WINSLOW, de l'Armée Américaine, Pilote à l'Escadrille 94
Remarquable pilote de chasse. Le 14 avril a abattu un avion ennemi dans nos lignes après un combat aussi rapide que brillant.

Alan F. Winslow

In the files at Dr. Gros's office in Paris may be found the following letter, written by Alan Winslow shortly before his transfer to the United States Air Service:

Dear Major Gros,
Please consider my letter of yesterday as hasty. I do not wish to join Naval Aviation and shall cancel the application there. I would not have hesitated to accept an army commission as first lieutenant. I was, however, a bit rumpled on receiving a second. But if I am not a good-enough sport and American to take what is given me, I am no good at all. Therefore I wish to accept my second lieutenancy in the army.

This letter is typical of Alan Winslow's spirit as a sportsman and a soldier. His disappointment at receiving a second lieutenancy was wholly reasonable. He was a trained pilot and had had already two months of service at the Front in a French squadron. Many airmen in America who had never seen France were being commissioned as first lieutenants, captains, and majors. Alan was not the only pilot in France who felt "a bit rumpled" at receiving a gold bar. But he preferred being at the Front as a buck private, if need be, to any possible reward of rank, and he arrived there as *Caporal Pilote* of Spad 152 the day before Christmas, 1917.

After his transfer to the United States Air Service, he was placed on active duty with the 94th Aero Squadron, the first combat unit which had been always American to be sent to the Front. The Escadrille Lafayette was, of course, the first squadron in the American Service; but it had previously been French, and even after it became the 103rd American Squadron, it was for some time attached to a French *groupe de combat* under French orders.

On April 14, 1918, the morning of the 94th's first day of service on the Front, Alan Winslow and Douglas Campbell started the ball rolling for American Aviation by shooting down two enemy single-seaters, almost over the Squadron Aerodrome at Toul. Without question this battle is the most spectacular in the history of the American Air Service. There was a strong northeast wind blowing, with heavy clouds at 300 to 500 metres. The first flight of the squadron was on *alerte* duty at the hangars, but on account of the threatening weather it seemed likely that there would be nothing to do. The telephone rang: "Enemy machines heard in the vicinity of Toul." Winslow and Campbell immediately went up in pursuit and were just leaving the ground when the German planes, an Albatross and a Pfalz, single-seaters, emerged from the clouds not 200 metres distant.

The combat was of less than three minutes' duration. Winslow forced his German to the ground, where the enemy machine turned over, partially wrecking it: and almost at the same instant Campbell shot his down in flames. Luckily the pilot of the burning machine had only 300 metres to fall and was thrown out when the *avion* crashed. Neither of the Germans was seriously hurt. The battle was witnessed by thousands of soldiers and civilians in Toul. One of them was slightly wounded in the ear by a bullet from Winslow's machine gun. He was overjoyed at the honour, as he called it, of having a *si bon souvenir* of the combat, and thanked Winslow most profusely and sincerely for it.

ALAN WINSLOW AFTER HIS VICTORY AT TOUL

From that time on, Winslow saw a great deal of the most active kind of service along the Front. On June 4, 1918, with two comrades of the 94th, he shot down a *biplace* far within the enemy lines; and on July 31, 1918, during a bitterly contested battle, was himself shot down within German territory. His left arm was shattered by an explosive bullet, but he managed to land before losing consciousness from the shock and loss of blood. A short time later, his arm was amputated above the elbow. After five months in German hospitals, he was returned to France, on January 9, 1919, being one of the last of the American prisoner aviators to regain his freedom.

SERVICE RECORD
CARROLL DANA WINSLOW, New York City.
SERVICE IN FRENCH AVIATION:
Date of enlistment: October 23, 1915.
Aviation Schools: October 25, 1915, to May 1, 1916.
Breveted: March 13, 1916 (Maurice Farman).
At the Front: Escadrille M.F. 44, May 3 to July 13, 1916.
  Escadrille N. 112, March 10 to April 30, 1917.
Final Rank: Sergent.

Carroll Dana Winslow

Winslow, having received his early training on the Maurice Farman, was not sent to the Escadrille Lafayette, but to the reconnaissance squadron, M.F. 44, a French unit. After two months at the Front he was sent to Pau for Nieuport training, and on August 10, 1916, he went to America on sick-leave. He returned in January, 1917, and after perfecting himself as a combat pilot, was sent on active duty a second time, to the French squadron, N. 112. After six weeks with this squadron he was granted his release for the purpose of joining the United States Air Service.

SERVICE RECORD
WALLACE CHARLES WINTER, Chicago, Illinois.
SERVICE IN FRENCH AVIATION:
Date of enlistment: June 25, 1917.
Aviation Schools: June 29 to November 28, 1917, Avord, Pau, G.D.E.
Breveted: September 15, 1917 (Caudron).
At the Front: Escadrille Spad 94, December 1, 1917, to January 1, 1918.
  Escadrille Spad 156, January 1 to March 8, 1918.
Final Rank: Caporal.
Killed in combat: March 8, 1918 (Champagne Sector).

DECORATIONS:
Croix de Guerre, with Star.

CITATION

Le 21 février, 1918

Le Général Commandant de la IVᵉ Armée cite à l'Ordre du Service Aéronautique:

Caporal de la Légion Étrangère WINTER, WALLACE, Mˡᵉ 9827, de l'Escadrille N° 156

Étant de patrouille le 19 janvier, 1918, a livré un vif combat à deux biplaces ennemis et a contribué à en abattre un en flammes.

Wallace Charles Winter

At Pau, Winter distinguished himself by the *finesse* and daring of his flying, and was specially commended by the Commandant for landing safely a machine which had been severely damaged in an aerial collision. Like a very few others, Winter was a man who seemed to take instinctively to flying; in the acrobatic class, his performance was that of an old pilot; he seemed to control perfectly the evolutions of his machine in *vrilles* and *renversements*, and in doing vertical *virages*, most difficult of all manoeuvres for a young pilot, he never slipped on the wing or nosed down toward the earth.

Winter went to the Front in December, 1917, joining Escadrille N. 94, and transferring in January to the N. 156. This latter was one of the few squadrons which received the small Morane monoplanes. With Winter in the N. 156 were Putnam and Shaffer, and though their machines were soon pronounced unsafe and no one was ordered to fly them, the four Americans were constantly over the lines on volunteer patrols. Winter was with Putnam when he shot down his second Boche, and for his part in the combat was decorated with the *Croix de Guerre*. Although the sector was at that time very quiet, he was constantly in the air, hunting the enemy far within his own lines, and his French comrades soon came to recognise in him an indomitable spirit of aggressiveness and action. Had he lived, he would have become a famous flyer; of that there can be no doubt.

On March 8, 1918, the eve of his transfer as a first lieutenant to the American Army, Winter made his last flight. It is characteristic of the man that, at the time, he was not even connected with the *escadrille*,

WINTER'S GRAVE

but simply waiting there for orders to report to American Headquarters, for he was not the type which searches for excuses to avoid flying. The commanding officer, out of courtesy to a man he liked, granted his request for a machine. In the mist of early morning, five little Moranes, swift and graceful as dragon-flies, rose from their aerodrome near Châlons and headed for the lines. A French pilot who was on the patrol is the only man who saw the fall.

Shortly after they reached the lines, he perceived a pair of German two-seaters well below him and attacked at once, plunging down at headlong speed. When close to the Boche, he found that his gun was jammed and sheered off to avoid the enemy's fire while clearing his *mitrailleuse*. Glancing over his shoulder at this moment, he saw another Morane diving straight on the German from behind; suddenly, when the distance between them was only a few yards, the wings of the Morane seemed to fold up and it plunged down, to disappear, its bracing cut away, undoubtedly, by German bullets. It was Winter.

All along the Front, from aerodrome to aerodrome, wherever American pilots were stationed, the news spread that Winter was dead, and his friends, saddened by the loss, added a new and heavy item to their account against the enemy.

SERVICE RECORD

HOUSTON WOODWARD, Philadelphia, Pennsylvania.
PREVIOUS SERVICE: American Ambulance, 1917.
SERVICE IN FRENCH AVIATION:
  Date of enlistment: July 14, 1917.
  Aviation Schools: July 24 to December 14, 1917.
    Avord, Juvisy, Pau, G.D.E.
  Breveted: September 30, 1917 (Caudron).
  At the Front: Escadrille Spad 94, December 16, 1917, to April 1, 1918.
  Final Rank: Caporal.
  Killed in combat: April 1, 1918, south of Mont-didier.
DECORATIONS:
  Croix de Guerre, with Palm.

CITATION

Le 29 avril, 1918
GROUPE D'ARMÉE DE RÉSERVE:
Citation à l'Ordre de l'Armée:
WOODWARD, HOUSTON (Américain), Caporal (Légion Étrangère) à l'Escadrille Spa. 94
  Pilote de chasse audacieux jusqu'à la témérité et recherchant opiniâtrément l'ennemi. Le 6 janvier, 1918, abattait un avion ennemi loin dans ses lignes. A disparu le 1 avril, 1918, au cours d'un combat contre plusieurs avions ennemis.

Houston Woodward

Woodward has left behind him a record as brilliant as it was brief—a story of sacrifice, of devotion to duty, of reckless, headlong courage. No finer words can be said of a soldier than those of his citation to the Order of the Army: *Pilote . . . audacieux jusqu'à la témérité et recherchant opiniâtrément l'ennemi.*

Sent to the Front on December 16, 1917, he joined the Spad 94, in a *groupe de combat* which contained some of the best fighting pilots of the French army. Austen Crehore was a member of the 94th, as was Marinovich, later to become a famous "ace." Inspired by the example of his comrades and burning with the ardour that counts neither odds nor cost, Woodward was in the air at every opportunity, flying alone for the most part and far into the enemy lines, where on many occasions he attacked single-handed large German formations. At such distances from friendly observation posts there is little hope of obtaining official confirmation, and though he made no useless claims, his comrades believe that more than one German plane was shot down on these lonely raids.

Woodward's bitter aggressiveness was a cause of concern to his superiors, who were immensely proud of their American recruit, but even threatened punishment for his rashness, in an effort to instil a drop of caution into a nature which literally did not know the meaning of fear.

Within three weeks after his arrival on the Front, Woodward scored an official victory—the sequel of a strange encounter. He was patrolling the lines alone, on the lookout for a formation of his comrades, due at any moment. Suddenly he made out a lone single-seater, weaving its way through bursts of shrapnel, and thinking that only one machine had come to join him he fell into formation with the newcomer, following above and behind. Up and down the lines the two paraded, the American following his companion's abrupt turns and changes of altitude, always behind and a little above. At last, as time was nearly up, the other *monoplace* banked, turned straight into the enemy lines and headed earthward with reduced motor. As it dropped below him, Woodward was astounded to see a pair of large black crosses on the wings—he had been following an Albatross! A quick dive and a burst from the Vickers sent the unconscious German hurtling down to crash near his own front lines.

On April 1, 1918, Woodward set out from the aerodrome at Le Plessis to patrol the ever-changing lines to the north. The clouds were thick and very low; south of Montdidier there was a combat against heavy odds. That is all we know. Months afterwards, when the enemy had been driven back and the tide of war had turned, the twisted wreck of a Spad was found in the desolation near Montdidier. It bore the number of Woodward's machine.

SERVICE RECORD

WARWICK D. WORTHINGTON, Paris, France.

SERVICE IN FRENCH AVIATION:
Date of enlistment: March 9, 1916.
Aviation Schools: March 15, 1916, to February 28, 1917, Buc, Étampes, G.D.E.
Breveted: September 24, 1916 (Farman).
At the Front: Escadrille C. 53, March 3, 1917, to February 13, 1918.
Final Rank: Sergent.

SERVICE IN U.S. AVIATION:
Commissioned First Lieutenant: February 18, 1918.
Instructor at American A.I.C., Tours, February 18, 1918, to Armistice.

DECORATION:
Croix de Guerre

Warwick D. Worthington

An eminent conversationalist, Worthington talked himself into the French Aviation in March, 1916. Although he was not a born pilot, he was distinctly a born hero, so that, in spite of ever-recurrent and ill-omened mishaps, he reached the end of an eventful novitiate by dint of much violent expostulation, and—be it here chronicled, a far greater display of admirable grit and determination—was breveted and sent to the Front. Worthington was one of the few pilots of the Lafayette Corps whose lot was cast among observation flyers. His work was quietly accomplished. It was none the less creditable. And the *Croix de Guerre* he wears bears witness to the esteem and admiration in which he was held by those under whom he served. His entire career was marked by an astonishing streak of ill-luck which would have broken the spirit of most men. Time after time he crawled hopefully from the wrecks of treacherous *coucous*, which, as he always volubly explained, had wilfully, and of malice aforethought, "done him dirt." And time after time he returned to his squadron, C. S3, to match his skill and courage against yet other recalcitrant ships, which, with few exceptions, consistently betrayed his confidence. Motors simply refused to run for him. And to this day pieces of splintered ash and mahogany, bits of frayed and weathered wing fabric, lie scattered along the battle-front of France, from the Ferme d'Alger to the dunes of Nieuport, in mute testimony to the constancy of Worthington.

He was deadly serious in his purpose. He had joined the service to fight, and every day spent away from the Front he counted as a day lost. Once upon a time he was sent from his squadron to the training centre at Le Plessis-Belleville to learn the dangers and the wiles of the new G. 6 Caudron. Upon reporting, what was his dismay to be told by the chief pilot that the G. 6, in its present state of evolution, had killed any number of novices and had been condemned for further flights until such time as a larger tail-fin could be manufactured and supplied in sufficient numbers to render all machines at the school reasonably safe. For once Worthington's perfect and phenomenally extensive command of the French language failed him. The chief pilot was adamant. No tail-fin, no flying, was the verdict.

Next morning Worthington was absent at roll-call. And for several days thereafter his absence constituted his chief claim to the attention of his superiors. Then, quite casually and simply, he returned and reported for duty. But he was not empty-handed. For he dragged with him, into the office of the thunderstruck Chief Pilot, two complete, large-size tail-fins for the G. 6. "You said no tail-fins, no flying," he explained. "Here are the tail-fins. May I fly?" And he was in earnest. It was no grandstand play; anything but a prank. He wanted to get back to the Front. Not being a soldier by training, only a fighter by nature, he had slashed through all the military precedents and red-tape that stood between himself and his ideal and had taken the only direct means to gain his end. He had had the tail-fins manufactured. The affair cost him some little time in the guard-house, the obvious sincerity of his motives being overshadowed by even more obvious disciplinary considerations. But he made shift, none the less, to carry his point; the tail-fins were mounted on a pair of Caudrons, and his training and rapid return to the Front accomplished in short order.

Worthington, throughout his service in the French Aviation, bore himself with the utmost credit, accomplishing bravely, faithfully, and in the face of consistently discouraging ill-fortune, every duty set him. His excellent record won for him a commission in the United States Air Service. He changed from horizon blue to khaki in February, 1918, and continued in active service to the end of hostilities.

SERVICE RECORD

HAROLD E. WRIGHT, Brooklyn, New York.

SERVICE IN FRENCH AVIATION:
Date of enlistment: March 20, 1917.
Aviation Schools: March 25 to September 8, 1917, Avord, Pau, G.D.E.
Breveted: July 18, 1917 (Caudron).
At the Front: Escadrille Spad 155, September 11 to December 23, 1917.
Final Rank: Sergent.

Harold E. Wright

Harold E. Wright's chief claim to distinction as an airman is due to the series of remarkable flights which he made during the summer of 1918, in the *Saturday Evening Post* sector. Flying the *avion* "Remington Typewriter" he had a long and bitter combat with Baron Richtofen, the greatest of German "aces." Richtofen escaped, but Baron Munchausen, the legendary king of ground-flyers, who was hovering at an immense height above the scene of the battle, received a mortal *coup* from the Wilson machine gun, and fell upward into the blue serene, hoist by his own petard, of which ammunition Sergent Pilote Wright had a plentiful supply. So far as is known this is Wright's only official victory.

SERVICE RECORD

WALTER R. YORK, Somerville, Massachusetts.

SERVICE IN FRENCH AVIATION:
Date of enlistment: June 25, 1917.
Aviation Schools: June 28, 1917, to March 1, 1918, Avord, Pau, G.D.E.
Breveted: December 2, 1917 (Caudron).
At the Front: Escadrille Spad 97, March 3, 1918, to Armistice.
Final Rank: Sous-Lieutenant.

DECORATIONS:
Croix de Guerre, with Palm.

CITATION

Le 10 *octobre,* 1918
GRAND QUARTIER GÉNÉRAL
DES ARMÉES DU NORD ET DU
NORD-EST, ÉTAT-MAJOR.

Le Général Commandant en Chef cite à l'Ordre de l'Armée:

YORK, WALTER, M^{le} 12287 (active), Sergent au 1er Régiment de Marche de la Légion Étrangère, Pilote Aviateur

Engagé volontaire pour la durée de la guerre, pilote de chasse remarquable par son courage, son sang-froid, et son mépris du danger. Ayant une haute conception de son devoir, attaque à fond ses adversaires et livre combat jusque très loin dans les lignes allemandes. Le 17 septembre, a abattu un appareil ennemi en flammes.

Le Général Commandant en Chef
PÉTAIN

Walter R. York

Walter York is one of the small group of Americans who have attained commissioned rank in the French army, having won this unusual distinction by good work over the lines, coupled with seriousness, devotion to duty, and a knowledge of French. York has been through many thrilling experiences, but perhaps none more exciting than the following, which we will let him relate in his own words:

> On September 15, seven of us went over with orders to attack and burn a certain *saucisse* at any cost. This particular *saucisse* was well in the German lines and the wind was dead against us for returning to our lines. Moreover, there were no clouds in the sky in which we could play a little game of hide and seek, should Fritz get us where he wanted us. When almost on the balloon, we saw a patrol of ten Fokkers, who, guessing what our business was, were turning to cut us off before we succeeded in reaching our objective. They just did beat us to it and fell on our patrol leader, and, contrary to custom, they attacked him first. I tried to disengage him and the attacking German let him go, but veering more quickly than I could, succeeded in placing himself behind me.
> From that minute the whole combat remains a confusion of

virages, renversements, and half-turns of *vrilles,* with the Boche generally ending up in the choice position, directly on the tail of my machine. A second *rat-tat-tat,* and a glimpse of incendiary bullets, was sufficient to make me abandon flying in a straight line. Manoeuvre as I would, I succeeded in finding him in my sights just once, and then only for an instant, not sufficient time to make a good correction. Frankly, I was up against a much better pilot than myself, a bird who could turn around on a dime and leave nine cents change. It seemed like an eternity that we had been fighting, when once again I looked over my shoulder to find him swinging the bright yellow nose of his machine into my tail. I tried to pull a mounting *virage,* but just in the middle of it, my motor spit a couple of times and my stick started turning slower and slower until it nearly stopped. No pressure on my *essence* gauge! There I hung, straight up and down in the air, presenting a perfect target that the worst shot in France couldn't miss. I knew it would be a matter of only a second before my machine would lose its speed, fall off into a wing-slip and then into a *vrille.*

If only my stick would keep on turning, and the Boche take a little more time before shooting, I should be safe, because in the *glissage* with my nose over, I could slip her into my *nourrice,* which is independent of pressure, and catch my motor. Can you guess my relief when, out of the corner of my eye, I saw another good old Spad dive from above, direct on the Fritz, and heard the rat-tat-tat of a pair of Vickers. I don't know exactly what happened after that, but I believe that the German, caught absolutely unawares, was shot down by the other Spad, which, by the way, was piloted by my roommate. When I came out of my *vrille,* I saw that the combat was over, and was well content to slide along home. We did not succeed in getting our *saucisse* and lost one lieutenant in flames. The patrol got one Boche officially and two others, probably. I did not see what passed with the others, having my hands full from the start, but it appears that another strong patrol of Fokkers was about to come to the rescue of their comrades, so our patrol had to beat it just as my own combat terminated. A pretty lucky escape for me. Two days later, three of us attacked by surprise this same band of Fokkers and had a sweet revenge. My roommate shot down one and I got another in flames.

ZINN AND HIS PILOT

SERVICE RECORD

FREDERICK W. ZINN, Battle Creek, Michigan.

PREVIOUS SERVICE: Foreign Legion (Infantry), August 24, 1914, to February 1, 1916. Wounded while with Legion.

SERVICE IN FRENCH AVIATION:
Date of enlistment: February 14, 1916.
Aviation Schools: February 17 to December 10, 1916, Étampes, Cazeaux, Pau, G.D.E.
Breveted (as mitrailleur-bombardier): August 29, 1916.
At the Front: Escadrille F. 24, December 12, 1916, to October 21, 1917.
Attached to the French Mission, American G.H.Q., Chaumont, October 21 to November 16, 1917.
Final Rank: Sergent.

SERVICE IN U.S. AVIATION:
Commissioned Captain: November 16, 1917.
Attached to American G.H.Q., Chaumont, November 16, 1917, to Armistice.

DECORATIONS:
Croix de Guerre, with Palm and Star.

CITATIONS

Citation à l'Ordre de l'Armée:

ZINN, FRÉDÉRIC, observateur à l'Escadrille F. 24

Engagé volontaire américain au 2ᵉ Étranger, a participé à toutes les opérations de ce corps d'août, 1914, à octobre, 1915. Grièvement blessé et passé dans l'aviation comme observateur, s'y est fait aussitôt remarquer par son sang-froid, son audace, et son mépris du danger. A fourni depuis le 10 avril, souvent sans protection, un grand nombre de reconnaissances photographiques lointaines qu'il a toujours menées à bien, malgré le tir de l'artillerie et les attaques des avions ennemis.

Citation à l'Ordre de l'Aéronautique:

ZINN, FRÉDÉRIC

Soldat de la nationalité américaine, s'est engagé dans l'armée française pour la durée de la guerre, blessé dans l'infanterie, a repris du service dans l'aviation en qualité d'observateur photographe.
A exécuté de nombreuses missions photographiques éloignées, sans protection et malgré la présence de nombreux avions ennemis. S'est toujours distingué par sa grand bravoure et son sang-froid.

Frederick W. Zinn

An adequate account of the war service of Frederick Zinn from August 24, 1914, when he enlisted in the Foreign Legion (Infantry), 1 until the Armistice, would greatly exceed the limits possible in a brief biographical sketch. His was an unusually varied experience, and his record, from the point of view of quality as well as length of service, one of the finest of the corps. In addition to the usual equipment of a *légionnaire, soldat de la deuxième classe*, Zinn carried with him to the trenches a good camera. He took numberless photographs during the campaign of 1914-15. War correspondents and photographers were not then permitted at the Front; but Zinn, who was both soldier and photographer, took his pictures without interference. They were in great demand in America. They were printed far and wide, in illustrated magazines and newspapers, and it was due to his fearlessness and his enthusiasm as an amateur photographer that Americans at home were able to have graphic pictorial accounts of life in the trenches during the first battles of the war.

Zinn was wounded during the 1915 Battle of Champagne which ended his career as an infantryman. After his release from hospital he entered French Aviation and became one of the three American observers and machine-gunners in the French service. As an observer he was able to continue in an official capacity his work in photography. In the old slow-flying Farmans, and later in Sopwiths, he went with his pilot on long photographic missions far into enemy territory, the two men often fighting their way back to the French lines and reaching them only by incredible good fortune.

Ten months of experience with the French in *corps d'armèe* work made him a valuable asset to the United States Air Service, and he was one of the first of the volunteers whose transfer was requested by the American authorities. This took place in October, 1917, and from that time until the close of the war, Zinn was on duty at the American G.H.Q. at Chaumont, at the First Air Depot, Colombey-les-Belles, and elsewhere. After the Armistice he went into Germany as chief of the American Mission for locating the graves of American airmen who had fallen in German-held territory.

Zinn's Squadron, Sop. 24

Appendix

I

MEMBERS OF THE LAFAYETTE FLYING CORPS RELEASED BY THE FRENCH GOVERNMENT BEFORE SERVING AT THE FRONT

ALLEN, SIDNEY T., St. Louis, Missouri.
Enlisted: July 19, 1917.
Released: September, 1917, because of defective eyesight.

APPLETON, W. K., JR., Nice, France.
Enlisted: July 15, 1916.
Previous Service: Foreign Legion (Infantry).
Released: December 16, 1916, because of inaptitude.
Returned: to the 170th Infantry regiment (French).

ATEN, ARTHUR M., Brooklyn, New York.
Enlisted: September 7, 1916.
Breveted: April 30, 1917.
Deserted to America: May 10, 1917.

BOSWORTH, CLARENCE M., New York City.
Enlisted: October 19, 1917.
Breveted: December 26, 1917.
Went to America April, 1918, on one month's leave of absence. Returned to France after the close of hostilities.

BOYESEN, ALGERNON, New York City.
Enlisted: January 15, 1916.
Released: March 8, 1916, because of inaptitude.

BROWN, STAFFORD L., Newton Center, Massachusetts.
Enlisted: July 21, 1917.
Released: September 12, 1917, for disciplinary reasons.

BULLEN, RICHARD N., Chicago, Illinois.
Enlisted: July 14, 1917.
Breveted: September 28, 1917.
Released: while at G.D.E., January 7, 1918, because of injuries received in a flying accident at Pau.

CARRÈRE, JOSEPH M., JR., New York City.
Enlisted: February 22, 1917.
Released: July 10, 1917, because of inaptitude.

COLLIER, EDWARD M., Bass Rocks, Massachusetts.
Enlisted: November, 1916.
Released: October 25, 1917, because of ill health.

COURT, ISIDORE, New York City.
Enlisted: July, 1916.
Previous Service: Foreign Legion (Infantry).
Released: February 15, 1917, because of inaptitude. (Entered Automobile Service French Army.)

DULON, LOWELL RICHARDS, New York City.
Enlisted: June 15, 1917.
Released: October 21, 1917, because of inaptitude.

EATON, SHERBURNE, Boston, Massachusetts.
Enlisted: March 25, 1917.
Released: September 1, 1917, because of inaptitude.

ELLIOTT, CHESTER A., Akron, Ohio.
Enlisted: August 2, 1917.
Breveted: October 22, 1917.
Released at G.D.E. February 1, 1918, upon his own request. Commissioned 2d Lieut. U.S. Air Service October 1, 1918.

ENDICOTT, JOHN, Boston, Massachusetts.
Enlisted: August 6, 1917.
Released: September 12, 1917, for disciplinary reasons.

FLYNN, JOSEPH, Philadelphia, Pennsylvania.
Enlisted: June 15, 1917.
Released: August 5, 1917, for dishonorable conduct.

FORD, TOD, Pasadena, California.
Enlisted: May 21, 1917.
Removed from flying training because of ill health August, 1917. Sent to America as member of French Mission. Released from French Service

and commissioned First Lieutenant U.S.A.S. Returned to France for technical and liaison duties.
FREY, WILLIAM.
Enlisted: May 6, 1916.
Breveted: September 7, 1916.
Deserted while on leave in America.
GIBSON, WILLIAM WALLACE, Savannah, Georgia.
Enlisted: July 13, 1917.
Released: September 23, 1917, because of inaptitude.
Commissioned Second Lieutenant U.S. Air Service and breveted at Tours.
GOURAUD, REGINALD G., Paris, France.
Enlisted: February 11, 1917.
Released: May, 1917, because of inaptitude.
GUEST, DAVID PORTER, Richmond, Virginia.
Enlisted: July 6, 1917.
Breveted: October 17, 1917.
Released: December 30, 1917, upon his own request.
HARRISON, JOHN B., JR., Bloomfield, New Jersey.
Enlisted: June 12, 1917.
Released: October 16, 1917, because of inaptitude. (Afterward joined British R.A.F.)
HEILBUTH, JOHN, Paris, France.
Enlisted: July 3, 1917.
Released: August, 1917, because of defective eyesight.
HICKSON, LESLIE, New York City.
Enlisted: July 30, 1917.
Breveted: September 27, 1917.
Released: January 18, 1918, upon his own request.
HOLDEN, MILTON W., Camden, New Jersey.
Previous Service. American Ambulance, 1917.
Enlisted: June 25, 1917.
Released: January, 1918, because of injuries received in a flying accident.
HOUGH, EDWIN A., Edgemere, Long Island.
Previous Service: Norton-Harjes Ambulance. (Received *Croix de Guerre* while in Ambulance Service.)
Enlisted: June 3, 1917.
Released: August 1, 1917, because of inaptitude.
HULL, MARK LESLIE, Mamaroneck, New York. and commissioned First Lieutenant U.S.A.S. Returned to France for technical and liaison duties.
FREY, WILLIAM.
Enlisted: May 6, 1916.
Breveted: September 7, 1916.
Deserted while on leave in America.

Enlisted: June 15, 1917.
Released: September 20, 1917, because of inaptitude.
KIRKWOOD, WILLIAM FRANCIS, Boston, Massachusetts.
Enlisted: August 1, 1917.
Released: October, 1917, because of inaptitude.
KOWALL, JOHN ROBERT, Roxbury, Massachusetts.
Enlisted: August 1, 1917.
Released: November, 1917, because of injuries received in a flying accident.
LEE, HENRY S., Cornwall, New York.
Enlisted: April 24, 1917.
Released: July 15, 1917, because of inaptitude.
LUDLAM, LESLIE, Montclair, New Jersey.
Enlisted: December 20, 1916.
Released: August 16, 1917, because of ill health.
McCREARY, JAMES B., JR., Buffalo, New York.
Enlisted: July 23, 1917.
Released: April, 1918, because of ill health.
McGINN, WILLIAM, Cincinnati, Ohio.
Enlisted: July 20, 1917.
Breveted: October 2, 1917.
Released: November 2, 1917, upon his own request.
MACKE, GORDON B., New York City.
Enlisted: June 29, 1917.
Breveted: September 26, 1917.
Released: at G.D.E. upon his own request.
MAGLEY, GUY BERTRAM, Joplin, Missouri.
Enlisted: September 1, 1916.
Released: October 14, 1916, because of inaptitude.
MANIERRE, HAROLD L., Chicago, Illinois.
Enlisted: July 15, 1917.
Released: August 16, 1917, because of inaptitude.
MILLER, ALVIN FORD, New York City.
Enlisted: September, 1916.
Released: May, 1917, because of defective eyesight.
MILLER, GEORGE, Kansas City, Missouri.
Enlisted: January 15, 1917.
Released: June, 1917, because of inaptitude.

Enlisted: June 15, 1917.
Released: September 20, 1917, becau of inaptitude.
KIRKWOOD, WILLIAM FRANCIS, Bostc Massachusetts.
Enlisted: August 1, 1917.
Released: October, 1917, because of i aptitude.

GIBSON, WILLIAM WALLACE, Savannah, Georgia.
  Enlisted: July 13, 1917.
  Released: September 23, 1917, because of inaptitude.
  Commissioned Second Lieutenant U.S. Air Service and breveted at Tours.
GOURAUD, REGINALD G., Paris, France.
  Enlisted: February 11, 1917.
  Released: May, 1917, because of inaptitude.
GUEST, DAVID PORTER, Richmond, Virginia.
  Enlisted: July 6, 1917.
  Breveted: October 17, 1917.
  Released: December 30, 1917, upon his own request.
HARRISON, JOHN B., JR., Bloomfield, New Jersey.
  Enlisted: June 12, 1917.
  Released: October 16, 1917, because of inaptitude. (Afterward joined British R.A.F.)
HEILBUTH, JOHN, Paris, France.
  Enlisted: July 3, 1917.
  Released: August, 1917, because of defective eyesight.
HICKSON, LESLIE, New York City.
  Enlisted: July 30, 1917.
  Breveted: September 27, 1917.
  Released: January 18, 1918, upon his own request.
HOLDEN, MILTON W., Camden, New Jersey.
  Previous Service: American Ambulance, 1917.
  Enlisted: June 25, 1917.
  Released: January, 1918, because of injuries received in a flying accident.
HOUGH, EDWIN A., Edgemere, Long Island.
  Previous Service: Norton-Harjes Ambulance. (Received Croix de Guerre while in Ambulance Service.)
  Enlisted: June 3, 1917.
  Released: August 1, 1917, because of inaptitude.
HULL, MARK LESLIE, Mamaroneck, New York.
MILLS, GORDON R., Chicago, Illinois.
  Enlisted: July 6, 1917.
  Released: October, 1917, because of ill health.
MOUVET, OSCAR, New York City.
  Previous Service: Foreign Legion (Infantry). Wounded in the Legion and cited in Regimental Orders.
  Enlisted: August 15, 1916.
  Released: April, 1917, because of inaptitude.
MUNSON, CURTIS B., New York City.
  Enlisted: July 23, 1917.
  Released: October, 1917, upon his own request.
OAKES, NATHAN, JR., Providence, Rhode Island.
  Enlisted: June 19, 1917.
  Breveted: October 15, 1917.

KOWALL, JOHN ROBERT, Roxbury, Massachusetts.
  Enlisted: August 1, 1917.
  Released: November, 1917, because of injuries received in a flying accident.
LEE, HENRY S., Cornwall, New York.
  Enlisted: April 24, 1917.
  Released: July 15, 1917, because of inaptitude.
LUDLAM, LESLIE, Montclair, New Jersey.
  Enlisted: December 20, 1916.
  Released: August 16, 1917, because of ill health.
MCCREARY, JAMES B., JR., Buffalo, New York.
  Enlisted: July 23, 1917.
  Released: April, 1918, because of ill health.
McGINN, WILLIAM, Cincinnati, Ohio.
  Enlisted: July 20, 1917.
  Breveted: October 2, 1917.
  Released: November 2, 1917, upon his own request.
MACKE, GORDON B., New York City.
  Enlisted: June 29, 1917.
  Breveted: September 26, 1917.
  Released: at G.D.E. upon his own request.
MAGLEY, GUY BERTRAM, Joplin, Missouri.
  Enlisted: September 1, 1916.
  Released: October 14, 1916, because of inaptitude.
MANIERRE, HAROLD L., Chicago, Illinois.
  Enlisted: July 15, 1917.
  Released: August 16, 1917, because of inaptitude.
MILLER, ALVIN FORD, New York City.
  Enlisted: September, 1916.
  Released: May, 1917, because of defective eyesight.
MILLER, GEORGE, Kansas City, Missouri.
  Enlisted: January 15, 1917.
  Released: June, 1917, because of inaptitude.
  Enlisted: June 10, 1917.
  Released: July 12, 1917, for disciplinary reasons.
SCHREIBER, EDWIN BOOTH, Anaconda, Montana.
  Enlisted: June 29, 1917.
  Released: Upon his own request for the purpose of joining U.S. Air Service.
  Killed in flying accident at Issoudun: August 8, 1918.
SEAVER, HORACE, Hartford, Connecticut.
  Enlisted: March 10, 1917.
  Released: August 13, 1917, because of injuries received in a flying accident.
SHIPLEY, WALTER B., Page, West Virginia.
  Enlisted: June 9, 1917.
  Breveted: December 10, 1917.
  Released: at the Front, March 22, 1918.

Released: December 12, 1917, upon his own request.
Later commissioned 2d Lieutenant U.S. Air Service and attached as instructor at Lake Charles, Louisiana.

POTTER, THOMAS, Westchester, New York.
Previous service: American Ambulance. (Awarded *Croix de Guerre* in Macedonia.)
Enlisted: June 21, 1917.
Breveted: November 10, 1917.
Released: November, 1917, because of inaptitude.

RIDLON, HUGH O. J., Chicago, Illinois
Enlisted: June 14, 1917.
Released: August 13, 1917, upon his own request.

ROCKWELL, GEORGE, Waterbury, Connecticut.
Enlisted: July 8, 1916.
Released: November, 1916, upon his own request.

ROLPH, JOHN F., JR., Centerville, Maryland.
Enlisted: July 31, 1917.
Breveted: September 28, 1917.
Released: November 11, 1917, upon his own request.

ROSS, RAYMOND T., Crawfordville, Indiana.
Enlisted: April 15, 1917.
Released: August 12, 1917, because of defective eyesight.

SAUL, JOSEPH ROE, Lancaster, New Hampshire.

SKINNER, SAMUEL W., Cincinnati, Ohio.
Enlisted: May 31, 1917.
Breveted: July 26, 1917.
Died: at G.D.E., October 16, 1917.

SPEERS, WALLACE C., Montclair, New Jersey.
Enlisted: June 19, 1917.
Released: August 1, 1917, because of ill health.

STONE, GERALD S., Spencer, Massachusetts.
Enlisted: August 2, 1917.
Breveted: October 29, 1917.
Released: January 13, 1918, while at G.D.E. upon his own request.

WAINWRIGHT, NEAL, Boston, Massachusetts.
Enlisted: July 6, 1917.
Released: November, 1917, because of ill health.
Enlisted in U.S. Army. Wounded and awarded D.S.C.

WILLOUGHBY, WESTEL R., Baltimore, Maryland.
Enlisted: July 9, 1917.
Breveted: December 4, 1917.
Released: January, 1918.
Commissioned Lieutenant U.S. Field Artillery.

WILSON, PIERRE M., Marseilles, France.
Enlisted: February 27, 1917.
Breveted: July 11, 1917.
Released: November, 1917, because of ill health.

II
THE DEAD

Sergent CHAPMAN, VICTOR.......................Killed in combat, June 23, 1916
Soldat DOWD, DENNIS...........................Killed in accident, August 11, 1916
Sergent ROCKWELL, KIFFIN YATES................Killed in combat, September 23, 1916
Sous-Lieutenant PRINCE, NORMAN.................Injured in accident, October 12, 1916 (Died of injuries, October 15, 1916)
Sergent McCONNELL, JAMES R....................Killed in combat, March 19, 1917
Sergent GENÊT, EDMOND C. C....................Killed, April 16, 1917. (Shot down by anti-aircraft fire)
Sergent HOSKIER, RONALD W.....................Killed in combat, April 23, 1917
Sergent BARCLAY, L. NORMAN....................Killed in accident, June 1, 1917
Caporal CHADWICK, OLIVER M....................Killed in combat, August 14, 1917
Soldat GRIEB, NORMAN..........................Killed in accident, August 28, 1917
Caporal BIDDLE, JULIAN CORNELL................Killed August 18, 1917. (Probably in combat)
Caporal MEEKER, WILLIAM H.....................Killed in accident, September 11, 1917
Sergent MACMONAGLE, DOUGLAS...................Killed in combat, September 24, 1917
Sergent CAMPBELL, A. COURTNEY.................Killed in combat, October 1, 1917
Soldat HANFORD, ROBERT M......................Killed in accident, October 15, 1917
Sergent PAVELKA, PAUL.........................Killed in accident, November 11, 1917
Caporal PALMER, HENRY B.......................Died of illness, November 12, 1917
Caporal SKINNER, SAMUEL.......................Died at G.D.E., November 12, 1917
Caporal FOWLER, ERIC..........................Killed in accident, November 27, 1917
Sergent TRINKARD, CHARLES.....................Killed in accident, November 29, 1917
Caporal WALCOTT, BENJAMIN STUART..............Killed in combat, December 12, 1917
Soldat STARRETT, FRANK E......................Killed in accident, January 3, 1918
Caporal SPENCER, DUMARESQ.....................Killed in accident, January 22, 1918

Caporal BENNEY, PHILIP P.	Wounded in combat, January 25, 1918 (Died of wounds, January 26)
Sergent TAILER, WILLIAM H.	Killed February 5, 1918. (Probably by anti-aircraft fire)
Sergent LOUGHRAN, EDWARD J.	Killed in combat, February 18, 1918
Sergent WINTER, WALLACE C.	Killed in combat, March 8, 1918
Captain COLLINS, PHELPS	Killed on patrol, March 12, 1918
Sergent WOODWARD, HOUSTON	Killed in combat, April 1, 1918
Sergent LEE, SCHUYLER	Killed in combat, April 12, 1918
Second Lieutenant ELY, DINSMORE	Killed in accident, April 21, 1918
Sergent STONE, DONALD E.	Killed in combat, April 21, 1918
Second Lieutenant CHAPMAN, CHARLES W.	Killed in combat, May 3, 1918
First Lieutenant BAYNE, J. ALEXANDER	Killed in accident, May 8, 1918
Caporal DREW, SIDNEY R.	Killed in combat, May 19, 1918
Major LUFBERY, RAOUL	Killed in combat, May 19, 1918
First Lieutenant JOHNSON, HARRY F.	Killed in accident, May 21, 1918
First Lieutenant OVINGTON, C. LANDRAM	Killed in combat, May 29, 1918
Sergent ASH, ALAN NEWTON	Killed in combat, May 31, 1918
Sergent PELTON, ALFRED DIGBY	Killed in combat, May 31, 1918
Second Lieutenant DAVIS, PHILIP W.	Killed in combat, June 2, 1918
Sergent NICHOLS, ALAN H.	Killed in combat, June 2, 1918
Sergent BLUTHENTHAL, ARTHUR	Killed in combat, June 5, 1918
Sergent CHAMBERLAIN, CYRUS F.	Killed in combat, June 13, 1918
Sergent BAYLIES, FRANK L.	Killed in combat, June 17, 1918
First Lieutenant HOBBS, WARREN T.	Killed by anti-aircraft fire, June 25, 1918.
Sergent BAUGHAM, JAMES HENRY	Wounded in combat, July 1, 1918. (Died of wounds, July 2)
First Lieutenant CLAPP, ROGER H.	Killed in accident, July 6, 1918
Sergent TUCKER, DUDLEY G.	Killed in combat, July 8, 1918
Sergent BOOTH, VERNON, JR.	Wounded in combat, June 25, 1918 (Died of wounds, July 10, 1918)
First Lieutenant LEHR, MANDERSON	Killed in combat, July 15, 1918
Sergent TYSON, STEPHEN	Killed in combat, July 19, 1918
Second Lieutenant MILLER, WALTER B.	Killed in combat, August 3, 1918
First Lieutenant SCHREIBER, EDWIN B.	Killed in accident, August 8, 1918
Caporal McKERNESS, WILLIAM J.	Killed in combat, August 15, 1918
First Lieutenant EDGAR, STUART E.	Killed in accident, August 17, 1918
Ensign TERRES, HUGH C.	Killed in accident, August 17, 1918
First Lieutenant GUNDELACH, ANDRÉ	Killed in combat, September 12, 1918
First Lieutenant PUTNAM, DAVID	Killed in combat, September 12, 1918
Sergent RHENO, WALTER D.	Died of illness, October 10, 1918
First Lieutenant WILSON, JOSEPH VOLNEY	Killed in accident, October 23, 1918
Second Lieutenant DOWD, MEREDITH L.	Killed in combat, October 26, 1918
Ensign TAYLOR, ELMER B.	Died of illness, October 27, 1918
Second Lieutenant DE KRUIJFF, THEODORE	Died of illness, November 6, 1918
Major PETERSON, DAVID McKELVEY	Killed in accident, March 16, 1919

III

WOUNDED

Sergent BALSLEY, H. CLYDE	June 18, 1916
First Lieutenant BAER, PAUL F.	May 22, 1918
Second Lieutenant BENOIT, LEO E.	December 13, 1917
Major BIDDLE, CHARLES J.	May 15, 1918
Sergent BIGELOW, STEPHEN	August 20, 1917
Sergent BUCKLEY, EVERETT T.	September 6, 1917
Sergent CHAPMAN, VICTOR	June 17, 1916
Ensign COATSWORTH, CALEB J., JR.	August 16, 1917
Caporal DOOLITTLE, RALPH	July 17, 1917
Adjudant FAIRCHILD, EDWIN B.	October 23, 1918
Captain HALL, JAMES NORMAN	June 26, 1917, and May 7, 1918
Sous-Lieutenant HITCHCOCK, THOMAS, JR.	March 6, 1918

First Lieutenant JOHNSON, HARRY F. .... January 20, 1918
Sergent KERWOOD, CHARLES. .... August, 1918 (Shot by a German sentry while attempting to escape from a prison camp)
Second Lieutenant LEWIS, DAVID WILBUR. .... September 7, 1918
Caporal MCKERNESS, WILLIAM J .... July 15, 1918
Sergent ROCKWELL, KIFFIN YATES. .... May 24, 1916
Lieutenant Colonel THAW, WILLIAM. .... May 24, 1916
Second Lieutenant WINSLOW, ALAN F. .... July 31, 1918

IV

PRISONERS OF WAR

Caporal BACH, JAMES J. .... Captured, September 23, 1915
Sergent WILLIS, HAROLD B .... Captured, August 18, 1917
    (Escaped October 13, 1918)
Sergent CHARTON, LOUIS. .... Captured, September 5, 1917
Sergent BUCKLEY, EVERETT T. .... Captured, September 6, 1917
    (Escaped July 1, 1918)
Sergent MCKEE, HERSCHEL .... Captured, February 8, 1918
Sous-Lieutenant HITCHCOCK, THOMAS, JR. .... Captured, March 6, 1918
    (Escaped August 28, 1918)
Sergent KERWOOD, CHARLES W. .... Captured, March 31, 1918
Caporal WHITMORE, HERMAN .... Captured, April 6, 1918
Caporal BUFFUM, THOMAS .... Captured, May 4, 1918
Captain HALL, JAMES NORMAN .... Captured, May 7, 1918
First Lieutenant BAER, PAUL FRANK. .... Captured, May 22, 1918
Caporal SHONINGER, CLARENCE B. .... Captured, May 29, 1918
Sergent BYERS, LESLIE L .... Captured, July 18, 1918
Second Lieutenant WINSLOW, ALAN .... Captured, July 31, 1918
Sergent SHAFFER, WALTER J. .... Captured, October 3, 1918
Captain FORD, CHRISTOPHER W. .... Captured, October 15, 1918

V

L.F.C. PILOTS IN ORDER OF ENLISTMENT

1914

LUFBERY, GERVAIS RAOUL ...... August 31
MASSON, DIDIER .... October
BACH, JAMES J .... December 10
THAW, WILLIAM .... December 24
HALL, BERT .... December 28

1915

CURTIS, FRAZIER .... February 28
PRINCE, NORMAN .... March 4
COWDIN, ELLIOT CHRISTOPHER .. March 5
CHAPMAN, VICTOR .... August 1
HILL, DUDLEY LAWRENCE .... August 3
WINSLOW, CARROL DANA .... August 19
JOHNSON, CHARLES CHOUTEAU
    September 2
ROCKWELL, KIFFIN YATES ... September 2
RUMSEY, LAWRENCE .... September 9
BALSLEY, H. CLYDE .... September 16
MCCONNELL, JAMES R .... October 1
PAVELKA, PAUL .... October 18

1916

HUFFER, JEAN .... January 1
HAVILAND, WILLIS B .... January 26
PRINCE, FREDERICK .... January 29

GENÊT, EDMOND CHARLES CLINTON
    May 24
ROCLE, MARIUS ROMAIN .... June 5
DUGAN, WILLIAM E., JR .... June 10
CAMPBELL, ANDREW COURTNEY, JR.
    July 20
HINKLE, EDWARD F .... July 20
MARR, KENNETH .... July 20
BRIDGMAN, RAY CLAFLIN .... July 24
JOHNSTON, ARCHIBALD .... July 28
DOLAN, CHARLES H., JR .... August 11
HORTON, DABNEY D .... August 16
MCCALL, GEORGE A .... September 1
MACMONAGLE, DOUGLAS .... October 3
PETERSON, DAVID MCKELVEY .. October 9
HALL, JAMES NORMAN .... October 11
DOOLITTLE, JAMES RALPH ..... October 16
ROUNDS, LELAND L .... October 16
DREXEL, JOHN ARMSTRONG ..... October 27
JONES, HENRY SWEET .... October 27
MOLTER, BENNETT A .... November 2
DONZÉ, ROBERT L .... November 7
BULLARD, EUGENE .... November 15
POLLOCK, GRANVILLE A ...... December 24
RHENO, WALTER D .... December 24

375

Rockwell, Robert Lockerbie	February 7
Zinn, Frederick W.	February 14
Soubiran, Robert	February 27
Worthington, Warwick D.	March 9
Dowd, Dennis	March 28
Littauer, Kenneth P.	March 29
Hoskier, Ronald Wood	April 5
Bigelow, Stephen	April 13
Hewitt, Thomas M., Jr.	April 13
Parsons, Edwin Charles	April 13
Barclay, Lief Norman	May 22
Lovell, Walter	May 22
Willis, Harold Buckley	May 22
Boal, Pierre	May 24
Chatkoff, H. Lincoln	May 24
Hamilton, Edgar G.	February 27
Trinkard, Charles	March 13
Gundelach, André	March 20
Jacob, Sereno Thorp	March 20
de Kruijff, Theodore	March 20
Loughran, Edward J.	March 20
Reno, Leonard M.	March 20
Wright, Harold E.	March 20
Malone, Charles T.	March 21
Jones, Charles Maury	March 26
Wild, Marcellus E.	March 29
Abbott, Wainwright	April 2
Biddle, Charles J	April 8
Stone, Donald E.	April 8
McKee, Herschel J.	April 12
Stanley, Alfred Holt	April 12
Stearns, Russell F.	April 12
Veil, Charles Herbert	April 12
Ovington, Carter Landram	April 20
Parker, Austin G.	May 2
Bush, Philip N.	May 9
Edgar, Stuart Emmet	May 9
Ford, Christopher W.	May 9
Tucker, Dudley G.	May 9
Dowd, Meredith L.	May 14
Bouligny, Edgar J.	May 15
Corsi, Edward J.	May 15
Terres, Hugh	May 15
Collins, Phelps	May 17
Baylies, Frank L.	May 21
Duffy, Nathaniel	May 24
Hanford, Robert M.	May 24
Moore, Robert L.	May 24
Shoninger, Clarence Bernard	May 24
Biddle, Julian Cornell	May 25
Faith, Clarence H.	May 25
Palmer, Henry Brewster	May 25
Tyson, Stephen	May 25
Willard, George Gale	May 26
Brady, Lester Strayer	May 28
Benney, Philip P.	May 31
Putnam, David F.	May 31
Sitterly, Glenn N.	May 31
Bluthenthal, Arthur	June 1
Lee, Schuyler	June 1
Booth, Vernon, Jr.	June 3
Chamberlain, Cyrus F.	June 3

1917.

Buckley, Everett T	January 6
Chadwick, Oliver M.	January 17
Huger, Daniel	January 26
Scanlan, Lawrence	February 8
Whitmore, John Joyce	February 8
Wilcox, Charles H.	February 8
Turnure, George E., Jr.	February 16
Kerwood, Charles W.	February 18
Pelton, Alfred D.	February 19
Stehlin, Joseph C.	February 19
Adams, John Russell	February 20
Baer, Paul Frank	February 20
Charton, Louis	February 20
Coatsworth, Caleb James, Jr.	February 20
Nordhoff, Charles B.	June 3
Walcott, Benjamin Stuart	June 3
Wass, William E.	June 3
Blake, Charles Raymond	June 4
Ponder, William Thomas	June 4
Davis, Philip Washburn	June 9
Drew, Sidney Rankin	June 9
Fowler, Eric A.	June 9
Glover, Clarence M.	June 9
Loomis, William F.	June 9
Benoit, Leo E.	June 10
Chapman, Charles W., Jr.	June 10
Cotton, John Rowell	June 10
Dock, George, Jr.	June 10
Gill, Joseph Francis	June 10
Hobbs, Warren Tucker	June 10
Miller, Walter B.	June 10
Saxon, Harold Young	June 10
Thompson, Clifton B.	June 10
Byers, Louis Leslie	June 13
Eldredge, Donald Herbert	June 13
Forster, Henry	June 13
Grieb, Norman	June 13
Hughes, Earl W.	June 13
McKerness, William J.	June 13
Kinsolving, Charles M.	June 13
Read, Robert E.	June 13
Sullivan, Upton	June 13
Wellman, William A.	June 13
Whitmore, Herman	June 13
Ash, Alan N.	June 15
Buffum, Thomas B.	June 15
Connelly, James A., Jr.	June 15
Sinclaire, Reginald	June 15
Bassett, Charles Chester, Jr.	June 17
Grey, Charles G.	June 17
Brown, Jasper C.	June 19
Cookson, Linn Palmer	June 19
Lewis, David Wilbur	June 21
Cushman, Alvin Alexander	June 22
Baird, Benjamin H.	June 25
Hitchcock, Thomas, Jr.	June 25
Johnson, Harry F.	June 25
McMillen, James H.	June 25
Rodgers, William B., Jr.	June 25
Taber, Leslie R.	June 25
Winter, Wallace Charles	June 25

MINISTÈRE DE LA GUERRE

Sous-Secrétariat d'État
de l'Aéronautique Militaire
et Maritime

République Française

Le Sous-Secrétaire d'État
de l'Aéronautique Militaire et Maritime
à M. Major Raoul Lufberry U.S.A.S.
19 Mai 1918

Le Président du Conseil, Ministre de la Guerre a décidé, sur ma proposition, d'accorder un souvenir aux quatre officiers directeurs et aux 214 pilotes du "Lafayette Flying Corps" qui, devançant l'élan de tout un peuple, sont venus prendre fraternellement dans les rangs Français, une belle part de périls et de gloire.

Ce souvenir consiste en un ruban bleu, semé d'étoiles, bordé des couleurs de France et d'Amérique, orné, en relief, de la tête de Sioux en argent, qu'ont glorieusement portée sur nos champs de bataille les avions de la première escadrille Lafayette.

Je suis particulièrement heureux de vous faire parvenir cet insigne, qui demeurera le témoignage reconnaissant de l'Aviation Française, fière de vous avoir compté parmi ses pilotes, et de la France toute entière, que vous avez bien servie.

Paris, le 23 Novembre 1918

CERIFICATE PRESENTED BY THE FRENCH GOVERNMENT TO THE PILOTS AND OBSERVERS OF THE LAFAYETTE CORPS

CLAPP, ROGER HARVEY............June 3	YORK, WALTER R................June 25
FERGUSON, FEARCHAR IAN........June 3	CAMPBELL, H. GORDON..........June 27
JUDD, DAVID E...................June 3	FAIRCHILD, EDWIN BRADLEY......June 27
LEHR, MANDERSON................June 3	KYLE, GEORGE MARION...........June 27
MEEKER, WILLIAM HENRY.........June 3	NICHOLS, ALAN H...............July 1
KENYON, HUGO N.................July 5	CRENORE, AUSTEN BALLARD.......July 16
CUNNINGHAM, ARTHUR LAWRENCE..July 7	STARRETT, FRANK ELMER.........July 19
BAUGHAM, JAMES HENRY..........July 10	RANDALL, JOHN F...............July 20
BAYNE, JAMES ALEXANDER........July 10	COOK, ALAN A..................July 21
CASSADY, THOMAS G.............July 10	COREY, RUSSELL B..............July 21
HOEBER, ROBERT B..............July 10	GUY, DAVID W..................July 21
LARNER, G. DE FREEST..........July 10	LOOMIS, RALPH LANE............July 21
MOSELEY, GEORGE CLARK.........July 10	STICKNEY, HENRY ELMER.........July 21
ROTHARMEL, KENNETH ALBERT.....July 10	TAILER, WILLIAM HALLET........July 21
SPENCER, DUMARESQ.............July 10	TAYLOR, ELMER B...............July 21
WINSLOW, ALAN F...............July 10	VAN FLEET, WILLIAM CAREY, JR..July 21
ELY, DINSMORE.................July 13	WILSON, JOSEPH VOLNEY.........July 21
FAUNT LEROY, CEDRIC GERALD....July 13	RAND, RUFUS R., JR............July 26
BULLEN, WILLIAM GRAHAM........July 14	BATCHELOR, HENRY, 3D..........August 1
EOFF, ROBERT GRIMSHAW.........July 14	GRIER, JAMES MURRAY...........August 1
PADEN, DAVID SHELDON..........July 14	SHAFFER, WALTER JOHN..........August 1
WOODWARD, HOUSTON.............July 14	BOGGS, ELLISON CONVERSE.......August 4

VI

L.F.C. PILOTS IN FRENCH SQUADRONS

I. COMBAT SQUADRONS

SPAD 3
  BAYLIES, FRANK L......................December 18, 1917, to June 17, 1918
  JUDD, DAVID E........................December 18, 1917, to January 22, 1918
  PARSONS, EDWIN C.....................April 24, 1918, to Armistice
DEPERDUSSIN 6
  THAW, WILLIAM........................December 24, 1914, to February 1, 1915
SPAD 12
  DOCK, GEORGE, JR.....................March 18, 1918, to Armistice
  STONE, DONALD E......................March 18 to April 21, 1918
  SAXON, HAROLD Y......................June 17, 1918, to Armistice
SPAD 15
  WILD, MARCELLUS E....................October 20, 1917, to March 30, 1918
  STEHLIN, JOSEPH C....................November 2 to December 12, 1917
  TUCKER, DUDLEY G.....................January 28 to July 8, 1918
  FORSTER, HENRY.......................June 1 to August 2, 1918
SPAD 23
  McCALL, GEORGE A.....................May 30 to September 9, 1917
  STANLEY, ALFRED H....................February 24, 1918, to Armistice
SPAD 26
  BRADY, LESTER S......................February 23 to April 13, 1918
SPAD 31
  SAXON, HAROLD Y......................January 21 to June 17, 1918
  DREW, SIDNEY R.......................March 25 to May 19, 1918
SPAD 38
  BACH, JAMES J........................August 29 to September 23, 1915
  HALL, BERT...........................Summer of 1915
  COWDIN, ELLIOT C.....................September 30 to November 10, 1915
  McMILLEN, JAMES H....................March 12 to September 27, 1918
  GUY, DAVID W.........................June 1, 1918, to Armistice
  PUTNAM, DAVID........................June 1 to June 14, 1918
  SHAFFER, WALTER J....................June 1 to October 3, 1918
  BYERS, LOUIS L.......................July 13 to July 18, 1918
  SITTERLY, GLENN N....................October 15, 1918, to Armistice
SPAD 48
  McCALL, GEORGE A.....................November 6, 1917, to April 23, 1918

SPAD 49
  COWDIN, ELLIOT C..................November 10, 1915, to January 15, 1916
  BRIDGMAN, RAY C...................April 13 to April 27, 1917
SPAD 62
  HUFFER, JEAN......................June 16, 1916, to March 15, 1917
  HUFFER, JEAN......................October 4, 1917, to February 18, 1918
SPAD 65
  COWDIN, ELLIOT C..................March 2 to April 18, 1916
  THAW, WILLIAM.....................March 28 to April 15, 1916
  BUCKLEY, EVERETT T................August 3 to September 6, 1917
  POLLOCK, GRANVILLE................October 16, 1917, to January 8, 1918
SPAD 67
  BENNEY, PHILIP P..................December 12, 1917, to January 26, 1918
  TAILER, WILLIAM H.................December 14, 1917, to February 5, 1918
  PONDER, WILLIAM T.................February 3 to February 17, 1918
  BROWN, JASPER C...................February 3, 1918, to Armistice
  SHIPLEY, WALTER B.................March 18 to March 22, 1918
SPAD 68
  MASSON, DIDIER....................September, 1915, to April, 1916
  TRINKARD, CHARLES.................September 1 to November 29, 1917
  SINCLAIRE, REGINALD...............December 4, 1917, to October 4, 1918
SPAD 69
  HORTON, DABNEY D..................June 15 to August 15, 1917
SPAD 73
  BIDDLE, CHARLES J.................July 28, 1917, to January 10, 1918
  CHADWICK, OLIVER M................July 28 to August 14, 1917
  BIDDLE, JULIAN CORNELL............August 11 to August 18, 1917
  JONES, CHARLES MAURY..............August 15, 1917, to January 21, 1918
  BAYLIES, FRANK L..................November 17 to December 18, 1917
  JUDD, DAVID E.....................December 1 to December 18, 1917
  BUSH, PHILIP N....................January 19 to July 21, 1918
SPAD 75
  HORTON, DABNEY D..................September 15, 1918, to Armistice
SPAD 76
  ELDREDGE, DONALD H................February 24, 1918, to Armistice
SPAD 77
  BUFFUM, THOMAS B..................March 24 to May 4, 1918
  WHITMORE, HERMAN..................March 24 to April 6, 1918
  CORSI, EDWARD J...................May 30, 1918, to Armistice
SPAD 78
  GLOVER, CLARENCE M................July 1, 1918, to Armistice
  VAN FLEET, WILLIAM C., JR.........July 1 to August 28, 1918
SPAD 79
  LEWIS, DAVID W....................February 27 to September 22, 1918
SPAD 80
  COATSWORTH, C. J., JR.............July 18, 1917, to March 20, 1918
  RHENO, WALTER D...................July 18 to September 15, 1917
  WILCOX, CHARLES H.................July 18, 1917, to January 18, 1918
  BAER, PAUL F......................August 14, 1917, to January 10, 1918
SPAD 81
  ADAMS, JOHN R.....................December 31, 1917, to March 13, 1918
  BAYNE, JAMES A....................March 3 to May 8, 1918
  BOGGS, ELLISON C..................April 21, 1918, to Armistice
SPAD 82
  BARCLAY, LEIF NORMAN..............April 12 to June 1, 1917
SPAD 83
  JOHNSTON, ARCHIBALD C.............April 27 to September 12, 1917
SPAD 84
  ROCLE, MARIUS R...................February 1 to July 15, 1917
  LOUGHRAN, EDWARD J................October 29, 1917, to February 18, 1918

  WALCOTT, BENJ. STUART.............October 29 to December 12, 1917
  BENOIT, LEO E.....................November 18 to December 2, 1917

Spad 85
  Bullard, Eugene..........................September 13 to November 11, 1917
  Chamberlain, Cyrus F................December 12, 1917, to January 9, 1918
  Johnson, Harry F.......................December 12, 1917, to January 9, 1918
  Ovington, Carter Landram...........December 12, 1917, to January 9, 1918
  Nichols, Alan H.........................December 19, 1917, to June 2, 1918
  Parker, Austen G........................December 19, 1917, to January 9, 1918
  Tyson, Stephen..........................December 19, 1917, to July 19, 1918
  Bayne, James A..........................March 1 to March 3, 1918
Spad 86
  McCall, George A.......................September 15 to October 22, 1917
  Larner, G. de Freest..................December 3, 1917, to June 15, 1918
Spad 87
  Wellman, William A....................December 3, 1917, to March 14, 1918
  Hitchcock, Thomas, Jr................December 10, 1917, to March 6, 1918
Spad 90
  Sullivan, Upton.........................January 8 to April 8, 1918
Spad 91
  Wass, William E.........................February 15 to November 4, 1918
Spad 92
  Charton, Louis..........................August 22 to September 5, 1917
Spad 93
  Donzé, Robert...........................May 20 to June 15, 1917
  Wells, Frank W.........................August 6 to December 23, 1917
  Bullard, Eugene........................August 27 to September 13, 1917
  Grey, Charles G........................November 26, 1917, to March 13, 1918
Spad 94
  Cremore, Austen B.....................December 1, 1917, to Armistice
  Winter, Wallace C.....................December 1, 1917, to January 1, 1918
  Putnam, David..........................December 12, 1917, to January 1, 1918
  Shaffer, Walter J......................December 16, 1917, to January 1, 1918
  Woodward, Houston...................December 16, 1917, to April 1, 1918
Spad 95
  Gundelach, André......................July 12 to September 8, 1917
  Adams, John R..........................August 12 to October 12, 1917
  Stehlin, Joseph C......................August 18 to October 2, 1917
Spad 96
  Moore, Robert L........................January 6 to May 1, 1918
  Booth, Vernon, Jr......................January 10 to June 25, 1918
  Ferguson, Fearchar I..................January 10, 1918, to Armistice
  Lee, Schuyler...........................January 10 to April 12, 1918
  Duffy, Nathaniel.......................April 25 to August 16, 1918
Spad 97
  York, Walter R..........................March 3, 1918, to Armistice
  Pelton, Alfred D.......................March 5 to May 31, 1918
Spad 98
  Chamberlain, Cyrus F................January 9 to June 13, 1918
  Johnson, Harry F.......................January 9 to February 16, 1918
  Ovington, Carter Landram...........January 9 to May 29, 1918
  Parker, Austin G........................January 9 to April 11, 1918
  Baugham, James H.....................June 27 to July 2, 1918
Spad 99
  Nordhoff, Charles B...................January 15 to July 11, 1918
  Thompson, Clifton B..................January 15, 1918, to Armistice
  Shoninger, Clarence B................February 22 to May 29, 1918
Spad 102
  Bigelow, Stephen.......................January 24 to February 8, 1917
  Pollock, Granville.....................July 15 to October 14, 1917
  Molter, Bennett A......................July 20 to August 1, 1917
  Haviland, Willis B.....................October 1, 1917, to January 1, 1918
  Ely, Dinsmore..........................February 24 to April 1, 1918
  Taylor, Elmer B........................April 1 to April 6, 1918
  Forster, Henry.........................April 10 to April 24, 1918

SPAD 103
  HALL, BERT.........................November 18 to December 20, 1916
  RENO, LEONARD......................July 23 to September 18, 1917
  TURNURE, GEORGE E., JR.............July 27 to December 16, 1917
  COLLINS, PHELPS....................September 19, 1917, to January 7, 1918
  HOEBER, ROBERT B...................December 19, 1917, to Armistice
  BATCHELOR, HENRY, 3d...............December 26, 1917, to March 1, 1918
  MCCALL, GEORGE A...................October 24, 1918, to Armistice
SPAD 112
  WINSLOW, CARROLL D.................March 10 to April 30, 1917
  ROUNDS, LELAND L...................August 3 to December 22, 1917
  HALL, JAMES N......................September 22 to October 3, 1917
  ROTHARMEL, KENNETH R...............February 25, 1918, to Armistice
SPAD 124 (ESCADRILLE LAFAYETTE)
  THÉNAULT, GEORGES, Capt. (French)..April 20, 1916, to January 16, 1918
  DE LAAGE DE MEUX, ALFRED, Lt. (French)..April 20, 1916, to May 23, 1917
  CHAPMAN, VICTOR....................April 20 to June 23, 1916
  MCCONNELL, JAMES R.................April 20, 1916, to March 19, 1917
  PRINCE, NORMAN.....................April 20 to October 14, 1916
  ROCKWELL, KIFFIN YATES.............April 20 to September 23, 1916
  THAW, WILLIAM......................April 21, 1916, to February 18, 1918
  COWDIN, ELLIOT C...................April 28 to June 25, 1916
  HALL, BERT.........................April 28 to November 1, 1916
  LUFBERY, RAOUL.....................May 24, 1916, to January 5, 1918
  BALSLEY, H. CLYDE..................May 29 to June 18, 1916
  JOHNSON, CHARLES CHOUTEAU..........May 29, 1916, to October 31, 1917
  RUMSEY, LAWRENCE...................June 4 to November 25, 1916
  HILL, DUDLEY.......................June 9, 1916, to February 18, 1918
  MASSON, DIDIER.....................June 19, 1916, to February 15, 1917
  MASSON, DIDIER.....................June 15, to October 8, 1917
  NUNGESSER, Lt. (French)............July 14 to August 15, 1916
  PAVELKA, PAUL......................August 11, 1916, to January 24, 1917
  ROCKWELL, ROBERT L.................September 17, 1916, to February 18, 1918
  HAVILAND, WILLIS B.................October 22, 1916, to September 18, 1917
  PRINCE, FREDERICK..................October 22, 1916, to February 15, 1917
  SOUBIRAN, ROBERT...................October 22, 1916, to February 18, 1918
  HOSKIER, RONALD WOOD...............December 11, 1916, to April 23, 1917
  GENÊT, EDMOND C. C.................January 19 to April 16, 1917
  PARSONS, EDWIN C...................January 25, 1917, to February 26, 1918
  BIGELOW, STEPHEN...................February 8 to September 11, 1917
  LOVELL, WALTER.....................February 26 to October 24, 1917
  HINKLE, EDWARD F...................March 1 to June 12, 1917
  WILLIS, HAROLD B...................March 1 to August 18, 1917
  MARR, KENNETH......................March 29, 1917, to February 18, 1918
  DUGAN, WILLIAM E., JR..............March 30, 1917, to February 18, 1918
  HEWITT, THOMAS M., JR..............March 30 to September 17, 1917
  CAMPBELL, A. COURTNEY..............April 15 to October 1, 1917
  BRIDGMAN, RAY C....................May 1, 1917, to February 18, 1918
  DOLAN, CHARLES H., JR..............May 12, 1917, to February 18, 1918
  DREXEL, JOHN ARMSTRONG.............May 12 to June 15, 1917
  JONES, HENRY S.....................May 12, 1917, to February 18, 1918
  MAISON-ROUGE, Lt. (French).........May 28 to October 6, 1917
  HALL, JAMES NORMAN.................June 16 to June 26, 1917
  HALL, JAMES NORMAN.................October 3, 1917, to February 18, 1918
  MACMONAGLE, DOUGLAS................June 16 to September 24, 1917
  PETERSON, DAVID MCKELVEY...........June 16, 1917, to February 18, 1918
  DOOLITTLE, JAMES RALPH.............July 2 to July 17, 1917
  VERDIER-FAUVETY, LOUIS, Lt. (French)..October 6, 1917, to February 18, 1918
  FORD, CHRISTOPHER W................November 8, 1917, to February 18, 1918
  COLLINS, PHELPS....................January 7 to February 18, 1918
  BAER, PAUL F.......................January 10 to February 18, 1918
  BIDDLE, CHARLES J..................January 10 to February 18, 1918
  WILCOX, CHARLES H..................January 26 to February 18, 1918
  TURNURE, GEORGE E., JR.............February 12 to February 18, 1918

SPAD 150
   STICKNEY, HENRY E. . . . . December 4, 1917, to Armistice
   VEIL, CHARLES H. . . . . December 18, 1917, to Armistice
   MOSELEY, GEORGE C. December 27, 1917, to February 4, 1918
   SPENCER, DUMARESQ. December 27, 1917, to January 22, 1918
   STEARNS, RUSSELL F. December 27, 1917, to February 24, 1918

SPAD 151
   PELTON, ALFRED D. . . . . September 27 to December 1, 1917

SPAD 152
   WINSLOW, ALAN F. . . . . December 24, 1917, to February 12, 1918
   DOWD, MEREDITH L. . . . . January 1 to February 6, 1918

SPAD 153
   LOOMIS, WILLIAM F. . . . . November 23, 1917, to February 19, 1918
   HOBBS, WARREN T. . . . . December 11, 1917, to January 15, 1918

SPAD 154
   ABBOTT, WAINWRIGHT. . . . . September 18, 1917, to September 3, 1918
   HAVILAND, WILLIS B. . . . . September 18 to October 1, 1917

SPAD 155
   GUY, DAVID W. . . . . December 2, 1917, to January 1, 1918
   WRIGHT, HAROLD E. . . . . September 11 to December 23, 1917

SPAD 156
   GUY, DAVID W. . . . . January 1 to June 1, 1918
   SHAFFER, WALTER J. . . . . January 1 to June 1, 1918
   WINTER, WALLACE C. . . . . January 1 to March 8, 1918
   PUTNAM, DAVID. . . . . February 7 to June 1, 1918

SPAD 157
   COOK, ALAN A. . . . . December 20, 1917, to July 20, 1918
   BAUGHAM, JAMES H. . . . . December 26, 1917, to June 27, 1918
   CASSADY, THOMAS G. December 26, 1917, to February 16, 1918
   JACOB, SERENO T. . . . . December 26, 1917, to September 8, 1918
   WILLARD, GEORGE GALE . . . . December 26, 1917, to January 13, 1918
   CONNELLY, JAMES A., JR. . . . . January 15 to June 27, 1918
   EOFF, ROBERT G. . . . . January 24 to March 27, 1918

SPAD 158
   DE KRUIJFF, THEODORE. . . . . December 6, 1917, to May 21, 1918
   RAND, RUFUS R., JR. December 6, 1917, to Armistice
   EDGAR, STUART E. . . . . December 11, 1917, to March 28, 1918
   RANDALL, JOHN F. . . . . December 11, 1917, to February 14, 1918
   HOBBS, WARREN T. . . . . January 15 to March 16, 1918

SPAD 159
   FAIRCHILD, EDWIN B. . . . . January 16, 1918, to Armistice

SPAD 162
   DOWD, MEREDITH L. . . . . February 6 to February 17, 1918
   BULLEN, W. G. . . . . March 13 to April 17, 1918

SPAD 163
   PONDER, WILLIAM T. May 12 to September 1, 1918
   CASSADY, THOMAS G. May 14 to September 8, 1918
   CONNELLY, JAMES A., JR. . . . . June 27, 1918, to Armistice
   COOK, ALAN A. . . . . July 20, 1918, to Armistice
   PADEN, DAVID S. . . . . September 6, 1918, to Armistice

SPAD 168
   JOHNSON, HARRY F. . . . . April 12 to May 21, 1918

SPAD 228
   BENOIT, LEO E. . . . . February 1 to August 25, 1918

SPAD 313
   COLLINS, PHELPS. . . . . September 2 to September 18, 1917

SPAD 314
   MCKEE, HERSCHEL. . . . . October 15, 1917, to February 8, 1918
   DONZÉ, ROBERT L. . . . . November 28, 1917, to March 22, 1918
   WHITMORE, JOHN J. . . . . May 13 to May 23, 1918

SPAD 315
   WHITMORE, JOHN J. . . . . November 24, 1917, to February 5, 1918

SPAD 391 (ORIENT)
   PAVELKA, PAUL. . . . . February 8 to June 15, 1917

SPAD 471 (DEFENSE OF PARIS)
    MASSON, DIDIER........................October 10 to October 28, 1917
    GILL, JOSEPH F........................Summer of 1918
SPAD 501 (ORIENT)
    BOULIGNY, EDGAR J.....................April 24 to June 14, 1918
SPAD 507 (ORIENT)
    PAVELKA, PAUL.........................June 15 to November 11, 1917
ESCADRILLE DE SAINT-POL (DUNKIRK)
    VAN FLEET, WILLIAM C., JR.............September 15 to October 30, 1918
    MOSELEY, GEORGE C.....................September 25 to November 5, 1918
    CAMPBELL, H. GORDON...................(Dates not known)

(*Note:* As nearly all French combat squadrons were finally equipped with Spad planes the former designation "Nieuport" is here omitted.)

II. BOMBARDMENT AND RECONNAISSANCE SQUADRONS

C. 11
    CHATKOFF, H. LINCOLN..................April 25 to June 15, 1917
C. 17
    HORTON, DABNEY D......................July 13, 1917, to January 5, 1918
C. 18
    MASSON, DIDIER........................March to September, 1915
F. 24
    ZINN, FREDERICK.......................December 12, 1916, to October 21, 1917
BR. 29
    TABER, LESLIE R.......................March 11 to March 17, 1918
    BLAKE, CHARLES R......................March 11 to September 3, 1918
SAL. 30
    MCCALL, GEORGE A......................May 29 to September 30, 1918
F. 36
    HUFFER, JEAN..........................July 13 to September 14, 1917
C. 42
    THAW, WILLIAM.........................March 26, 1915, to January 29, 1916
M.F. 44
    WINSLOW, CARROLL D....................May 3 to July 13, 1916
C. 46
    ROCLE, MARIUS R.......................1917
    SITTERLY, GLENN N.....................March 26 to August 20, 1918
    MCKERNESS, WILLIAM J..................May 12 to August 15, 1918
C. 53
    WORTHINGTON, WARWICK D................March 3, 1917, to February 13, 1918
BR. 66
    HUGHES, EARL W........................January 14 to June 15, 1918
C. 74
    LITTAUER, K. P........................October 16, 1916, to January 2, 1918
    TAYLOR, ELMER B.......................February 1 to April 1, 1918
    FORSTER, HENRY........................February 1 to April 10, 1918
V. 97 (DEFENSE OF PARIS)
    BALSLEY, H. CLYDE.....................February 15 to April 1, 1916
    JOHNSON, C. C.........................February and March, 1916
V.B. 106
    LUFBERY, RAOUL........................October 7, 1915, to April 10, 1916
V.B. 108
    COWDIN, ELLIOT C......................May 1 to August 15, 1915
    PRINCE, NORMAN........................May 20 to July 1, 1915
    CHAPMAN, VICTOR.......................August 10 to September 22, 1915
F. 110
    HUGHES, EARL W........................October 6, 1918, to Armistice
SOP. 111
    GUNDELACH, ANDRÉ......................September 24 to December 21, 1917
V.B. 113
    PRINCE, NORMAN........................July 1, 1915, to February 15, 1916

BR. 117
    KERWOOD, CHARLES W. ....November 21, 1917, to March 31, 1918
    KINSOLVING, CHARLES M. ....November 21, 1917, to June 16, 1918
    LEHR, MANDERSON......................November 21, 1917, to July 1, 1918
    KYLE, GEORGE M.......................December 26, 1917, to July 1, 1918
    WILSON, JOSEPH V.....................November 21, 1917, to July, 1918
BR. 120
    CLAPP, ROGER H.......................January 15 to May 15, 1918
    COTTON, JOHN R......................January 15 to September, 1918
BR. 134
    ASH, ALAN N.........................February 23 to May 31, 1918
    RENO, LEONARD......................June 4 to July 18, 1918
BR. 213
    ROCLE, MARIUS R....................(Dates not known)
BR. 224
    FORSTER, HENRY....................April 24 to May 3, 1918
BR. 227
    BLUTHENTHAL, ARTHUR..............March 17 to June 5, 1918
SOP. 255
    HORTON, DABNEY D.................January 5 to February 18, 1918
C. 305
    MOORE, ROBERT L..................November, 1917, to January 1, 1918

VII
TRANSFERRED TO U.S. AIR SERVICE

First Lieutenant ABBOTT, WAINWRIGHT
Second Lieutenant ADAMS, JOHN RUSSELL
First Lieutenant BAER, PAUL F.
Captain BALSLEY, H. CLYDE
First Lieutenant BAYNE, J. ALEXANDER
Second Lieutenant BENOIT, LEO E.
Major BIDDLE, CHARLES J.
First Lieutenant BLAKE, CHARLES RAYMOND
Captain BOAL, PIERRE
Second Lieutenant BOULIGNY, EDGAR J.
Second Lieutenant BRADY, LESTER S.
Captain BRIDGMAN, RAY C.
First Lieutenant BROWN, JASPER C.
First Lieutenant BUSH, PHILIP N.
Captain CASSADY, THOMAS G.
Second Lieutenant CHAPMAN, CHARLES W.
First Lieutenant CLAPP, ROGER H.
Captain COLLINS, PHELPS
Second Lieutenant COOKSON, LINN PALMER
First Lieutenant COTTON, JOHN R.
Major COWDIN, ELLIOT C.
First Lieutenant CUNNINGHAM, ARTHUR L.
Second Lieutenant DAVIS, PHILIP W.
First Lieutenant DOLAN, CHARLES H., JR.
First Lieutenant DONZÉ, ROBERT L.
Second Lieutenant DOWD, MEREDITH L.
Major DREXEL, JOHN ARMSTRONG
First Lieutenant DUGAN, WILLIAM E., JR.
Second Lieutenant EOFF, ROBERT G.
First Lieutenant EDGAR, STUART E.
Second Lieutenant ELDREDGE, DONALD H.
Second Lieutenant ELY, DINSMORE
Second Lieutenant FAITH, CLARENCE H.
Major FAUNT LEROY, CEDRIC G.
Major FORD, CHRISTOPHER W.
Second Lieutenant GIBSON, WILLIAM W.
Second Lieutenant GILL, JOSEPH FRANCIS

Major HUFFER, JOHN F.
First Lieutenant JACOB, SERENO T.
Captain JONES, CHARLES MAURY
First Lieutenant JONES, HENRY SWEET
Captain JOHNSON, CHARLES CHOUTEAU
First Lieutenant JOHNSON, HARRY F.
Captain JOHNSTON, ARCHIBALD C.
Second Lieutenant KENYON, HUGO N.
First Lieutenant KINSOLVING, CHARLES M.
Second Lieutenant DE KRUIJFF, THEODORE
First Lieutenant KYLE, GEORGE M.
Captain LARNER, G. DE FREEST
First Lieutenant LEHR, MANDERSON
Second Lieutenant LEWIS, DAVID WILBUR
Major LITTAUER, KENNETH P.
First Lieutenant LOOMIS, WILLIAM FITCH
Major LOVELL, WALTER
Major LUFBERY, RAOUL GERVAIS
Major MARR, KENNETH
First Lieutenant MCMILLEN, JAMES H.
Second Lieutenant MILLER, WALTER B.
Captain MOLTER, BENNETT A.
First Lieutenant NORDHOFF, CHARLES B.
First Lieutenant OAKES, NATHAN
First Lieutenant OVINGTON, CARTER LANDRAM
Major PETERSON, DAVID McK.
First Lieutenant POLLOCK, GRANVILLE
First Lieutenant PONDER, WILLIAM T.
First Lieutenant PUTNAM, DAVID E.
Captain ROCKWELL, ROBERT LOCKERBIE
Second Lieutenant ROCLE, MARIUS R.
First Lieutenant RANDALL, JOHN F.
First Lieutenant ROUNDS, LELAND L.
Second Lieutenant ROTHARMEL, KENNETH A.
First Lieutenant SCHREIBER, EDWIN B.
Major SOUBIRAN, ROBERT

Captain GREY, CHARLES G.
First Lieutenant GUNDELACH, ANDRÉ
First Lieutenant GUY, DAVID W.
Captain HALL, JAMES NORMAN
Captain HILL, DUDLEY L.
First Lieutenant HOBBS, WARREN T.
First Lieutenant WELLS, FRANK W.
First Lieutenant WILCOX, CHARLES H.
Second Lieutenant WILLARD, GEORGE GALE
Second Lieutenant WORTHINGTON, WARWICK D.

First Lieutenant STICKNEY, HENRY E.
Lieutenant-Colonel THAW, WILLIAM
Second Lieutenant THOMPSON, CLIFTON B.
First Lieutenant TURNURE, GEORGE E., JR.
First Lieutenant VEIL, CHARLES
First Lieutenant WASS, WILLIAM E.
Second Lieutenant WILLOUGHBY, WESTEL R.
First Lieutenant WILSON, JOSEPH VOLNEY
Second Lieutenant WINSLOW, ALAN
Captain ZINN, FREDERICK

VIII
TRANSFERRED TO U.S. NAVAL AIR SERVICE

Ensign BAIRD, BENJAMIN H.
Lieutenant (J.G.) BASSETT, CHARLES CHESTER, JR.
Lieutenant (J.G.) BATCHELOR, HENRY, 3d
Ensign BULLEN, WILLIAM G.
Ensign CAMPBELL, H. GORDON
Ensign COATSWORTH, CALEB J., JR.
Ensign COREY, RUSSELL B
Ensign CUSHMAN, ALVIN A.
Ensign FORSTER, HENRY
Ensign GRIER, JAMES MURRAY
Senior Lieutenant HAVILAND, WILLIS B.
Ensign HUGER, DANIEL
Lieutenant (J.G.) JUDD, DAVID E.

Ensign LOOMIS, RALPH L.
Lieutenant (J.G.) MOSELEY, GEORGE C.
Ensign PARKER, AUSTIN G.
Lieutenant (J.G.) READ, ROBERT E.
Ensign RENO, LEONARD M.
Ensign RODGERS, WILLIAM B., JR.
Second Lieutenant STEARNS, RUSSELL F. (U.S. Marine Aviation)
Ensign SULLIVAN, UPTON S.
Ensign TABER, LESLIE R.
Ensign TAYLOR, ELMER B.
Ensign TERRES, HUGH
Ensign VAN FLEET, WM. C., JR.
Ensign WILD, MARCELLUS F.

IX
L.F.C. PILOTS, WHO REMAINED IN THE FRENCH SERVICE

Sergent BOGGS, ELLISON C.
Sergent BUCKLEY, EVERETT T.
Caporal BYERS, LOUIS L.
Sergent CHATKOFF, H. LINCOLN
Adjudant CONNELLY, JAMES A., JR.
Adjudant COOK, ALAN A.
Sergent CORSI, EDWARD J.
Sergent CREHORE, AUSTEN B.
Sergent DOCK, GEORGE, JR.
Sergent DUFFY, NATHANIEL
Sergent FERGUSON, FEARCHER I.
Adjudant FAIRCHILD, EDWIN B.
Sergent GLOVER, CLARENCE M.
Sous-Lieutenant HAMILTON, EDGAR G.
Sous-Lieutenant HITCHCOCK, THOMAS, JR.
Sergent HUGHES, EARL W.
Sergent HOEBER, ROBERT B.

Sergent HORTON, DABNEY D.
Sergent MCCALL, GEORGE A.
Sergent MCKEE, HERSCHEL
Adjudant MASSON, DIDIER
Sergent PADEN, DAVID S.
Sous-Lieutenant PARSONS, EDWIN C.
Adjudant RAND, RUFUS R., JR.
Officier-Interprète de 3ème Classe DE ROODE, CLIFFORD
Sergent SAXON, HAROLD Y.
Sergent SHAFFER, WALTER J.
Caporal SHONINGER, CLARENCE B.
Adjudant SINCLAIRE, REGINALD
Adjudant SITTERLY, GLENN N.
Adjudant STANLEY, ALFRED HOLT
Sergent WILLIS, HAROLD B.
Sous-Lieutenant YORK, WALTER R.

X
OFFICIAL VICTORIES

LUFBERY, RAOUL GERVAIS	17	BLAKE, CHARLES RAYMOND	1
BAYLIES, FRANK L.	12	BOGGS, ELLISON C.	1
PUTNAM, DAVID	11	CAMPBELL, H. GORDON	1
BAER, PAUL F.	9	CHAPMAN, VICTOR	1
CASSADY, THOMAS G.	9	CHAPMAN, CHARLES W., JR.	1
LARNER, G. DE FREEST	8	COLLINS, PHELPS	1
PARSONS, EDWIN C.	8	COWDIN, ELLIOT C.	1

Biddle, Charles J	7	Dolan, Charles H., Jr.	1
Ponder, William	7	Eldredge, Donald H.	1
Connelly, James A., Jr.	6	Eoff, Robert G.	1
Peterson, David McKelvy	5	Gundelach, André	1
Thaw, William	5	Guy, David W.	1
Grey, Charles G.	4	Haviland, Willis B.	1
Hall, Bert	3	Hoeber, Robert B.	1
Hall, James Norman	3	Johnson, Charles Chouteau	1
Huffer, Jean	3	Jones, Henry S.	1
Jacob, Sereno T.	3	Kenyon, Hugo N.	1
Prince, Norman	3	Lee, Schuyler	1
Sinclaire, Reginald	3	Loomis, William F.	1
Turnure, George E., Jr.	3	Lovell, Walter	1
Veil, Charles H.	3	Marr, Kenneth	1
Wilcox, Charles H.	3	Nichols, Alan	1
Abbott, Wainwright	2	Nordhoff, Charles B.	1
Baugham, James	2	Paden, David S.	1
Corsi, Edward J.	2	Reno, Leonard M.	1
Crehore, Austen B.	2	Rounds, Leland L.	1
Fairchild, Edwin B.	2	Sitterly, Glenn N.	1
Ford, Christopher W.	2	Soubiran, Robert	1
Hitchcock, Thomas, Jr.	2	Stehlin, Joseph C.	1
Rheno, Walter D.	2	Stickney, Henry E.	1
Rockwell, Kiffin Y.	2	Walcott, Benjamin Stuart	1
Saxon, Harold Y.	2	Wass, William E.	1
Shaffer, Walter J.	2	Wilson, Joseph V.	1
Stanley, Alfred H.	2	Winter, Wallace C.	1
Wellman, William A.	2	Woodward, Houston	1
Winslow, Alan F.	2	York, Walter R.	1

Total 199

www.ingramcontent.com/pod-product-compliance
Lightning Source LLC
Chambersburg PA
CBHW021958160426
43197CB00007B/178